Lincoln and the Politics of Slavery

Civil War America

Peter S. Carmichael, Caroline E. Janney,
and Aaron Sheehan-Dean, *editors*

This landmark series interprets broadly the history and culture of the
Civil War era through the long nineteenth century and beyond. Drawing
on diverse approaches and methods, the series publishes historical works
that explore all aspects of the war, biographies of leading commanders,
and tactical and campaign studies, along with select editions of primary
sources. Together, these books shed new light on an era that remains
central to our understanding of American and world history.

Lincoln

AND THE

Politics of Slavery

The Other Thirteenth Amendment and the
Struggle to Save the Union

DANIEL W. CROFTS

The University of North Carolina Press
Chapel Hill

This book was published with the assistance of the
Anniversary Fund of the University of North Carolina Press.

Designed and set in Miller by Rebecca Evans
Manufactured in the United States of America

The University of North Carolina Press has been a member
of the Green Press Initiative since 2003.

JACKET ILLUSTRATION: ambrotype of Abraham Lincoln by Preston Butler,
Springfield, Ill., Aug. 13, 1860, Library of Congress, Prints and Photographs
Division, LC-DIG-ppmsca-17159; Lincoln letter accompanying the "Prospective
Thirteenth Amendment, Transmitted to the Governor of North Carolina by
President Abraham Lincoln and Secretary of State William H. Seward,
March 16, 1861," courtesy of the State Archives of North Carolina.

Page vi: Lincoln letter, courtesy of the State Archives of North Carolina.
Page viii: text of the proposed thirteenth amendment, courtesy of the
State Archives of North Carolina.

Library of Congress Cataloging-in-Publication Data
Crofts, Daniel W., author.
Lincoln and the politics of slavery : the other Thirteenth Amendment
and the struggle to save the union / Daniel W. Crofts.
pages cm
Includes bibliographical references and index.
ISBN 978-1-4696-2731-1 (cloth : alk. paper)
ISBN 978-1-4696-2732-8 (ebook)
1. Lincoln, Abraham, 1809–1865—Political and social views.
2. United States. Constitution. 13th Amendment—History.
3. Slaves—Emancipation—United States—History—19th century.
4. Slavery—Law and legislation—United States—History. I. Title.
E457.2.C935 2016   973.7092—dc23
2015032054

For my students at
TRENTON STATE COLLEGE
and
THE COLLEGE OF NEW JERSEY,
1975–2014

To His Excellency,

The Governor of the State of North Carolina,
Raleigh.

Washington, March 16, 1861.

Sir:

I transmit an authenticated copy of a Joint Resolution to amend the Constitution of the United States, adopted by Congress and approved on the 2d of March, 1861, by James Buchanan, President.

I have the honor to be,

Your Excellency's obedient servant,

Abraham Lincoln

By the President:

William H. Seward.
Secretary of State.

Enclosure: 1861, March 2. Joint Resolution adopted by Congress. Copy.

Contents

PUBLIC 7.   RESOLUTION.

THIRTY-SIXTH CONGRESS OF THE UNITED STATES,

AT THE SECOND SESSION

BEGUN AND HELD AT THE

CITY OF WASHINGTON IN THE DISTRICT OF COLUMBIA

ON MONDAY THE THIRD DAY OF DECEMBER ONE THOUSAND EIGHT HUNDRED AND SIXTY.

JOINT RESOLUTION to amend the Constitution of the United States.

Resolved by the Senate and House of Representatives of the United States of America in Congress assembled, That the following article be proposed to the legislatures of the several States as an amendment to the Constitution of the United States, which, when ratified by three-fourths of said legislatures, shall be valid, to all intents and purposes, as part of the said Constitution, viz :

ARTICLE XIII. No amendment shall be made to the Constitution which will authorize or give to Congress the power to abolish or interfere, within any State, with the domestic institutions thereof, including that of persons held to labor or service by the laws of said State.

WM. PENNINGTON,
Speaker of the House of Representatives.

JOHN C. BRECKINRIDGE,
Vice-President of the United States,
and President of the Senate.

Approved March 2, 1861.

JAMES BUCHANAN.

Figures and Table

Lincoln and the Politics of Slavery

Prologue

The Bread Pill

Most Americans were sound asleep during the wee hours after midnight. It was already Inauguration Day—Monday, March 4, 1861. But the United States Senate struggled on through the night, paralyzed by a filibuster.[1] The session had only hours to run. Congress would expire no later than noon, and Abraham Lincoln was about to become president. The issue at hand was a proposed amendment to the U.S. Constitution specifying that Congress could not interfere with slavery in the states where it existed. The amendment was designed to reassure white Southerners that they could safely remain in the Union. Lincoln's election four months before on the Republican Party's antislavery platform had stirred an uproar in the South. Seven slave states in the Deep South, from South Carolina west to Texas, already had seceded and begun to form a separate government, the Confederate States of America. They would not tolerate Lincoln, a "Black Republican." But eight slave states in the Upper South, home to two-thirds of white Southerners, clung uneasily to the Union, and no shots had yet been exchanged.

Just days before, the House of Representatives had narrowly mustered a two-thirds majority in favor of the amendment. The Senate would need the same margin to send it to the states for ratification. If the Senate did not act during the next few hours, the amendment would die. Secessionists wanted the amendment stopped. Were ordinary white Southerners to get the idea that slavery would be safe in the Union, the case for an independent South would unravel. Hard-line Republicans had their own reasons for wanting the amendment stopped. They demanded that the Constitution be "obeyed rather than amended." Any seeming concession would condone the South's outrageous behavior. So Louis Wigfall, the Texas duelist and Confederate agent, droned on into the night, as did "Bluff Ben" Wade, the bluntly anti-Southern senator from Ohio. Anxious conciliators, who saw the amendment as a possible means of bringing about peaceful reunion, sat tight and hoped to outlast its opponents.[2]

James Murray Mason. "They were unable to agree to give you anything more than this wretched bread pill." *Congressional Globe*, 36:2 (Mar. 4, 1861), 1388. Photograph by Mathew Brady, Library of Congress, Prints and Photographs Division, Brady-Handy Photograph Collection, LC-BH82- 3489 A.

Occasionally the Senate's discussion was animated by give and take. The disgruntled Virginia Democrat James Murray Mason led the effort to shunt the amendment aside. Tall, imposing, clad in homespun, and with a chaw of tobacco lodged permanently in his cheek, Mason had given up on the United States. He wanted Virginia to align with the seceded states of the Deep South. He therefore condemned the amendment as a "wretched bread pill," designed to delude the patient "under the belief that he has taken a salutary medicine"—when in fact he had taken only a placebo, containing "crumbs of bread." Mason loftily spurned the proposed reassurance. Any danger to slavery in the states was "remote." Virginia's "principal grievance" was "the great territorial controversy." Virginia and the slave states demanded security for their "rights in the common Territories." It was an irrelevant subterfuge to promise that Congress never would interfere with slavery in the states. The soon-to-be Confederate diplomat hated the bread pill but would be obliged to accept it if the filibuster failed. A month before, the voters in his home

Stephen A. Douglas. "When there is a disease of the mind which the patient imagines to be a physical malady, but which is imaginary only . . . a bread pill . . . is the best medicine possible." *Congressional Globe*, 36:2 (Mar. 4, 1861), 1388. Late 1850s, Library of Congress, Prints and Photographs Division, Brady-Handy Photograph Collection, LC-BH82- 2460 C.

state had delivered an emphatic two-to-one verdict against secession. He had to vote for any Union-saving measure that Congress might enact.[3]

Stephen A. Douglas, the amendment's floor manager, rejected Mason's evasions. The feisty Illinois Democrat had been at sword's points with the Southern wing of his party for the past three years. The Little Giant, so-called because his massive head was mounted on a stubby torso, was not to be taken lightly. Nobody could match his verbal virtuosity or his gift for rapid-fire repartee. Douglas insisted that the proposed amendment spoke directly to the most emotionally charged anxieties felt by ordinary white Southerners. "Secessionists and disunionists," he exclaimed, had incessantly repeated that it was "the fixed purpose of the North" to change the Constitution and "abolish slavery in the States by an act of Congress!" He was no friend of the Republican Party, and during his 1858 Senate campaign against Lincoln he had repeatedly tried to fasten the abolitionist label on his opponent. But that was for effect. Douglas knew better. Lincoln and other Republican leaders always vowed that they had neither the power nor the intention of interfering with slavery in the states where it existed. Douglas knew too that moderate Republicans had carried the amendment through to House passage. So he cheerfully accepted the bread pill idea. The "best doctors" sometimes administered bread pills, he reflected, to counteract "a disease of the mind." A placebo was the correct way to treat a patient who thought himself to be suffering from a "physical malady" that is "imaginary only." Secessionists feared that the amendment would "pacify" the South, Douglas charged, because it would show people there that the North was "determined to do them justice."[4]

Douglas also derided Mason's claims about the significance of the "the great territorial controversy." He pointed out that Republicans had quietly given ground with regard to the territories. They had just voted to organize three western territories—Dakota, Colorado, and Nevada—with no reference to slavery. Even though they had the power to impose their long-sought formal prohibition of slavery in the territories, they had chosen not to do so. In effect, Republicans validated the position Douglas himself had long held—that the controversy about slavery in the territories could best be resolved at the territorial level, not dragged into national politics. He thought that Republican scare tactics had created a monster. By demanding that slavery be barred from arid western territories where it never would have taken root, Republicans had roused the equally pig-headed Southern Rights clamor. If the South had any tangible grievance, Douglas insisted, it was a concern about the future safety of slavery in the states, and the amendment addressed that directly.[5]

The leading Senate Republican, New York's William Henry Seward, who only a year before had been the odds-on favorite to win his party's presidential nomination and who more recently had been selected to become secretary of state, chose not to remain at the Capitol that fateful night. Instead he allowed Douglas to take charge. Improbably, the two were for the moment allied. Both Seward and Douglas gave priority to accommodating the Upper South's embattled Unionists, who had managed so far to gain the upper hand and hold their states in the Union. The amendment would help. Congressman John A. Gilmer of North Carolina, who advised both Seward and Douglas, cheerfully agreed that the South needed only a few bread pills to cure its madness. But the bread pills would take time to work. They would be useful only if the short-term crisis could be defused.[6]

The Upper South's Unionists therefore beseeched their Northern allies to avoid a military showdown with secessionists. They warned that any shots fired in anger might kill the Union cause in Virginia, North Carolina, Tennessee, and across the Upper South. But hard-line Republicans were in no mood to listen. They insisted that lawless seizure of federal property in the Deep South had to be stopped. They believed that secessionists would back down if confronted by unmistakable evidence that the federal government stood ready to use force against them—or that a few battlefield victories would quickly restore the Union.[7]

Seward did not know whether Lincoln remained open to conciliation. A week before, he had told the president-elect to tone down his inaugural address, because he feared the draft version Lincoln had shown him would be seen in the South as a call to arms. Seward then ran himself into the ground attempting to persuade Lincoln to rethink his approach. But Seward was so uncertain whether Lincoln had heeded his advice that he penned a brief note on March 2 refusing to serve as secretary of state. This was a desperate, high-stakes gambit—Seward hoped to jolt Lincoln away from any immediate showdown with the South. So for Seward the amendment was only one part of an excruciating puzzle. But it was a part in which he had a direct stake—he was its author. And even as hard-line Republicans were doing their best to scuttle the amendment, Douglas specified that it had Seward's support.[8]

The handsome new Senate chambers, which had opened for use just two years before, presented a startling spectacle during the hours after midnight, early on March 4. Half the senators were "asleep on the sofas, and some in their seats," noted a reporter for *Harper's Weekly*. The galleries had long since emptied. "Repeated motions for a recess were made." But Douglas, "with bull dog tenacity," refused to give in. At last, just before 5:20 A.M., "the ayes and noes were called for, and the Resolution passed by 24 to 12—just the necessary two-thirds."[9] Both houses of Congress had agreed to offer the bread pills. Only the future would reveal whether they would have the desired effect.

As the early spring dawn began to lighten the Capitol's gleaming white marble, few in Washington knew or cared what the Senate had just done. Its vote came much too late to make the Monday morning newspapers, and the story was sure to be crowded aside on Tuesday by the momentous events of the upcoming day. Jubilant Republicans thronged the capital to celebrate their party's crowning achievement. More than a few hungrily anticipated a division of the loaves and fishes. All eyes were on the lawyer-politician from Illinois who stood ready to wield power.

Lincoln delivered his inaugural address from the east front of the Capitol early that same afternoon, amid bright sunlight and a stiff breeze. Never had a speech been more keenly awaited. The vast national crisis overshadowed an occasion marked in quieter times more by ceremony than by substance. The new president hoped to contain and reverse the secession movement. To do that, he needed to arrest the dangerous spiral toward war and preserve the peace. Lincoln's text included many of Seward's conciliatory suggestions. "We are not enemies, but friends," he pleaded. "We must not be enemies." He urged his "dissatisfied fellow countrymen" in the South to reconsider their recent actions. Neither he nor the Republican Party, Lincoln insisted, would "interfere with the institution of slavery in the States where it exists." Noting that Congress had just passed a constitutional amendment to rule out such a possibility, he announced that he had "no objection" to making explicit what he always had thought implicit in the Constitution. In short, the man who would come to be known as the Great Emancipator came to power having just accepted a prospective constitutional amendment that barred any attack on slavery in the slave states.[10]

We know, of course, that Lincoln proved unable to prevent war. Six weeks after his inauguration, the Confederate government opened fire on Fort Sumter in the harbor of Charleston, South Carolina, and Lincoln then called for 75,000 soldiers to be raised from all the states. Rival waves of patriotic fervor swept both the North and the South. Four additional slave states—Virginia, North Carolina, Tennessee, and Arkansas—reversed course to align with the Deep South. Both sides thereby stumbled into a far more bloody and protracted war than could have been imagined in early 1861. Nobody ever expected such a "fundamental and astounding" result—as Lincoln so memorably noted four years later in his second inaugural address—with slavery, "the *cause* of the conflict," brought to an abrupt end and the status of four million former slaves dangerously and urgently unresolved.[11]

THE HOUSE AND SENATE's last-minute approval of the would-be thirteenth amendment—and Lincoln's endorsement of it—has long since disappeared from sight. It was never ratified by more than a handful of states because the war it was designed to avert started six weeks later. During the course of that war, the ground rules that remained in place through March 1861 were swept completely away. A war originally waged to restore "the old Union as it was" became a war to create a new Union in which slavery had no place. The actual Thirteenth Amendment, ratified in 1865—four years and one war later—specified exactly the opposite of the original version. The two Thirteenth Amendments—the one that did not become part of the Constitution in 1861 and the one that did in 1865—bookend the most critical four years in American history. And it is the 1865 version we choose to remember, especially after seeing Steven Spielberg's 2012 film *Lincoln*.

Why then, it may be asked, should we read about such an odd curiosity as the other thirteenth amendment? Something so contrary to the mainstream national narrative seems strangely out of place. It is bound to give Americans today an uneasy feeling—surprised to learn that both houses of Congress approved it and relieved to know that it was never ratified. Wasn't it merely transitory, hatched on the fly amid an unprecedented crisis, and best forgotten? Weren't Republicans who put forward the amendment acting out of character and abandoning their values in ways they never would have done except in face of a grave emergency? Does the amendment really reveal anything worth knowing about?

A full answer to these key questions requires a book, but the reader is entitled to a brief defense in advance of the chapters that follow. The prospective thirteenth amendment of 1861 reminds us that hardly any white Americans on the eve of the Civil War expected emancipation in the foreseeable future. Abraham Lincoln, as we shall see, judged that slavery would last for a century or more. He and other Republican leaders always stated that they had no power to liberate slaves and no intention of doing so. The idea that slavery in the slave states was untouchable had a long pedigree, and it was accepted by almost all antislavery politicians during the decades before the war. States that wanted slavery could have it.

Leading Republicans endlessly asserted that they stood with the Founding Fathers. They wanted to block the expansion of slavery, and they looked forward to its eventual disappearance. But they recognized that white Southerners would have to take the initiative. Republicans considered themselves good constitutional conservatives, not dangerous radicals. Unwilling to take seriously the outrageous "Black Republican" caricature propagated on the Southern hustings, Republicans walked blindly into a grave crisis. They did not anticipate war—certainly not a titanic four-year struggle—and they did not envision themselves as emancipators.

Today we assume that the Civil War was fought to end slavery, but we forget that no Republican supported in advance using armed force to bring about such an "astounding" result (Lincoln's adjective, as already noted). The Union army went south to quell the rebellion, not to emancipate slaves— only to find that the two were inextricably interconnected. The war emboldened slaves to flee their bondage, to aid the Union army, and to volunteer for combat. The war changed everything—most especially the willingness of white Northerners to continue tolerating slavery—and ultimately made it possible to adopt the real Thirteenth Amendment.

The story of the other thirteenth amendment also shines a damning light on the late antebellum South's political leaders, especially its powerful nucleus of Deep South Democrats. They exaggerated the dangers the white South faced. At work here, in part, was the very nature of Southern political discourse. Rival partisan entrepreneurs sought to identify threats to popular liberty—and to smear their opponents for displaying insufficient zeal in blocking such threats or for insidiously collaborating with the South's enemies. It became standard procedure for political orators to warn that the South was menaced by abolitionism. These accusations likely resonated because white Southerners presided over a system of forced labor while they pretended that black slaves were content. Endless affirmations that slavery was a "positive good" for everyone involved never quite banished the fear that ferocious rebels might lurk behind inscrutable black masks. White Southerners were predisposed to be suspicious.[12]

The Deep South's political leaders did see a deadly threat in late 1860, but not the supposed threat to slavery. A politician faced with sudden loss of power and position experiences a fear that nonpoliticians never encounter. When Jefferson Davis saw his constituents flock to the secession cause during the weeks after Lincoln's election, he and his counterparts faced a choice. Should they still lead by riding the new wave, or should they abdicate? Whether or not they thought secession made sense (Davis had doubts, and he was far from the only one), they reflexively decided to keep leading. A kind of groupthink was at work. If many others are headed up the same blind alley with you, it can't be all bad and there must be strength in numbers.

Their answer, however, was hardly the only one imaginable. In the winter of 1860–61, whites in the Upper South also were emphatically proslavery— but not prosecession. Most non-Democratic political leaders in Virginia, North Carolina, and Tennessee, aided by a sprinkling of Union Democrats, warned that secession was utterly reckless and suicidal. It would lead to war, and war could destroy slavery and revolutionize Southern society. Until forced to choose sides in that war, the Upper South deplored the drive for Southern independence.[13]

Secession was the most calamitous example of bad judgment in all of American history. It was designed to counteract a supposed danger to slavery—even though Republicans insisted that they would only restrict its "territorial enlargement" (again, Lincoln). Southern secessionists spurned the proffered constitutional amendment, fractured the Union, and started a war. They paid no heed to abundant historical evidence that slavery was particularly vulnerable during wartime. Instead, they removed their states from the protection of the Constitution and provoked growing numbers of Northerners to demand an end to slavery, the apparent taproot of the rebellion.

After Lincoln issued the Preliminary Emancipation Proclamation in September 1862, his secretary of the treasury, Salmon P. Chase, observed that Southern slaveholders had fallen victim to collective "insanity." Had they stayed in the Union, they might have kept slavery "for many years to come." No party or public feeling in the North "could ever have hoped" to touch it. But instead slavery had been "madly placed in the very path of destruction." And who had placed it there? —the slaveholders themselves.[14] In the end, secession destroyed slavery.

THIS BOOK HAS TWO BASIC ELEMENTS. First, it focuses on the effort to enact the other thirteenth amendment. This never has been done before. In the several excellent modern studies of secession, the amendment gets no more than cursory treatment, fuzzy on specific details and at points simply misinformed. It is often repeated—incorrectly—that the amendment would for the first time have incorporated the word "slavery" into the Constitution. In fact, it paraphrased the circumlocution of the original Constitution. Even if deeply rooted, slavery was a national embarrassment both in 1787 and in 1861. It is also frequently stated that the amendment could never have been changed. A version that could not have been touched without consent from every state was indeed under consideration for a time. But that version was dropped, so the actual amendment approved by the House and Senate stated simply: "No amendment shall be made to the Constitution which will authorize or give to Congress the power to abolish or interfere, within any State, with the domestic institutions thereof, including that of persons held to labor or service by the laws of said State."[15]

The amendment was only one facet of the North-South sectional crisis that would culminate in civil war. To understand the impasse this supposed palliative was created to remedy, one must distinguish between *slavery in the states* and *slavery in the territories*—remember the sharp exchange between Douglas and Mason at the start of this Prologue. Even vociferously antislavery members of the Republican Party—for example, Pennsylvania Congressman Thaddeus Stevens and his Illinois counterpart Owen Lovejoy—agreed that slavery in the states could never be abolished by the federal government. On the other hand, all Republicans—and not just the party's more militant wing—insisted that slavery should be prevented from expanding into the territories. Douglas and his Republican allies attempted to reassure white Southerners that slavery was secure in the states where it existed, so there was no reason to break up the Union.

The endlessly debated issue during the secession winter—and the years leading up to it—was slavery in the territories. Promoters of the would-be constitutional amendment attempted to change the topic. They reasoned that slaves did not live in the territories; they lived in the slave states. And hardly any slaveholders intended to take their slaves to the territories. But the amendment often was received coldly. Many white Southerners, aware that Republicans had already said that they would not interfere with slavery in the slave states, dismissed the amendment as an inconsequential gesture or even a deliberate insult. Historians have often agreed. The amendment was "not likely to do much to mend matters," wrote the eminent Roy Franklin Nichols. "Could not something real be done?" Viewed in retrospect, however, the amendment looks all too real. Nichols's eminent counterpart, David Potter, judged the territorial issue an empty sideshow that was "largely exhausted"—but the amendment "now seems an appallingly greater concession to the South."[16] Somehow, the elephant in the room became marginalized while an irritating mouse remained the center of attention. *Lincoln and the Politics of Slavery* will redirect attention to the larger of these two creatures.[17]

This book's second basic element involves an inquiry into the tension between history as it actually unfolded and history as it is remembered. Americans tend to read back into history what we would like to find there—a nation "conceived in liberty," where slavery never really belonged; squadrons of slaves riding the underground railroad to freedom, secreted in the hidden passages of homes opened to them by public-spirited white Northerners; and a civil rights movement in the 1950s and 1960s, supported by all right-thinking people, that decisively ended racial discrimination and made American practices square with American ideals. We want history to be a source of inspiration and reassurance. We crave "a chronicle of national greatness" and shun "reminders of what seems shameful or demeaning," writes historian David Lowenthal. We create a "yearned-for past," altered to accommodate "present needs," and we "reshape our heritage to make it attractive in modern terms."[18]

Americans today find it difficult to accept that slavery once loomed large in the United States and that slaveholders wielded formidable political and economic power. We find it difficult to imagine that slavery once was normal, taken for granted, and very much a given. We thereby fail to see the country as it was. Our image has no place for a Republican Party and an Abraham Lincoln who pledged not to interfere with slavery in the states where it existed and who knew the law was on the side of slaveholders when they attempted to recapture fugitive slaves. The comforting legend of an underground railroad, historian David Blight reminds us, creates the impression that principled white Northerners fatally weakened the slave system even before the war started and assured that America's "race problem" would be "banished by emancipation." We forget Lincoln's lament to his Kentucky friend Joshua Speed: "I confess I hate to see the poor creatures hunted down, and caught, and carried back to their stripes, and unrewarded toils; but I bite my lip and keep quiet." Even if repelled by the injustices of slavery, Northerners generally, like Lincoln, gave priority to maintaining "their loyalty to the constitution and the Union."[19] We also tend to overlook the ugly reality that African Americans living in the free states before the Civil War were shamefully excluded from economic or educational opportunities and from public life. Racial stigmas, the perverted stepchild of slavery, were (and are) national and not simply Southern.

The other thirteenth amendment runs contrary to uplifting national mythology. Twenty-first century American sensibilities, combined with a near-universal tendency to exalt Lincoln, obscure the situation in 1860–61. It makes no sense to us that professedly antislavery Republicans, including Lincoln, all could vouch that they had neither the power nor the intention of touching slavery in the states where it existed. We assume they must have been kidding. But we assume wrongly. Lincoln and his fellow Republicans disliked slavery. They hoped it would disappear eventually. But they had no blueprint to get from here to there. They counted on white Southern slaveholders to realize—at some point in the distant future—that free labor would create a more prosperous and productive society than slave labor. Neither Lincoln nor the Republican Party expected to fight a war to revolutionize Southern society.

Today we rightly honor Lincoln as the Great Emancipator, but during the troubled months following his election as president, the last thing on his mind was the long-run future of slavery in the United States or the many indignities and hardships suffered by American slaves. Historians often depict Lincoln as someone who came to office with a clear view of the road ahead, determined to do what needed to be done.[20] In fact, the president-elect had no time to ruminate on the matters he had discussed with Speed years before. Even if the South had acquiesced quietly to his victory, Lincoln faced a daunting task in staffing his administration.[21] As it became plain that he would inherit the gravest political crisis ever to confront a new president, he could not have spared a moment to think about slavery or slaves.

Steven Spielberg's fine movie creates the impression that Lincoln always wanted to do what he did do in 1865—use the leverage of the presidential office to persuade Congress to ratify the Thirteenth Amendment that abolished slavery. But Spielberg's *Lincoln* lacks a time dimension. It does not touch the situation just four years earlier when Lincoln accepted a radically different thirteenth amendment that would have precluded the one for which he is now celebrated. Spielberg's many viewers need to be aware that Lincoln became the Great Emancipator only after earlier having vowed that he had no such intention.

Starting with the mental framework of the early twenty-first century, we assume that all the players on the stage in late 1860 and early 1861 recognized that the showdown moment between slavery and freedom had arrived. We seek an easily understood morality tale in which brutal slaveholders and their political allies found themselves confronting the victors of the 1860 election, whose antislavery commitment would win favor with Amnesty International. Several contemporary historians do indeed depict Republicans as virtual abolitionists who welcomed a war for emancipation.[22] But they read the evidence selectively. To be sure, many militant hard-core Republicans in New England and the New England exodus regions to the west did see Lincoln's election as the first big step that might lead eventually to emancipation. Because these Yankees hated slavery, hyperbolic white Southerners decided that all Republicans were bloodthirsty abolitionists. The mass panic that swept the South in November and December also was fueled by the dreaded erosion of Southern political power and a hot-tempered anger at the North for refusing to heed Southern warnings that a Lincoln victory would have serious consequences.

Even though we assume that slavery was the crux of the matter, Southern secession created an immediate problem far more pressing than the long-run future of slavery. What secession principally threatened, Northerners judged, was orderly constitutional governance. If the Southern states had the right to break up the Union simply because they had lost an election, they gravely endangered what historian Russell McClintock felicitously identified as "America's unique experiment in self-government, whose example was to have inspired the overthrow of monarchy and the spread of republican principles throughout the world."[23] Explosive Northern anger, the deadly counterpart and mirror image of its Southern twin, was driven far more by the spectacle of secessionists seizing federal property and dishonoring the American flag than by the maltreatment of Southern slaves.[24]

The pages that follow challenge the popular image of the Civil War as a Homeric epic in which the boys in gray and the boys in blue bravely jousted with each other. Their sacrifices, or so we tend to see it, were part of a splendid ritual that ultimately reknit the national fabric. Here, too, the American wish to have a history we can feel good about gets in the way of understanding what actually happened. The war began with a catastrophic breakdown of governance. It brought wholesale violence and misery on a scale that nobody could have imagined in advance and that still staggers the imagination today. But somehow the war must be seen as purposeful and fulfilling—and conducted according to some kind of logical script. Because the war ultimately ended with the Union restored and slavery abolished, we assume that it must have been entered into and conducted by farsighted leaders who had clear objectives in mind—so that its outcome somehow was predetermined or foreordained. This version of history cannot easily be squared with the uncertainties and messy realities through which people lived and died during the 1860s.[25]

THIS BOOK DIVIDES INTO FOUR PARTS. The first part establishes the antebellum context. Its initial chapter considers how abolitionists struggled to reconcile their hatred of slavery with the U.S. Constitution, which most Americans understood to allow slavery in the states that wished to have it. William Jay, the central personality in this chapter, sought to "denationalize" slavery by making it entirely a matter of state law and absolving the federal government from any role in sustaining it. The second chapter traces the rise of the political antislavery movement. It shows how three pioneering leaders—Joshua Giddings, Salmon P. Chase, and Charles Sumner—continued the struggle to "denationalize" slavery. They would abolish it in the District of Columbia, prevent its spread to new territories, exempt the federal government from responsibility for fugitive slaves, limit the interstate slave trade, and bar new slave states from entering the Union. But the quest for electoral success created pressures to pull back from a broad-focus antislavery agenda. The third chapter shows that the Republican Party, established in the mid-1850s, was dominated by moderates—most notably, Lincoln. They insisted that the territorial issue alone best demonstrated the party's antislavery principles while at the same time respecting the Union and the Constitution. Republicans of all types distanced themselves from abolitionists and emphasized that they posed no threat to slavery in the states where it existed.

This book's second part, "Origins of the Other Thirteenth Amendment," traces its emergence in December 1860 and January 1861. The fourth chapter, entitled "Mutual Misconceptions," examines the irreconcilable explanations of current reality that arose in the prosecession Deep South, the Republican North, and the conditionally pro-Union Upper South. None of the contending parties accurately understood the situation in which they found themselves, and each managed to downplay its lethal potential. Chapter 5 centers on New York senator William Henry Seward, soon to be Lincoln's secretary of state, who recognized sooner than most Republicans that the secession epidemic in the Deep South created an imminent threat of war. To counteract the most emotionally charged issue that divided North and South, he drafted the constitutional amendment to bar any interference with slavery in the states where it existed. Chapter 6 introduces Seward's counterpart in the House of Representatives, Ohio's Thomas Corwin, a prominent veteran who headed a special committee to address the crisis and sponsored an amendment similar to Seward's.

The book's third part, "Debating the Other Thirteenth Amendment," recaptures the diversity of opinion that swirled in January and February 1861. Chapter 7 describes how the amendment's supporters—conciliatory Republicans and antisecession Southerners—tried to make common cause. This chapter profiles seven key House members and concludes with the startling pro-Union victories in early February, when large popular majorities in Virginia and Tennessee rejected secession. Chapters 8 and 9 address the internal debate within the Republican Party in January and February. Conciliators who supported the constitutional amendment said that it would strengthen the Upper South's Unionists, who held their states out of the secession vortex. But those who represented New England districts and the New England exodus areas to the west faced intense constituent pressures to "not give an inch." Those pressures are at the heart of chapter 8. Hard-line Republican leaders disavowed all intention of attacking slavery in the states where it existed but argued that it would be wrong to offer concessions in the face of secessionist recklessness; the Constitution should be "obeyed rather than amended." The unyielding stance of the Upper North's spokesmen is the subject of chapter 9.

The fourth part of the book spotlights the would-be thirteenth amendment's brief moment on the national stage. Chapter 10 details the improbable achievement of the conciliators during the last week of the congressional session in late February and early March 1861 as they assembled wafer-thin two-thirds majorities in both the House and the Senate. The eleventh chapter begins with Lincoln's inaugural address on March 4, which vowed that he would not touch slavery in the states and announced that he could accept the amendment. But the Fort Sumter crisis derailed all efforts to contain the crisis. Seward and the Upper South's Unionists wanted to abandon Sumter in order to deprive Confederates of the pretext for starting a war. Lincoln decided, however, that he could not voluntarily relinquish the beleaguered outpost. An armed clash at Sumter between Union and Confederate forces on April 12 and 13, 1861, carried the belligerents across the Rubicon. So the amendment's potential as a peacemaker never was realized, and it stands today as a curious and troubling reminder of an era when slavery appeared to be a fixed presence in American life. Chapter 12 shows that the amendment, even though quickly made obsolete by the outbreak of war, nonetheless was ratified by six states (Kentucky, Ohio, Rhode Island, Maryland, Illinois, and the future state of West Virginia) between April 1861 and February 1862.

Two epilogues and a bibliographical postscript conclude the book. The first epilogue enlarges on the now-familiar story, as dramatized by Spielberg—how Congress, during the last year of the war, approved the real Thirteenth Amendment that abolished slavery. Ohio congressman James M. Ashley, who denied that slavery ever had constitutional legitimacy, spearheaded the struggle to make the actual words of the national charter square with his long-held beliefs. Both in early 1861 and in early 1865, secretive political horse-trading was needed to cobble together two-thirds majorities, and the chief trader for both of the diametrically opposite amendments proved to be William H. Seward, aided by surreptitious lobbyists. The second epilogue shows how the first section of the Fourteenth Amendment— the enlarged definition of national citizenship, and the requirement that states provide equal protection, due process, and privileges or immunities to all citizens—was crafted in 1866 by yet another Republican congressman from Ohio, John A. Bingham, the most radical dissenter from the prewar political consensus that slavery in the states could never be touched by the federal government. Bingham believed that the promise of equality always was implicit in the Constitution; he insisted that it be made explicit. He thereby created what has become the Constitution's most important section. The bibliographical postscript explores what other historians have and have not understood about the stillborn thirteenth amendment of 1861. There are clear reasons why it has been distorted or overlooked. The topic is especially awkward for those who lionize Lincoln and those who imagine that Republicans before the war cheerfully embraced the abolition cause.

In the end, *Lincoln and the Politics of Slavery* tells a cautionary tale. If we impose our own values on the past and imagine that historical actors saw the world just as we do, we distort the historical record. The same problem arises when we pick and choose among these actors and hand out gold stars to the ones whom we consider like-minded. The message is plain. We do not live in the mid-nineteenth century, and Abraham Lincoln never can be our contemporary in the early twenty-first century. When we ignore historian David Lowenthal's wise admonition—"the past is a foreign country"—we impair our ability to understand that past.[26]

PART I

The Antebellum Context

1

The Abolition Movement and the Problem of the Constitution

William Jay hardly could believe his ears. He hated slavery as much as anyone, but he also believed that abolitionists dared not minimize the immense challenges they faced. What upset Jay were the debates at the fifth annual meeting of the American Anti-Slavery Society (AA-SS), held in New York City in May 1838, which showed that a majority of his fellow delegates embraced what he considered a "vile heresy."[1] They insisted that the Constitution of the United States forbade slavery. Even though the slave system had grown ominously during the previous half century, shielded by an array of state laws and apparent national sanction, Jay's critics contended that slavery lacked any legal basis. If the Constitution were correctly interpreted, they proclaimed, it must be seen as an antislavery document. Congress could legislate against slavery, and abolition could begin forthwith.

Jay had played a key role in founding the AA-SS five years before at Philadelphia. Son of the eminent John Jay, William Jay tried to show how abolitionists could combat slavery while staying true to the Constitution. He persuaded his colleagues "to fully and unanimously recognize the sovereignty of each State to legislate exclusively on the subject of slavery." He feared that it would be "fatal to the cause" to contend otherwise. Unless abolitionists "acknowledge[d] the existence of slavery under State authority," in "strict accordance to the Constitution," their position would be untenable. Those who opposed slavery should make their case "within the limits of the Constitution," Jay argued, by using the press, the right of petition, and the right to assemble. He anticipated that "the great mass of the northern people" would, before long, bring pressure on their representatives in Congress to rule slavery out of bounds wherever it was a matter of federal rather than state jurisdiction—in the District of Columbia, in new territories west of the Mississippi, and on the high seas. He believed the constitutional power of Congress to take these three steps could not be "rationally questioned."[2]

William Jay. "Our Fathers, in forming the Federal Constitution, entered into a guilty compromise on the subject of slavery." Jay, *Miscellaneous Writings on Slavery* (Boston: John P. Jewett, 1853), 217. Sketch by Charles Martin in Jay, *Miscellaneous Writings on Slavery*, frontispiece, courtesy of the Maine Historical Society.

William Jay once wrote that "our fathers, in forming the Federal Constitution, entered into a guilty compromise on the subject of slavery." His words carried special weight. No other abolitionist had such a direct link to the Founding Fathers.[3] John Jay had not been a delegate at the Constitutional Convention in Philadelphia in 1787, but soon afterward he joined with Alexander Hamilton and James Madison to write the influential *Federalist Papers*, which made the case for ratifying the Constitution. John Jay's experience as a diplomat persuaded him that the United States needed a stronger central government than it had under the Articles of Confederation. But he was also a leading opponent of slavery, and he well knew that the slave interest had exacted a high price in framing the Constitution.

In several ways, the national charter provided special benefits for slaveholders. It allowed the international slave trade to continue for twenty years. It awarded slave states extra weight in the House of Representatives and the Electoral College—they gained the right to count three-fifths of their enslaved inhabitants in addition to all of their free inhabitants. By the 1830s, this "overrepresentation" gained the slave states twenty-five extra members of the House and twenty-five extra electoral votes in selecting a president.[4] The Constitution also pledged that the federal government would protect the states against "domestic Violence"—a cryptic reference to slave insurrections. And it asserted that "Persons held to Service or Labour" (that is, slaves) who escaped from one state to another were to be "delivered up" rather than "discharged."

Some delegates at Philadelphia in 1787 regretted that slavery was so em-

The Antebellum Context

Gouverneur Morris. He said "what many
of the delegates knew in their heart, but
deeply wished not to acknowledge or
discuss." Garrett Epps, *Democracy Reborn:
The Fourteenth Amendment and the Fight
for Equal Rights in Post–Civil War America*
(New York: Henry Holt, 2006), 3. Drawing
by Pierre-Eugène du Simitière, Library of
Congress, LC-USZ62-45482.

bedded in the Constitution, but only Pennsylvania's Gouverneur Morris plainly spoke his mind. "Upon what principle is it," he inquired, "that the slaves shall be computed in the representation? Are they men? Then make them citizens, and let them vote. Are they property? Why, then, is no other property included? The houses in this city [Philadelphia] are worth more than all the wretched slaves who cover the rice swamps of South Carolina." Morris tartly explained the significance of increased representation for slave states. It meant that "the inhabitant of Georgia and South Carolina who goes to the Coast of Africa, and in defiance of the most sacred laws of humanity tears away his fellow creatures from their dearest connections and damns them to the most cruel bondages, shall have more votes in a Government instituted for the protection of the rights of mankind, than the Citizen of Pennsylvania and New Jersey who views with a laudable horror, so nefarious a practice." He would "sooner submit himself to a tax for paying for all the negroes in the U[nited] States, than saddle posterity with such a Constitution." Morris's eloquence could not budge the practical mind-set that dominated the convention. His proposal to exclude slaves from the formula for representation, and to base it instead on "free inhabitants," won support from only a single state.[5]

Blunt candor set Gouverneur Morris apart. He said "what many of the delegates knew in their heart, but deeply wished not to acknowledge or discuss," modern legal scholar Garrett Epps has written. Among the other leading men of the time, John Jay stood closer to Morris in his hatred of slavery than anyone else. The founder and president of the New York Manumission Society, Jay repeatedly tried to end slavery in his home state. Finally in 1799, during his term as governor, he had the satisfaction of signing into law the state's gradual emancipation act. In his earlier role as an American diplomat, Jay angered Southern slaveholders. The important treaty between Great Britain and the United States that he negotiated in 1795 had been ill-received in the South, in part because it failed to secure compensation for the thousands of American slaves liberated by the British army during the Revolution.[6]

William Jay not only inherited his father's scruples against slavery but also gave them new force and intensity. While maintaining his family's commitment to the Episcopal Church, he also became deeply involved with the new religious stirrings of his era. His leadership in the American Bible Society prefigured his involvement in a broad spectrum of reformist-evangelical causes. Jay's commitment to antislavery deepened when he discovered, in 1826, that Gilbert Horton, a free black man who once had lived near Jay's home in Westchester County, New York, was being held as a slave in the District of Columbia. As Jay learned more about the tawdry matter, he kept asking why a locality under the exclusive jurisdiction of Congress even allowed slavery. Soon he spearheaded a petition to request that Congress abolish slavery in the District. "Were the free States to will it," he wrote, "slavery would cease at the capital of the republic." He believed that "the progress of knowledge and religion" eventually would compel white Americans to reconsider their addiction to slavery. Ending it in Washington would have "a salutary influence."[7]

Jay knew that abolitionists faced an uphill fight in the battle to sway public opinion. "Multitudes of good people who abhor slavery," he wrote, nevertheless feared that abolitionists were "a set of dangerous fanatics" whose ideas would trigger slave rebellions and destroy the Union. Accordingly, the privileged insider with the sterling pedigree advised his friends to frame their arguments carefully. They must heed the constitutional boundaries that "forbid all other than moral interference with slavery in the Southern States." He wanted abolitionists to show that emancipation offered a safer future than continued expansion of the slave system. [8]

At the same time, Jay urged abolitionists to take the lead in defending the interests of the free states. He pinpointed the grave constitutional issues raised when the House of Representatives voted to reject petitions calling for the abolition of slavery in the District of Columbia. The right of petition was "one of the most unequivocal and undoubted of all constitutional rights" and it was "expressly guaranteed" by the First Amendment. Freedom of the press enjoyed similarly high constitutional protection, also in the First Amendment, and yet postal officials removed abolitionist newspapers from the mails and burned them.[9]

When abolitionist men and women petitioned Congress to bar slavery from the federal territories and the District of Columbia, they stirred the ire of South Carolina's great champion, John C. Calhoun, who protested against any such "intermeddling" by those who considered slavery "sinful and immoral." He warned that "the first battle is to be fought in this District and in the Territories"—that abolitionists hoped to carry "these exposed points" and thereby initiate "a direct and dangerous attack on the institutions of all the slaveholding States." It was the "universal sentiment" among abolitionists, Calhoun charged, that "abolition in the District was the first step to abolition in the States." He urged fellow Southerners not to "yield" or "give ground." They should demand their constitutional rights and insist that the federal government give "increased stability and security to the domestic institutions of the States."[10]

During the 1830s, when the abolition movement gained unprecedented visibility and stirred deep controversy, Jay was among its most forceful spokesmen. His stature resulted from "the influence of his pen"—he was a gifted writer and publicist but not an effective platform speaker. Poor eyesight and chronic ill health typically kept Jay at home. He never attempted the stern regimen of itinerant abolitionist oratory that vaulted Theodore Dwight Weld, for example, to prominence. An outbreak of rioting in New York City in 1834 against abolitionists and the city's beleaguered black residents stirred Jay's power with words. His scathing polemic published months afterward, *Inquiry into the Character and Tendencies of the American Colonization and American Anti-Slavery Societies*, established his reputation in abolitionist circles. His subsequent writings industriously unearthed gut-wrenching specifics from Southern sources about the ill treatment of slaves—and he demanded that others share his moral outrage. His compendious *View of the Action of the Federal Government in Behalf of Slavery*, published in 1839, showed that supporters of slavery had repeatedly enlisted the assistance of the federal government when it suited their needs. He thereby undermined the argument that Congress could refuse abolitionist petitions, on the grounds that matters involving slavery concerned only the states.[11]

Jay scorned Southern warnings that continued abolition agitation might drive the slave states out of the Union. It was one thing to make idle threats, in hopes of intimidating the North. But if slaveholders actually attempted disunion, they would transform themselves from "our fellow countrymen and citizens" into "foreigners who had discarded our friendship and connection." Northern antislavery sentiment, "at present chiefly confined to the religious portion of the community," would become more universal if the South disrupted the Union. Resentful at seeing the nation "torn asunder," Northerners would no longer allow slaveholders to reclaim fugitives. So Jay dismissed Southern threats to dissolve the Union—they were not "the result of mature determination" but were instead outbursts of passion. He was unable to see how secession would "tend to guard and perpetuate the institution of slavery." If "insulated from the sympathies of the whole civilized world," the South would become a pariah nation. Sooner or later, "stung with insults and injuries," it would "appeal to arms." It could then be invaded by hostile armies. "The standard of emancipation would be reared, and slavery would expire in blood." Because secession would be so "preposterous and disastrous," he concluded, "we may reasonably presume it will not occur."[12]

What Jay considered unimaginable did, of course, happen. To anticipate briefly, this book's central concern will be the political crisis that flared into civil war in April 1861. The focus here will be the root issue that divided North and South—the security of the slave system in the states where it existed. The ostensible sticking point at the center of national political controversy during the 1840s and 1850s—the future of slavery in the territories where it did not yet exist—was in reality a proxy for the root issue. Growing numbers of white Southerners concluded, like Calhoun, that the effort to bar slavery from the territories or the District of Columbia was simply a smokescreen and that the antislavery movement's real goal was to weaken and eliminate slavery in the states. A conviction that slavery was no longer safe in the Union fueled the Southern Rights and secession movements. In the end, the Deep South spurned a last-minute Republican offer to amend the Constitution, so as to make explicit that slavery in the states where it existed lay beyond the reach of Congress.

Let us return to the 1830s, when the vanguard of principled reformers decided that "the guilty slumber of the nation" must be challenged. An articulate and irrepressible nucleus of young Northerners announced that slavery had become an urgent moral problem. Every slave had the right, they insisted, to *immediate, unconditional emancipation.* William Lloyd Garrison's *Liberator* started to publish in 1831, soon to be followed by the *Weekly Emancipator*, edited by William Goodell with support from Arthur and Lewis Tappan. The New England Anti-Slavery Society was organized in 1832; during the following year Great Britain emancipated its slaves in the West Indies, and a new national organization was created—the AA-SS.

The Antebellum Context

It boldly vowed "to convince all our fellow-citizens, by arguments addressed to their understandings and consciences, that Slaveholding is a heinous crime in the sight of God, and that the duty, safety, and best interests of all concerned, require its *immediate abandonment*, without expatriation." By emphasizing a moral imperative and calling for immediate action, abolitionists rejected gradualism and ignited an intense national controversy regarding slavery.[13]

Abolitionists initially thought that slavery could be terminated through persuasion—that "reason and truth" might exert a "moral influence" to awaken the consciences of slaveholders.[14] This noble hope was destined to disappointment. However inspired, imaginative, and persistent—and they were all of these—the proponents of immediate emancipation ran into a wall of hostility in the white South. The slave system was deeply entrenched and growing rapidly. A booming interstate slave trade fueled the explosive growth of cotton cultivation in the Deep South, which supplied the essential raw material for industrial manufacturing in both the United States and western Europe. Whites in the slaveholding states closed ranks in the face of criticism and did their best to stifle the abolition message. Immediatists were warned repeatedly that their lives would be in danger if they ever came South. Many whites in the free states likewise rejected any challenge to the proslavery status quo. Influential Northern elites—"gentlemen of property and standing"—encouraged antiabolition mob violence or turned a blind eye when an urban rabble took the initiative. Abolitionists were widely regarded as unreasonable troublemakers. "To say that slavery ought to be immediately abolished," Jay recalled, "was sufficient cause for the clergyman to lose his pulpit and the merchant his credit."[15]

Almost all white Americans of the era considered it axiomatic that "only the states could abolish or in any way regulate slavery within their jurisdictions" and that "the federal government had no power over slavery in the states." Jay and the pioneering abolitionists who founded the AA-SS specifically renounced any legal right to interfere with slavery in the states where it existed. They thereby accepted what historian William Wiecek dubbed the "federal consensus." From the start, however, the "federal consensus" made members of the AA-SS uncomfortable. Suffocated by the gradualism that previously constrained the antislavery community, they believed that slavery should be abolished immediately. Their "momentous shift in outlook" was coupled with the hope that "moral suasion" might persuade slaveholders to renounce their undeserved dominion over other humans. Members of the AA-SS also pondered ways in which the slave system might be attacked and weakened, even while heeding constitutional barriers that forbade interference with slavery in the states.[16]

Those who would end slavery while respecting the Constitution had to walk a fine line. The AA-SS acknowledged "the exclusive right" of each slave state to legislate in regard to slavery. Congress had "no right to abolish slavery in the Southern States"—it could be "lawfully abolished" only by the legislatures of the states "in which it prevails." Moreover, the AA-SS specified that "the exercise of any other than moral influences to induce such abolition" was unconstitutional, and it cautioned slaves against "vindicating their rights by resorting to physical force." But as we have seen, the AA-SS also thought it both legal and desirable to terminate the federal government's involvement with and support for the slave system. It asserted that Congress had the constitutional right to abolish slavery in the District of Columbia, to prohibit it in territories and new states, and to end the domestic slave trade. Immediatists also soon decided that the federal government had no responsibility for recapturing escaped slaves. Aware that slavery had been uprooted from the free states during and after the Revolution, opponents of slavery hoped that slaveholders in the slave states likewise might come to see the wisdom and justice of emancipation.[17]

For several years, Jay's idea about the Constitution appeared to be generally accepted among abolitionists. For example, the Massachusetts Antislavery Society acknowledged in August 1835 that "no change in the slave laws of the Southern States can be made, unless by the Southern Legislatures. Neither Congress nor the Legislatures of the free States have authority to change the condition of a single slave in the slave States." Jay was "not aware that there was a man or woman belonging to an antislavery society who entertained a different opinion."[18]

But the late 1830s were a time of yeasty ferment within the abolitionist movement. A substantial faction suddenly emerged to proclaim that slavery was unconstitutional and that Congress had the power to act against it in the slave states. Matters came to a head in May 1838 at the fifth annual meeting of the AA-SS in New York City, when Alvan Stewart of Utica, New York, attempted to strike from the AA-SS constitution the clause that recognized the right of the slave states to control the institution within their own borders. The ensuing two-day debate marked him as the pioneering leader among immediatists who rejected the "federal consensus." A tall and powerful speaker whose evangelical awakening transformed him from a prosperous lawyer into an ultra-abolitionist, Stewart already led the New York State Anti-Slavery Society. He called for a new definition regarding the Constitution's relationship to slavery—that the two were entirely inconsistent with each other and that the Constitution, if correctly understood, actually was an antislavery document. He insisted that the Fifth Amendment to the Constitution—which stated that no person should be "deprived of life, liberty, or property, without due process of law"—meant that slavery lacked any legal basis. Congress therefore could abolish slavery nationwide "simply by passing a declaratory statute carrying into effect the spirit and intention of the Fifth Amendment." At least forty-six of the eighty-four who attended the convention of the AA-SS in 1838 in New York City sided with Stewart, but not the two-thirds necessary to alter the organization's basic statement of purpose that had been agreed to five years earlier. The breach was destined to persist.[19]

Stewart's view of the Constitution hinged on a sleight of hand. Downplaying the concessions that slaveholders extracted during the Constitutional Convention in 1787—notably the three-fifths clause and the fugitive slave clause—he contended that an amendment adopted just four years later, in 1791, negated the 1787 compromises and transformed the Constitution into an antislavery document. Historian Jacobus tenBroek observed that Stewart was "not concerned with historic meanings or precedents." He combined a "bold imagination" with a "disregard for historical fact." His whole argument was "a priori, hypothetical, [and] suppositional." He wanted to establish "great moral, political, [and] constitutional truths."[20]

Stewart subsequently persuaded a number of other leading abolitionists—including Lysander Spooner, William Goodell, James G. Birney, Jane Swisshelm, and Joel Tiffany—that Congress had the power to abolish slavery in the states. They charted a definition of paramount national citizenship that superseded state law, based on the comity clause in article 4, section 2, which guaranteed to the citizens of each state "all Privileges and Immunities of Citizens in the several States." By this line of thought, a person who qualified for citizenship in one state could not be held as a slave in another—and Congress had the power and the responsibility to end slaveholding in all the states, just as in the territories and the District of Columbia. So, too, they read article 4, section 4 of the Constitution, which guaranteed each state a republican form of government, to mean that state laws upholding slavery were unconstitutional. It was an "absurdity," thundered Goodell, to say that "there can be *constitutional* slavery in the United States."[21]

Abolitionists who believed slavery incompatible with the Constitution insisted that the Declaration of Independence's promise of equality—"that all Men are created equal, that they are endowed by their Creator with certain unalienable rights, that among these are Life, Liberty, and the Pursuit of Happiness"—had been grafted onto the Constitution and was part of the fundamental law of the United States. The Declaration's "mighty moral discovery," wrote Stewart, made slaveholding "a base hypocrisy, a violation of our engagements to mankind, and to God." He and like-minded immediatists contended that the Constitution's preamble—"we the people of the United States"—specifically echoed the reference to "all men" in the Declaration and thereby linked these two key foundational documents. But the efforts to define an antislavery Constitution through article 4 and the Declaration's vision of equality suffered from the same defects as Stewart's reading of the due process clause. Each required a mix of tunnel vision and historical amnesia. Rather than recognize that the Founding Fathers had decided grudgingly to tolerate an institution that was too deeply rooted to eradicate, abolitionists who saw the Constitution on their side teased out specific words and phrases to establish that slavery lacked any legal validity. Repeatedly, concluded historian Aileen Kraditor, they insisted that the Constitution "was in reality very different from what everyone thought it was."[22]

William Jay felt "great uneasiness for the future" when he found that many of his fellow abolitionists ignored what he considered a constitutional imperative. He peppered his correspondence with complaints about the "folly" and "utter absurdity" of Stewart's seductive stance. It effectively abandoned moral suasion and "virtually recommend[ed]" the use of "*military power*" against the slave states. If Congress were to legislate against slavery in the states, Jay warned, "bloodshed and national calamity" would result. He decided the oath he had taken as a county judge to support the Constitution made it impossible for him to continue playing a role in antislavery societies. He also noted that he had just completed a revised version of his influential book, *Inquiry into the Character and Tendencies of the American Colonization and American Anti-Slavery Societies*, which confidently defended abolitionists against the accusation that they intended to interfere with slavery in the slave states. That segment of the book would now have to be rewritten to include "painful and humiliating confessions."[23]

Viewed narrowly, those who imagined an antislavery Constitution were deluded visionaries. But if viewed from a longer perspective, it becomes apparent that they glimpsed something transcendent and that they ultimately set in motion the most fundamental rewriting of the Constitution ever to occur. Of course a war had something to do with that, too. In the pages that follow we shall read more about two Ohio congressmen, James M. Ashley and John A. Bingham, the truest heirs to Stewart's vision of an antislavery Constitution.

The best-remembered leader of the abolitionist movement, William Lloyd Garrison, developed a view of the Constitution that was antithetical both to Jay's and to Stewart's. Garrison decided in the early 1840s that the Union and the Constitution were hopelessly tainted by concessions to slaveholders and compromises with slavery; he thereupon famously labeled the Constitution "a covenant with death and an agreement with hell." He condemned "the people of the North" for having made a "fatal compromise" with "Southern oppressors" that resulted in slavery being "nourished, protected and enlarged." Wendell Phillips, the most dynamic spokesman for Garrison's wing of the movement, issued a pamphlet, *The Constitution, A Pro-Slavery Compact*, a historically based case that the Founding Fathers had "consciously incorporated protection for slavery into their Constitution." James Madison's recent book, based on notes taken in 1787 during the Constitutional Convention, convinced Phillips that the Constitution was designed to appease slaveholders and provide national sanction for the slave system—most notably through the three-fifths clause that increased the political weight of slaveholding states, the reopening of the African slave trade for twenty years, and the fugitive slave clause. To explain the rapid growth of the slave system in his own time, Phillips noted that slaveholders dominated the federal government, trampled the rights of the free states, and made "the courts of the country their tools." In his view, anyone who voted or held office was "responsible for the sin of slavery."[24]

Garrison's "no government" and "non-resistance" wing of the movement, which before long came to dominate the AA-SS, maintained that all compulsory laws were sinful—including laws that William Jay had long maintained would be eminently constitutional and desirable, such as an act by Congress to abolish slavery in the District of Columbia. Jay was "as strong an advocate of emancipation as lived," but his family roots in the world of realpolitik also set him apart from the "come outers," who argued that existing political and religious institutions were so corrupted by slavery that a person of conscience must separate oneself from them. He saw a flawed Constitution that nevertheless gave opponents of slavery several potential levers. He knew that slavery had embedded itself in American economic, social, and political life, that it could not simply be wished away, and that individuals could not divorce themselves from the collective problem.[25]

During the 1840s and 1850s, a fourth and ultimately the most consequential element of the antislavery movement took shape. Opposition to slavery gradually became a political force, small at first with the two presidential campaigns of the Liberty Party in 1840 and 1844, then more formidable with the formation of the Free Soil Party in 1848. Not until the mid-1850s, however, did a tidal wave of growing Republican Party strength in the free states vault political antislavery to the fore. From that point onward, the antislavery movement focused on electing more Republicans to office. The three groups of cutting-edge immediatists—those who tried with Jay to live within the "federal consensus," those who like Stewart rejected it to proclaim an antislavery Constitution, and Garrisonians who spurned the proslavery Constitution—all found that they must share the antislavery stage with calculating politicians who gave priority to winning elections. Indeed, political antislavery effectively pushed abolitionists to the wings of the stage. But the stage itself would not have existed without the pioneering labors of the early abolitionists. Their agitation, historian Eric Foner emphasizes, "helped to establish the context within which politicians like Lincoln operated."[26]

Mainstream Republicans constantly reiterated that the federal government had no power to touch slavery in the states where it existed, and they were disinclined to pursue any antislavery agenda other than territorial restriction. Some Republicans also wanted to curtail slavery in the District of Columbia and to limit federal responsibility for recovering fugitive slaves. But the party's 1860 presidential candidate, Abraham Lincoln, considered it divisive for the party to adopt a position on any slavery-related issue other than the territories—and so he quietly ruled out of bounds those in the party who wanted to condemn the Fugitive Slave Act or call for emancipation in the national capital. On balance, Republicans were content to await protracted and gradual antislavery advances. Lincoln once mused that slavery might last another century.[27]

But if Republicans as a party carefully circumscribed their antislavery agenda, the emerging Republican coalition included many individuals, both prominent and humble, who were immediatists at heart and who hoped that antislavery might triumph sooner rather than later. Joshua Giddings, Salmon P. Chase, and Charles Sumner—each to be discussed in the next chapter—sought to "denationalize" slavery. That is, they would divorce the federal government from any responsibility for upholding or sustaining the slave system and leave the matter entirely to the slave states. What this meant in practice was equivalent to the program championed by William Jay and the other immediatists who accepted the "federal consensus"—abolishing slavery in the District of Columbia and in the territories, refusing to admit additional slave states to the Union, severely restricting or the eliminating the interstate slave trade, and (after 1850) repealing the Fugitive Slave Act. This agenda appealed to many Republican rank and file. But militant Republicans did not speak for the entire party, and the stance assumed by the national party in its victorious 1860 campaign gave short shrift to those who favored more immediate action.[28]

After retreating from the AA-SS, William Jay became an unaffiliated abolitionist freelance. He turned down an overture from the Liberty Party in 1840 because several of its leaders, including Alvan Stewart, had attempted to wrench the AA-SS away from his views of constitutional propriety. But he remained an active writer for the abolition cause, so much so as to lose his Westchester County, New York, judgeship. Several years later Jay's horror at the Texas annexation and the Mexican War did draw him into the Liberty Party, the first time he had identified with any political party, although he remained vigilantly opposed to those who believed the federal government had the power to end slavery in the states. He championed the Wilmot Proviso, which attempted to prevent the spread of slavery to territory acquired from Mexico, and he took heart at the Free Soil insurgency's "wonderful progress" in 1848. "The seed the abolitionists have been scattering for years," he exulted, "is evidently germinating and exhibiting a vigorous growth."[29]

Was the course of history moving in Jay's direction? At times he thought not. He excoriated Daniel Webster for supporting the Compromise of 1850 and the "atrocious Fugitive-Slave Act." The latter imposed obligations on the federal government that the fugitive slave clause of the Constitution had left the states to resolve, Jay fumed, and it "nearly demolished" the "moral bulwark raised against slavery in times past by the religious sentiment and the respect for the rights of man." He condemned the "stupendous iniquity" of the Kansas-Nebraska Act, which repealed the Missouri Compromise's restriction on the westward expansion of slavery, and he feared that it opened the door to future proslavery aggressions in the Caribbean and Central America. The "disgraceful" assault on Charles Sumner by Preston Brooks in May 1856 alarmed the aging Jay and renewed his fears of civil war. The "plaudits" showered on Brooks in the South revealed "an extinction of the moral sense in the slave-holding community."[30] But Jay rejoiced when the Republican Party rose to challenge the Slave Power. The Republican platform was consistent with his long-held ideas, even though it lacked the moral intensity and the broad scope of his immediatism. His understanding of the Constitution did, however, directly anticipate that of Giddings, Chase, and Sumner—the left wing of the emerging Republican Party. Their quest to denationalize slavery, like his, involved more than territorial restriction.

Jay died in 1858, having "set an example to the class most able and least willing to oppose the curse of slavery." Notable among those who mourned Jay's passing was his fellow abolitionist Frederick Douglass, who pronounced a solemn eulogy at the leading African American church in New York City, Shiloh Presbyterian. "We have, as a people, too few real friends even among our professed friends," Douglass observed, "and we have now lost one of the truest and best of that few." With the pen his "weapon of choice," Jay had "affirmed all the leading principles of modern Abolitionism" and "the great cause of human freedom" even before the movement became organized. Consistent with his long-held constitutional views, which rejected any congressional power to legislate regarding fugitive slaves, Jay willed some of his estate to promote the "safety and comfort" of fugitives. This was, Douglass affirmed, "the crowning act, the most glorious climax to a great and benevolent life." [31]

2

Antislavery Politics and the Problem of the Constitution

Joshua Giddings, newly elected to the House of Representatives, fearlessly stood his ground in February 1839 as "the greatest confusion prevailed." Although repeatedly "called to order for arguing the abolition question," he kept speaking. The sanitized shorthand preserved in the *Congressional Globe* only hints at the upheaval stirred by the Ohio firebrand's blunt words. Horrified by the "barbarous spectacle" of public auctions on the grounds of the U.S. Capitol at which slaves were bought and sold, and sickened by the way his "Northern friends" in the House allowed themselves to be intimidated by "Southern Bullies," the tall, barrel-chested frontiersman from the Western Reserve insisted that "the seat of the government could not be long continued in the District of Columbia with the existence of the slave trade therein." He therefore opposed appropriating money to build a bridge across the Potomac River. Southerners denounced Giddings's "gross calumnies and foul aspersions" and called for his arrest, but he boldly persevered. He refused "to remain silent and witness my country's disgrace."[1]

Born in 1795, Giddings was a self-educated attorney. He was elected to the House in 1838 as a Whig from a district in the northeastern corner of Ohio where New Englanders clustered and where antislavery and abolition sentiment was intense. Forthright and outspoken, he soon became "the most effective antislavery agitator in Congress." James Brewer Stewart, his biographer, has written that Giddings, like abolitionists such as Alvan Stewart and Lysander Spooner, "overlooked the basic predicaments others saw in the Constitution." He could not admit to himself "the Constitution's proslavery nature." His understanding of politics derived from his religious outlook. His "faith in the conversion experience" led him to transcend "political life as it was" so as to promote what "he fully expected it soon *would be*."[2]

Giddings, however, actually held federal office. So he was obligated to take into account things as they actually were, and he could not see the Constitution as a purely antislavery document. He decided it did allow the

Joshua R. Giddings. "I was compelled to . . . witness my country's disgrace." Giddings to "Dear Sir," Feb. 26, 1839, Joshua R. Giddings Miscellaneous Papers, New-York Historical Society, quoted in James Brewer Stewart, "Joshua R. Giddings, Antislavery Violence, and the Politics of Congressional Honor," in *Abolitionist Politics and the Coming of the Civil War* (Amherst: University of Massachusetts Press, 2008), 124. Library of Congress, Prints and Photographs Division, Brady-Handy Photograph Collection, LC-BH82- 5251 C.

original thirteen states to maintain slavery if they so chose. But he insisted that the Founding Fathers wanted to "denationalize" slavery—to relieve the federal government of responsibility for upholding it. In his view, neither slavery nor the slave trade in the District of Columbia had any constitutional basis. He likewise objected to transforming federal territories into slave states, to employing federal soldiers to hunt escaped slaves in the Florida Territory, or to using the navy to protect the coastwise slave trade. Neither the federal government nor the free states, Giddings asserted, had any obligation to help slaveholders recover fugitives.

In the eyes of most Americans in the 1830s and 1840s, including most Northerners who disliked slavery, the argument that Congress simply could legislate slavery out of existence was a fiction, far divorced from political reality. Notwithstanding the castles in the sky constructed by Stewart, Spooner, and others, slavery had sturdy constitutional and legal foundations that could not be wished away. Historian David Potter once astutely observed that most Americans who wanted slaves to be free also "wanted the Constitution, which protected slavery, to be honored, and the Union, which was a fellowship with slaveholders, to be preserved." Though "committed to values that could not logically be reconciled," they nonetheless

The Antebellum Context

sought ways "to oppose slavery and to cherish a Constitution and a Union which protected it."[3]

So the emerging political antislavery movement of the late 1830s and 1840s had to address the problem of the Constitution. Those who attempted to steer the antislavery impulse into the realm of electoral politics confronted political arrangements and assumptions that conflicted with an idealized system imagined by those who saw the Constitution as an antislavery document. To be sure, the purists who founded the Liberty Party in 1840 included Alvan Stewart and others who shared his utopian views. They wanted to show that they stood apart from the corruption of the two national political parties, especially from Henry Clay's Whig Party, which enjoyed the allegiance of many antislavery voters. But the Liberty Party never really played a political role or sought electoral success; it appealed principally to a hard core of committed abolitionists. By the late 1840s it had become an inconsequential rump.[4]

The pioneering antislavery politicians had to pursue a different course than the Liberty Party, even though some of them—most notably Salmon P. Chase—toiled for a time as Liberty men. Unlike the purists, however, Chase and others like him tried to widen the antislavery appeal in the hope of achieving electoral success. They grudgingly accepted that the slave states might manage their own affairs without outside interference, but they denied that that federal government had any responsibility to help maintain slavery. Like William Jay, they wanted to abolish slavery in the District of Columbia, exclude it from the territories, forbid the creation of new slave states, and stop the interstate slave trade. They also saw fugitive slaves as a state responsibility, not something that should involve the federal government. In 1848, Chase succeeded, as we soon shall see, in shepherding most Liberty Party supporters into a larger political coalition.

The focus of this chapter will be three notable pioneers in the political antislavery movement—Giddings, Chase, and Charles Sumner. Starting in the late 1830s and the early 1840s and spurred by the handful of dissenters in Congress, the antislavery campaign became a larger part of national political discourse than ever before. But as political opposition to slavery grew and matured, it also became less driven by immediatist and evangelical sensibilities. The war with Mexico (1846–48) and the controversy over slavery extension widened the political antislavery movement's base while at the same diminishing its scope. Between 1846 and 1861, the issue of slavery in the territories grew to overshadow all others.

As we shall see, the rise of the Republican Party in the mid-1850s reduced the expansive agenda of the early political antislavery movement to a single least common denominator—a commitment to prevent slavery from expanding into the territories. Republican managers worried that any additional antislavery demands—regarding fugitives, the slave trade, new slave states, or the District of Columbia—would narrow the party's appeal. Republicans disliked slavery, hoped that it eventually would disappear, and believed that the South exercised disproportionate power in the Union. But Republicans also accepted that white Southerners had the law on their side in those states where slavery existed.

Let us resume with the outspoken Giddings. He frequently ran afoul of the so-called gag rule, through which leaders of the Democratic and Whig Parties attempted to bar antislavery discussion from the House of Representatives. When abolitionists petitioned Congress in 1836 to end slavery in the District of Columbia, Henry L. Pinckney of South Carolina attempted to quash the petitions and put Congress on record that it would be "unwise, impolitic, and dangerous" to touch slavery in the District. Pinckney also wanted Congress to specify that it possessed "no constitutional authority to interfere in any way with the institution of slavery in any of the States." Anticipating Calhoun, he explained that abolitionists hoped to use "this District as a lever" or an "entering wedge" but that their true objective was *"general emancipation"*—"they never will be satisfied with anything short of it." Pinckney proposed to "crush out" their hopes "by saying to them, plainly and distinctly, that this Government possesses no power whatever by which they could be aided in their views. Satisfy them that they have no hope in relation to the States, and they will soon cease to trouble us in relation to the District."[5]

At first glance, it would appear that Pinckney had hit on a successful strategy. He won large House majorities for his resolutions ruling out interference with slavery in the District and laying aside or ignoring all petitions having to do with slavery. Although most Northern Whigs opposed Pinckney on the District and the gag, all Southerners and almost all Democrats voted with him. Pinckney's resolution forbidding interference with slavery in the states passed by a nearly unanimous vote, 182–9.[6]

But one of the nine was former president John Quincy Adams, who put up a spirited fight. During wartime, he cautioned, "there are many ways by which Congress not only have the authority, but are bound to interfere with the institution of slavery in the States." And war was more than a remote possibility: American ambitions for Texas threatened war with Mexico, which also had the potential to create conflict with Britain or France. "Your own Southern and Southwestern States" could become "the battle-field upon which the last great conflict must be fought between slavery and emancipation," Adams warned. "From the instant that your slaveholding States become the theatre of war, civil, servile, or foreign, from that instant the war powers of Congress extend to interference with the institution of slavery in every way by which it can be interfered with."[7]

Congress had no power to "meddle" with slavery, Adams noted several years later, so long as the slave states kept it "within their own bounds." But if the slave states were to seek the aid of the federal government in putting down an insurrection, that use of the "war power" potentially would change everything. The "laws of war" that operated during wartime included the power to emancipate slaves. Before attempting "to plant the lone star of Texas and slavery on the walls of Mexico," Adams cautioned, Southerners should think twice about the likelihood that war with Mexico would lead to war with Great Britain.[8]

Adams befriended and deeply influenced Giddings. Although Adams cared most about civil liberties and did not share Giddings's evangelical mentality, the two worked closely together, especially in early 1842, when both audaciously ignored the gag and created an uproar in the House. Giddings focused on the case of the *Creole*, an American ship involved in the coastwise slave trade. In 1841, a cargo of slaves seized control of the *Creole* and forced the captain to sail to the Bahamas. Giddings insisted that the federal government had no power to uphold slavery on the high seas and no basis for demanding that Britain return the absconding slaves. Southerners were outraged that Giddings saw no problem with a slave rebellion on an American ship. His Southern Whig colleagues joined with almost all Democrats to censure him. Giddings thereupon resigned his seat. Several months later he was triumphantly reelected. In the Western Reserve, if not elsewhere, voters welcomed a militant antislavery stance that spurned white Southern sensibilities.[9]

Although the gag was finally repealed in December 1844, Adams and Giddings had little chance to celebrate. A month before, Democrat James K. Polk had been elected president on an expansionist platform that called for annexing Texas, and the lame-duck administration of President John Tyler maneuvered to secure Texas through a joint resolution of both houses of Congress. Adams, Giddings, and a number of other antislavery Northerners did their best to block the resolution. They complained that a proslavery conspiracy orchestrated the Texas movement, that it would drag the United States into a war with Mexico, and that American soldiers would be needed to secure slavery in Texas and prevent runaways. Most Whigs opposed annexation, but Democrats and a handful of Southern Whigs supported it. Adams considered the vote on Texas "the heaviest calamity that ever befell myself and my country."[10]

In January 1846, Giddings once again threw the House into turmoil when he challenged the Democratic Party to follow through on the other part of its expansionist campaign—to secure all of Oregon ("54° 40′ or fight"). He knew that most Whigs wanted nothing to do with any Democratic drives for territorial expansion, but he and Adams and a number of other antislavery Whigs sided with western Democrats, who were ardent for Oregon. The free states deserved the right to expand to the northwest, Giddings insisted, because acquiring Texas had created a majority of slave states in the Senate and surrendered "the free labor of the North" to the control of "a slaveholding oligarchy."[11]

Giddings recognized that asserting American rights to Oregon might lead to war with Great Britain, but better war "with all its horrors" than continued submission to "slaveholding power." If war did occur, he predicted, it would cripple the slave system. The "people of the North" would awaken "to sever the cords which have so long, unconstitutionally, bound us to the putrescent carcass of slavery." The bondsmen of the South, he warned, would have every motive to welcome British liberation. "I would not be understood as desiring a servile insurrection," Giddings observed. He hoped "the downtrodden sons of Africa in our Southern States" would use "quiet and peaceful means" to secure their freedom. "But if they cannot regain their God-given rights by peaceful measures, I nevertheless hope they will regain them; and if blood be shed, I should certainly hope that it might be the blood of those who stand between them and freedom, and not the blood of those who have long been robbed of their wives and children and all they hold dear in life." Were "blood and massacre" to accompany "the struggle for liberty of those who for ages have been oppressed and degraded, my prayer to the God of Heaven shall be, that *justice—stern, unyielding justice*—may be awarded to both master and slave." In short, war would bring "the death of slavery." The man who defended the slave rebels on the *Creole* five years before thereby cemented his reputation, in the eyes of his critics, as a reckless firebrand who cheerfully welcomed the slaughter of Southern whites. His words were destined to be endlessly quoted for the next fifteen years, whenever a proslavery speaker wanted to show that antislavery politicians were trying to stir up slave insurrections.[12]

And there was a geopolitical kicker. Not only would war with England cripple the American slave system, Giddings predicted; it also would bring within the grasp of the United States "the Canadas, Nova Scotia, and New Brunswick, adding, at least, six new States to the northern portion of the Union." These would "restore to the North that balance of power which was surrendered up by the acquisition of Texas." Giddings thereby contemplated something that continued to intrigue a number of antislavery Northerners—an expanded Union that embraced part or all of Canada and that did not necessarily include all the slave South.[13]

Polk's demand in May 1846 that Congress declare war against Mexico irrevocably reshaped the political antislavery movement. Giddings might risk war to acquire all of Oregon, because he hoped such a war might have antislavery consequences, but he regarded war with Mexico as a war for slavery. Many in the free states had doubts about the war against Mexico, but only Giddings and Adams and dozen other Whigs in the House, mostly from Massachusetts and Ohio, dared to vote against it. Disgusted by the way most Whigs reluctantly voted appropriations for the war, even including his mentor Adams, Giddings began to look for allies elsewhere. He was intrigued to find that antislavery Democrats led by Pennsylvania's David Wilmot demanded that slavery be forbidden in any territory acquired from Mexico. Meanwhile so-called Conscience Whigs used the same issue to spur a revolt against the state party in Massachusetts. Might there be a way to bring all antislavery elements together in a new party? Giddings visited New Hampshire to stump for John P. Hale, a leading antislavery Democrat, and he corresponded with Salmon P. Chase, who had worked for years in their home state of Ohio to make the militantly antislavery Liberty Party a counterweight to the two major parties.[14]

Like Giddings, Chase had New England antecedents. Born in 1808 to a large family in a small New Hampshire town, he had risen through his own efforts rather than any inherited advantages. He presented "a striking figure," writes his biographer, John Niven—"tall, big-boned and well-muscled, clean shaven and immaculately dressed." Chase established himself as an attorney in Cincinnati, the Queen City of the West, directly across the Ohio River from Kentucky. He and the city's modest cluster of New Englanders were appalled by antiblack and antiabolition riots that flared in 1836 and 1841, and Chase took the lead in devising new legal and political strategies to limit and reverse the power of proslavery interests. His keen mind, facile pen, strong voice, and driving ambition soon elevated him to statewide and national prominence.[15]

Chase and Giddings thought alike regarding the Constitution. Both be-

Salmon P. Chase. "The allegation against us of an intention to interfere with slavery in the states . . . prejudices against us many worthy and sensible people, who think that the Constitution authorizes no such interference." Chase to Gerrit Smith, May 14, 1842, in *The Salmon P. Chase Papers*, vol. 2, *Correspondence, 1823–1857*, ed. John Niven (Kent, OH: Kent State University Press, 1996), 97. Library of Congress, Prints and Photographs Division, LC-B813- 1747 B.

lieved that it absolved the federal government of any responsibility for up-holding slavery—in the territories, in the District of Columbia, and on the high seas. Only the slave states themselves could pursue fugitives, and in so doing they had no claim to support from the federal government or the free states. Chase filed a learned brief to this effect with the U.S. Supreme Court in the celebrated Van Zandt case. He considered slavery "a creature of state law" that should be "confined within those states which admit and sanction it." It had no "constitutional warrant" outside those states. At the same time, Chase cautioned against an indiscriminate assault on "all the positions of the enemy." He knew that "many worthy and sensible people" saw no constitutional basis for interfering with slavery in the slave states.[16]

Chase thought that the Liberty Party could become the nucleus for some-thing more formidable—if it differentiated itself from the "unnecessary odium" that attached to the abolitionist label. Thousands who were "averse to identifying themselves with Abolitionists in name" had been deterred from antislavery politics. He therefore proposed that the Liberty Party direct its energies "against the unconstitutional encroachments of the Slave Power" but leave it to the slave states themselves to determine "the best mode of negro emancipation." He dared to hope that several slave states soon might voluntarily renounce slavery and that "the example of these would speedily

The Antebellum Context

be followed by the rest." The Liberty Party could attract antislavery-inclined men from both the Whig and Democratic Parties, Chase believed, so long as it occupied a "broad enough & large enough" ground.[17]

Chase also labored to distance the fledgling Liberty Party from abolitionists such as Stewart and Spooner, who considered the Constitution an antislavery document. He considered it unrealistic and counterproductive to demand that the federal government abolish slavery in the states. He hoped to win the party's 1844 presidential nomination for William Jay, well known for his conservative reading of the Constitution. Chase's Cincinnati associate Gamaliel Bailey, editor of the *Philanthropist*, noted in Jay's favor that he was "associated with the *revolution*, through his distinguished father." But Jay's detractors countered that the reclusive, well-born patrician lacked a public presence and would appeal only to "a very select class." Jay did nothing to encourage Chase, and the idea proved stillborn.[18]

Chase played a leading role in writing the 1844 Liberty Party platform. It promised to rescue the "National Government" from "the grasp of the slave power," a "privileged aristocracy" of "two hundred and fifty thousand slaveholders." It did not specifically disavow Alvan Stewart's hobbyhorse, but it did categorize slavery as "strictly local" and dependent entirely on "State legislation, and not on any Authority of Congress." Its call for "the absolute and unqualified divorce of the General Government from slavery" showed that the Liberty Party stood for denationalization rather than immediate abolition. Three years later, in June 1847, William Goodell and the wealthy New York philanthropist Gerrit Smith, who believed that the Constitution "made slavery illegal everywhere," seceded from the main body of the Liberty Party. The larger remaining faction of the party, led by Chase, accepted that slavery was legal in the states that practiced it, even though unconstitutional in the territories and based entirely on state law.[19]

In 1848, many former antislavery Whigs and Democrats, prominent among them Giddings, together with the Chase faction of the Liberty Party, abandoned their previous party allegiances and joined together to create the new Free Soil Party. They vowed to stop slavery from entering the new territories acquired from Mexico—this was the so-called Wilmot Proviso. Their broader objective was to draw support from both national parties and give the proponents of denationalization the political muscle to move the country toward ultimate emancipation. Chase urged opponents of slavery to yoke together in new partisan fellowship. He also hoped the antislavery insurgency might accelerate his own individual advancement.[20]

To emphasize the bipartisan basis for the new party, Free Soil managers in 1848 orchestrated a national ticket headed by former president Martin Van Buren, a Democrat, and Charles Francis Adams, a Conscience Whig and son of John Quincy Adams, who had just died in February. Chase drafted the Free Soil platform. It echoed the 1844 Liberty platform in promising "to rescue the Federal Government" from the control of "the *Slave Power*." It stated that slavery depended on "State laws alone" and should not be allowed to expand—"no more Slave States and no more Slave Territory," and "no more compromises with Slavery." It obliquely advocated emancipation in the District of Columbia. Unlike the 1844 Liberty platform, however, which included a quasi-Garrisonian blast at the fugitive slave section of the Constitution, the Free Soil platform in 1848 steered clear of the fugitive issue. Those who imagined an antislavery Constitution could take comfort from complimentary references to the Constitution's preamble and the due process clause. But the Free Soil platform in 1848 made explicit what was only implicit in the Liberty platform of 1844—state laws upholding slavery could not be "repealed or modified by the Federal Government. . . . We therefore propose no interference by Congress with Slavery within the limits of any State." The Free Soil stance thereby anticipated the consensus view of the political antislavery movement in the decade-plus to come—slavery was a regrettable presence in the United States, and the entire country would be better off if it were ended, but national power could not be used to compel the slaveholding states to change their ways.[21]

The Van Buren–Adams ticket attracted more robust support than the Liberty Party had in 1840 or 1844. The top two Free Soil states in 1848 were Vermont and Massachusetts, where it polled 29 percent and 28 percent, respectively, with New York and Wisconsin close behind at over 26 percent each. The Free Soilers collected no electoral votes, but they did affect the outcome in at least two states. A large Free Soil breakaway of pro-Van Buren "Barnburner" Democrats in New York allowed Whigs to carry the largest state in the Union. But in Ohio, the Free Soil Party drew away antislavery Whigs and thereby delivered the state to the Democrats, and the same may also have occurred in Indiana. In no state, however, did the Free Soil Party gain support from all voters whom it might potentially have attracted. Antislavery Whigs such as William H. Seward, Abraham Lincoln, and Thaddeus Stevens stumped for the Whig presidential candidate, Zachary Taylor, and argued that the Whig Party provided the best means to secure antislavery objectives. Antislavery Democrats such as Hannibal Hamlin, Thomas Hart Benton, and John Wentworth likewise championed their party's nominee, Lewis Cass.[22]

The 1848 election in Ohio demonstrated both the limitations of anti-slavery politics and its future potential. Van Buren polled only 11 percent in the state overall, but he ran much stronger in the Western Reserve, Gid-dings's home base, where he won a plurality victory. Free Soil incursions forced Ohio's Whigs to intensify their antislavery appeals. The Whig candidate for governor, Seabury Ford, narrowly survived because he refused to support Taylor and thereby appeased Free Soilers. The state's Whig senator, Thomas Corwin, who will loom large in the pages to come, "traversed the whole state, speaking to large assemblies and to small, at the principal points and in obscure villages" to proclaim that Taylor was "a man of anti slavery opinions and sympathies." Corwin thereby held down Van Buren's totals. Most Ohio voters outside the Western Reserve clung to their previous party allegiances so that Free Soilers, Chase ruefully lamented, were ground "between the upper & the nether millstone." Viewed in retrospect, however, the 1848 campaign ended the era when Whigs and Democrats monopolized Ohio politics and framed partisan discourse there. Historian Stephen Maizlish shows how the 1848 antislavery insurgency effectively undermined the Whig Party in the Western Reserve and lay the foundations for a new state-wide political order in the decade to come.[23]

A trio of Free Soilers—Chase, John P. Hale, and Charles Sumner—won seats in the U.S. Senate in the late 1840s and early 1850s. When the legislatures in Ohio, New Hampshire, and Massachusetts proved to be closely divided between the two major parties, strategically positioned increments of Free Soil legislators found themselves able to use balance-of-power tactics to secure Senate seats. Chase's long labors thereby yielded him a handsome reward. But the intricate backroom maneuvers and sharp elbows that secured his victory left a sour taste in many mouths.[24]

The three Free Soilers found it difficult to wield much influence in Washington, DC. Many Whigs and most Democrats regarded them as deluded troublemakers and political pariahs. The trio were shoved to the political margins and excluded from the corridors of power. The situation on the other side of the Capitol appeared more promising, at least initially. A dozen Free Soilers were elected to the House in 1848, and they held the balance of power between the two major parties. Their first act was to block the reelection of Speaker of the House Robert C. Winthrop, a conservative Massachusetts Whig. By so doing, however, they alienated many antislavery Whigs.[25]

Free Soilers and antislavery Whigs frequently acknowledged, during the protracted debates leading up to the Compromise of 1850, that slavery in the states was beyond the reach of the federal government. Congress had "no right to interfere with slavery by legislation beyond the sphere of our constitutional powers," Chase observed. "We have no power to legislate on the subject of slavery in the States." Instead, it was the "duty" of Congress to "abstain from interference with it in the States." But Congress also had a duty "to prevent its extension." Chase took pains to rebut the argument, recently made by Daniel Webster, that conditions of climate, soil, and rainfall would bar slavery from the territorial west without overt legislative prohibition. Only "positive law" could prevent the expansion of slavery, Chase insisted, and Congress had an "imperative and sacred" responsibility to enact such a law.[26]

Several antislavery leaders in the House made the same distinction between congressional power over slavery in the states and congressional power over slavery in the territories. Horace Mann of Massachusetts, who replaced John Quincy Adams, had been elected with Whig and Free Soil support. Mann abhorred slavery and insisted that it not be allowed to expand, but he denied that the "great body of the people" in the free states ever proposed to overstep the South's constitutional rights. They would not agitate "the question of slavery in the States." George W. Julian, an Indiana Free Soil representative, insisted that Northern antislavery men had the right to articulate their "moral convictions," but he denied that they intended to disrupt slavery in the states. "The subject is beyond our control," he acknowledged; we "disclaim all right on the part of Congress to touch the institution of slavery where it exists." Lewis D. Campbell of Ohio, an antislavery Whig, likewise stated that "the great mass of all parties in my State disclaim all design to interfere with your 'peculiar institution,' in all States where it constitutionally exists." But he stoutly defended the Wilmot Proviso. He also rejected the idea that free men were obliged to hunt fugitive slaves or that free women were obliged to refuse charitable refuge to runaway women.[27]

Thaddeus Stevens, the outspoken Pennsylvania egalitarian then serving his first term in the House, called slavery "the most absolute and grinding despotism that the world ever saw." All "free citizens" of the United States were responsible for perpetuating a "great evil." But he nonetheless vowed to stand by "all the compromises of the Constitution." He confessed that he "greatly dislike[d]" some of these compromises, "and were they now open for consideration, they never should receive my assent. But I find them in a constitution formed in difficult times, and I would not disturb them." Because of these compromises, Stevens admitted, "Congress has no power over slavery in the States. I greatly regret that it is so; for were it within our legitimate control, I would go, regardless of all threats, for some just, safe, and certain means for its final extinction. But I know of no one who claims the right, or desires to touch it within the States."[28]

Such avowals to respect the Constitution hardly satisfied those who represented the slave South. Robert Toombs of Georgia, echoing Calhoun's earlier lament, deplored "the fierce and bitter denunciations" of slavery voiced by Northerners. Even though they appeared to accept "some, at least, of the constitutional obligations to protect slavery," they did so in a manner that made white Southerners suspicious—they "hold these obligations inconsistent with good conscience, and they therefore denounce the institution as 'a covenant with Hell,' and struggle earnestly for its overthrow." Toombs insisted that the South must have "equality" to enter the territories and warned that Southerners would "stand by our arms" rather than allow "the will of the majority" to become "the supreme law of the land."[29]

The Compromise of 1850, originally proposed by Henry Clay, allowed California to enter the Union as a free state. But to sweeten this bitter pill for the South, the compromise refused to bar slavery from two immense new western territories, Utah and New Mexico. Instead it allowed residents there to resolve the matter for themselves. The key element that made the compromise acceptable to the South was the Fugitive Slave Act, which established a mechanism to make the federal government responsible for the recovery of slave runaways. Both during the 1850 debates and thereafter, the Fugitive Slave Act became a lightning rod for antislavery Northerners, prominent among them Charles Sumner.

Sumner was an unlikely and atypical politician. Fluent in French, German, Italian, and Spanish, a legal scholar and orator in the classical mode, the tall and imposing Bostonian had been drawn to antislavery and antiracism by a powerful ideology—that removing barriers to social advancement would enable individuals to realize their potential. He never held public office before winning the Senate seat from Massachusetts, and he lacked the common touch that those in public life either possess by instinct or learn to cultivate. "His intensity and seriousness dampened light conversation," wrote his biographer David Donald. "He had no sense of humor." Reviled by some as "a one-idead abolitionist agitator," Sumner arrived in Washington as a man without a party.[30]

Like other antislavery politicians, Sumner recognized that the Constitution, despite "all its imperfections," secured "a larger proportion of happiness to a larger proportion of men, than any other Government."[31] But he vehemently opposed the idea that the Constitution obliged the free states or the federal government to recapture fugitives. His maiden Senate speech

Charles Sumner. "Our lives are cast under a Constitution, which, with all its imperfections, secures a larger proportion of happiness to a larger proportion of men, than any other Government." Sumner to Wendell Phillips, Feb. 4, 1845, in Irving H. Bartlett, ed., "New Light on Wendell Phillips: The Community of Reform 1840–1880," *Perspectives in American History* 12 (1979): 138. Engraving, Library of Congress, Prints and Photographs Division, LC-DIG-pga-00048.

in August 1852 noted that those who opposed slavery were put down as "sectional," while "its supporters plume themselves as national"—with the result that "a national Whig is simply a slavery Whig, and a national Democrat is simply a slavery Democrat." Instead, he insisted that freedom was national and slavery sectional. The Founding Fathers—George Washington, Thomas Jefferson, Benjamin Franklin, Alexander Hamilton, and John Jay—made their opposition to slavery so plain that "not one of them" could be nominated in 1852 as a presidential candidate by either of the two major political parties.

Sumner insisted that slavery was based only on state law. In certain ways it was tolerated by the federal government, but he pushed back against the idea that either the Declaration of Independence or the Constitution could be construed as proslavery. The Constitution contained "no power to make a slave or to support a system of slavery." Taking an expansive view of the Tenth Amendment, which reserved to the states or the people "the powers not delegated to the United States by the Constitution," Sumner contended that "Congress could not establish slavery in the national territories or protect it in the District of Columbia." Nor could it admit new slave states, exercise jurisdiction over fugitive slaves, or countenance slavery under the American flag on the high seas. Slavery was "a local institution, peculiar to the States." Under the Constitution, Congress could not "legislate, either for its abolition in the States or its support anywhere."[32]

The Antebellum Context

Even though Sumner conceded that Congress had no power to remove slavery from the states, he stood far outside the conventional wisdom of the moment. His theatrical performance rejected the "finality" of the Compromise of 1850 and took dead aim at the Fugitive Slave Act. The latter, he proclaimed, overrode the fundamental laws of the free states regarding trial by jury and habeas corpus. Just as the colonies had made the Stamp Act of 1765 a "dead letter," so the free states were entitled to spurn the Fugitive Slave Act. A law that ran counter to "public conscience" and "could be enforced only by the bayonet" was "no law."[33]

Horrified as Southerners were to hear Sumner's "extraordinary speech" and his broadside against the Fugitive Slave Act, they did agree that slavery was "a State institution where it exists." If it were a national institution, reasoned Senator George Badger, a North Carolina Whig, "it would be liable to national control; and it would be liable, for aught I know, to abolition by national authority." But Badger contended that slavery, "like many other State institutions," was "entitled to a certain degree of aid . . . from the General Government." In particular, the states had a constitutional basis to regard the return of fugitive slaves as a national responsibility—until recently it had been "admitted by all hands to be perfectly within the scope of our authority under the Constitution." Badger dismissed Sumner's "mischievous" effort to deny the slave states legitimate national protection. Sumner really hoped to abolish slavery, Badger contended, but his ideas were "utterly impracticable," because "no sane man" believed it possible to liberate three million slaves, and "no sane man believes it to be desirable, if it were possible."[34]

Stephen A. Douglas of Illinois, the architect of the Compromise of 1850 and its Fugitive Slave Act, complained that Sumner had placed himself in an impossible position. Having taken an oath "to support and sustain the Constitution of the United States," he had no right to pick and choose or to denounce as unconstitutional a law "which has been passed for the purpose of carrying the Constitution into effect." His objections really were "objections against the Constitution, rather than against the law." If he believed that the Constitution violated "the law of God," he should not continue to hold public office. But Chase rose to defend Sumner. The Founding Fathers had intended that the national government avoid "all jurisdiction over the subject of slavery," Chase argued, and Congress had "no power to legislate on this subject." He predicted that Sumner's understanding of the Constitution would ultimately prevail and that it would "sweep this law from the statute-book." Chase did not know when "the hour for its repeal will arrive," but, he promised, "you may rely upon it." His prophecy was not fulfilled on

August 26, 1852. That afternoon, Sumner's motion to overturn the Fugitive Slave Act collected exactly four votes in the Senate—the three Free Soilers (himself, Chase, and Hale), plus Benjamin Wade of Ohio, an antislavery Whig elected with Free Soil votes.[35]

BY LATE 1852 the political antislavery movement reached a low ebb. Most Free Soil Democrats returned to their earlier party allegiance, so that John P. Hale, the Free Soil nominee for president, barely polled half the vote his party had attracted in 1848. But persistent Free Soil loyalties prevented Winfield Scott, the Whig standard bearer, from consolidating the non-Democratic vote in the free states. And while Free Soilers eroded Scott's strength in the North, Whig turnout in the Deep South collapsed, prompted by suspicions that Scott and his party could not be counted on to support the Compromise of 1850. With Whigs whipsawed by defections both North and South, the 1852 election resulted in a Democratic wave. Franklin Pierce of New Hampshire, a "Northern man with Southern principles," swept the presidential election by carrying all but two free states and all but two slave states. Buoyed by votes from recent immigrants, Democrats also amassed huge margins in both houses of Congress, and the Free Soil contingent in the House shrank to three.[36]

But political antislavery's apparent demise was deceptive. The partisan status quo of the previous two decades that pitted Whigs against Democrats encountered a series of shocks that both included and transcended North-South divisions. The pace of social and economic change accelerated in the late 1840s and early 1850s. Unprecedented numbers of new immigrants surged to the United States from Ireland and Germany. A burst of railroad construction encouraged Americans to uproot and move west, and it rewarded larger companies that could sell goods in volume to distant markets. The California Gold Rush fired the imaginations of many restless souls and poured a stimulating volume of new precious metal into the national economy. New communications technologies—the telegraph and inexpensive daily newspapers—made it more difficult for candidates to straddle polarizing issues and eroded support for national political parties. Growing numbers of voters, disenchanted with both Whigs and Democrats, searched for new political homes.[37]

Antislavery forces, galvanized by new provocations, also rebounded to become stronger than ever before. In January 1854, Senator Stephen A. Douglas of Illinois introduced the Kansas-Nebraska bill. It called for repeal of the Missouri Compromise, which had prohibited slavery in western territories north of 36° 30′. Chase, Sumner, and several other "Independent Democrats" from the House issued a rousing "Appeal" that denounced the Kansas-Nebraska bill as "a gross violation of a sacred pledge," "a criminal betrayal of precious rights," and part of an "atrocious plot" to convert the unsettled West into "a dreary region of despotism, inhabited by masters and slaves." Douglas exploded at the "Abolition confederates" for raising a "tornado" of "falsehood." Chase stood his ground. He and Sumner were "but two in a body of sixty-two," he noted; they knew they did not have "the sympathies of this body with us." Their only offense, Chase continued, was to "deny the nationality of slavery." They had never proposed to "interfere" with "any State of the Union upon that subject." But they did insist that the territories should be "preserved from slavery" and that the federal government should stand "on the side of liberty."[38]

Douglas prevailed. The Kansas-Nebraska bill passed both houses of Congress and was signed by President Pierce. But the issue ignited a prairie fire of protest that swept across the free states. Antislavery Northerners suspected the worst—a naked grab by proslavery forces to wrest control of a region that had been legally off-limits to slavery since 1820—and they resolved to resist. "Come on, then, gentlemen of the slave States," New York senator William H. Seward announced. "Since there is no escaping your challenge, I accept it in behalf of the cause of freedom. We will engage in competition for the virgin soil of Kansas, and God give the victory to the side which is stronger in numbers as it is in right."[39] For the next several years, settlers from the free and slave states swarmed into the contested territory, amid mutual recrimination and well-publicized infringements of each other's rights.

Events in Kansas had a major impact on the existing system of national parties. Antislavery Whigs denounced their Southern counterparts for dissolving the glue that held the party together. "Our Southern brethren knew full well that no northern Whig can in any way favor this measure and live," complained Ohio's outspoken radical Ben Wade. They had "compelled every northern Whig to become their political enemy, or to betray his constituents." Wade grimly promised to "accept the issue thus tendered." He was determined to "drive slavery back, and confine it within the States where it exists." The South had "put the North at defiance, and declared a sectional war for mastery." But it would regret having roused the free states from their torpor. "The Constitution of the United States was a hard bargain for the North," Wade observed, as he echoed the point Thaddeus Stevens made four years earlier. With the repeal of the Missouri Compromise, "all further compromises are at an end." Those who tried to humiliate the North, Wade anticipated ominously, "must be hunted down like the Tories of the Revolution."[40]

Free Soil absolutists jousted with moderates to place their stamp on the anti-Nebraska movement. In some places, those who were militantly anti-slavery gave the insurgency a more radical stance. A platform adopted at Jackson, Michigan, in July 1854, called for repeal of the Fugitive Slave Act and abolition in the District of Columbia. The incoming Michigan governor, Kinsley S. Bingham, likewise spoke out to "restrict and denationalize slavery" in his inaugural address in January 1855—he wanted no slavery in the nation's capital, none in the territories, "no slave catching under national law," and "no slave trade in American vessels." Wisconsin Republicans, also first meeting in Madison in July 1854, called for repeal of the Fugitive Slave Act and for admitting no new slave states. The state's "most influential antislavery leader," Sherman M. Booth, wanted slavery abolished, not just contained.[41] But moderates more often controlled the first efforts to define an official position for the anti-Nebraska fusion movement in the summer of 1854. Mainstream Whigs in Ohio regarded Free Soilers as "reckless, irrational extremists" and insisted on a platform that was silent on the Fugitive Slave Act and other controversial matters. Illinois Free Soilers also proved willing to downplay the antislavery measures that Jay and Chase had long championed. Opponents of the Kansas-Nebraska Act in Indiana called simply for restoring the Missouri Compromise, a stance that fell short of complete territorial restriction. And everywhere across the Lower North, anti-Nebraska promoters disavowed the dreaded "abolitionist" bugaboo.[42]

A significant increment of Northern Democrats also considered the Kansas-Nebraska Act an intolerably high price to pay for maintaining their partisan allegiances. Lyman Trumbull, Kinsley Bingham, John Wentworth, Gideon Welles, Hannibal Hamlin, and many other future Republicans abandoned the Democratic Party in 1854.[43] Across the North, and especially in New England and in the New England exodus regions to the West, the Kansas issue confronted Democrats with a painful choice. Even though fully half the Democrats in the House from the free states voted against Kansas-Nebraska, the party suffered massive Northern losses in 1854. But the Democratic Party as a political organization carried forward, albeit in weakened form, whereas the Whig Party did not. Democratic control of the presidency and both houses of Congress provided the leverage to maintain organizational cohesion and whip doubters into line. Democratic newspaper editors received sharp reminders that their lucrative public printing

The Antebellum Context

contracts hung in the balance. The most energetic and talented Northern Democrat, Douglas, threw himself into the struggle. The Little Giant relentlessly marshaled his forces, plugged gaps in his lines, and enabled the shrunken party to survive.[44] But Kansas inflicted a high price indeed on Democrats. Dominated after 1854 by its Southern wing, the party became increasingly unable to maintain itself in the free states. Instead, Democrats struggled to fend off accusations that they were willing instruments of the Slave Power conspiracy.[45]

Many Northern Whigs hesitated initially to give up on their national party. Conservative heirs to Daniel Webster, such as Robert C. Winthrop and Thomas Corwin, remained hopeful that they could maintain and rebuild ties to Southern Whigs. The most visible antislavery Whig, William H. Seward, faced a difficult reelection battle that likely hinged on keeping the party together in the New York legislature.[46] But intense demands for new kinds of reforms gnawed at Whig allegiances. Efforts to impose temperance legislation and prohibit alcohol had become more overtly partisan in the early 1850s than ever before. The state of Maine pointed the way in 1851 by enacting the so-called Maine Law, which banned the sale of alcohol. Reformers in other states took heart from Maine's example. "Although the antislavery and anti-liquor crusades focused on differing social evils and the leadership of the two movements was not identical," historian William E. Gienapp wrote, "the crusades sprang from similar moral impulses." Temperance eroded ties to the two major parties, just as the campaign for the Wilmot Proviso had done several years before. The Whig Party, which had long been more attractive to voters with an evangelical-reformist orientation, found itself especially bedeviled by third-party temperance enthusiasts. Free Soil partisans often embraced the new issue, eager to capitalize on its appeal to evangelically oriented voters who found both alcohol and slavery morally distressing.[47]

An even more disruptive challenge to existing party arrangements arrived on the heels of the antiliquor movement. High levels of immigration from Ireland and Germany in the latter 1840s and early 1850s fueled an anti-immigrant and anti-Catholic backlash. Hostility to immigrants was "closely connected to the temperance movement," Gienapp noted, because hard-drinking Irish men and Germans who socialized with lager beer symbolized a threat to reformist cultural norms.[48] The anti-immigrant impulse, which fed into the so-called Know Nothing movement, suddenly vaulted to political prominence in 1854 and 1855, just when resentment at the Kansas-Nebraska Act was most intense. During this key interval, it was difficult to disentangle the various strands of insurgency. Indignation about Southern efforts to control the federal government and the western territories often overlapped with resentment at immigrants and campaigns to legislate against alcohol. But it was the anti-immigrant upheaval that posed "the biggest threat to the unity, the invincibility, and indeed the very existence of the Whig Party," historian Michael F. Holt concludes.[49]

In 1854 and 1855, the anti-immigrant American Party, which grew out of the Know Nothing movement, gained the inside track in many states and appeared well positioned to build a new national party. It swept to victory in Massachusetts and Maryland, and it ran well in many other states. As late as the spring of 1856, "American" Know Nothings appeared to offer the principal challenge to Democrats in the upcoming fall election. But just as Whigs and Democrats were being scissored by North-South acrimony, the newly minted American Party found itself threatened by the same force. Northern Know Nothings (dubbed "Know Somethings"), sensitive to grassroots sentiment in their home districts, objected to heavy-handed Southern efforts to make Kansas a slave state. The American Party South then realized that its Northern allies had become an albatross.

The gap that separated Northern and Southern members of the American Party became a chasm in May 1856 when two celebrated incidents made the Slave Power a more immediate menace to Northern sensibilities than immigrants. A proslavery militia attacked Lawrence, the free state capital of Kansas. Two days later, South Carolina congressman Preston Brooks ambushed Charles Sumner as he sat at his desk in the U.S. Senate and beat him senseless with a heavy cane. Of the two provocations, Gienapp wrote, "the attack on Sumner was more important in producing Northern indignation." Amid an uproar about the fates of "bleeding Kansas" and "bleeding Sumner," the Republican Party suddenly emerged as the principal opposition party in the North. Republicans brought together most former Whigs and Know Nothings from the free states, all former Free Soilers, plus a significant number of antislavery Democrats. Republicans also attracted temperance enthusiasts, whose cultural outlook dovetailed with the anti-immigrant impulse.[50]

Republicans without exception accepted that slavery in the states where it existed lay beyond the reach of outsiders. William H. Seward, for example, claimed in 1855 that he did not know anyone "who maintains or supposes that the Government of the United States has the lawful authority or the right to abolish slavery in the States of this Union." And Chase labored to convince abolitionist Theodore Parker that working to have slavery "*denationalized*" offered a "practical" path, unlike the "dangerous" delusion of pretending "that Congress can legislate abolition within slave-states." To be sure, Republicans generally disliked slavery and believed that the South exercised disproportionate power in the federal government. At the same time, however, they recognized that slaveholding white Southerners had the law on their side in the states where slavery existed.[51]

The Republican Party platform, adopted at the party's first national convention in June 1856, insisted that slavery lacked any constitutional sanction in the territories and denounced at length the Kansas policies of the Pierce administration. But it steered clear of any threat to slavery in the states—it cryptically acknowledged "the rights of the States," albeit without making explicit that those rights included the right to hold slaves. The Republican platform was also silent on two divisive issues—the Fugitive Slave Act and slavery in the District of Columbia—both of which tended to estrange moderates in the party from those who saw slavery as an urgent moral problem. The platform did laud one part of the Constitution prized by those who thought it an antislavery document—the due process clause—but it protested infringements of due process in the territories, not the states. While Republicans embraced "the principles promulgated in the Declaration of Independence," they breathed no hint that these principles might include racial equality.[52] On balance, the Republican Party positioned itself close to the center of the political spectrum in the free states. Nevertheless, many in the South and some in the North insisted that Republicans threatened both slavery and the Union.

The rise of the Republican Party made the North-South gap deeper and more fundamental than ever before. Northern opposition to slavery and Southern power in the Union triggered a white Southern proslavery reaction, and the two conflicting tendencies fed off each other. Each side saw itself as a victim, with its basic rights endangered by an aggressive rival. Many white Southerners considered themselves under siege. In their view, a powerful antislavery movement in the free states sought to control the territories, end Southern equality in the Union, and potentially menace the slave system. Growing numbers of Northerners took the opposite view. They interpreted Southern determination to legalize slavery in the territories as evidence that a "slave power conspiracy" wanted to spread slavery not just to the territories but also to the free states.

North-South polarization generated by the presidential campaign in 1856 was both ominous and unprecedented. Republicans nominated John C. Frémont, "the Pathfinder," a romantic figure famed for his exploring expeditions in the West, who had made a fortune in the California Gold Rush. Frémont's wife was Jessie Benton, daughter of the powerful Missouri Democrat Thomas Hart Benton. With hindsight, we know that she monopolized the talent in the marriage—and that her husband was a spectacularly unqualified presidential candidate. Frémont's nomination, Gienapp wrote, was both "a triumph of image over achievement" and "an act of grave irresponsibility." His subsequent failures as a Civil War military commander would reveal someone who was egocentric and inept.[53]

But Frémont's incapacity was not the issue in 1856. Because he was the Republican Party's first presidential nominee, his candidacy became a line in the sand. Growing numbers of prominent Southerners insisted that his election "would be the end of the Union" and "a declaration of war." Democrats smeared "Black Republicans" as reckless incendiaries who stood poised to upend the social and economic order and destroy white racial supremacy.[54]

Frémont did not run strongly enough to gain the presidency, but he captured eleven free states and a plurality of Northern votes. Republicans persuaded majorities of voters across New England and the Upper North that their interests were menaced primarily by the Slave Power. Frémont kindled a passionate response. His supporters "streamed to Frémont picnics and rallies" in New England and its westward offshoots and considered themselves part of "a great moral crusade." Their chants reverberated—"Free Soil, Free Labor, Free Men, and Frémont!" The menace of a "slave power conspiracy" galvanized a huge turnout. Even today, many counties, towns, neighborhoods, and streets in the Upper Midwest and the Pacific Coast bear the magic name Frémont and testify to the intensity his candidacy aroused.[55]

Frémont's "victorious defeat" (Gienapp's phrase) positioned the Republican Party as the principal opposition party to the Democrats in the free states and the second strongest party in the nation, even though it attracted hardly any support in the white South. In more than a century and a half since then, no new party has managed to duplicate what Republicans accomplished in 1856.[56]

Giddings, Chase, and Sumner all gained stature amid the political earthquake of 1856. No longer marginal scolds, they became respected members of a rising political party that appeared well positioned for future success. They believed slavery should be denationalized and that, at the very least, its expansion must be blocked. Their antislavery zeal put them ahead of the Republican mainstream, which put all its antislavery eggs in the territorial basket, but they defined the party's ideological core and gave it "backbone." Giddings won reelection to the House and took satisfaction that Frémont carried Ohio. The patriarch of the political antislavery movement dared to hope that slavery's days were numbered. The Democrats had taken advantage of a temporary legislative majority in Ohio to claim Chase's Senate seat. But he rebounded even before the Republican Party coalesced at the national level and was elected as governor of Ohio in October 1855, the first Republican to win the top office in a major state. To do this, he had to reach out surreptitiously to Know Nothings even while maintaining support from those who wanted an antislavery focus. But Chase was disappointed the next year when Republicans bypassed him for the presidential race and gave the party's nomination instead to Frémont. Sumner's martyrdom transformed him from an isolated maverick to a cherished symbol of interconnection between civil liberties and antislavery. His Senate chair, which stood empty for the next three years as he recovered from the terrible beating, became a standing rebuke to the slave power. He would fill the Senate seat from Massachusetts for the rest of his life.[57]

The Republican Party, Abraham Lincoln, and the Problem of the Constitution

President Franklin Pierce glumly took stock in December 1856 as his term sputtered towards its end. Four years before, the handsome, affable New Hampshire Democrat had come to Washington with plans to strengthen his party and quell North-South antagonisms. Instead, he disastrously mismanaged the new Kansas Territory and thereby wrecked his administration. The *New York Herald*, normally a Democratic newspaper but estranged from the party by the Kansas issue, summarized the case against Pierce. Among the emigrants to Kansas were a few "rabid abolitionists" and a few malcontents from Missouri who wanted to make the new territory a slave state. Although the president should have disdained both factions and recognized that most people coming to Kansas cared nothing about the slavery controversy, he instead had interfered "directly and openly, by taking the side of the slave interest." The resulting tumult made it appear that Pierce had tried "to force slavery upon the people of Kansas with fire and sword."[1]

In November 1856, the Democratic Party did manage to retain the White House and it regained a majority in the House of Representatives. Its control of the Senate also was assured. But the party was far weaker than it had been four years before. Its presidential candidate, James Buchanan, lost eleven of the sixteen free states to John C. Frémont, candidate of the upstart Republican Party. Pierce's home state of New Hampshire, long a Democratic stronghold, fell to the Republican onslaught. Frémont and former president Millard Fillmore, candidate of the American Party, together outpolled Buchanan by almost a three-to-two margin in the free states and by almost four hundred thousand votes nationwide. Northern Democrats, who had been trounced in the 1854 congressional elections, amid resentment at the Kansas-Nebraska Act and the sudden growth of political nativism, enjoyed only limited success in 1856 as they tried to rebuild their shattered ranks. The Democratic Party maintained its grip on national power because it dominated the South—and because its opponents in the free states split the anti-Democratic vote. Pierce, who had swept into office four years before with thumping Electoral College margins both North and South, prepared to limp away from the wreckage.

Pierce attempted to explain what had gone wrong. His occasion for doing so was the annual message, presented each year in December when Congress convened. In it the president mourned that many "otherwise good citizens" had been "inflamed into the passionate condemnation of the domestic institutions of the Southern States" and had fallen into "temporary fellowship with the avowed and active enemies of the Constitution." Who was responsible? Pierce pulled his punches and never used the word "Republican," but his complaint about "mere geographical parties" plainly insinuated that Republicans were sheltering these enemies. While "pretending to seek only to prevent" the spread of slavery, they had provided cover for those who "are really inflamed with the desire to change the domestic institutions of the existing States." Unless checked, this "revolutionary" assault on the Constitution would end in "fratricidal carnage"—with "burning cities, and ravaged fields, and slaughtered populations" as the nation sank into "civil and servile war."[2]

Pierce's startling valedictory met with a frosty reception. The *New York Times* complained that this "sweeping and indecent assault upon the motives and character of the Republican Party" was "the most unbecoming and malignant party diatribe we have ever seen from so high a quarter." Its "studied falsification of political history" libeled the two million voters who disapproved of his leadership, and it was "flatly contradicted" by the evidence. The *New York Herald* chimed in to condemn the president's "pettifogging misrepresentations of the facts of history." The "false issues and false pretenses of poor Pierce's message" marked him as a pawn of "the Southern disunion faction." His words were "remarkable and reckless," wrote historian Elizabeth Brown Pryor, the embittered parting shot from a repudiated lame duck.[3]

Pierce's put-down ignited a lively scrum in the U.S. Senate. This give-and-take in some respects rehashed the recent presidential campaign. Partisans on all sides sought to pin blame for the unsettled Kansas situation and to interpret the election results to their own advantage. But the discussion also addressed weightier themes. Within the past year, a new political party had coalesced in the free states and established itself as one of the two principal national parties. Its presidential candidate had carried eleven states. What did Republicans stand for? And what did their "victorious defeat" portend?[4] Republicans plotted to do more than bar slavery from the territories, Pierce charged. In reality, they threatened slavery in the states where it existed. And that would place the nation on the high road to disunion and civil war. Pierce thus created the occasion for a public airing of matters central to this book. Did the Republican Party menace slavery? And should white Southerners have seen Republicans as a deadly threat?

Albert Gallatin Brown, a Mississippi senator and an assertive radical, often took more extreme positions than other Southern Democrats. He accused Republicans of playing a deceptive double game—and he was ready to name names. Massachusetts senator Henry Wilson stated that there was "no power under the Constitution to interfere with slavery in the States," but he then told audiences that they had a responsibility to aid "three and a half millions of bondsmen groaning under nameless woes."[5] If slavery was to be abolished "by and through the influence of the northern people," Brown reasoned, that meant it would happen "without consultation with the Southern people, and against their will." Brown condemned Wilson's adroit and "disingenuous" evasions. "Does it matter to us whether you claim the power to interfere with slavery in the States, or whether you exercise the power without claiming it?" Brown also noted that New York senator William H. Seward had once stated that "slavery can and will be abolished, and you and I can and will do it."[6] What did he mean by that language, Brown asked, "if he did not contemplate an attack on slavery in the States?" Such "bold declarations" from "high quarters" promised to overthrow slavery "whenever they shall have the power to do so."[7]

Brown also insisted that Republicans during the recent election campaign had collaborated closely with "the ultra abolitionists in the North." William Lloyd Garrison, notwithstanding his no-government principles, had stated, "If I had a million of votes, I would give them all to Frémont," and "in the midst of the canvass, Fred Douglass, the free negro, took down the name Gerrit Smith [from the masthead of his newspaper], and ran up the name of John C. Frémont." Republicans miscalculated, Brown concluded, if they thought "the Southern people could submit quietly and tamely" to having war made "upon $2,000,000,000 of Southern property, and upon the peace and quiet of every Southern family." He and Virginia's James Murray Mason insisted that Frémont's election would indeed have led to "dissolution of the Union." Brown's polemic did not impress the *New York Herald*. It was "contemptible and ridiculous" to charge Frémont's supporters with favoring "the abolition of slavery everywhere." With a few exceptions, they were "honest, Union loving, conservative and law-abiding men."[8]

But Northern Democrats, led by Michigan's Lewis Cass, showed that the clamor extended far beyond the Deep South's firebrands. The elderly veteran—who had been Andrew Jackson's secretary of war, then ambassador to France, and in 1848 the unsuccessful Democratic candidate for president—would soon be appointed Buchanan's secretary of state. Cass commended Pierce for calling attention to "the real state of things" and warning of dangers that "no man could have foreseen or anticipated a few years ago." Southerners had reason to believe that a "large portion" of the Republican Party would prevent any new slave states from entering the Union, repeal the Fugitive Slave Act, and abolish slavery in the District of Columbia. Slanderous newspaper attacks on "slavery and slaveholders" suggested that "the hearts and minds of the people of the northern and northwestern States" had been so twisted that the issue was "not now about the extension of slavery so much as about its existence."[9]

Cass, still reeling from the huge Republican surge that upended Michigan's Democrats and assured that his Senate seat would go to a Republican, judged that "vast numbers of voters" in the free states had decided that slavery "was abhorrent to them" and had "cast their ballots, as they thought, against it." Even if not yet ready to take "extreme measures" against "the institution itself," many in the North now saw slavery as "one of those terrible evils with which there should be no truce nor peace." In so doing, they gave little heed to the South's constitutional rights. Southerners, having been "attacked and vilified" and feeling "oppressed and dishonored," might not remain in the Union. Cass saw no "right of secession under the Constitution," but he predicted that the Union could not be kept together by force.[10]

Cass complained that "false-hearted" Americans who opposed slavery had dishonored themselves by promoting their cause in the foreign press and holding up their country "to the detestation of the world." Cass and South Carolina senator Andrew P. Butler singled out a recent essay in the *Edinburgh Review*, "The Political Crisis in the United States," that had attracted wide notice on both sides of the Atlantic. "Read the article," Butler exclaimed. Even though "artful" and "ably-written," it "appealed for foreign aid to put down one section at the expense of another" and thus tried to enlist "a foreign and rival press to make war on your brethren." Here Butler overreached. William Henry Hurlbert, the young author of the offending piece, did call attention to the way in which "the great religious community of the Northern States" and "the most respectable and energetic classes of Northern society" had become "agitated on the question of Slavery." Although the author stated that he shared these sentiments, he recognized too that the rise of political antislavery had stirred "ferocious exasperation" and a rule-or-ruin recklessness in the South. He warned that the impasse

The Republican Party, Lincoln, and the Constitution

had the potential to split the Union and ignite a war of "more than ordinary ferocity."[11]

Republicans mounted a spirited counterattack against Pierce's strictures. Asserting their allegiance to the Constitution and the Union, they scorned the idea that they menaced the slaveholding states, and they differentiated themselves from abolitionists. The president's "extraordinary and unprecedented" message accused large numbers of Northerners of a "want of fidelity to their constitutional obligations, and of hostility to the Union and the Constitution," complained New Hampshire senator John P. Hale, the former Free Soil leader. In Hale's view, Pierce had erected an outrageous straw man. Even "the most radical and the most ultra" men and women in Hale's acquaintance denied "that Congress had a right to interfere with Slavery in any State in this Union." When Southern senators rebutted to point out that such opinions could be found in the writings of abolitionist Lysander Spooner and in a monthly publication entitled *Radical Abolitionist*, sponsored by Gerrit Smith, Hale dismissively pointed out that neither was a Republican. "Every man who is cognizant of the state of public opinion in any northern State," Hale insisted, would agree that "practically there is nobody there who contends that Congress has the power to abolish slavery in the States." Hale stated that he and the members of the Republican Party appealed "to the enlightened consciences of those who hold slaves" and counted on "the influence of moral, humane, and philanthropic principles." He wanted slavery to end but did not want "to see the Constitution amended to give me the power to do it." He knew the Constitution prevented the federal government from interfering with slavery in the states where it existed.[12]

Henry Wilson, a target of Brown's barbs, chimed in to reject the idea that Congress or the federal government had "the power to abolish slavery in the States of this Union." He did allow that the political abolitionist Gerrit Smith, who had polled approximately two thousand votes nationwide on the Radical Abolition ticket in the recent presidential election, believed that slavery was unconstitutional both in the territories and in the states. Smith believed the Declaration of Independence provided the foundation for "an anti-slavery Constitution." Wilson vowed that Republicans also venerated the "sublime" doctrines propounded in Jefferson's Declaration, but they did not believe that the men who framed the Constitution intended "to give Congress the power to abolish slavery in the slaveholding States." The 1.3 million who had voted for John C. Frémont "maintain no such doctrine, never have maintained it, do not claim any such power, and never intend to usurp it." He and other Republicans disagreed with Spooner, who had made the most extensive case that slavery was unconstitutional. He had read Spooner's book, Wilson stated, but "while I admit it to be a work of great learning and power, I do not assent to it."[13]

Wilson also demonstrated that Garrison and his associates saw the situation differently than the Republican Party. The Boston abolitionist had written that "every enlightened friend of freedom" would prefer Frémont to Buchanan or Fillmore, because the Republican Party would resist the extension of slavery into the territories. But Garrison also insisted that the Republican Party was hopelessly tarnished because of "its fidelity to the United States Constitution" with all its "pro-slavery compromises." Although sympathetic to Frémont, Garrison had remained true to his principles and had not voted. Wilson did, however, commend the "Garrison Abolitionists" for having "devoted their lives and their property, and incurred contumely and reproaches, for the cause of the bondsmen of America." They were "men of great ability" who had "studied the slavery question in all its aspects." Those who dismissed them as fanatics could learn from them.[14]

Although the *New York Herald* contemptuously dismissed Pierce's and Brown's complaints about the rank and file of Frémont supporters, its flamboyant editor, James Gordon Bennett, seconded "every word of reproof" that the Mississippi senator directed at Wilson and Seward. Bennett had wanted Frémont to run a campaign focused narrowly on Pierce's Kansas debacle. The frustrated editor had been confounded to find that those who also saw slavery as a moral problem gravitated to the Frémont campaign, and he blamed them for the candidate's defeat. Wilson was "a thoroughly trained sectional demagogue" whose campaign speeches had been "more or less tinctured" with abolitionism, Bennett charged, and Seward was "an anti-slavery fanatic" whose instincts were the same as Garrison's. Unlike Garrison, Seward never called directly for "the abolition of slavery in the Southern States, constitution or no constitution, Union or no Union." But his claims of attachment to the Constitution were hypocritical, because he always worked "to array the North against the South" and to stigmatize Southern slaveholders as a despotic governing class. Support from the likes of Wilson and Seward had placed Frémont "in a false position in the central States," Bennett charged, and did much "to damage his cause among their conservative people, who love the whole Union, and who know what the constitution requires of all good citizens."[15]

Wilson and Hale insisted, however, that the Republican Party supported the Constitution and the Union unconditionally. No Republican had threatened secession, Hale noted. Only Southern malcontents threatened to dis-

The Republican Party, Lincoln, and the Constitution

rupt the Union, and Republicans would not allow that to happen. Wilson reported having traveled thirty thousand miles in fourteen free states during the preceding two years, but he had "never yet heard one word uttered claiming power in Congress, or proposing to usurp power in Congress, to abolish slavery in the slaveholding States." Like Jackson and Webster, Republicans believed "the Constitution as it is should be preserved." Wilson therefore indignantly rebutted Pierce's "charge of disunion against the Republican Party"—it came with "an ill grace from the chief of a party which has in its ranks every political disunionist of the United States." But Wilson understood that Republicans needed a more centrist image to compete successfully in 1860. His biographer notes that the Massachusetts senator made it his mission to "mute the more stridently antislavery voices of the party and persuade the voters that Republicans, who neither favored violent action against the slaveholders nor threatened disunion, could safely be entrusted with the nation's government." Writing privately, Wilson complained that radical abolitionists had "but little idea of the load they put upon our friends in New Jersey, Pennsylvania, Indiana and Illinois." The "disunion cry" had beaten Republicans in 1856, and it could happen again.[16]

Cass unwisely targeted Massachusetts senator Charles Sumner's "inflammatory" comments about "the rape of a virgin territory, compelling it to the hateful embrace of slavery." Sumner's "unpatriotic metaphor betokens a prurient imagination," Cass complained. Wilson pounced. His colleague's "forced absence from this body for the last seven months"—after having been savagely beaten on the floor of the Senate in May 1856 by South Carolina congressman Preston Brooks—had "touched the sensibilities of every honorable man in America." Although Sumner's physical condition was such that he could not yet speak for himself, Wilson was confident that Sumner had honestly articulated the "sentiments and opinions" of Massachusetts and ultimately would return to his seat. The soil of Kansas had been "bathed in the blood of brave men for the sole offense of loving liberty," Wilson observed, much as in the slaveholding states, where "free speech and a free press are known only in theory."[17]

Other Republican senators also challenged Pierce. Lyman Trumbull of Illinois complained that the president tried to fasten on Republicans "sentiments and opinions which we disclaim and disavow." Pierce's message and Brown's pronouncement were contrived to alienate "one section of this Union from the other." Republicans entertained "no views hostile to the Union or the Constitution." They opposed allowing slavery to expand to "free territories" but had no wish "to interfere with slavery in any of the States of this Union." By deliberately obscuring "the very great difference between these positions," Southerners "impute to us that which we have solemnly declared we are opposed to." Trumbull also warned against breaking up the Union in response to the results of a presidential election. "The great principle, lying at the bottom of the institutions of the country, and of the Constitution itself, is, that we must acquiesce in the decision of the majority, constitutionally expressed." It could not be that "the Constitution contains within itself the elements of its own destruction."[18]

The influential William Pitt Fessenden of Maine then castigated Pierce for having "studiously misrepresented facts" by attacking "the principles and motive of the great majority of the people of the free States" and accusing them of wanting "to interfere with the question of slavery in the States." Like Henry Wilson, he thought that Pierce and his defenders in the Senate conflated a "small, powerless" group of radicals with the Republican Party. Gerrit Smith's "ultra-Abolitionists" did profess that "under the Constitution there is power to abolish slavery in the States," and they wanted "to exercise that power," but their numbers were "very few" and they had no representation in Congress. Fessenden forcefully insisted that Republicans had "never maintained the doctrine that we had a right to interfere, or desired to interfere, with the institution of slavery in the States."[19]

The Senate debate regarding the president's message soon spilled over into the House. First to speak was Ohio's youthful John Sherman, who already had established himself as a talented insider. Sherman noted that the Republican Party had formed to oppose the extension of slavery into new territories. As such, it was a coalition that brought together persons with differing outlooks. Among its supporters were a few "genuine abolitionists" who believed that "Congress had the power, and that it was its duty to abolish slavery in the states." A larger class of "anti-slavery men, of much greater numbers, influence, and ability," also acted with the new party, Sherman observed. They were "honestly, ably, and fearlessly represented" by his Ohio colleague Joshua Giddings, who believed that Congress had both the power and the duty "to prohibit slavery in the District of Columbia and in the national dock-yards, and also the commerce in slaves between the several States." But Giddings's views were "no more ingrafted upon the Republican platform" than those of the "genuine abolitionists." Instead, the "great mass" of Frémont supporters from the old Whig and Democratic parties wished only to stop the spread of slavery to the territories and "never held to any sentiment that affects or impairs the constitutional rights of the South." The rank and file of Republicans, Sherman insisted, were "the conservative ele-

The Republican Party, Lincoln, and the Constitution

ments of the northern States—men of property, men of information, men who sanctioned the compromises of 1850." They had neither the wish nor the design "to interfere with slavery in any Southern State."[20]

Sherman took sharp exception to Pierce's innuendo that Republicans intended to violate the Constitution and abolish slavery. Republicans had neither the power nor the intention to do any such thing, the Ohio congressman observed, though they had "no doubt—and in this the voice of the civilized world will concur," that white men in the slave states had an interest in moving from slave labor to free labor. The president's "groundless imputation" that Republican successes would lead to "burning cities, ravaged fields, and slaughtered populations" struck Sherman as ironic—only on "the plains of Kansas" had such scenes been enacted, "but he ascribes to the Republican Party the very results which his own policy has produced." Looking to the future, Sherman hoped that Kansas would be admitted to the Union as a free state. If it were not, and if instead "force and fraud" were used to impose slavery on it, then the "sense of wrong" generated across the North by the repeal of the Missouri Compromise would fester and grow.[21]

Three years later, in January 1860, when Southern Democrats blocked him from being selected Speaker of the House, Sherman recalled that he had made but a single speech in Congress "on the subject of slavery." That came when he had "spread upon the record my opinions on the subject" in answer to "what I regarded as an improper remark made by President Pierce." He made it plain then that he "never sought to trample upon the rights of citizens of the Southern States." The opinions he expressed then were ones that he continued to hold, Sherman vowed, "and they are the opinions of the body of the Republicans."[22]

Maine's Israel Washburn spurned Pierce's "groundless" accusations. Washburn vowed that Republicans sought "only to do that for which they have constitutional warrant, and they know and admit that they have no right to interfere with slavery in the States." But the president claimed "that he knows better" and that Republicans actually plotted "to revolutionize" the government. His "calumnious misrepresentations" lacked "the slightest foundation in fact" and marked him as a "flippant libeler."[23]

Southern Democrats in the House, led by John Letcher of Virginia, challenged the Republicans by harping about Sherman's Ohio colleague Joshua Giddings. As we have seen, the outspoken veteran had stated a decade before that he looked forward to the day when "the down-trodden sons of Africa in our Southern States" would regain "their God given rights." Giddings hoped that "peaceful measures" would secure this outcome, but he feared that blood might be shed by "those who stand between them and freedom." He anticipated the "approaching dawn" of a "political and moral millennium," when "the legitimate powers of this Government" would "do justice to the slave." What does this mean, asked Letcher, the future governor of his state, if not "direct interference with slavery wherever it exists"?[24]

Giddings defended himself, though hardly in a way that marked him as an orthodox Republican. He explained that the Declaration of Independence was "the chief corner-stone, the basis, the foundation of the Republican Party." In his view, its language about the right to "life, liberty, and the pursuit of happiness" had been "transferred to and perpetuated in the Constitution." The link between the Declaration and the Constitution had then been made explicit in the Fifth Amendment, which provided that "no person shall be deprived of life, liberty, or property, without due process of law." Giddings therefore believed that the law was already on the side of those oppressed as slaves, and he hoped that their oppression might end "without the unnecessary shedding of human blood."[25]

Frequently reiterated affirmations of Republican conservatism weighed on the prophetic Giddings, by then the senior member of the House. He felt marginalized by Sherman. Long an isolated gadfly who had stood outside both the Democratic and the Whig Parties, sustained only by his militantly antislavery constituents in Ohio's Western Reserve, Giddings longed to be part of a mainstream movement that would exercise real power. But his position in the Republican Party was precarious. His colleagues publicly saluted his "firmness and integrity" and observed that he had "successfully withstood" pressures that would have swept away "almost any one of his weaker adversaries." But privately they urged him to be "cautious and prudent"—not to push the party toward "advanced ground." Already in declining health, he was passed over for renomination in 1858.[26]

Matthias H. Nichols, an obscure Ohio Republican who rarely exposed himself to the rough-and-tumble of House debates, complained that the president had unfairly stigmatized the Republican Party. In fact, antislavery sentiments were bipartisan. Democrats in his western Ohio district, Nichols reported, had falsely charged that he voted to extend slavery to Kansas and to enforce "the infamous fugitive slave law" there. Here and elsewhere in the North, Democrats had vied with Republicans for the free soil mantle. Nichols considered it outrageous that Pierce and his "coadjutators" were scaremongering about disunion and questioning the right of the people to elect a president of their choosing. Republicans had "sought redress at the ballot-box" in a perfectly constitutional manner. Had they been successful, nobody could have had any legitimate basis for disrupting the Union.[27]

As Sherman and others noted, the gap separating Republicans and abolitionists was wide. For most Republicans, that was just as it should be. But the minority of Republicans who viewed slavery as an urgent moral problem had to explain to their abolitionist friends why partisan politics was the proper arena for pursuing moral objectives. They also had to explain how they squared their allegiance to the Constitution with their commitment to a cause that had proven difficult to pursue under the Constitution. It was not an easy sell.

In June 1857, abolitionist William Goodell, an outspoken champion of the idea that the Constitution was an antislavery document, penned a pessimistic assessment of the situation to George Washington Julian, the former Free Soil congressman from Indiana and the Free Soil candidate for vice president in 1852. Julian had enthusiastically joined the Republican Party and played a conspicuous role at its first national convention in Philadelphia in 1856. Goodell, writing for the American Abolition Society, bluntly complained that the antislavery cause had languished. After a generation of agitation, slaves were still in bondage, their numbers had greatly increased, "no effective measures" to bring about their liberation had occurred in any slave state or in the District of Columbia, and an "atrocious" Fugitive Slave law had been enacted. Persistent efforts to limit the expansion of slavery had failed, most recently in Kansas, and an emboldened "Slave power" had secured the Supreme Court's Dred Scott decision, which affirmed that slaveholders had a right to own slave property in the national territories. Meanwhile, the political antislavery movement remained confined by a self-imposed strait jacket—it accepted that "*slavery where it exists* should be left undisturbed."

The "friends of liberty" should act more aggressively to bring about "immediate and unconditional abolition," Goodell insisted. Two decades before abolitionists had broken "the long, dreary, dead calm" and laid bare "the horrors and abominations of Slavery." They had forced slavery's defenders to abandon their earlier claims that the federal government had "no constitutional control or jurisdiction over the Slavery question." Instead, slaveholders themselves had torn apart "the web of wicked compromises" and demanded the right to take slaves into "territories and free States where there are no local laws in their favor." By proclaiming "the Nationality of Slavery,"

The Antebellum Context

its defenders had "unwittingly proclaimed our National Guilt, admitted our National responsibility, and taught us our National duty."[28]

Although Julian's papers do not show how he responded to Goodell, he did preserve the draft of a public letter he wrote several months later to Thomas Wentworth Higginson, who represented a group of radical disunion abolitionists who wanted the free states to separate from the slave states. Higginson, who had led an 1854 Boston mob that attempted to rescue a fugitive slave from federal custody, would emerge in 1859 as one of John Brown's key supporters. In replying to Higginson, Julian took the opportunity to explain and defend his involvement with the Republican Party. His response spoke directly to the concerns Goodell had also raised.

Julian contended that Republicans stood committed to the key elements of "essential anti-slavery truth"—barring slavery from federal territories, abolishing it in the District of Columbia "and all places under the exclusive jurisdiction of the Federal Government," and opposing the admission to the Union of new slave states. They demanded "the restriction and national discouragement of slavery, as the forerunner of other measures, moral or political, which shall work out its peaceable overthrow." Julian depicted the Republican Party as the legitimate heir to "our Republican fathers," who cherished the Declaration of Independence and never contemplated the "diabolical folly" of a "permanent union of such incompatible elements as freedom and slavery." They wrote a Constitution "made necessary by the state of the times" that "compromised to some extent the freedom of the colored race." It "did not avow the doctrine of Federal interference with slavery in the states," but Julian was confident that the Founding Fathers expected slavery to end, and "like them, I am for the *extinction* of slavery."

Julian affirmed that "slavery must be abolished" and that Republicans ought not "be ashamed to avow this as our ultimate purpose." But he nonetheless politely distanced himself from the abolitionist disunionists. He counted on "the awakening humanity of the people" to transform the Union from being "a citadel of slavery" and a "prison-house of the slave." He hoped that principled antislavery politics would kindle "a love of liberty" and bring about a "moral and political regeneration." But he did accept that some abolitionist criticisms of the Republican Party were valid. "Noisy demonstrations of excited political contests" and the narrow pursuit of "immediate success" were a poor way to advance correct "principles." Some Republicans, Julian admitted, so trusted "in the power of numbers" that they pursued "dishonorable coalitions and shallow expedients." Worst of all, some Repub-

The Republican Party, Lincoln, and the Constitution

licans explicitly scorned "abolitionism." They thereby blurred the distinction between proslavery and antislavery politics, and they forfeited any claim to being "the friend of the slave."[29]

George W. Julian was a Republican with a difference. A protégé to the aging Joshua Giddings, Julian would subsequently wed Laura Ann Giddings, the old patriarch's favorite daughter. Unlike most Republicans, who never would have corresponded with the likes of Goodell or Higginson, Julian tried to identify common ground shared by antislavery politicians and outright abolitionists. Inevitably, he exaggerated. It was disingenuous to conflate his own advanced views with mainstream Republican positions, which focused on territorial restriction. Few other Republicans would have insisted that "liberty is dearer to us than the Union." His hatred of slavery and his belief in human equality were rooted in his Quaker heritage. They were not widely shared in his home state of Indiana, which he considered "the most pro-slavery" and antiblack of all the free states. He brought to politics an atypical moral urgency.[30]

THE FOUR YEARS BETWEEN 1856 and 1860 were a perplexing time for Republicans who wanted antislavery to be a meaningful program rather than an empty slogan. As the party positioned itself to win the prize that eluded its grasp in 1856, it marginalized the militants—notably Giddings—and worked diligently to widen its appeal in the free states. Republican managers knew that they needed to reassure conservative former Whigs and Know Nothings who had voted for the American Party ticket in 1856 and who thereby held the balance of power in the key Lower North states—Pennsylvania, Indiana, and Illinois. Republicans acknowledged that they could not touch slavery where it existed, but they held out hope that sensible white Southerners would come to see that free labor had huge economic advantages over slave labor—that self-motivated workers were better workers than slaves. In the long run they hoped the United States would become all free, but in the near term the Republican Party would simply restrict the expansion of slavery.

Everyone understood the political logic of the Republican stance. Frémont had swept New England and the New England settled states to the west—the Upper North. Victory had eluded Republicans in 1856 because they failed to consolidate the anti-Democratic vote in the Lower North. Former president Millard Fillmore collected almost four hundred thousand votes in the free states on the American Party ticket, enough to allow Democrat James Buchanan to slip through and win the presidency. Fillmore and

Frémont together outpolled Buchanan in New Jersey and Illinois and ran him a dead heat in Pennsylvania and Indiana. To claim the Lower North, Republicans plainly needed to win over Fillmore's supporters, most of whom were former Whigs. So Republicans had to deflect accusations that they were irresponsible, dangerous radicals. Republicans also needed to craft an economic program that offered hope to those whose economic prospects had been blighted by the so-called Panic of 1857. In Pennsylvania especially, a protective tariff was considered a sure-fire antidote for hard times in the coal and iron industries.[31]

But calls for partisan expediency balanced uneasily against efforts to make sure that Republicans actually stood for something. Many rank-and-file Republicans in the Upper North—New England, upstate New York, northern Ohio and Illinois, and the new states of Michigan and Wisconsin—regarded an aggressive antislavery stance as a moral or religious imperative. They wanted the party to repeal the Fugitive Slave Act, abolish slavery in the District of Columbia, and find ways to accelerate the end of slavery in the South—and they pressured party leaders in the Upper North to heed their will. Salmon P. Chase echoed the same points in his private correspondence. He regretted that Republicans had, in 1856, narrowed their focus "to the mere question of freedom or slavery for Kansas" and thereby had downplayed "the great real issue before the country" (he and James Gordon Bennett held diametrically opposite interpretations of the 1856 campaign). Chase worried too that "a class of Republicans" stood ready "to get rid of earnest antislavery men" and to "debase our standard & our aims."[32] Even though Chase was a key builder of the party, his views placed him outside the consensus among nuts-and-bolts Republican managers. They knew that the Upper North alone was insufficient to do the job. They feared that a pronounced Upper North tilt would ruin the party's chances in the Lower North.

Abraham Lincoln played an absolutely central role in creating the Illinois Republican Party. He was, in the opinion of historian David Donald, its "principal architect." He deftly reached out across the political spectrum—not just to Whigs but to disaffected Democrats and to evangelical Free Soilers such as Owen Lovejoy. He also maintained friendships with members of the American Party, many of whom shared his Whig antecedents, and at the same time he cultivated German Americans. Lincoln encouraged militant opponents of slavery from northern Illinois to ally with former Whigs and Americans from central and southern Illinois. At the same time, he tried to damp down the doubts of erstwhile Whigs and Americans, who hesitated to accept political fellowship with purported abolitionists. When the party coalesced in 1856, he took to the stump and did his best to persuade former Whigs and Americans to cast ballots for John C. Frémont. Even though that effort fell short, nobody doubted that Lincoln had become the party's leader in one of the three key states that Republicans knew they had to win.[33]

Lincoln became an articulate champion of mainstream Republican ideas. He repeatedly emphasized that the Founding Fathers—Washington, Jefferson, and Madison—opposed slavery in the territories, just as Republicans now did. Unlike former Free Soilers, however, Lincoln recognized that the South also had a constitutional right to recapture runaway slaves. Although he found the Fugitive Slave Act distasteful, he would accept it so long as alleged fugitives had the right to a fair trial. We have noted already his pithy private summation—"I confess I hate to see the poor creatures hunted down, and caught, and carried back to their stripes, and unrewarded toils," he wrote to a close friend, "but I bite my lip and keep quiet."[34] When Chase told him that it was "indispensable" for Republicans to support repeal of the Fugitive Slave Act, Lincoln pointedly disagreed. Were the next Republican National Convention to take such a position, he predicted, it would "explode the convention and the party."[35]

Lincoln achieved national visibility in 1858 when he challenged Stephen A. Douglas, the incumbent senator. His contest with the Little Giant, highlighted by their seven debates, is one of the most storied set pieces in all of American history. Douglas was the leading Democrat in the free states, with more stature than the incumbent president, James Buchanan. He was also a superb debater, "doubtless the most formidable legislative pugilist in all our history," in the opinion of historian Allan Nevins. By any objective standard, the one-term congressman who had been out of office for a decade was outclassed. But Lincoln knew Douglas well and was not intimidated. He set up a David-versus-Goliath match, with himself as David.[36]

Lincoln could not run a conventional campaign against Douglas. The big issue that year was the Buchanan administration's effort to admit Kansas to the Union as a slave state under the Lecompton Constitution, and Douglas stood with the Republicans against Lecompton. Douglas and the Republicans also found fault with the Supreme Court's Dred Scott decision, which affirmed the right to take slaves to territories even if majorities there did not want slavery. So Lincoln was obliged to differentiate himself from the incumbent in other ways. Lincoln insisted that he, like the Fathers, disliked slavery and looked forward to its eventual disappearance, whereas Douglas had no moral quarrel with it, claimed not to care whether it was voted up or voted down, and in fact harbored a "covert *real* zeal" for its spread.[37]

When speaking in public Lincoln endlessly professed confidence that stopping the spread of slavery to the territories would be the first step toward ultimately ending it, but his private surmise was more pessimistic. Lincoln scholars never have paid sufficient attention to the anguished lament he wrote in 1855 to George Robertson, an eminent Kentucky jurist, who several decades before had looked forward to "the peaceful extinction of slavery." Lincoln sadly suggested that history had taken a wrong turn and that there was "no peaceful extinction of slavery in prospect for us." Shortly after the Revolution "nearly half the states adopted systems of emancipation at once," but "not a single state has done the like since." The Russian czar would "resign his crown," Lincoln bitterly observed, "sooner than will our American masters voluntarily give up their slaves." One must conclude that territorial restriction was, for Lincoln, a barren hope, a necessary ploy to secure the allegiance of voters who yearned for slavery's demise.[38]

Lincoln and Douglas deliberately exaggerated their differences. They certainly did disagree regarding slavery: Lincoln saw it as a moral problem, and Douglas did not. But Lincoln stretched the evidence to say that Douglas's "*declared* indifference" to slavery—his "don't care" attitude—concealed a "covert *real* zeal" for its spread. Lincoln also overreached when he tried to link Douglas to the Dred Scott decision and claimed that Douglas had conspired with Supreme Court Chief Justice Roger B. Taney to nationalize slavery. Douglas likewise overreached when he tried to tar Lincoln as a "Black Republican" abolitionist—someone who saw things the same way as "Father Giddings, the high priest of abolitionism," "Parson Lovejoy," and "Fred Douglass, the negro."[39]

Lincoln's understanding of the relation between slavery and the Constitution marked him as a moderate conservative on the spectrum of Republican thought. But today many historians, eager to show that Lincoln always intended to abolish slavery, tend to place him with the radical forefront. They see his rhetorical assaults on "the monstrous injustice of slavery"—a "gross outrage" that was understood as a "great wrong" in "all civilized nations"—as glimpses of the real Lincoln. But they give short shrift to the way Lincoln positioned himself as a Northern centrist. He disagreed with those who would "defy all constitutional restraints, resist the execution of the fugitive slave law, and even menace the institution of slavery in the states where it exists." At the same time he rebuked proslavery Southerners who

Abraham Lincoln. "I have no purpose directly or indirectly to interfere with the institution of slavery in the States where it exists. I believe I have no lawful right to do so, and I have no inclination to do so." Debate with Stephen A. Douglas, Ottawa, Illinois, Aug. 21, 1858, in *The Collected Works of Abraham Lincoln*, 3:16. Ambrotype by Preston Butler, Springfield, Illinois, Aug. 13, 1860, Library of Congress, Prints and Photographs Division, LC-DIG-ppmsca-17159.

would "claim the constitutional right to take to and hold slaves in the free states—demand the revival of the slave trade; and demand a treaty with Great Britain by which fugitive slaves may be reclaimed from Canada."⁴⁰ Lincoln's modern admirers downplay his frequently repeated point during his 1858 debates with Douglas—that he would not interfere with slavery "in the States where it exists." He had no right "to quarrel with Kentucky, or Virginia, or any of the slave States, about the institution of slavery." They could "do as they pleased" and "decide the whole thing for themselves."⁴¹

Lincoln's "constitutional vision"—his insistence that the Constitution embraced the Declaration of Independence with its memorable promise of equality—impresses many historians. "The Declaration was Lincoln's ace card," one wrote, "his incontrovertible proof that the Founding Fathers wanted slavery dead and gone."⁴² Lincoln frequently claimed the Declaration for himself while insisting that Douglas had lapsed from the true faith of the Founders. But Lincoln carefully qualified his reading of history. The Fathers "found the institution of slavery existing here." They "knew of no way to get rid of it at that time." Instead, they tried to limit slavery by forbidding it in parts of the national domain and by ending the African slave

The Antebellum Context

trade in twenty years. Lincoln would follow their gradualist example—and he had private fears that it would be similarly ineffectual. His reverence for the Constitution always prevented him from taking any advanced antislavery stance.[43]

When Lincoln disavowed interference with slavery in the states, some historians suggest, he merely was play-acting and throwing up a deceptive facade. Their Lincoln, like the pioneering vanguard in the political antislavery movement, decided long before the war began that slavery was entirely a state institution without any national countenance under the Constitution. If true, Douglas was on target in 1858 when he depicted Lincoln as an abolitionist fellow traveler, and white Southerners had reason to identify Lincoln and the Republican Party as a deadly menace. For now, let us remember that Lincoln spent the summer and fall of 1858 fending off such accusations from Douglas. Had Lincoln indeed been an abolitionist at heart, then he misrepresented himself to Illinois voters during his campaign against Douglas—and he likewise deceived the hardheaded Republican managers who selected the presidential candidate two years later.[44]

We are getting ahead of the story. In 1858, Lincoln remained an afterthought. He attracted national notice for running a spirited campaign against the incumbent. But in the end he fell short, and Douglas retained his U.S. Senate seat. The conspicuous front runner and odds-on favorite for the Republican presidential nomination in 1860 was William H. Seward. The New York senator had stood back in 1856. He and his political manager, Thurlow Weed, were unwilling to risk Seward's political future by trying to lead a brand-new political party. But Seward would not stay on the sidelines in 1860. He eagerly positioned himself as the nominee-in-waiting. Hiding behind a smokescreen of delphic generalities, Seward attempted to distance himself from discussions of "political or partisan questions." Instead, he traveled in 1859 to Europe, where he was treated as a virtual head of state.[45]

But it never was easy for Seward to separate himself from those who understood North-South disagreements in stark moral terms. Several times during his career, he faced the challenge of trying to maintain popular majorities for moderately antislavery mainstream political parties when a more ideologically pure third party threatened to split the antislavery vote. He tried to reach out rhetorically to those who gave moral absolutes a higher priority than electoral success. Most famously, just before the presidential election of 1848, Seward spoke at Cleveland, in the heart of Ohio's Western Reserve, when the Free Soil Party appeared poised to lure antislavery Whigs away from their customary political allegiances and thereby throw the state

The Republican Party, Lincoln, and the Constitution

to the Democrats—as in fact happened. He then declared, "Slavery can be limited to its present bounds, it can be ameliorated, it *can* be and *must* be abolished and you and I can and must do it." He predicted that a time would come when "any constitutional guarantee" enjoyed by slavery would be "relinquished." "Whenever the public mind shall will the abolition of slavery," he predicted, "the way will open for it." For those who might worry that "this is all too slow," Seward suggested—"well then, go faster, if you can, and I will go with you." These quasi-abolitionist pronouncements offered no plan of action but were instead designed to secure a political objective, and they were coupled with an admonition to act peacefully, "in the spirit of moderation and benevolence, not of retaliation and fanaticism."[46]

Seward faced the same conundrum again in October 1858—when a third-party ticket headed by Gerrit Smith, who embraced Alvan Stewart's ideas about an antislavery Constitution, threatened to siphon off votes needed by New York Republicans. Speaking in Rochester, New York, Seward set out to persuade voters that he and the Republican Party looked forward to the triumph of freedom over slavery. "Are you in earnest?" he began. When his audience failed to stir, he posed the question again. This time he was rewarded with "intense applause." "So am I," he exclaimed. He then described the struggle between freedom and slavery as an "irrepressible conflict between opposing and enduring forces" to determine whether the United States would become "entirely either a slave-holding nation, or entirely a free-labor nation." That sort of language pointed directly, Democrats charged, "to interference with the institution of slavery" wherever it existed. But Seward always maintained that he relied on a peaceful process, through which white Southerners would become aware that emancipation was consistent with their own self interests. No interference with Southern constitutional rights ever would take place.[47]

The Supreme Court's *Dred Scott* decision complicated Republican efforts to stand as good constitutional conservatives. A majority of the court invalidated the Missouri Compromise, three years after it already had been repealed as part of the Kansas-Nebraska Act, on grounds that Congress had no power to interfere with the property rights of slaveholders who might wish to take their slaves to the territories. The court thereby challenged the bedrock principle that held the Republican Party together. Consequently, President James Buchanan could lecture Republicans about respecting the right of every citizen to take his property, including slaves, "into the common Territories belonging equally to all the States, and to have it protected there under the Federal Constitution." And if Southern property rights could not be secured in the territories, he implied, then they also were endangered in the states where slavery existed. Republicans utterly disagreed. They believed Congress had the power to exclude slavery from the territories, and they wanted that power exercised. But they disavowed either the power or the wish to touch slavery in the states. Republicans took strong exception to the position defined by the Court and championed by Buchanan. Lurking behind the campaign to foist slavery on the territories, they charged, was an insidious plot to make slavery legal in all the states, North as well as South. Iowa senator James Harlan, for example, warned that Buchanan's reasoning was "as applicable to the States as to the Territories"—and that the logic of asserting a constitutional right to take slaves to territories led inexorably to making slavery legal everywhere in the nation. Harlan likewise discounted Southern threats to break up the Union if their constitutional rights were not observed. He and other Republicans could not believe that the South might act in such a flagrantly self-destructive manner.[48]

Republican managers emphasized their party's constitutional bona fides as the next presidential election loomed. John Brown's abortive raid on Harpers Ferry, Virginia, in October 1859, triggered Southern and Democratic Party complaints that Republicans countenanced antislavery violence. Putting as much distance as possible between themselves and Brown made obvious political sense. "John Brown was no Republican," Lincoln insisted when he spoke at New York City's Cooper Union in February 1860, "and you have failed to implicate a single Republican in his Harper's Ferry enterprise." To suggest otherwise was "simply malicious slander."[49]

Republicans eagerly wooed former Whigs who had voted for Millard Fillmore in 1856 and thereby prevented Frémont from carrying the big states in the Lower North—Pennsylvania, Indiana, and Illinois. These voters needed to be reassured that Republicans were constitutional conservatives. So the Republican platform, adopted at the party's national convention in Chicago in May 1860, denounced "the lawless invasion by armed force of the soil of any state or territory, no matter under what pretext, as among the gravest of crimes." Republicans also pledged, even more specifically than they had in 1856, to "the maintenance inviolate of the rights of the states, and especially the right of each state to order and control its own domestic institutions according to its own judgment exclusively." As in 1856, the Republican platform said nothing about slavery in the District of Columbia or fugitive slaves. Party managers were not about to take positions that might deter prospective supporters.[50]

Republicans combined their constitutional affirmations with a vigorous indictment of slavery in the territories. They condemned the "dangerous political heresy" propounded in the Dred Scott decision, which asserted that slavery was legal in all territories. Freedom was the "normal condition" of the territories, Republicans insisted; the right to liberty was guaranteed by the due process clause of the Fifth Amendment. But the original draft of the platform said little about the Declaration of Independence, and that left Joshua Giddings so dissatisfied that he threatened to walk out of the convention. To avoid such an open break in party ranks, the convention voted to appease Giddings with a bold declaration that "the principles promulgated in the Declaration of Independence," specifically including the language that "all men are created equal," had been "embodied in the Federal Constitution." The embattled old warrior thereby won a satisfying symbolic victory.[51]

The principal task confronting Republicans at the Chicago convention was to nominate their strongest candidate for president. Seward was the odds-on favorite, but his detractors worried about his appeal in the Lower North. With party managers concerned to damp down suspicions that Republicans were abolitionists in disguise, Seward carried the stigma of occasionally having given rhetorical sanction to radical ideas. Until the convention met, however, no clear alternative to the New York senator had emerged. But the convention's galleries stampeded for the home-state favorite, the "Rail-splitter" from central Illinois, while Lincoln's astute promoters worked feverishly among the delegates to make him the consensus candidate of the Lower North. On the third convention ballot, they succeeded. Lincoln's greater "availability" involved other matters in addition to slavery-related ones. He was more acceptable to former American Party nativists than Seward, who had long championed immigrant rights. And Lincoln—soon to be Honest Abe—also was presented as the best candidate to turn the page on the notorious graft and malfeasance that marred the Buchanan administration.[52]

Lincoln staged a classic "front porch" campaign. He remained at home in Springfield, Illinois. He thereby honored the tradition that barred a presidential candidate from overtly advancing his own cause. Behind the scenes, however, he adroitly called the shots. At his behest, surrogates fanned out across the free states. In the Upper North, led by Seward, they emphasized Lincoln's principled antislavery commitment as demonstrated in his 1858 campaign against Douglas. In the Lower North, especially in Pennsylvania and Indiana, they emphasized his responsible constitutional conservatism and his stance on bread-and-butter issues—the protective tariff, homestead legislation, and a Pacific railroad. Everywhere Republicans depicted themselves as the true heirs of the Founding Fathers. Lincoln was well aware of Southern threats to disrupt the Union, but he discounted them. "The people of the South have too much of good sense, and good temper, to attempt the ruin of the government," he wrote privately in August 1860—"at least, so I hope and believe."[53]

Had he been able to eavesdrop surreptitiously amid the crowds that gathered in courthouse towns across the rural South that summer and fall to listen to political oratory, Lincoln might have been more alarmed. There speakers "vied with one another in their efforts to arouse the greatest resentment," historian Roy Franklin Nichols once observed. "Many a listener undoubtedly jumped to the conclusion that all Yankees were abolitionists, and that the non-slave states were solidly in league to destroy the South." A witch's brew of "fear and dread, resentment and defiance" swirled. Ominous questions lurked: "What was to be done if Lincoln were elected?" and "Could the South afford to stay longer in the Union?"[54]

Lincoln faced three opponents. The Democratic Party ruptured in 1860, with Southern insurgents supporting Vice President John C. Breckinridge on a Southern Rights ticket rather than Stephen A. Douglas, the nominee of national Democrats. Southern Whigs and Americans, calling themselves the Constitutional Union Party, nominated former Tennessee senator John Bell. Lincoln gleaned precious little support in the South, and he was not even on the ballot in many slave states. But in the North, and most especially in the three pivotal states of the Lower North, he ran well ahead of Frémont's 1856 vote. Lincoln thereby swept the free states and earned a decisive majority in the Electoral College. Even though six of ten voters nationwide supported one of the other three candidates, his plurality victory could not be questioned.

THIS CHAPTER CONCLUDES by calling attention to the seemingly off-the-reservation ideas championed by the most unrepentant Republican radical, John Armor Bingham, an Ohio congressman. The heir and legatee to the battle-scarred Giddings, Bingham represented a district in eastern Ohio that included four counties in the Ohio River Valley—Columbiana, Carroll, Harrison, and Jefferson. The district lay south of the one in the Western Reserve that Giddings had represented, but many of its residents were deeply anti-slavery, and it had polled a significant Free Soil vote.[55] Bingham, who resided after 1851 in Cadiz, the seat of Harrison County, had been a loyal Whig, not a Free Soiler. He played a prominent role in the anti-Nebraska insurgency of 1854 that consolidated the antislavery vote and lay the foundations for

The Republican Party, Lincoln, and the Constitution

the Republican Party. He was elected to Congress that year as a Republican and took his seat in December 1855. He would remain in the House for all but two of the next eighteen eventful years.[56]

Bingham looms large in this book because at the end of the antebellum era he was an outspoken heretic regarding the federal government's power over slavery in the states where it existed. His understanding of the Constitution set him apart from almost all other Republicans in Congress. Plainly influenced by abolitionist theorists who propounded the gospel of an anti-slavery Constitution, he contended that slavery deprived some persons of "life, liberty, and property" without "due process of law" and therefore was inconsistent with the Fifth Amendment to the Constitution. He also believed that slavery contradicted article 4 of the Constitution, which specified that "the citizens of each state shall be entitled to all the privileges and immunities of citizens in the several states." Not least, Bingham viewed the Declaration of Independence, with its promise of equality, as the foundation of American constitutionalism; slavery, he decided, was incompatible with the Declaration. In 1866, he took the lead in weaving all three strands together and placing them in the Constitution—"No State shall make or enforce any law which shall abridge the privileges or immunities of citizens of the United States; nor shall any State deprive any person of life, liberty, or property, without due process of law; nor deny to any person within its jurisdiction the equal protection of the laws." Rightly dubbed "the father of the Fourteenth Amendment," Bingham is an overlooked giant of the Civil War era.[57]

Between 1856 and 1860, Bingham repeatedly challenged the constitutional consensus. His maiden speech to the House in March 1856 excoriated the Kansas territorial legislature for making it a capital crime to assist runaway slaves and a felony to challenge the right of slaveholders to own slaves. "Our immortal Declaration and our free-written Constitution," he declared, had established "the self-evident truth that life and liberty belong of right to every man." Under the Constitution, Kansas could not abridge "freedom of speech or of the press," and it could not deprive persons of liberty "without due process of law." Although Bingham's complaint here was directed against a territorial legislature, the logic of his argument struck at the legal foundations supporting slavery in the states—the Constitution, he insisted, "guarantees to each man personal liberty."[58]

Bingham renewed his assault on constitutional taken-for-granteds in January 1857. He lit into the "monstrous proposition" that the Constitution sanctioned "traffic in slaves." Adopting a position long articulated by Giddings, Bingham conceded that the original thirteen states had "retained to themselves a monopoly in the horrid crime of slavery" but that new states created after the Constitution went into effect had no right to "enslave [their] own children, and sell them like cattle." Neither could any of the national territories establish slavery. The Constitution specified that "*no person* shall be deprived of life, liberty, or property without due process of law," and it made "no distinction either on account of complexion or birth." It forbade the spread of despotic institutions and required that all new states and territories uphold "the equality and brotherhood of the human race." Bingham's Constitution demanded "the absolute equality of all, and the equal protection of each."[59]

In February 1859, Bingham castigated the Oregon Territory's application for statehood because its proposed state constitution denied free negroes the right to own property, to sue in court, and even to reside in the state. In so doing, Oregon violated the privileges and immunities clause, he charged, because hundreds of thousands of free negroes enjoyed citizen rights in other states and therefore were citizens of the United States. Anticipating matters that would dominate the national agenda in the immediate postwar era, Bingham accepted "that a State may restrict the exercise of the elective franchise to certain classes of citizens of the United States," but it could not "exclude a law abiding citizen of the United States from coming within its Territory, or abiding therein, or acquiring and enjoying property therein."[60]

In April 1860, Bingham reiterated his view that any expansion of slavery beyond the original thirteen states was inconsistent with the Constitution — and that the antislavery provisions of the Northwest Ordinance should have been applied to all territories and future states. He took to task the many white Southerners who would "annul the great law of human progress" and the bedrock free labor principle—that "they who cultivate the land shall possess it." Although the South threatened to resist the election of a Republican president "to the extremity of disunion and civil war," Bingham was confident that "there can be no conflict of arms between the great sections of this Union." He looked to the "the power of public opinion" to quash "secession and treason" and to make war "an impossibility." Public opinion would also be the "final arbiter" of the Supreme Court's assertion, in the Dred Scott case, that slaveholders had an unlimited right to carry slavery to all the territories.[61]

Bingham's ties to Giddings plainly shaped his outlook. When Bingham first arrived in Washington, the two roomed together at the same boardinghouse on First Street SE (now the site of the Jefferson Building, part of the Library of Congress). Bingham took the lead in enlisting more than one hundred other Republicans to salute Giddings with a farewell gift in early 1859 when the aging patriarch, by then the longest-serving House member, finally ended his career in the capital. [62]

Although Giddings no longer served in Congress, he and Bingham remained in touch. On January 14, 1861, two months after the presidential election, Bingham poured out his heart in a letter to the old stalwart. "We are surrounded by traitors North and South against the Constitution," Bingham fumed. Toombs and Hunter and Benjamin and Jeff Davis proposed "to strike down Liberty by Secession"—while Seward and Sherman proposed "to betray Liberty to the Conspirators by compromise." Could anything still be done to avert the sellout? "Unless the people come to the rescue," Bingham prognosticated, "we are sold and *cast* down not by Secession—but by the Treachery or Timidity of Republicans." [63]

Bingham stood almost alone in early 1861. Many Republicans were prepared to amend the Constitution so as to safeguard slavery in the states from interference by Congress. Those Republicans who opposed any such amendment typically dismissed it as unnecessary, on grounds that they had neither the power nor the intention of disrupting slavery where it existed. Hardly anybody besides Bingham imagined that the Constitution might in the future abolish slavery and affirm equal rights for all.

PART II

Origins of the Other
Thirteenth Amendment

4

Mutual Misconceptions

Joseph Holt tore open the letter from his brother in Mississippi and read with amazement. Writing on November 9, 1860, Robert Holt announced that the election of Abraham Lincoln, just three days before, was "a declaration by the northern people" that they intended to "emancipate the Slaves of the South." Joseph Holt, postmaster general in James Buchanan's cabinet, kept reading. His excited brother was convinced that "poison, knives and pistols" had been distributed to slaves by abolitionist agents. Public sentiment in Mississippi, he reported, was "almost unanimously in favor of an immediate withdrawal from the Union" and establishing "a government of our own."[1]

The letter from Mississippi darkened the older brother's already grim mood. Stoic and solitary, he was grieving the death of his wife, just months before. Now came this awful news from a younger brother who had long looked up to him. Joseph Holt knew that his home state of Kentucky would be caught in the middle if the Union disintegrated. He knew too that the Holt family would be hopelessly fractured. And he dreaded the excruciating dilemma that might soon face the Buchanan administration—whether force should be used to challenge secession. Convinced that disunion sentiment resulted from an irrational misconception, Holt implored his brother "to exert his influence in allaying the phrenzy." But Robert Holt scoffed at Joseph Holt's naive "devotion to the Union." People in the North were "marked by dishonesty, injustice, rapacity, and an infernal greed," Robert Holt fumed. Between them and the South there was "nothing in common." The only possible outcome was "complete separation" and "immediate secession." Throughout the "planting states" there was "scarcely a show of opposition to it." Moreover, he continued, "it is a movement not of the leaders, but of the masses whom the leaders could not control if they would. The conviction is strong and universal, and I share it fully, that submission by the South is now death."[2]

This chapter will examine the mutually irreconcilable explanations of current reality that took shape during the five months that followed the presidential election. Our focus will be the three most consequential groupings—the prosecession Deep South, the North (especially the Republican North), and the conditionally pro-Union Upper South.[3] A glimpse ahead to the ghastly blood-drenched battlefields during the next four years reveals that the potential consequences of the disunion movement were difficult to see in advance. Opinion leaders North and South found ways to interpret the situation so as to obscure or conceal its lethal potential. The gap between what each side thought it knew—and what it turned out not to know—became painfully apparent only after the guns opened at Sumter in April 1861.

THE CATALYST THAT ROUSED the Deep South to an impulsive fury was, of course, the presidential election. Viewed in retrospect, Lincoln's victory appears foreordained. The core logic of his candidacy was to carry the Lower North, where Frémont had faltered. The electoral vote of the Lower North, if added to that of the Upper North, would create a majority in the Electoral College. It also worked in Lincoln's favor that his three opponents divided the remainder of the vote. But the fact of Lincoln's election rudely shocked the South. The sting was felt throughout the slave states, but it was most intense in the Deep South. White Southerners had heard endlessly that "Black Republicans" planned to destroy slavery and confer equal citizen rights on ex-slaves. It seemed inconceivable in the white South that such an unholy combination of fanatics and opportunists might win the election and actually wield power. Surely people in the free states never would elevate some obscure Illinois lawyer to the office once held by Washington, Jefferson, and Jackson.

So for white Southerners, the election did not—as usually would happen—quiet the partisan jousting that had roiled the country. Instead, its outcome posed far more fundamental questions. At stake now was the South's allegiance to the nation itself. White Southerners suspected the worst. They believed that Black Republicans had belittled and insulted them and soon might try to revolutionize their social order. Then, especially across the Deep South, they discovered that their kinfolk and neighbors saw the situation just as they did. Suddenly a moment of collective catharsis crystallized. They would follow their hearts and trust their instincts. A correspondent in Texas described for the *New York Herald* the "blind resentment which disregards all considerations of material interest." Any "submission" to the "coming administration of Lincoln" would fix "a moral slur upon Southern society."

It would compromise "the honor of every Southern man and woman" and would constitute "an admission of inferiority." Public opinion in the Deep South "had gone beyond reason and calculation," historian Roy F. Nichols observed. The "plain people" were "fearful and angry."[4]

The secession groundswell in the Deep South took hold with remarkable speed. On Monday, November 19, less than two weeks after the presidential election, the citizens of Columbus, Mississippi, gathered at the Lowndes County courthouse, which was "filled to the brim." They eagerly adopted resolutions that charged "a number of our sister States" with having violated both "the spirit and letter" of the Constitution by denying the South equal access to the territories, by interfering with the slave system so as "to promote servile insurrections," and by "producing a spirit of hatred" that could lead to civil war. Those attending the meeting resolved "*unanimously* with great applause" to "*discard and renounce all former political names and party organizations*" and to urge that the upcoming state convention end the state's ties to the Union. In the opinion of Beverly Matthews, the local member of the legislature, the Columbus meeting was "characteristic of every other held" across Mississippi and Alabama in mid- to late November.[5] That same week, on November 23, a resident of Albany, Georgia, cautioned an Illinois relative that the Deep South was in dead earnest and "sure" to go. The "masses" as well as the politicians were "all for secession." Why? "The working class of men" suspected that "in the course of events the *negroes* will be free and deprive them of their labor and become their equals." Another "Union loving" Southerner reported, also on November 23, that the Deep South was certain to secede. Disunionists had flagrantly misrepresented Lincoln as "an *ultra abolitionist* of [the] Wendell Phillips or Sumner school" who was "bent on interfering with slavery *in the States*."[6]

In secessionist eyes, either you were a Southern patriot who stood ready to resist oppression just as the Founding Fathers had in 1776, or you were a traitor to the South who would willingly submit to Black Republican rule. A profoundly absolutist secession mindset in the Deep South persuaded those with doubts to lie low and keep to themselves. So-called cooperationists who thought that the slave states might better act together, rather than follow the one-state-at-a-time script initiated by South Carolina, were brusquely shunted aside. It was not a time for principled dissent; the imperatives of community solidarity demanded both unanimity and speed. One Alabama observer reported an intense popular drive to "agree to *no* compromise whatever," to "separate immediately," and to "form a Southern confederacy as soon as possible." The people were "far ahead of the politicians" and "calmly

Mutual Misconceptions

determined." Old and young, rich and poor—all seemed "willing to die in defense of their principles." Another report from Alabama cautioned that there was "no other feeling than that for secession." Anyone who believed that there was "any considerable body of men" in the Deep South who were "even silently opposed to secession" was "deceived."[7]

South Carolina set the upheaval in motion just days after the presidential election. The state legislature voted unanimously to call a state convention, members of which were elected by voters on December 6, 1860. The convention met on December 17, and just three days later, on December 20, it severed the Palmetto State's ties to the Union. This drama was followed immediately in late December and early January by the riveting first phase of the Fort Sumter crisis—when war almost broke out in Charleston harbor and South Carolina batteries fired at a Union ship, the *Star of the West*. Between January 9 and 23, 1861, five other Deep South states followed South Carolina's brazen lead, with Texas close behind in February. As the seven seceding states exited the Union, their senators and representatives departed from Washington, DC, pausing long enough only to deliver farewell speeches. Delegates from the seven self-proclaimed independent states met on February 4 in Montgomery, Alabama, as the Provisional Congress for the Confederate States of America. Within a week they had written a constitution and designated Jefferson Davis and Alexander Stephens as president and vice president, respectively, of the chrysalid nation.[8]

Deep South political leaders rapidly embraced and reinforced the besieged mindset sweeping their home region. Rather than try to deflect the clamor, they validated it. Georgia's Howell Cobb, the U.S. secretary of the treasury and Joseph Holt's colleague in the Buchanan cabinet, stood tall among the public men from his region. But he promptly resigned his post in early December and issued a startling polemic to justify his actions. Cobb warned that the Republican Party was committed to "immediate and unconditional abolition in every State" and that Lincoln planned to build up a party in the South to promote "this insidious warfare upon our family firesides and altars." He pooh-poohed any hopes for a Union-saving compromise and announced that "equality and safety in the Union are at an end." Cobb knew that he was talking nonsense. He and other Southern leaders did dread the possibility that Lincoln might try to lure nonslaveholders away from proslavery political allegiances. But it was irresponsible demagoguery to insinuate that the Republican Party intended to stir slave insurrections or that it favored immediate abolition.[9]

Yet many prominent Deep South spokesmen echoed Cobb. Georgia senator Alfred Iverson, for example, charged that Republicans planned first to use their "power and patronage" to drive slavery from the Upper South. They would encourage "incendiarism, John Brown raids, murderings, poisonings, and revolts." The border states would succumb to the abolition onslaught because they could "get along without slavery"—their "soil and climate" were "appropriate for white labor." In the Deep South, however, slavery was essential "to cultivate our cotton, our rice, and our sugar fields." But the continued influx of slaves from the Upper South would be too much of a good thing in the Deep South, where the numbers of slaves would increasingly exceed the numbers of whites. Hemmed in "on all sides," the Deep South would face racial apocalypse. The federal government would ultimately demand "universal emancipation" and ignite "such scenes of murder between the two races as have never been seen or heard of in the world's history." Iverson's half-baked scare tactics insinuated that his constituents had for decades suicidally overreached. Deep South planters had eagerly bought slaves throughout the antebellum era, and some even had called for reopening the African slave trade. Iverson deftly turned conventional thought and practice upside down. He grimly predicted that the presumed asset of a black labor force was, in fact, a deadly menace.[10]

Georgia's senior senator, Robert Toombs, likewise purported to fear slavery's strangulation. Northerners had "told us for twenty years that their object was to pen up slavery within its present limits—surround it with a border of free States, and like the scorpion surrounded with fire, they will make it sting itself to death." The Republican Party's "main purpose" was "final and total abolition." They intend to "war against slavery until there shall not be a slave in America, and until the African is elevated to a social and political equality with the white man." This sort of secession hysteria transformed random prognostications made by hard-line antislavery absolutists into the fixed policy of the Republican Party, even though no front-line Republican—and certainly not Lincoln—ever talked about stinging scorpions. Yet one modern scholar takes these irresponsible theatrics at face value and uses them to provide the title for a recent book.[11]

Mississippi senator Albert Gallatin Brown refused to hold out any "delusive hopes" of reconciliation. William H. Seward, he recalled, had once told a large audience that "slavery must be abolished, and you and I must do it." Brown also vowed that an unnamed Republican congressman had just confided that "we never mean to ground our arms until we have emancipated the last slave in America." Because Republicans had persuaded the "rising generation" of Northerners "to hate the Southern people," the South's only security lay in independence.[12]

NORTHERNERS, especially Northern Republicans, initially saw secession as the work of a small oligarchy. It was predictable that this fanatical minority exercised greatest influence in South Carolina, always the most estranged and particularistic of the slave states. In 1832 and again in 1850, South Carolina took the lead in confronting the federal government only to find that other slave states would not follow. Republicans hoped that the palmetto rebels, desperate to reopen the African slave trade or to nullify the tariff, would again overplay their hand and demonstrate secession's utter folly. Before long, ordinary South Carolinians would realize that they had been cruelly duped, and they would expel the secessionist conspirators from power. No other state would follow South Carolina's horrid example, and no general war would result.

But instead, secession spread like wildfire across the Deep South. So the Northern framework for understanding the situation had to be modified. Many Republicans decided that the Gulf States, inspired by South Carolina's outrageous example, were playing a high-stakes game of extortion. Southern political leaders surely did not intend to destroy the Union. Instead, Republicans saw secession as a bold gambit, designed to secure humiliating concessions and to overturn the results of the presidential election. It appeared that Deep South oligarchs, acting with deliberate calculation, had temporarily deluded the honest masses and blinded them to their true interests. Even though the secession experiment was being conducted on a wider scale than a single state, Republicans assumed that the outcome would be the same. By endangering seven states rather than just one, the conspirators would forfeit public trust. When ordinary white Southerners awakened to discover how recklessly their supposed leaders had acted, they would push back. The scheme to create a separate Southern nation would crumble, and no general war would result.

The Northern mindset drew strength from what Republicans knew about themselves. The more Republicans heard about an abolitionist conspiracy to trample the Constitution and destroy slavery, the less inclined they were to take the secession movement seriously. Southern "political demagogues," one Pennsylvania Republican newspaper complained, were guilty of "unscrupulous misrepresentation." Their "reckless assertions" had led the "Southern people" into thinking that Lincoln would "incite the slaves to servile insurrection, or in some other undefined and undefinable way, secure their emancipation!" Either secessionists were charlatans, who deliberately roused fears they knew had no basis in fact, or they were deluded fools. Whichever the case, they had demonstrated their incapacity to lead and renounced any claim to have their alleged grievances respectfully considered.[13]

Most Northerners found it impossible to comprehend the reality of Southern estrangement or to entertain the possibility of an extensive mass panic that the Deep South's leaders "could not control if they would." It was easier to assign blame than to recognize how rapidly the foundations of the Union were crumbling. What might be called the "blame narrative" seemed to make sense. Surely the culprits were the Deep South's treacherous political leaders—led by Mississippi's Jefferson Davis, Georgia's Robert Toombs, and Louisiana's Judah Benjamin, the top three Southerners in the Senate. They had manufactured the bogus inquisition to deny Stephen A. Douglas the Democratic presidential nomination. They had insisted that Southern slaveholders had a non-negotiable right to settle in the territories and that this right would have to be "protected" whether or not any slaveholders wished to exercise it. Having demonstrated that they would rule or ruin the Democratic Party, the Deep South's leaders orchestrated the postelection frenzy to snatch victory from the jaws of defeat. Their purported "compromise" proposals were thinly concealed blackmail—a threat to hold the Union hostage because they disliked the outcome of the presidential election.

One leading Senate Republican, William Pitt Fessenden of Maine, had it all figured out. He was convinced that Jefferson Davis did not expect that "any thing is to come of this uproar." His object was simply "to demoralize the Republican Party" by extorting "a recognition of what he *assumes* to be the Constitutional rights of the South." Fessenden vehemently opposed any such "ignominious surrender." Republicans should "yield nothing to rebellion." And they should not admit to having done anything wrong. He favored facing "the worst of it *now*." If Republicans were to abandon "all the principles we have been contending for," he warned, it would destroy "the confidence of our people in our capacity and firmness." Fessenden was fixated by the danger of "northern weakness." The "victors" must not give in to the "vanquished." The free states never could "secure the respect of the South" if they were to "run like cowards" and show themselves to be "so utterly devoid of manliness." Instead, the true course for the North was to sit tight and count on the "Conservative men in the South to arrest this tide of madness." Southerners would have to recognize that "the idea of peaceable secession is simply absurd," and they would have to find a face-saving way to escape the trap of their own making.[14]

Another of Fessenden's Senate colleagues, Lyman Trumbull of Illinois, viewed the situation similarly. He accused Jefferson Davis of demanding that the federal government "abdicate" to a mob. Davis and his secessionist friends were "undermining the foundations of the Constitution" and running the risk of civil war. Yet they "modestly ask us to have peace by submitting to what they ask!" Trumbull insisted that Republicans had no role to play in resolving the crisis. They had not injured the South, and they would not do so in the future. Their party's only fault was to have "elected its candidate for the Presidency." Trumbull deplored efforts to "pick out an isolated passage from Mr. Lincoln's speeches, or from the speeches of some extreme man," and to pretend that the South was in danger. This kind of deliberate and persistent "misrepresentation" had warped "the minds of the people of the South." But if one looked at "the public course of the President elect, at his avowed opinions, at the platform upon which he is elected, you will find nothing that interferes in the least with the rights of the South." Trumbull predicted that Lincoln, once in office, would demonstrate conclusively that the South enjoyed the same rights as heretofore. His administration would show by its acts—and "that is the only way we can ever show it to the South"—that popular "misapprehensions" were entirely unwarranted.[15]

But it became increasingly apparent during January that the situation in the South had acquired a mad momentum of its own and that its leaders no longer led. Republicans had been "willfully and wickedly misrepresented," charged New York Republican representative Charles H. Van Wyck. Ordinary white Southerners, "in their blind infatuation, believe that we intend to overrun, devastate, and destroy the Southern States, and liberate their slaves by force." They had gotten this misinformation from Southern leaders, who knew that slavery was not endangered but who had nonetheless whipped up "the worst passions of your people." These supposed leaders had failed the first test of leadership—and "now you say you cannot control them." Van Wyck scoffed at the idea that Republicans should "surrender" to preserve the peace by accepting a compromise. "What have we to concede? We have done you no wrong, and propose none." The key question, he insisted, had nothing to do with slavery. It was, instead, did "the white freemen of the nation" have the right to elect a president of their own choosing? The South's leaders had "created the storm" under false pretenses and would have to bear the consequences. By trying to dissolve the Union by force, "you leave us with only one course—to oppose force by force."[16]

Under these grave circumstances, some moderate Republicans—let us designate them as "conciliatory"—decided that their party needed to play a more active role in defusing the crisis and reversing the slide toward war. While the Deep South's leaders attempted to bully the free states, conciliatory Republicans reasoned, they also were bullying the border slave states, a term typically used to include North Carolina and Tennessee. Secessionists castigated pro-Union leaders in the Upper South as "submissionists," who refused to stand squarely for Southern Rights. Conciliatory Republicans saw an opening and urged their party to reach out to "the bold true-hearted Union men" in the Upper South who were "standing firmly and nobly against the madness which seeks to involve the whole South in the treason of South Carolina."[17]

Earliest and most prominent among the emerging conciliators were New York senator William Henry Seward and his alter ego, Thurlow Weed, editor of the *Albany Evening Journal*. As we shall examine in fuller detail in the next chapter, Weed took the public lead in floating conciliatory trial balloons and providing cover for his ally. They first put their heads together on November 15 and remained in close communication during the weeks and months to come. Through the editorial columns of his newspaper, Weed attempted to drive home what he saw as the unpleasant new realities. Republicans, he warned, ought not "deceive ourselves with the impression that the South is not in earnest." On the contrary—a spasm of "blind vengeance" had "taken hold of all classes" in the Deep South and "crush[ed] out" allegiance to the Union. "Acting in utter ignorance of the intentions, views and feelings of the North," the Deep South's masses "are, in their readiness for civil war, in *advance* of their leaders." These leaders well knew that "Mr. Lincoln will administer the Government in strict and impartial obedience to the Constitution and Laws," Weed judged, but they had cynically misled their constituents. Why? They knew that "if they wait for a provocation, none will be furnished." But the leaders had lost control of the situation, and Republicans had "to deal with things as they are."[18]

Republicans should be prepared to make concessions, Weed contended, because "a victorious party can afford to be tolerant." Many Southerners were "blinded by passion" and should be treated with "moderation and forbearance." He boldly suggested that Republicans might shelve their longstanding demand to ban slavery from all federal territories. Slavery never could take root in the arid West and Southwest, he insisted, and with Lincoln in power nobody would try to impose slavery on a territory where it was unwanted.[19]

Weed's alleged "compromise" of party "principle" met with a cold response. "Stiff-backed" Republicans pounced on the "weak-kneed" Weed. New York's other U.S. senator, Preston King, a hard-line Republican, mourned to Weed that "nothing could have surprised me more than you did" when he started editorializing for concessions. In the eyes of the Northern public, Seward distanced himself from Weed. It was, as we shall see, all for show. Seward privately shared Weed's fears that Republicans could not just sit still and wait for the troubles to blow over.[20]

IN THE UPPER SOUTH, a larger spectrum of responses followed Lincoln's election. Some localities favored secession, but others did not. In contrast to the Deep South, many border state Southerners wanted the Union preserved. They too were dismayed by Lincoln's election, but they were equally dismayed by the Deep South's hot haste in breaking up the Union. They insisted that the South should contend for its rights within the Union. And they feared that secession endangered the slave system itself. William B. Campbell, a former governor of Tennessee, tried to persuade an Alabama cousin that secession was "unwise and impolitic," liable to speed "the ruin and overthrow of negro slavery," and sure to jeopardize "the freedom and liberty of the white man." Campbell condemned irresponsible Deep South politicians for leading the stampede. Secession threatened to divide the South, Campbell warned; his state and Kentucky never would be "dragged into a rebellion."[21]

Judge Samuel Smith Nicholas, of Louisville, Kentucky, wrote a widely circulated pamphlet to rebut the case for secession. He dismissed the territorial issue as "the flimsiest pretext for so mighty a revolution." Even if Republicans were to legislate against slavery in the territories, it would change nothing. The United States owned no territory "into which slavery could be introduced, by any encouragement," in the foreseeable future. Nicholas likewise ridiculed secessionist claims that Republicans stood ready to interfere with slavery in the states where it existed. Those who pretended to see such a danger were "hypocritically stimulating" a fear that they did not themselves feel. Kentucky, which "lies right in the path of any such aggression," scorned this "paltry pretext for disunion." Nicholas also condemned secessionists for complaining about something almost unknown in the Deep South, the loss of fugitive slaves. The erosion of fugitives was confined to

Origins of the Other Thirteenth Amendment

the border states, which understood that secession was a remedy "worse than the disease." Those clamoring for Southern independence would place "another Canada upon our immediate border" and would assure that "for every fugitive we now lose we should certainly lose at least ten after disunion on the slave line."[22]

During January and February, the Upper South refused to follow the Deep South's lead. In the eight slave states of the Upper South, immediate secession failed to take hold, stifled either in the legislatures or in state-wide elections. Many Republicans tended, however, to downplay or ignore the conditional nature of these apparent pro-Union victories. Instead, the antisecession surge in the border states corroborated the mainstream Republican idea that secession was the work of an insidious minority. That minority had boldly stampeded the Lower South. But two-thirds of white Southerners lived in the Upper South. So long as these states stayed true to the Union, Northerners assumed, secessionists could not claim to speak for the entire South, nor could they sustain an independent Southern nation. They would not dare to fight the North without support from the Upper South, and in the end they would back down.[23]

Most border state Unionists placed themselves, however, in the soon-to-be-untenable position of insisting that the federal government renounce any use of force against the seceding states. However much they deplored what secessionists had done, Unionists generally provided them cover. "The moment you wage war, you array the entire South, as one man, in behalf of the person that is attacked," observed unconditional Unionist Horace Maynard, an East Tennessee congressman. Coercion would create a situation "as when a brother is assailed," and "all his brethren rush to his rescue, not stopping to inquire whether, in the context, he be right or wrong." His Southern Opposition Party colleague, James M. Leach of North Carolina, likewise warned that war waged "on brethren of the same blood and a common lineage" would turn his state against the Union. It would be "the height of folly and madness and wickedness" if the federal government attempted "to coerce a State." That would "rally every slave State of the Union together." Maynard and Leach exaggerated, but not by that much. When Lincoln fatefully requested in mid-April that all the states supply troops to put down the rebellion, that did indeed propel four pivotal Upper South states—Virginia, North Carolina, Tennessee, and Arkansas—into the Southern Confederacy. Hundreds of thousands of prewar conditional Unionists turned on a dime.[24]

The Upper South's self-proclaimed Unionists harshly criticized the Republican Party. Like other white Southerners, they deplored Republican success in the presidential election, and they feared that Republicans misunderstood what was happening in the South. The most assertive pro-Union newspaper in the Upper South, William G. Brownlow's *Knoxville Whig*, castigated Republicans for failing to recognize the seriousness of the secession threat. "You have never regarded these Disunionists of the South as being in *earnest*," Brownlow complained, "but have looked upon them as *blustering for effect*." Lyman Trumbull, "a gentleman supposed to speak the sentiments of the President elect," had spoken dismissively of the secession movement and acted as if the Republican Party had no responsibility to face up to "the triumphant march of revolution" as it swept across the Lower South. Instead, Republicans opposed "every scheme brought forward for a compromise" and appeared blind "to the ruin which threatens the Union."[25]

Brownlow also denounced the Chicago platform "as interpreted by the Ultra Republicans." Nobody in the South would submit to a federal government that attempted "to deprive us of our slave property." On this matter, Brownlow emphasized, "there has never been any difference between the Border States and the Cotton States." Union men in the South contended that no attempt to touch slavery ever would be made, and they counted on Republicans to provide tangible guarantees to that effect. But if Lincoln attempted otherwise, he would find that "the whole South, including the Border States, is a unit."[26]

Brownlow's qualifier here—"as interpreted by the Ultra Republicans"— deserves scrutiny. Some Republicans indeed hoped that banning slavery from the territories might be the first step on the road to abolition. For two decades, hard-liners in the political antislavery movement demanded that slavery be "denationalized"—that the federal government's responsibility for the slave system be ended. They would prevent slavery from expanding to the territories, abolish slavery in the District of Columbia, stop the interstate slave trade, especially on the high seas, prevent any new slave states from entering the Union, and require that any rendition of fugitives be managed at the state level. They considered it intolerable that the slave system had grown and grown with no end in sight.

The Republican Party, led by Lincoln, officially steered clear of this protoabolition agenda. His priority was to expand the Republican base— especially in the Lower North, where a conservative Whig outlook persisted. He knew that the Ultra Republican agenda could thwart the party just as it stood on the cusp of success. But he also knew that the single issue of territorial restriction, the political antislavery movement's least common denominator, was a prerequisite to appeasing the ultras and holding the party together. A good deal of special pleading and even cynicism accompanied the argument that territorial restriction was the first step on the road to ultimate extinction. The party needed the votes of those who had moral objections to slavery and wanted it to end soon. So leading Republicans had motive to magnify the consequences of territorial restriction even though few of them imagined that slavery might disappear in the foreseeable future. In the last chapter, we noted Lincoln's private pessimism—there was "no peaceful extinction of slavery in prospect for us."[27]

Can a case be made that secessionists accurately understood Republicans—that the party's promise not to interfere with slavery was simply a facade? Did the radical tail wag the Republican dog? Did Republicans in fact have a plan to undermine and destroy the slave system? Occasional bits of evidence did seem to point in that direction. For example, in Massachusetts, William S. Robinson, the outspokenly antislavery columnist for the *Springfield Republican*, who used the pen name "Warrington," complained that some Republican newspapers were "trying to represent that we are *less* aggressive than we really are." He scoffed at assurances that nobody in the North intended "to interfere in any manner with existing Southern institutions within the states." Instead, Robinson would "deal frankly with the South." He candidly warned Southerners that they ought not believe what Republicans were telling them. To be sure, Republicans would not "interfere by congressional action," but they certainly did hope to weaken the slave system—and "the slaveholders and their doughface allies" were correct to suspect as much. If Southerners were determined to defy "the spirit of this age" and attempt "to hold on to slavery" and all the "despotic institutions" necessary to keep it in place, they should indeed "get out of the Union."[28]

Joshua Giddings was no longer a member of Congress, but he still hoped "to make my influence felt on the great subject that has occupied my life." He indignantly rejected the idea that the Republican Party, once in power, should be as solicitous toward slaveholders as "the old Whig party." Giddings demanded, instead, that Republicans "exert the constitutional powers of government in favor of liberty [and] against oppression and slavery *wherever it holds exclusive jurisdiction.*" This meant, as he had reiterated for more than twenty years, that slavery had no legitimate basis in the territories or the District of Columbia and that the federal government could not return fugitive slaves or protect the coastwise slave trade or admit new slave states to the Union. Any enactments by Congress upholding slavery were "in direct violation" of the due process clause in the Constitution's Fifth Amendment, which specified that "no person shall be deprived of life, liberty, or property

Mutual Misconceptions

without due process of law." Giddings considered the departure of the Gulf States good riddance. If the border states chose not to follow them and wished instead to remain in the Union, they would have to emancipate their slaves. He had long believed that slavery and the Union were incompatible.[29]

Another example of assertive over-the-top Republican hostility to slavery, at least of a rhetorical variety, may be found in letters written by Lincoln's law partner, William Herndon. Sickened by all talk about "cowardly compromises," he repeatedly lectured Senators Charles Sumner and Lyman Trumbull against any "flinching" or "backing down," and he hoped that "no influential Republican" would bend "to the blustering threats of the Disunionists." Liberty and slavery were utterly antagonistic, Herndon thought, as juxtaposed as "Civilization and barbarism." They could not "co-exist on the same soil." Instead, "one or the other must perish," and he wanted this "natural war" and "inevitable struggle" to continue until "slavery is *dead, dead, dead.*" Were the Republican Party to forsake its responsibility, Herndon was ready to "tear it down and help to erect a new party that shall never cower to any slave driver."[30]

As secessionists saw things, Robinson, Giddings, and Herndon were bold truth-tellers who candidly revealed the true aims of the Republican Party. But in retrospect it seems irresponsible to give them such credit. Neither Robinson nor Giddings nor Herndon nor anyone else with their views carried weight in high Republican councils. Samuel Bowles, who edited the *Springfield Republican*, knew that Robinson resonated with his many hardline readers. But the editorial stance in Bowles's newspaper was moderate and conciliatory. He blamed anti-Republican scaremongers, such as the *New York Herald* and the *Boston Courier*, for their absurd distortions. It caused "incalculable mischief," Bowles complained, to accuse Lincoln of favoring an abolitionist agenda and promoting an "amalgamating of the white and black races." Giddings occupied a precarious position in the Republican Party. His colleagues urged him to be "cautious and prudent," and not to push the party toward "advanced ground." As we have seen, he was passed over for renomination in 1858, ending his long tenure in Congress. Herndon continued as Lincoln's law partner, but not, according to Herndon's biographer, David Donald, as "the recipient of Lincoln's political confidences." At a time when the Republican Party was attempting to broaden its appeal to conservative ex-Whigs, the "indiscreet and impolitic" Herndon presented a problem. His "ultra views" regarding the South and slavery were unwelcome at a time when the party preferred "minced words and carefully chosen phrases." By 1860, he was "definitely out of the main political current in Illinois."[31]

NEW CROSSCURRENTS OF misconception and misunderstanding swirled in early 1861 as the country careened toward disintegration and possible war. The apparent good news coming from the Upper South tempted Northerners to lose sight of the disturbing drama fast playing out in the Lower South. There the architects of a new Confederate nation were busily at work preparing to confront Lincoln with a fait accompli when he took office on March 4. Northern optimists persuaded themselves that the Upper South had pulled the rug out from under the secession movement, which necessarily would wither. But a large element of wishful thinking was at work here. Even if conceived in hothouse haste, the Confederate nation was fast becoming a reality. The mid-nineteenth century was the classic era of nationalist revolutions. Few in the North understood, however, that most whites in the Deep South had transformed their allegiance overnight from the United States to something else entirely.[32]

So Northerners often lost sight of the situation's explosive potential. They dismissed as play-acting the purported withdrawal of seven Deep South states from the Union. They tried to wish secession away or to imagine that it could be reversed. Even conciliatory Northerners, who were more likely than hard-liners to see the danger ahead, continued to hope that pro-Union white Southerners could persuade their deluded secessionist counterparts to reconsider. At the same time, Northern hard-liners impatiently warned secessionists to climb down off their high horse. Hard-liners generally expected, however, that a veiled threat of force, rather than the actual use of force, would produce the desired results.

Few saw the situation so clearly as Thurlow Weed. "The World has never witnessed judgment so perverted, passion so reckless, or madness so blind, as that which is precipitating Slavery upon its own destruction," he solemnly editorialized on January 18, 1861. Weed recalled what John Quincy Adams had "so forcibly proved" a quarter century before—that slavery "owed its existence" to the protections it enjoyed under the Constitution. By "voluntarily divorc[ing] themselves from the Constitution," the seceding states were taking a fateful step that would lead to emancipation "by violence, and through blood." Weed himself, though "deeply imbued with Emancipation sentiments and sympathies," continued his quest to avert "this great calamity—or greater blessing, as Providence designs." He wished that his voice "in favor of mutual concession and forbearance" could be "stronger and more potent." But while promising to do "all in our feeble power for Peace," Weed bluntly warned the "Southern people" to recognize the potentially "appalling consequences of Civil War."[33]

Mutual Misconceptions

An armed collision became increasingly likely. As the Confederate government consolidated its authority in the Deep South, the federal government continued to occupy two coastal fortifications—Fort Sumter, in the harbor of Charleston, South Carolina, and Fort Pickens, near the entry to the harbor at Pensacola, Florida. Confederates beefed up an arsenal of long-range cannons near both sites, especially Sumter, and demanded their surrender.

The Upper South's conditional Unionists implored their Northern friends to relinquish Sumter and Pickens. Any clash of arms, they warned, could destroy the tentative pro-Union advantage in the Upper South. "The only thing now that gives the secessionists the advantage of the conservatives," North Carolina congressman John A. Gilmer told William H. Seward, "is the cry of coercion—that the whipping of a slave state, is the whipping of slavery." He wanted to extinguish this dangerous firebrand. The experience of going "out into the cold for a while," Gilmer hoped, would diminish popular enthusiasm for independence in the Deep South and lead eventually to voluntary reunion. If "we are to have fighting at Sumter or Pickens," he cautioned, "it is what the disunionists have most courted, and I seriously apprehend that it will instantly drive the whole South into secession."[34]

Northerners were not the only ones who failed to judge the situation accurately. In retrospect, Gilmer's hope for a peaceful outcome to the crisis appears unconvincing, the wish the father of the thought. He assumed that the nationalist revolution in the Cotton States could be reversed so long as an armed collision was averted. Gilmer did have some basis for his outlook. As the Upper South searched, in the words of historian Nelson Lankford, for "an uncharted middle way between extremes," it still seemed possible that the peace might hold and that the border states might yet play a mediating role. The drive for Southern independence stalled when popular majorities in the eight Upper South states routed secession in early 1861. By so doing, they upended the partisan status quo and threatened to send Southern Rights Democrats into the political wilderness. New Union parties, poised to take power in the Upper South, would have marginalized slaveholders more than any grouping ever to hold office in a slaveholding state. Secessionist efforts "to create a united South," historian David Potter once observed, "divided the South as never before." When Lincoln took office on March 4, eight slave states remained in the Union, two-thirds of white Southerners lived in those states, and nobody knew how events would soon play out.[35]

The inability of Southern Unionists to discern the future will always be overshadowed, however, by the abject blindness afflicting Southern secessionists as they sleepwalked heedlessly into what became the ultimate catas-

Origins of the Other Thirteenth Amendment

trophe. The Republican Party posed no threat to slavery in the imaginable future. But war did. The flamboyant abandon often displayed by secession enthusiasts contrasts jarringly with the actual outcome of their abortive revolution. It was commonly said in the Deep South that "a lady's thimble will hold all the blood that will be shed." And if it did come to war, there was widespread confidence that "one Southron can drive before him five Yankees." Young white men in Alabama were "all in favor of disunion," one observer reported, "and would not object to just enough war to show the Yankees how easily they could whip them if occasion required."[36]

Southerners often assumed that the free states were too disunited to challenge the Deep South—that chronic Northern partisan divisions and ethnic rivalries, along with latent class tensions, had left the federal government paralyzed. Someone who observed the North in the winter of 1860–61 could point to plenty of corroborating evidence. Instead of putting aside their respective agendas in the face of crisis, the North's Democratic and Republican Parties continued initially to snipe at each other. Some of the North's most shrill anti-Republican newspapers announced that secessionists had "well founded apprehensions" that justified their apparent "rashness." The party "which put the reins of power into Lincoln's hands," the *New York Daily News* announced, was dominated by an "abolition mania." Its "sole object" was "the liberation of the negro." Faced with a "Republican mob" that was determined "to interfere with slavery," the South's "young men" would "flock to arms unanimously" and "fight for their homes." Lincoln, by contrast, would face the impossible task of rallying "the millions of Northern men who opposed him at the polls."[37]

Far north in the Yankee heartland, Marcellus Emery, editor of the *Bangor Daily Union*, urged Maine's Democrats to stand "shoulder to shoulder" and demand that Republicans support a "reasonable and just compromise." Absent that, "not a Democrat will be found who will raise an arm against his brethren of the South." Any use of force against the South, he insisted, would boomerang and would instead make permanent the rupture of the Union. Republicans needed to know that "the North is not a unit on coercion." None of those who voted Democratic in Maine in 1860 would cross the state line on an "errand of subjugation."[38]

The *New York Herald* kept insisting that overwhelming majorities in the free states had swung around to favor the Crittenden Compromise, which specified that slavery would be protected in territories south of 36° 30′, now held or "hereafter acquired." Republicans viewed this as an abject surrender—it was far more than the conciliatory Thurlow Weed would offer, and we have glimpsed how poorly his suggestions were received within his party. But lengthy procompromise petitions circulated, especially in Boston, New York City, and Philadelphia, and imposing delegations of merchants descended on Washington, DC, to deliver these documents. Insisting that Crittenden's handiwork was the only way to reverse the slide toward war, the *Herald*, which had the largest daily circulation in the world, called on Republicans to change their tune and quit thwarting majority sentiment in the free states.

Republicans suspected, with good reason, that Democrats had partisan motives for talking compromise. The *Herald* made no secret of its wish to create a "Great Re-Union Party of the Future" that would exclude hard-line ultra Republicans. "The Wades, Sumners, Fessendens, Hales, Greeleys, Phillipses and Garrisons" all would be "thrown overboard." These "radical revolutionary Republicans," the *Herald* speciously claimed, demanded an antislavery war that would "exterminate the white race in the South, and set the negro free from the Ohio to the Rio Grande." From this dubious source came advice for Lincoln. He should "strike out boldly for Union and for peace" by embracing "a Union compromise" that would secure the allegiance of the "border slave States" and attract Union Democrats such as New York's John A. Dix, who had recently joined Buchanan's cabinet. By placing his political future in the hands of a new party, Lincoln could avoid "civil war and its attendant horrors." Lincoln had every reason to spurn all such advice. He and other Republican leaders, already ill-disposed to compromise, had even less motive to do so when prodded by the *Herald*. By creating a partisan scrum, it obscured the actual danger of war. Meanwhile, the Republican rank and file in the Upper North remained adamantly anticompromise.[39]

Northern fractiousness was misleading, and the South misunderstood it. By January the secession movement stirred an increasingly combative attitude in the free states. Northerners lionized Major Robert Anderson and his beleaguered contingent at Fort Sumter, in Charleston harbor. When South Carolina cannons fired on January 9 at the Union resupply ship the *Star of the West*, a war fever swept the North. Within days the Ohio legislature unanimously pledged "the entire power and resources" of the state to prevent disunion and to uphold "the Constitution and laws of the General Government." John A. Gurley, a Republican House member from Cincinnati, promised on January 16 that citizens of his state would "rally as one man to defend the Union." He warned the South not to misjudge matters: "It has been supposed that the people of the West are divided in sentiment on this subject, and that a large number of them will side with those who

Origins of the Other Thirteenth Amendment

are now seeking to destroy the Government." But Westerners never would "submit to the Mississippi river being controlled by any power except that of the Union," he continued, and he ominously predicted that a "mighty storm" was gathering. Although "slow to anger," tens of thousands in the West would "overleap all party lines" and stood poised to rush into combat.[40]

Influential House Democrats such as Indiana's William S. Holman and two of his Illinois colleagues, Isaac N. Morris and John A. McClernand, insisted that Northwesterners "would not consent that the Union should be destroyed." They valued the Union above all and wanted it restored. To that end, they were ready to support a Union-saving compromise. But they bitterly condemned what was happening in the Deep South—the forced seizure of "forts, arsenals, [and] custom houses"—accompanied by the bald claim that any use of force against secession would constitute coercion. "The sooner we make up our minds to resist disunion the better," Morris warned. McClernand, who claimed to speak for "nearly all the Northwestern Democrats in Congress," denied that any state had a "lawful or constitutional right" to secede. He was especially incensed that Louisiana's departure from the Union potentially blocked upriver access down the Mississippi to the Gulf of Mexico. The Kentucky-born McClernand, soon to be elevated to military command, considered war "the greatest calamity that could befall the country," but he detested secession as "madness" and was determined "to defend and maintain the integrity of the Union." He dismissed Southern claims that it would be "coercion" to "stay the violent and lawless hand that would tear down the noble structure of our Government."[41]

The constitutional amendment to affirm the safety of slavery in the states where it existed—this book's focus—was designed to cut through these mutual misconceptions and get at the core issue that underlay all North-South acrimony. Samuel S. "Sunset" Cox, a prominent Democratic representative from Ohio, defined the problem squarely. The South's "real grievance," he judged, was a fear of "slave insurrections and abolition." Convinced that Lincoln was "elected on a principle of hostility to the social systems of the South," white Southerners persuaded themselves that a deadly menace loomed. They dreaded "a conflict for supremacy" that would pit blacks against whites and potentially bring about the "equality of the negro with ourselves and our children." However farfetched, such fears were widely held.[42]

The staple of political combat during the 1850s had been the territorial issue—a disagreement about the future of slavery in regions where it did not exist or in regions not even owned by the United States. Fugitive slaves created a secondary source of irritation, but one overshadowed by the territories. Douglas Democrats and most Republicans accepted, albeit grudgingly, the Fugitive Slave Act, but they opposed making the Kansas Territory a slave state, and they rejected the claim that the South had a federally protected right to carry slavery into all territories.

The architects of the amendment asked, in effect, that the contending parties all step back, take a deep breath, and quit tying themselves in knots. Billows of hot oratorical air and untold gallons of printer's ink had been expended to make the case that Republicans were enemies of the South and the slave system because they rejected Southern rights in the territories. As this drumbeat continued, many ordinary Southerners came to assume that Republicans were outright abolitionists, eager to use political power to destroy the slave system. Republicans indignantly pushed back against these accusations. They saw a mountain of misinformation—evidence that the South remained a closed society, unable to participate in a free exchange of ideas. They assumed that ordinary white Southerners were ideological captives, held in thrall by an overbearing elite and unable to tell fact from fiction. One New York newspaper judged that Southern nonslaveholders were helpless pawns who had been "practiced upon and made to believe that the North aims at abolition"—and that abolition would "make the negroes their equals."[43]

In a situation so fraught with misperception, the constitutional amendment appeared to offer something plain and straightforward—something that might break the spiral of finger pointing. It offered a direct answer to the core accusation that dogged Republicans, and it enabled them to show that they were not abolitionists. It captured a moment in time before anyone could contemplate the dynamic that would be unleashed by the start of warfare. Because the amendment was designed to prevent a war, it became irrelevant once the war broke out.

And the ironies ran even deeper. The effort to strip away the confusion and reduce the problem to its essentials turned out to contain the most central misconception of all. Before long, Northerners who never could imagine using armed force against the slave system found that war forced them to do just that. By mid-1862, growing numbers of Northerners saw the situation— and saw themselves—through different eyes. They increasingly blamed slavery as the source of the war itself. To prevent any such catastrophe from ever again happening, they resolved to do exactly what the amendment had promised they never would do. But all of this was outside the realm of possibility during the winter and early spring of 1861.

Origins of the Other Thirteenth Amendment

MUCH THAT HAS BEEN written about the North-South sectional crisis and the coming of the war leans one way or the other. Historians may try to distance themselves from the positions of the protagonists, but they often bring residual sectional sensibilities to their work. Eric Foner and Kenneth Stampp lean North. The North's free labor ideology reflected "the optimism and self-confidence of northern society," Foner writes. It directly threatened the South, which had no choice but to fight because the interests of the two sections were "diametrically opposed." Stampp likewise depicted North and South as fundamentally antagonistic. He dismissed all talk of compromise as "fraudulent" and celebrated the northern public's refusal to appease disunionists. His sympathies lay with stiff-backed Northerners who stood ready to fight—and who soon fought for emancipation as well as for reunion. William Cooper, by contrast, leans South. He depicts Jefferson Davis as a responsible moderate who would have welcomed a Republican overture, and he faults Lincoln for refusing to offer him anything. Cooper also writes that the Republican Party was committed to "the eventual destruction of slavery," because stopping its expansion was the first step toward getting rid of it. He thereby tends to validate the case for secession. In the end, Cooper's view is the mirror image of Foner's and Stampp's. All three of these fine historians see stark opposites that were destined to collide. By adopting either a Northern or a Southern frame of reference, all three almost inevitably find themselves identifying with an injured party.[44]

In my view, however, the historian should try to stand apart from both sides in the secession crisis tangle and explain how each misunderstood the other. That is the approach I have tried to follow here, and I am in good company. Lincoln and the Republican Party "were incredulous of all threats of disunion," David Potter noted, because they could not picture themselves as a menace to the South. They rode "blindly toward a crisis" and refused to see that the South might be in earnest. In short, Potter concluded that "neither North nor South had anything more than a muddled understanding of what was at issue between them, or what they wanted from each other." And both sides miscalculated perilously. "The South had no idea how ruthlessly its northern Democratic allies were prepared to deal with anyone who tried to tamper with the Union," he wrote. Likewise, "The North had no idea how fiercely Southern Unionists who valued the Union for themselves would defend the right of other Southerners to reject it for *them*selves and to break it up without being molested."[45]

Potter's insights deeply inform the work of historians Michael F. Holt, William Gienapp, and Russell McClintock. Holt contends that white Southerners exaggerated the danger posed by the Republican Party. They looked at Northern resentment about excessive Southern power in the Union—what Republicans called Slave Power—and thought that they saw a desire to revolutionize the Southern social order. They failed to see that Republicans principally intended to displace the Southern-dominated Democratic Party, not to interfere with slavery. "For most Republican voters," Holt writes, "Lincoln's victory and Democratic defeat was the only triumph over the South, the slave power, and slavery they required." Gienapp likewise emphasized Northern anxieties about Slave Power. Rather than attacking "slavery or Southerners," Republicans charged that the Slave Power—an aristocratic, conspiratorial elite—threatened "to stamp out all liberties of northern white men." This claim "struck a responsive chord in the minds of countless northerners, most of whom had no sympathy for a crusade to abolish slavery in the South." McClintock likewise recognizes that only a minority of Northerners had qualms about "the morality of slavery" and "the plight of the slaves." Instead, what fundamentally alarmed Northerners and gave life to the Republican Party was a fear that the South's "despotic planter-aristocrats" intended to use the power of the federal government to "destroy the Northern way of life." Both sides acted as they did, McClintock concludes, to defend themselves against dangers that they magnified all out of proportion: "The more Southern leaders fought to extend slavery through federal legislation and ultimately the Supreme Court, the more Northerners were convinced of the reality of a slave power conspiracy and acted to limit its might; and the more Northerners tried to restrict slavery and the influence of Southern planters, the more Southerners were convinced . . . that a frenzied antislavery North was trying to destroy slavery in the Southern states." [46]

William Freehling, a self-proclaimed Potter heir, likewise finds the North-South relationship fraught with misunderstanding. Linked by shared values and institutions, the two sections overlapped in many ways. Few in the North wished to meddle with the South. And until late 1860, white Southerners who opposed disunion appeared to hold the high cards. So the sudden rise of the Confederate nation and the outbreak of civil war were unexpected; most Northerners and Southerners were astonished by the sequence of events that followed Lincoln's election. Freehling depicts a South that was far from united. Many in the Upper South remained unpersuaded by proslavery polemics and continued to imagine that slaves and slavery might drain away toward the Gulf. He gives special emphasis to the Deep South's gnawing fear that the Upper South harbored a fifth column of "traitors" who stood ready to "plant a Republican Party inside the South." Secession, in his eyes, was a desperate gambit, designed to force the Upper South to take sides. Freehling, in contrast to Cooper, studies the South but does not side with the South. He treats all participants in the sectional conflict with respectful sympathy while never losing sight of the great paradox—that disunion led directly to abolition.[47]

Potter's wise example, writes historian Edward Ayers, "helps us set aside the easy assumptions we often make about how the Civil War evolved." Having looked in depth at two localities—Franklin County on the southern border of Pennsylvania and Augusta County in Virginia's Shenandoah Valley—Ayers finds that the protagonists on both sides stumbled into a conflict that few either wanted or expected. Ayers, like Potter, believes that white Northerners and white Southerners "shared a great deal" and yet lost sight of how much they shared. A majority of Franklin County residents voted for Lincoln, but they did not consciously throw down a gauntlet. They wanted neither war nor abolition. They did think, however, that the South exercised too much power in the Union, and they wanted to change that. Whites in Augusta County failed to understand "the deep appeal the Republicans held for men who cared little about slavery as it stood." The Virginians Ayers studied did not at first crave a separate destiny for the South, and they overwhelmingly spurned those who thought secession the right response to Lincoln's election. But they would not tolerate the use of force against secession.

Most directly pertinent to our study here, Ayers rejects the idea that the North went to war purposefully to end slavery. He questions whether "a war that began as a fight to maintain the Union with strong protections for slavery" ought to "be seen as inherently antislavery from the beginning." And so do I.[48]

5

The Seward Amendment

The train rumbled east through the bleak early winter landscape of upstate New York. It was Saturday afternoon, December 22, 1860, three days before Christmas. Thurlow Weed, editor of the *Albany Evening Journal* and the master political tactician of his generation, looked forward to getting home. For most of the past week, he had journeyed to Springfield, Illinois, and back. Creature comforts were at best haphazard in the early days of rail travel, and the sixty-three-year-old likely found his exertions tiring. But his last hours on the train must have been intense. At Syracuse, Weed was joined by his closest political ally, William Henry Seward, who was eager to find out what Weed had learned during consultations with the president-elect, Abraham Lincoln.[1]

For more than thirty years, the tall, secretive, soft-spoken Weed had promoted the political fortunes of Seward, four years his junior. They had enjoyed many successes. As governor of the most populous state in the Union from 1839 to 1843 and then U.S. senator starting in 1849, Seward became the most conspicuous national leader among antislavery Whigs and, after 1855, the most high-profile Republican of all. Seward framed ideas in a compelling manner. He was an optimistic nationalist who believed that history was on his side.

Seward had been sorely tempted to seek the Republican presidential nomination in 1856. Weed feared, however, that no Republican could win that year, and he knew too that Seward's long-standing opposition to nativism made it unlikely that he could maximize Republican strength.[2] But Seward and Weed planned assiduously during the next several years as Republican prospects steadily improved. They thought they had the inside track only to see it vanish before their eyes. In May 1860, as explained in chapter 3, the Republican Party spurned Seward, the odds-on favorite before the convention, and instead selected Lincoln as its presidential nominee. Both New Yorkers were stunned. But Weed and his protégé overcame their chagrin and campaigned loyally for the ticket.

In early December, Lincoln secretly offered Seward the top position in his cabinet, secretary of state. Unwilling to fuel public curiosity by conferring personally with the president-elect, Seward sent Weed to Springfield as his intermediary. Weed's visit was designed to find out what authority Seward might wield in the new administration. Was the offer from Lincoln to his former rival merely a gesture? Or did the president-elect intend to give Seward a major policy role? Would he have a say in selecting others for the cabinet? Above all, what did Lincoln think about the startling turn of events in the South?

Seward and Weed had watched with dismay during the weeks after Lincoln's election on November 6 as Deep South extremists, led by rabid South Carolinians, rushed to abandon the Union. Twice that month they consulted face to face, and on both occasions Weed then wrote editorials for his widely read newspaper to suggest how the situation might be stabilized. He insisted that Republicans dared not ignore the fast-intensifying crisis. They should, instead, look for ways to ameliorate the South's perceived grievances. It would be irresponsible, the editor stated, for Republicans simply to say that "*we* have done nothing wrong and have nothing to offer."[3]

Weed's advice was not what the Republican rank and file wanted to hear. Outraged by the behavior of Deep South secessionists, hard-line Republicans vehemently opposed any compromise of core party "principle." They chastised the "weak-kneed" Weed for proposing to "back down." "What is this world coming to," wailed George P. Morgan of Skaneateles, New York. "Every man you meet says they will never vote a Republican ticket again if such a thing is done." The hornet's nest of criticism prompted both Weed and Seward to deny that Weed's editorializing met with Seward's approval. Seward deliberately adopted a deceptive facade and pretended to be unconcerned about developments in the South. All of this was for show. Seward had enlisted Weed to float trial balloons, and both viewed the Republican reaction ominously. Only gradually did astute young Henry Adams realize that "Weed's motions, compromises and all, had been feelers on Seward's part."[4]

The two New Yorkers deliberately forewarned Lincoln of their concerns by having Weed's newspaper publish an outspokenly conciliatory editorial on December 17 just as he departed for the West. In it, Weed stated that his party should give priority to preserving the Union. By winning the election, Republicans had guaranteed that federal power would not be misused to foist slavery on the territories. The controversy over slavery in the territories therefore was "obsolete" and "the conflict between Freedom and Slavery" was resolved. No territorial government in the foreseeable future would, he

Thurlow Weed. "In the border Slave States there are tens of thousands of anxious, devoted Union men who ask only that we should throw them a plank which promises a chance of safety." *Albany Evening Journal*, Jan. 9, 1861. Library of Congress, Prints and Photographs Division, Brady-Handy Photograph Collection, LC-BH82- 4505 A.

reasoned, attempt to establish slavery, and Republicans no longer needed to prohibit overtly something that was not about to happen in the first place. Weed went even further. He thought that Republicans should also accept the current arrangement through which the New Mexico Territory, the one part of the western domain south of the old Missouri Compromise line of 36° 30′, had legalized slavery. This apparent concession would bring no tangible disadvantage, Weed thought, because the arid Southwest (the present-day states of New Mexico and Arizona, plus southern Nevada) could not support plantation slavery. Only a few dozen slaves, the personal attendants of Southern army officers stationed there, lived in New Mexico in 1860.[5]

Weed also considered concessions appropriate because a few shrill Northerners had demanded "the Abolition of Slavery everywhere." They refused to accept that "Our Fathers found Slavery so deeply seated . . . that they could not form a Union without recognizing and tolerating it." However much Republicans looked forward to slavery's "ultimate extinction," they needed to acknowledge that "it exists in the Southern States under the Constitution."

Origins of the Other Thirteenth Amendment

By opposing all compromise and risking war, Republicans served neither the national interest nor narrow party interests. If war did follow, Republicans needed to be able to say that "we have done our duty in endeavoring to preserve peace."[6]

Weed and Seward both judged it essential to offer a symbolic concession on the territorial issue in order to reverse the secession epidemic then sweeping the South. But Weed learned during his Springfield visit that Lincoln saw the situation differently, and he must have conveyed this news to Seward with a heavy heart. The president-elect reacted guardedly to Weed's "heavy broadside," the editor later recalled, and hoped that his apprehensions would prove to be "unfounded." As Lincoln saw it, sensible Southerners already understood that the Republican Party posed no menace to them.[7]

Yet Lincoln's stance created a seemingly insurmountable chasm between him and the pro-Union element in the South. He would not bend an inch toward them on the territories. Any compromise regarding slavery in the territories must be opposed, he insisted to his lieutenants, "as with a chain of steel." He would not "shift the ground" on which he had been elected. Stopping the spread of slavery was the glue that held Republicans together. For Lincoln, considerations of principle and politics coincided. It would be "the end of us"—that is, the Republican Party—to "surrender to those we have beaten."[8]

What would Lincoln offer instead? He entrusted Weed with a brief memorandum for the guidance of Senate Republicans. The president-elect specified that he would enforce the fugitive slave clause of the Constitution. But he would exempt ordinary citizens from having to "assist in its execution," and he would safeguard against free men "being surrendered as slaves." He also called for repeal of any state laws that conflicted with the Fugitive Slave Act. In exchange, Southerners would need to agree that "the Federal Union must be preserved."[9]

Weed and Seward regarded Lincoln's suggestions as insufficient. The politically divisive issue remained, as it had been all along, slavery in the territories. To be sure, some secession-inclined Southerners pointed to nonenforcement of the Fugitive Slave Act as a major provocation. But the sudden new attention given this long-dormant issue had come about because it was the only tangible grievance secessionists might identify. They had said little about fugitive slaves until the weeks after Lincoln's election. And on this issue, he stood ready to meet them halfway. The president-elect thought the South entitled to a properly framed fugitive slave law, which the free states could not legitimately obstruct.[10]

The Seward Amendment

The territorial issue, by contrast, presented an insoluble dilemma. It brought together the broadest possible spectrum of Northern antislavery opinion. Those who saw slavery as immoral and looked forward to its disappearance accepted the idea that, as a first step, it should be prevented from expanding. Republicans loved to present themselves as heirs to the Founding Fathers, who anticipated that the Republic would eventually rid itself of slavery. None other than Thomas Jefferson once tried to get Congress to exclude slavery from all the territories. Even though that did not happen, Congress did in 1787 enact the famed Northwest Ordinance, which barred the institution from territories north of the Ohio River.[11] As we have seen in the last several chapters, Republicans who hated slavery wanted more than territorial restriction. They would also have absolved the federal government and the free states from any responsibility for returning fugitive slaves; abolished slavery in the District of Columbia; attempted to end the interstate slave trade, especially when it involved ships on the high seas; and blocked the admission to the Union of any more slave states. But if hardliners could not get the party to accept this wider agenda, they insisted that the party's stance against territorial expansion must remain unqualified, absolute, and irrevocable.

Unfortunately, Southern Rights proponents demanded the exact opposite—an unlimited right to take slaves to the territories. Slaveholders might not have had the incentive or inclination to exercise that right—because none of the existing territories had the rainfall or climate to sustain plantation agriculture—but the Supreme Court had validated the abstract right in the Dred Scott decision. It thereupon became an axiom of Southern Democratic politics that the right to take slaves to the territories was a defining symbol of Southern equality in the Union. Without this right, white Southerners insisted, they would be humiliated, dishonored, and stigmatized as inferiors and second-class citizens. Rather than submit tamely to any such disgrace, they would resist. It also had become a Southern Democratic mantra that any interference with the alleged right to take slaves to territories would be the first step toward attacking it in the states where it existed. So it was that doctrinal absolutists, North and South, fixated on the territories. The extremes reinforced each other and worked together to pull the knot tighter.[12]

Having indicated to Weed that he would not accept any territorial concessions, Lincoln turned the conversation to "cabinet-making." Weed was not happy to learn that Lincoln intended to offer cabinet seats to Salmon P.

Chase and Montgomery Blair, both Seward's antagonists and advocates of a hard-line Southern policy. Lincoln's choice to represent New England would not be Seward's friend, Charles Francis Adams of Massachusetts, but rather Gideon Welles of Connecticut, who was likely to align with Chase and Blair. Weed had one more card to play. Following up on a suggestion that Seward had made by letter to Lincoln, the editor bid to appoint to the cabinet two Unionists from the Upper South who had no ties to the Republican Party. By so doing, Lincoln might help to quiet the uproar in the slave states. Lincoln doubted whether any prominent non-Republican Southerner would accept such an offer, but he finally yielded to the extent of promising to offer a slot to the leader of the so-called Southern Opposition Party in the U.S. House, John A. Gilmer of North Carolina.[13]

Better than anyone else, historian David Potter has pinpointed the significance of Weed's December 22 rendezvous with Seward. "What comments were exchanged on that trip from Syracuse to Albany is not recorded," Potter wrote in 1942, "but it is scarcely too much to say that, somewhere along the route, the active leadership of the Republican Party passed from Seward to Lincoln, and the cause of territorial compromise received a blow from which there was no recovery."[14]

Until May 1860, Seward had been the presumed leader of the Republican Party. From May to December 1859, he had toured Europe and the Mediterranean. Throughout, "he was fêted and hailed as if he was already the next president."[15] But the Republican convention displaced him in favor of the more "available" Lincoln. Seward's visibility at the center of public life, seemingly his great strength, proved instead a vulnerability. His antislavery rhetoric worried party moderates and conservatives, because it made him sound like the hard-liner that he wasn't. He also refused to bend his long-time proimmigrant stance to appease politically influential nativists. And he found his reputation for probity clouded by the wheeler-dealer manipulations of his friend Weed, the party boss in New York State.

The blow plainly stung. Some months later, when warned that a faction of patronage seekers would be disappointed if one of their number did not receive a plum appointment, Seward vented a keen frustration: "Disappointment! You speak to me of disappointment! To me, who was justly entitled to the Republican nomination for the presidency, and who had to stand aside and see it given to a little Illinois lawyer! You speak to me of disappointment!"[16] But politics is a stern game, and Seward had no real choice but to swallow that disappointment. He certainly did so—by traveling thousands of

William H. Seward. "The peacemaker be forever blest!" John Greenleaf Whittier, quoted in Hyatt H. Waggoner, ed., *The Poetical Works of Whittier* (Boston: Houghton Mifflin, 1975), 332. Daguerreotype, ca. 1850, J. H. Whitehurst, Chicago History Museum.

miles across the Upper North to deliver campaign speeches. In the estimate of his biographer, Walter Stahr, Seward "did more than any other man to achieve the election of Lincoln."[17]

Seward showed himself a team player—or so we are endlessly told—because he expected to become the power behind the throne. Although he had lost the great prize itself, he hoped that a relatively inexperienced new president would come to rely on a right-hand man who knew his way around Washington. He had played such a role for Zachary Taylor a dozen years before, and he would do the same with Lincoln. Seward's stature in the party, combined with his energetic barnstorming during the campaign, all but assured that Lincoln would offer him the top slot in the cabinet. Once in office, he would control and dominate the "simple Susan" who had been elevated beyond his depth. This line of thought has a long history. Historian Michael Burlingame recently unearthed an intriguing recollection penned more than a century ago by Charles Francis Adams Jr., who "knew and admired Seward." Adams judged that Seward "thought Lincoln a clown, a clod, and planned to steer him by . . . indirection, subtle maneuvering, astute wriggling and plotting, crooked paths. He would be Prime Minister; he would seize the reins from a nerveless President; [and] keep Lincoln separated from other Cabinet officers."[18]

Origins of the Other Thirteenth Amendment

We must, however, take careful account of the immediate circumstances during which Seward attempted to impress his ideas on Lincoln. The evidence is overwhelming that Seward was motivated principally by his anxiety about the South and his fear that the unexpected crisis could lead to war unless deftly handled. From Weed's initial trial balloons in November and December, designed to move Lincoln away from a rigid position on slavery in the territories, through to March and early April, when Seward tried to persuade the new president to retreat from Fort Sumter, the would-be prime minister gave priority to policy. The traditional Seward story, in short, has matters inside out: in trying to get Lincoln to rethink Republican orthodoxy, Seward sought no narrow or personal advantage. Matters of substance overshadowed all else during the secession winter.

But Seward risked much as he tried to introduce fresh thinking. Newspapers buzzed with speculation when he retreated to his home in upstate New York in mid-December. En route he conferred with Weed, just before the editor headed west to meet with Lincoln. Seward's close friend Israel Washburn, a Maine congressman who was about to become the state's governor, anxiously asked him to explain Weed's "most unfortunate article," which unjustly depicted Republicans as "rogues and humbugs" rather than "statesmen and patriots." Worst of all, Washburn thought, "is that you are known to have been in Albany when it was written." Many House Republicans believed that "it speaks for you without the slightest doubt." To maintain his position in the Republican Party, Seward pretended to distance himself from Weed and to insist that Weed's editorials were entirely his own doing. At a time when "the weak brethren weep and tear their hair," young Henry Adams reported to his brother, Seward was "chipper as a lark" and swearing that "everything was going on admirably." When a number of hard-line congressmen from New England and Wisconsin gathered at the Adams household in early December, Seward stood out as "a perfect giant" who was "really firm": "There's no shake in him. He talks square up to the mark and something beyond it." Seward's buoyant, if cryptic, optimism reassured his listeners that the troubles facing the country would yet be peacefully resolved.[19]

The high-stakes struggle between Lincoln and Seward has long been blurred. Even the great David Potter, perhaps the most gifted American historian, did not fully comprehend Seward's role. Potter described him as Lincoln's "agent" in Washington.[20] But Seward was more a self-appointed negotiator between Lincoln and the Southern Unionists whom Republicans counted upon to save the Union. And Seward was compelled to dissimulate.

The Seward Amendment

He came to understand that Lincoln was not about to make the concessions for which the Unionists pleaded, but he dared not reveal how unyielding Lincoln really was. Ironies abounded. Republicans bypassed Seward in 1860 because they feared his supposed taint of radicalism. But Lincoln soon showed that he rather than Seward actually shared more ideological affinity with Republican hard-liners. Seward's jaunty facade concealed grave anxieties. In private he attempted to move Lincoln in a conciliatory direction. He had some hope that this effort might prove successful—he needed Lincoln, to be sure, but Lincoln also needed him.

Historian Russell McClintock has succinctly framed the divergence between the two Republican principals. Lincoln gravitated toward hard-line Republicans, for whom "the idea of even discussing concessions in the face of armed rebellion was outrageous." Secessionist provocations, especially the wholesale expropriation of federal property and military installations, made many Northerners itch to fight back. But cooler heads kept pointing out that it was the Union men of the Upper South who made the most telling pleas for conciliation. Nothing would be conceded to secessionists, who spurned all efforts to resolve the crisis. Seward did his utmost behind closed doors to persuade the Upper South's Unionists that their needs would be met. McClintock notes that both Lincoln and Seward attempted to strike a balance between "firmness and magnanimity" and that both were engaged in a complex "double game" with each other. But Lincoln held the high cards, and Seward lacked the leverage to move him in a more conciliatory direction.[21]

Weed departed the train in Albany, and Seward proceeded south toward New York City. On arriving there, he checked in at the Astor House where he finally ate at 9:00 P.M. His arrival coincided, however, with the annual dinner of the New England Society, which attracted a number of dignitaries and a large, fashionable crowd. Seward had earlier declined an invitation to the event, but when unforeseen circumstances brought him to the hotel, he found it impossible to avoid a late-evening summons to the ballroom. Speaking impromptu, and with no chance for preparation, he bravely predicted that the ties binding the American Union together were stronger than those that threatened to tear it apart. As in any large family, there were bound to be disagreements, but these could be overcome. In sixty days, he predicted, "a more cheerful atmosphere" would reveal itself.[22]

The next day was Sunday, December 23, and Seward paused in New York. Not until evening did he board a sleeping car that carried him down what we now call the Northeast Corridor. If he were in a contemplative frame of mind, he could not help but reflect on history's unpredictability. A year before, he had been the odds-on favorite to win the Republican nomination, but the great prize went instead to the lesser-known but more "available" Lincoln. Like almost all other Republicans, both Seward and Lincoln underestimated the disunion movement. Until Lincoln's victory took place, Republicans scorned the idea that it might trigger a grave crisis. It had been a centerpiece of the Republican campaign to say that the South had too much invested in the Union to destroy it. Thus Seward himself, the week before the election, had belittled "these Southern statesmen and politicians" who threatened to tear down "this government and this constitution" and "dissolve the Union." Their scare tactics were an empty bluff, he reassured his listeners at a large campaign rally in New York City; Southerners knew perfectly well that the election would bring to power "men who will leave slavery in the United States just exactly where it is now." Republicans were convinced, as Potter phrased it, that "secession was a mere rhetorical weapon, devised to frighten the electorate, but not for a moment seriously intended to be used, except by the most ultra of the fire-eaters." If the free white men of the North voted for Lincoln, Republicans predicted, the Union would not only survive but be strengthened. The South had long exercised outsized power in the federal government. It could give up some of its undeserved advantages without suffering hardship or danger. Republicans vowed that they had neither the power nor the intention of attacking slavery in the states where it existed.[23]

But the South's reactionary revolutionaries marched to a different tune. Within days of the presidential election, South Carolina set in motion the chain of events that rapidly severed its ties to the Union and ignited an unprecedented conflagration across the Deep South. On December 20, as Seward awaited Weed's return from Springfield, South Carolina unilaterally declared its independence. The Palmetto State's incorrigible incendiaries astutely played their trump card. Their action created a situation in which the federal government would have to either acquiesce in disunion or use force to prevent it. Knowing that the use of armed force against a sister slave state would be intolerable to most white Southerners, South Carolina boldly challenged the other slave states to stand with her or against her. Soon Mississippi and Florida fell into line. "Cooperationists" who considered separate state secession unwise were more numerous in Alabama and Georgia, but within weeks they lost control of their states. Georgia's secession cut the moorings that still tethered the remaining two Deep South states, Louisiana and Texas.[24]

The astonishing events that unfolded in the Deep South revealed that traditional political leaders such as Mississippi's Jefferson Davis and Georgia's Robert Toombs could not deflect the secession rampage, even had they been disposed to do so. They had unleashed forces that no longer could be controlled. Throughout the summer and fall, historian William J. Cooper has written, they "predicted ruin for the South should the Republicans win." They thereby fueled the uproar that rabid Deep South extremists fanned into a raging fire. Soon many supposedly responsible Deep South leaders embraced the disunion cause. A notable case in point, as we have seen, was Georgia's Howell Cobb, the secretary of the treasury, who suddenly resigned in early December and made the nonsensical claim that the Republican Party was committed to "immediate and unconditional abolition in every State." Increasingly, secessionists insisted that the South could not turn back. Joseph Holt's Mississippi brother depicted a white-hot movement "not of the leaders, but of the masses whom the leaders could not control if they would," with the only possible outcome "complete separation." "We spit upon every plan to compromise," roared one newspaper editor. "A Southern man who would now offer to compromise with the Northern States is a traitor to the South."[25]

Officially, however, Davis and Toombs insisted that prompt Republican acceptance of the compromise proposal promoted by Kentucky senator John J. Crittenden would bring the disunion movement to a screeching halt. But the Crittenden Compromise was an unlikely panacea. It created an ominous precedent that Republican must "apologize and beg forgiveness"—Lincoln's tart phrase—for having carried the presidential election. And it trampled Republican sensibilities by specifying that slavery would be federally protected in all territories south of 36° 30′, now held or "hereafter acquired." Weed had been denounced for proposing a far less drastic concession. "Protection" had been inserted to satisfy those who insisted that Dred Scott be applied somewhere in the territorial domain even if not in all the territories. Worse, the language about "hereafter acquired" seemed to Republicans an open invitation to conquer a Caribbean slave empire. When Davis and Toombs said that Crittenden's handiwork would be acceptable to them if Republicans would accept it too, they likely were posturing, confident that Republicans would refuse. This was no compromise, Republican senator William Pitt Fessenden charged, but rather an "ignominious surrender."[26]

During Seward's absence from Washington, a special committee of thirteen senators had been appointed to address the crisis. Their deliberations placed him and the four other Republicans on the committee in an awkward position. Crittenden's dubious handiwork was already being touted around the country as the key to sectional reconciliation and peace. To reject it outright would play into the hands of secessionists. But Seward now knew that Lincoln spurned any territorial compromise, let alone one so weighted down with objectionable features as Crittenden's. If Seward intended to accept the cabinet offer, he had no choice but to follow Lincoln's lead. That meant doing what he had so far avoided—coming out squarely against the Crittenden Compromise. At the same time, he wanted to offer something tangible in its place.[27]

Freshly arrived in Washington on Monday morning, December 24, Seward immediately consulted with the four other Republican members of the Committee of Thirteen—Jacob Collamer of Vermont, James W. Grimes of Iowa, Benjamin F. Wade of Ohio, and James R. Doolittle of Wisconsin. This was a responsible group, with Wade a more outspoken radical than the others. The four had voted against the Crittenden Compromise two days before, and Seward now added his vote to theirs. The group decided, however, to submit an alternative to the Crittenden plan. Grimes had already drafted a proposal to put the Republican Party on record regarding three points: to amend the Fugitive Slave Act so as to secure the alleged fugitive a trial by jury, to "respectfully" request that the states "repeal or modify" any laws that might "contravene" either the Constitution or federal laws (this circumlocution referred to so-called personal liberty laws, enacted by several Northern states, that potentially narrowed the scope of the Fugitive Slave Act), and to amend the Constitution so that Congress could not "abolish or interfere" with slavery in the states where it existed. Seward coined the actual language for the amendment, carefully phrased to avoid adding the word "slavery" to the Constitution. It read as follows: "No amendment shall be made to the Constitution which will authorize or give to Congress any power to abolish or interfere, within any State, with the domestic institutions thereof, including that of persons held to labor or service by the laws of said State."[28]

Weed's fingerprints were all over this counteroffer. The smoking gun is a letter to Weed from James E. Harvey, who confidentially informed the editor, "We made a little step forward yesterday in the Committee of 13, and Seward behaved exceedingly well by taking up our proposition without a waver, and presenting it. I sent it to the Tribune last night. That spikes their guns about interference in the states, which is not believed by the men who charge it."[29]

Plainly Weed enlisted Harvey, a premier journalist and key Washington insider, to act as his go-between, and the evidence suggests that Harvey reached out to Grimes and Collamer even before Seward's return to Washington. Could Weed have taken such a significant step on his own authority? Just possibly, but not likely. The message from Harvey could be read to suggest that Seward learned about the constitutional amendment and agreed to support it only after arriving in Washington. But it also could mean that Harvey did not fully understand what Seward's astute long-ago biographer, Frederic Bancroft, concluded—that Weed and Seward "were working together like the two hands of one man" during the secession crisis. I think that Seward and Weed must have agreed to go for the amendment before Weed reached out to Harvey.[30]

If so, the amendment was part of the discussion on the afternoon train ride between Syracuse and Albany on December 22. And that raises a key question: Had the amendment also been a topic of conversation between Weed and Lincoln? Weed's memoirs describing his Springfield visit, published years later, do not mention the amendment, but a key piece of contemporary evidence strongly implies that Weed and Lincoln must have discussed it. On the evening of December 26, Seward updated Lincoln on what the Senate Republicans were doing. He reported that the five members of the Committee of Thirteen had "offered three propositions which seemed to me to cover the ground of the suggestions made by you, through Mr. Weed, as I understand it." The first item on Seward's list was the proposal "that the Constitution should never be altered, so as to authorize Congress to abolish or interfere with slavery in the States." I do not think Seward would have written as he did unless he thought that Lincoln wanted the amendment.[31]

Historian William J. Cooper regards the Seward letter as proof that Lincoln deftly lined up Republican support for the amendment—and that Weed and Seward were acting at his behest. This may be true; certainly Lincoln eventually did accept it in his first inaugural address. But Weed may well have taken the lead on the amendment in December. Just as he persuaded Lincoln to offer a cabinet post to Gilmer, Weed may also have gotten the president-elect to acquiesce temporarily in the amendment palliative. It is conspicuous, as Cooper agrees, that Lincoln tried to conceal his stance on the amendment. Lincoln's alleged instructions were oral, not written, and he soon backtracked. Shortly afterward, on December 28, Duff Green, an old acquaintance of Lincoln's from Ann Sprigg's boardinghouse, arrived in Springfield to talk up the Crittenden Compromise. He had been dispatched by James Buchanan. But Lincoln told Green that he did "not want any amendment to the Constitution."[32]

Knowing that the Deep South remained hell-bent on disrupting the

Union, one may conclude that the constitutional amendment was insignificant and meaningless. Secessionists instead demanded immediate enactment of the Crittenden Compromise. They set the bar there, Seward told Lincoln, because they thought Republicans were "not going to concede" to their ultimatum.[33] Southern demands for a federally protected right to hold slaves in present and future territories made the Crittenden proposal unacceptable to Republicans. But neither Southern slaveholders nor their slaves yet lived in the territories. The proposed constitutional amendment involved the states—where slaves and slaveholders and nonslaveholders already did live. In reality, the amendment addressed the core impulse that created the secession movement—a suspicion or fear that the victors in the 1860 election stood poised to undermine slavery in the states. The amendment enjoyed unanimous support from the five Republicans on the Committee of Thirteen. And two of them explained at length why Southerners should take their work seriously.

James Doolittle of Wisconsin forcefully defended the Republican Party and the president-elect against accusations that they menaced slavery in the states. The 1860 Republican Party platform left slavery to each state's "own judgment exclusively," and there were "no Republicans to be found" who thought otherwise. During Lincoln's debates with Stephen A. Douglas in 1858, Doolittle emphasized, Lincoln had vowed that he had "no purpose, directly or indirectly, to interfere with the institution of slavery in the States where it exists. I believe that I have no lawful right to do so, and I have no inclination to do so." Lysander Spooner had advanced the "unfounded" idea that the Constitution "abolishes slavery," Doolittle observed, and many Southerners now took the polar opposite position that the Constitution was "slavery-extending." But Doolittle contended that the Constitution must be "neutral." It "never could have been formed at all" under either the Spooner theory or the Dred Scott theory. The men who framed it carefully left the matter of slavery to be determined by each state. Doolittle condemned the unreasonable and alarmist accusation that Republicans ultimately intended to so enlarge "the number and power of the free states" that they would be able "to amend the Constitution itself, and give the Federal Government the power to abolish slavery in the States." He urged his Southern colleagues to "quiet the alarm" among their people and quit insinuating that Republicans had the same objective as abolitionists, many of whom were "as anxious for the dissolution of the Union" as the "extremists upon the Gulf of Mexico."[34]

Ben Wade of Ohio also challenged Southern malcontents. They falsely claimed that Republicans were "mortal enemies" who stood ready "to trample their institutions under foot." Republicans had been depicted, he complained, as "John Brown men," eager to launch violent attacks in the slave states—"a thing that no Republican ever dreamed of or ever thought of." In fact, Republicans never pretended that they had any right "to interfere with your peculiar institution." The South was about to "break up this Government" and "involve us in war and blood," because of a "groundless suspicion" that Republicans would do "that which we stand everywhere pledged not to do." Wade recognized that Republicans always disapproved of slavery and insisted that it not be allowed to expand, but slavery in the States was "out of our jurisdiction," and Republicans had "no designs upon it." Wade's reassurances deserve notice—he was no obscure backbencher but rather one of the most outspoken Republican radicals.[35]

Officially the Committee of Thirteen failed. It was "unable to agree upon any general plan of adjustment," according to the formal report it made to the full Senate, issued the last day of December. But Seward's proposed constitutional amendment obtained committee approval, eleven to two. In addition to support from the five Republicans, it picked up four of five Southern votes and two of the three from Northern Democrats. Both Jefferson Davis and Stephen A. Douglas accepted it. If not a "general plan of adjustment," it nevertheless defined a small patch of common ground amid the otherwise polarized situation.[36]

Peace hung by a thread in early January 1861. The Deep South's rush out of the Union accelerated. Secessionists continued to seize federal forts and arsenals, and rumors swirled that a hostile force might be about to strike at Washington, DC. Newspapers reported that a federal flotilla was headed South. Finally, on January 9, artillerymen employed by the self-proclaimed independent entity of South Carolina fired on a ship in U.S. service, the *Star of the West*, as it approached Fort Sumter at the mouth of Charleston harbor. The ship turned back and federal forces did not return fire, but an intensifying war fever gripped the free states. All talk of conciliation appeared pointless and irrelevant.

"Seward is evidently very low-spirited," Henry Adams surmised on January 8. He blamed the changed countenance of the previously ebullient New Yorker on the situation in the Upper South. Seward hoped that "the border-states would not go," but he recognized that "all depends on Virginia." Were Virginia to follow the Deep South out of the Union, Adams inferred, it might be impossible to avoid war.[37] At this ominous juncture, however, Seward announced that he would speak to the Senate. His acceptance of Lincoln's offer to join the cabinet had just been made public. Seward's prospective speech stirred a frenzy of anticipation. Conciliators hoped that he was "about to extend the olive branch." But hard-liners, among them his wife, Frances, implored him not to deviate. Salmon P. Chase begged him to avoid any "surrender of principle." His friend and Senate colleague James W. Grimes warned of a potentially "quite disastrous" movement afoot in the House Republican caucus to rebuke Seward if he lowered the party standard.[38]

Seward's pending speech had historical resonance. It was bound to be seen through the lens of what had occurred eleven years before, on March 7, 1850, when the Senate's all-time greatest orator, Daniel Webster of Massachusetts, delivered the most controversial speech of his life. His voice "rang out like a trumpet . . . with a roll of thunder in it," historian Robert Remini wrote; it was "powered by a massive chest that sent it hurtling great distances." The "Godlike Daniel" also mesmerized audiences with his "large, deep-socketed black eyes . . . [which] glowed like coals in a furnace."[39] Webster's Seventh of March speech contended that slavery would never spread to the territories, so there was no need to prohibit it there; that white Southerners were entitled to a strengthened fugitive slave law; and, above all, that Union mattered more than slavery. Those who considered slavery a grave moral problem erupted in fury. The most devastating rebuke to Webster was penned by the abolitionist poet John Greenleaf Whittier:

> So fallen! so lost! the light withdrawn
> Which once he wore!
> The glory from his gray hairs gone
> Forevermore! . . .
> Of all we loved and honored, naught
> Save power remains; . . .
> All else is gone; from those great eyes
> The soul has fled: . . .
> Walk backward, with averted gaze,
> And hide the shame![40]

The U.S. Capitol was "thronged like an inauguration day" on Saturday morning, January 12, 1861. Crowds surged toward the north side of the immense building—where the Senate's handsome new quarters had opened just two years earlier. Natural light suffused through its skylight, a "colored glass roof." Its sixty-six polished mahogany desks, two for each of the thirty-three states in the Union, perched on a striking, floral-patterned purple carpet. The original desks dated from 1819, when the Capitol was reopened after having been burned by the British during the War of 1812. Almost two centuries later, those same desks—along with newer ones built to mark the admission of additional states—remain in use, as does the 1859 Senate chamber. By midday, a "great audience" numbering "many thousands" packed the Senate's galleries. The section reserved for women was "radiant with beauty and fashion." Reporters congregated behind the presiding officer's desk. A mass of humanity jammed the hallways. The persistent undertone of anxious whispering suddenly hushed at twenty minutes before one o'clock as Seward rose to speak.[41]

Slight in stature and lacking the long-dead Webster's oratorical prowess, Seward nonetheless had a gift for memorable phraseology and an expansive, optimistic view of the future. No other senator could match his ability to articulate the case for "free labor." For the past decade he had confidently predicted that the retrograde system of American slavery would not endure, that "ultimate emancipation" was predestined, and that it would unfold without violence or convulsion. He anticipated that slaveholders would willingly "yield" to the "beneficent" values of the age, just as snow melts away in the warm springtime sun.[42]

The events of November and December had startled Seward. Sooner than other Republicans, he realized that the whirlwind sweeping the Deep South was not just play-acting. Only three days before he spoke, South Carolina cannons had taken aim at the *Star of the West*. The unimaginable was on the verge of happening—the United States stood on the brink of civil war. Could anything be done to move the nation back from the precipice?

"It has been my fortune to have witnessed nearly all the great occasions in Congress during the last twenty years," wrote James E. Harvey, the elite Washington correspondent for the *Philadelphia North American* (his private labors at Weed's behest have already been noted). "No recent event, even among the many startling ones which have exercised the public mind, has excited more comment, or produced a profounder sensation, than Mr. Seward's speech." Even "radical secessionists, who professed an unwillingness to hear any terms," listened intently.[43] Seward especially commanded attention because it was assumed that he spoke for the incoming Republican administration. It had just been announced that he would become Lincoln's secretary of state. With Lincoln still a relative unknown in official Washington, observers inevitably saw the New York senator as his spokesman. But we now know that the two had secretly jousted for the previous six weeks and that they disagreed regarding the hour's key issue.

As Seward stood before the Senate and the nation, he faced a seemingly impossible dilemma. He had to heed Lincoln's views, yet he was eager to reach out to Southern anti-secessionists. And they kept insisting that disunion could be averted only if Republicans offered the South a territorial compromise. So Seward tried to change the subject—he pleaded for a "truce" to the endless "dogmatical" debates regarding slavery in the territories. Instead, the western territories might be admitted into the Union as two big states, he suggested, so as to bypass the territorial phase. To counter the South's other most emotionally charged complaint, Seward proposed amending the Constitution to prohibit any interference with slavery in the states where it existed. Finally, he reminded white Southerners that their rights within the Union were secure, whereas "the horrors of civil war" would make any of their perceived grievances look trivial by comparison.[44]

Underlying Seward's speech was the hope that secession could be confined to the Deep South. Weed, his political manager, kept imploring Republicans to distinguish between the "true Patriots" in the Upper South who were trying to save the Union and the "traitors" in the Cotton States who were trying to destroy it. He challenged the idea that any Republican concession countenanced secession. Quite the opposite—"in the border Slave States," Weed insisted, "there are tens of thousands of anxious, devoted Union men who ask only that we should throw them a plank which promises a chance of safety." As we have seen, Lincoln quietly gave Seward and Weed permission to offer a seat in the cabinet to North Carolina congressman Gilmer, a leading Unionist. Two-thirds of white Southerners lived in the Upper South. If these eight states held fast against secession, Seward reasoned, the uproar in the Deep South might be contained and ultimately reversed.[45]

Seward's speech elicited a bewildering array of responses. Moderates both North and South voiced at least qualified approval, but secessionists and Southern Rights advocates howled in protest. Seward hadn't offered any compromise worth considering, they insisted. His empty posturing showed instead that Black Republicans planned to ride roughshod over the South. Northern antislavery ideologues were equally miffed. "I deplore Seward's speech," Charles Sumner fumed. Thaddeus Stevens was "mortified and discouraged." Abolitionist Wendell Phillips sneered that Daniel Webster's support for the Compromise of 1850 had been "outdone" and that "Massachusetts yields to New York the post of infamy which her great Senator has hitherto filled." Even Frances Seward feared that her husband stood "in danger of taking the path that led Daniel Webster to an unhonored grave."[46]

Webster's ghost plainly lurked. But John Greenleaf Whittier reacted differently to Seward's speech than he had to Webster's. An abolitionist but also a Quaker, Whittier dreaded war. He thanked Seward "in the sweet and holy name of peace, for wise calm words that put to shame passion and party."

> If, without damage to the sacred cause
> Of Freedom and the safeguard of its laws—
> If, without yielding that for which alone
> We prize the Union, thou canst save it now
> From a baptism of blood, upon thy brow
> A wreath whose flowers no earthly soil have known,
> Woven of the beatitudes, shall rest,
> And the peacemaker be forever blest![47]

Although some abolitionists grumbled that the pacifist Whittier gave higher priority to preventing war than to opposing slavery, his verse effectively silenced those who reviled Seward as a second Webster. Young Henry Adams, who closely observed Seward during the secession winter, witnessed only one moment when the normally "immovable" New Yorker "felt what was said of him"—when "he opened the envelope and read the sonnet which the poet Whittier sent to him from Amesbury."[48]

But could the "baptism of blood" be averted? That dread question hung over everything in early 1861, its answer inscrutable.

6

The Corwin Amendment

Thomas Corwin became part of the folklore of American history on February 11, 1847. That afternoon, the tall, heavyset, fifty-two-year-old Ohio Whig made a sensational speech in the U.S. Senate to condemn the American war against Mexico. One key passage from his memorable oration stood out: "If I were a Mexican, I would tell you, 'Have you not room in your own country to bury your dead men? If you come into mine we will greet you with bloody hands, and welcome you to hospitable graves.'"[1] Irrevocably thereafter, Corwin was remembered either as a courageous dissenter who dared to speak his mind—or as a traitor who gave aid and comfort to the enemy while American troops were in combat.

When a career gets reduced to a single snapshot, a great deal of essential context gets omitted and the image itself may not be in focus. Corwin's 1847 declamation created such an uproar because he was formidable, not a marginal scold prone to reckless theatrics. Why did this successful mainstream politician make such an outburst? To answer that question, we must learn more about one of the most significant public lives of the antebellum era. As the North-South sectional crisis scissored the political institutions of the country, Corwin understood sooner and better than most of his contemporaries the lethal potential of controversy regarding slavery in the territories. He opposed the war to gain territory because it endangered the Union. The real treason, he presciently insisted, was heedless conquest, which was bound to bring a collision between North and South "on a point where neither will yield." It could potentially "light up the fires of internal war, and plunge the sister States of this Union into the bottomless gulf of civil strife." Antislavery leaders, who hated the war, immediately heralded Corwin as a prospective presidential candidate. But he was destined to disappoint them. He hoped to heal the breach between North and South, not widen it. His object, historian Michael Morrison has noted, was to hold together both the Union and the Whig Party.[2]

This chapter will address the sequel, fourteen years later, to Corwin's celebrated critique of the Mexican War. In late 1860 and early 1861, the fires he had warned about in 1847 were close to igniting. Seven Deep South states were seceding, and peace hung by a thread. Could anything be done? According to one retrospective source, Corwin privately feared that "all the efforts for compromise will come to nothing" and that too many men on both sides were "like bull-dogs eager for the fray."[3] Yet he made a last-ditch effort to head off disaster. This was to be his valedictory. He was already sixty-six, and he lived in an era of shorter life expectancy. But he summoned up enormous energy during his last months in Congress. He should be remembered at least as much for what he attempted to do in early 1861 as for what he said in early 1847—indeed, the two moments are inseparably interconnected.

Corwin's political home was the Whig Party, and historian Michael F. Holt has reminded us that he was conspicuous among those Whigs who abjured sectionalism. His loyalties to party and nation were symbiotic, and he remained a man without a true political home after his party disappeared.[4] By the late 1850s, however, he knew that the Whig Party was no more. After five years out of the public spotlight, he secured the 1858 Republican nomination for a seat in Congress. To do this, he accepted the lead of his constituents—most Whigs in his hometown of Lebanon and the surrounding region in southwestern Ohio had become Republicans. Corwin easily regained the post he had occupied a generation before during the 1830s. Although technically a freshman, he was regarded as an elder statesman. He had served as governor of Ohio, U.S. senator (when he gave his famous speech), and secretary of the treasury in Millard Fillmore's cabinet. If someone with his stature felt comfortable calling himself a Republican, the party could hardly have been committed to a radical antislavery agenda.

Corwin's return to the House coincided with the protracted speakership contest of December 1859 and January 1860. The Republican nominee for Speaker, John Sherman of Ohio, ran into an orchestrated buzz saw of Southern hysteria. Sherman and many other Republicans had routinely endorsed a book written by an obscure North Carolinian, Hinton Helper, who urged Southern nonslaveholders to challenge the dominant planter elite. Sherman's hyperbolic critics concluded, outrageously, that the Ohio congressman had in effect encouraged John Brown's raid at Harpers Ferry in October 1859. Corwin, alarmed by the overheated rhetoric, tried to defuse it with a light touch. He had grown tired, he confessed, of hearing that Republicans were Brown's accomplices and guilty of wholesale "treason, murder, robbery, and arson." None of his colleagues, Corwin vowed, had been "at Harper's

Ferry with a pike in his hand, pushing it into the bosom of a Southern gentleman." Republicans were not abolitionists. They were "conservative" and "law-abiding." They disliked slavery in just the same way that Washington and Jefferson did, and they shared with the Founding Fathers the hope that some day slavery might disappear.[5]

Corwin was fifteen years Abraham Lincoln's senior. Both were ardent western Whigs who shared Kentucky roots. But Corwin made his mark much sooner. At a time when young Lincoln was splitting rails in rural Illinois, Corwin had moved onto the national stage. He was a celebrated stump speaker who could charm audiences with his wit and good humor. The two probably crossed paths in Congress in the late 1840s—Corwin was among the leading Whigs in the Senate when Lincoln served his single term in the House. But their interactions were hardly even superficial. In 1850 Lincoln wrote a patronage letter on behalf of a friend to Corwin, then the treasury secretary, in which Lincoln surmised that Corwin might have "a slight general recollection of me; though nothing more."[6]

In 1858 Lincoln became more visible by running a close but losing race against Stephen A. Douglas, the incumbent U.S. senator from Illinois. That same year, Corwin emerged from political retirement to reclaim the House seat that he first held decades earlier. Both Lincoln and Corwin had become Republicans, but Lincoln had given up his Whig allegiances sooner than Corwin. Lincoln's efforts to become better known outside his home state— part of his dark-horse strategy in pursuit of the Republican presidential nomination—brought him to make several speeches in Ohio in September 1859, a month before the state elections. Deferential and self-deprecating, Lincoln warned his audiences that they were accustomed to hearing "such speakers as Corwin, and Chase, and Wade, and many other renowned men," and that they ought not "raise your expectations to that standard."[7]

Lincoln's Ohio visit initiated an exchange of letters between the two Whigs-turned-Republicans. Corwin was glad to find Lincoln "earnest in the wish for general success in the coming contest" but disappointed to learn of Lincoln's prediction that "a moderate man," if nominated by Republicans for president in 1860, "would loose Illinois by 50,000." Corwin countered by worrying that a moderate nominee offered the only hope of carrying Indiana and Pennsylvania—"without which we may fight bravely and die gloriously, but the poor Republic will remain in the hands of the spoilers." Corwin hoped that the "Northern Opposition" would simply state that "Congress had the power to make law for territories, and cease the subject there." But he feared that the 1860 contest might be "a hopeless one for us"—Republi-

The Corwin Amendment

cans were "just so fixed that we cannot succeed with a Conservative or [an] Extreemist."[8] Plainly the old veteran and the about-to-be rising star were taking their measure of each other. They discovered that they talked the same language even if their prognostications diverged.

Just one year later, Lincoln stood on the cusp of victory in the presidential contest. State elections in Indiana, Ohio, and Pennsylvania in October 1860 foreshadowed a Republican sweep one month later. Plainly Lincoln had read the situation with more insight than Corwin—Republicans could indeed attract Northern moderates without alienating those who had an ideological aversion to slavery. The key had been to find the right nominee.

But just as the celebrations were about to begin, Corwin dispatched a warning to Lincoln. He enclosed copies of letters sent to him privately from two former Southern Whigs, both of whom feared that Lincoln's election victory might ignite a firestorm in the South. Corwin therefore encouraged Lincoln to announce "his conservative views in the strongest light" as soon as the votes were counted. Corwin's two correspondents, Waddy Thompson, a former South Carolina congressman, and William L. Hodge, formerly of New Orleans, hoped to blunt the Southern response to Lincoln's election. "Do you know the man," Thompson asked Corwin, "and will he be conservative?" If he announced as much immediately after his election, it might "do much good, and perhaps prevent seceding movements." Hodge similarly voiced hope that Lincoln would be "highly conservative" and "a perfectly safe man for the South and so they would find him if they only remain quiet." But Hodge feared that danger was "imminent"—secessionists were positioned to act quickly both in South Carolina and in Georgia. If a single drop of blood was shed, "the whole South would be in flames and beyond all control." Hodge conceded that "there is a good deal of the *brag* game in it at the South but there is also quite too much of the reality." A postelection statement from Lincoln would "greatly strengthen the hands of the Union men at the South," and it "would calm the timid men there, who think Mr. Lincoln intends to liberate all their slaves." Hodge knew that Lincoln had no such intention. He knew too that "a dissolution would be the knell of slavery." But, he observed, "you cannot persuade them to that."[9]

Corwin accompanied the enclosures to Lincoln with his own closely reasoned letter. He commended the two authors for their "good sense" and "general character" and for their "knowledge of the tone and feeling of the south." As representatives of "the Union men (all old Whigs) in the south," they wished "to prevent the first step in an attempt at secession." Corwin recognized that a statement from Lincoln right after the election might seem

Origins of the Other Thirteenth Amendment

to admit that Southerners had real cause for "the apprehension of evil." He worried too about a related potential downside. "Under no circumstances," he cautioned Lincoln, "must these Southern men be allowed to suspect, that we are timid or afraid of them." It should be "gravely pondered" whether any statement would be "proper or prudent"—and "of course for yourself to determine." But Corwin was inclined to agree with Thompson and Hodge. He suggested that "some confidential friend" could address "a letter on the subject of Southern affairs" for Lincoln to answer "in your own way." The paramount need was to prevent any Southern state, motivated by "false pride," from taking "some mad step, which once adopted, leads to dangers which those who take it had not the discretion to foresee." Corwin would not, he assured Lincoln, abandon "any principle, for which we have contended." Instead, he hoped "to allay the unfounded fears of good men and render impossible the evil movements of bad men." Lincoln should remember, Corwin concluded, that "magnanimity displayed by a conqueror, is not merely an amiable quality, but very often coincides with wise policy."[10]

A week later, and just days before the election, Corwin forwarded a similar letter to Lincoln, written by S. W. Spencer of Chestertown, Maryland, a neighbor of Corwin's old friend U.S. senator James A. Pearce, a Whig-turned-Democrat. Spencer gave Lincoln the benefit of the doubt for having been "a firm and consistent Whig" who cherished "the principles of Henry Clay." Spencer feared, however, that many in the South thought otherwise. They associated Lincoln not with Clay but with the radical faction of the political antislavery movement—with Giddings, Sumner, and Owen Lovejoy. His election would "create a profound sensation in all the Southern States—The Wolf is really upon us now." The "secessionists further South will be in a perfect frenzy," Spencer warned, and even in Maryland, "this old conservative State," feelings of "uneasiness and distrust" were apparent. As soon as the election was decided, Spencer hoped, Lincoln should give "an authoritative exposition of his principles in regard to the slavery question."[11]

Lincoln did indeed admire Clay. He lauded Clay's rare eloquence, judgment, and will—and his "deep devotion to the cause of human liberty." But Lincoln also thought it tragic that Clay never had been able to move Kentucky toward gradual emancipation. As the nominee of a party that included many former Democrats who did not share his own warm regard for Clay, Lincoln distanced himself from the compromising statecraft of the Great Pacificator.[12]

Corwin's Southern friends read the situation accurately. As we have seen, Lincoln's election as president in early November 1860 triggered mass panic

Thomas Corwin. "You believe that, ultimately, the great Abolition party, which you always magnify in your imaginations fifty or one hundred times beyond its proper proportions, will obtain control of the Republican Party." *Congressional Globe*, 36:2 (Jan. 21, 1861), A74. U.S. Bureau of Engraving and Printing.

across the South, especially the Deep South. For years Southern Democrats had insisted that "Black Republicans" threatened the survival of slavery in the states where it existed. Rather than wait to find out whether Lincoln would actually seek to revolutionize the Southern social order, secessionists insisted on setting up a separate Southern government. This was exactly the impasse Corwin had feared in 1847. He had noted then that "men of all parties" in the free states opposed slavery expansion, whereas Southerners "would contend to any extremity for the mere *right*" to expand slavery to the territories, even though they had "no wish to exert it." In so doing, Southerners ignored the key distinction that antislavery politicians always made—that they would not disturb slavery in the states where it existed.[13]

Corwin found himself in the midst of efforts to limit and reverse the secession surge. When the lame-duck session of Congress convened in early December 1860, a month after Lincoln's election, the House voted immediately to appoint a special committee to consider "the present perilous situation of the country." Several dozen hard-line Republicans opposed setting up the committee, but they were outvoted by a large margin, 145 to 38. The Speaker of the House, New Jersey's William Pennington, then appointed one member from each of the thirty-three states. Observers credited him with selecting "moderate and conciliatory" colleagues wherever he could do so. The committee's daunting task was to formulate a Union-saving arrangement.[14]

Origins of the Other Thirteenth Amendment

Corwin agreed to head the House Committee of Thirty Three. This vantage point made him keenly aware how extraordinary the crisis had become. He continued to update Lincoln with pithy assessments of the fast-worsening situation. Few people could see so readily what was happening both North and South. Corwin's letters to Lincoln were anything but encouraging. "I have never, in my life, seen my Country in such a dangerous position," he wrote. "I look upon it with great alarm." Just at the time the Committee of Thirty Three first met, Corwin returned to the idea that Lincoln make a public statement—the same idea he had floated more than a month before. On December 10 he forwarded to Lincoln a letter to this effect from John A. Gilmer, the North Carolinian who led the Southern Opposition Party in the House.[15]

Corwin corroborated Gilmer's message—people in the North were "not well informed as to the excitement prevailing in the South." It seemed "to border on madness," Corwin recognized, "and so it may appear to others who believe with me, that no adequate cause for it exists." But Corwin insisted that Lincoln had to recognize "that you and the great body of the Republican Party have been misrepresented and are pretty and very generally misunderstood in that part of the Union." Corwin vouched strongly for the "purity" of Gilmer's motives. He knew him well and regarded him as one of the "best men in the public service." When Thurlow Weed arrived soon afterward in Springfield to suggest offering Gilmer a cabinet seat, Corwin's words likely resonated. Lincoln was amenable to including one Southern non-Republican in his cabinet, and Gilmer appeared to be the logical choice.[16]

But neither Corwin's letter nor the enclosed message from Gilmer made pleasant reading for Lincoln. Gilmer hoped Lincoln would issue a statement of his conservative intentions. Warning that "apprehensions of real danger to them and their peculiar institution" had "seized the people of my section," Gilmer urged Lincoln to disavow any intention of interfering with slavery where it existed. He also suggested that "a generous and patriotic yielding of your section" would "settle and quiet the disturbing question of slavery in the Territories." Corwin recognized that Gilmer's request might seem "unreasonable." But Corwin assured Lincoln that Gilmer spoke for "the great majority if not the entire body of Conservative men in the South." Corwin also suggested that Lincoln visit Washington, where he could better assess the situation than in Springfield. Many "sincere Union men" from the South had "expressed a great desire that you should come here *soon*," Corwin noted, so that they "might see and converse with you."[17]

Lincoln, however, resisted. He would not make any fresh statement, nor

The Corwin Amendment

would he travel to Washington. His conservative sentiments were already "in print, and open to all who will read." He was willing only to reiterate the obvious in "private and confidential" messages to Southerners he trusted, such as Georgia's Alexander Stephens:

> Do the people of the South really entertain fears that a Republican administration would, directly, or indirectly, interfere with their slaves, or with them, about their slaves? If they do, I wish to assure you, as once a friend, and still, I hope, not an enemy, that there is no cause for such fears. The South would be in no more danger in this respect, than it was in the days of Washington. I suppose, however, this does not meet the case. You think slavery is right and ought to be extended; while we think it is wrong and ought to be restricted. That I suppose is the rub. It certainly is the only substantial difference between us.

Lincoln was not about to back down on the territories. Repeatedly, as we have seen, he cautioned his friends to oppose a territorial compromise "as with a chain of steel." "The tug has to come, and better now, than any time hereafter." He considered it "out of the question" to "shift the ground" upon which he had been elected.[18]

A frustrated Corwin wrote to Lincoln on Christmas Eve. "There is an epidemic of insanity raging all over this country," he mourned, "and I am not sure we can prevent the lunatics from destroying each other." Corwin blamed "wounded pride, personal ambition, party strife and an almost total want of old fashioned patriotism" for having worked "with a fury unknown to any former crisis which has occurred in my life time. I still hope, but am compelled to believe there is great danger, which nothing but firm and prudent measures can avert." As yet the Committee of Thirty Three had failed to reach any agreement. Corwin would not make slavery "the normal condition of all territory *to be conquered*," he indignantly noted, but he would "yield much" regarding "territory we already possess." He hoped to end the controversy by bringing all remaining federal territory into the Union, "making *states* of it all, leaving them as the pact of 1850 declares they may, to come in, with or without slavery as they may ordain."[19]

A few days before, Baltimore congressman Henry Winter Davis had brought forward the key part of just such a plan in hopes of circumventing the explosive territorial snarl. If the New Mexico Territory—today's New Mexico, Arizona, and southern Nevada—were admitted as a state, it would bring into the Union all the remaining land south of the 36° 30′ line owned by the United States. New Mexico nominally would be a slave state, even though its arid climate made it unsuited for plantation slavery. Those clamoring for federal protection of slavery in territory south of 36° 30′—a key part of the much-heralded Crittenden Compromise—would find the rug pulled out from under them.[20]

Henry Winter Davis had worked closely with Corwin in early 1860 when they each helped pull together a coalition of former Whigs and moderate Republicans to organize the House of Representatives. This experience gave Davis a high estimate of the Ohio veteran. Before the presidential election, Davis wrote a long letter to his cousin David Davis, one of Lincoln's key Illinois promoters. Henry Winter Davis suggested that Corwin was the right person to hold the top position in Lincoln's cabinet, secretary of state, because he would give "more confidence and quiet to the country there than any other man."[21] The Maryland representative explained to his cousin that Corwin's "moderate speeches" the previous winter, when bitter North-South polarization threatened to paralyze the House, did much to resolve the impasse. "For the first time since I have been in Congress," Davis wrote, Corwin articulated "the real views and feelings of the people of the free states." Davis also commended Corwin's role in the presidential election campaign. He and John Sherman reassured "the great mass of Fillmore[']s friends and of the old Whigs to join Mr. Lincoln." They thereby undercut "the wild things said and attempted by a few mad men"—and the insidious argument that Lincoln's election might threaten the peace of the Union.

Henry Winter Davis also explained why political arithmetic should incline Lincoln to follow a moderate course. The "Whigs of the country" must be his "chief supporters." Henry Clay and Daniel Webster both showed that slavery would never take hold in the territories without "positive law" to support it, so that "no law is in fact necessary for its exclusion." Were he to follow their lead, Lincoln could isolate the "secessionists and Southern democrats" who demanded legislation to extend or protect slavery in the territories. Large majorities could be assembled to thwart them—"not only all northern Republicans but almost half and probably two thirds from the South of those opposed to the democrats will vote together—besides many democrats from the north and the south." What seemed obvious to Davis failed, however, to take in account the sensibilities of those who had a moral aversion to slavery. As we have seen, hard-liners saw only treachery and failure when they contemplated the legacies of Clay and Webster.

The second prong of the Committee of Thirty Three's key proposals—a constitutional amendment protecting slavery in the states—took shape soon

The Corwin Amendment

after Henry Winter Davis presented his New Mexico statehood plan. The constitutional amendment originated when four Republicans met to devise a response that would telegraph their conciliatory impulses without giving ground on the territorial issue. They pondered the appeal made to them by Thomas A. R. Nelson of East Tennessee, a decided Unionist, who tried to explain why "the South considered Mr. Lincoln's election as a blow aimed at slavery in the States, and for its extermination."[22]

Within a few days, and somewhat to his own surprise, a leader emerged from this group of four Republicans. Charles Francis Adams, like Corwin, had just been elected to the House in 1858. But he too was neither young nor a political newcomer. The son of John Quincy Adams and the grandson of John Adams, he had been a "Conscience Whig" in the 1840s and the Free Soil candidate for vice president in 1848. When Adams subsequently became a Republican, he brought to the new party an illustrious family legacy and a valuable symbolic link.[23]

On December 28, Adams asked the committee to consider a prospective constitutional amendment to forbid interference with slavery in the states where it existed. He would also specify that any future change to this amendment would have to originate in a slave state and be accepted by every state in the Union: "No amendment of this Constitution having for its object any interference within the States with the relation between their citizens and those described in section second of the first article of the Constitution as 'all other persons,' shall originate with any state that does not recognize the relation within its own limits, or shall be valid without the assent of every one of the States composing the Union."[24] Adams plainly intended that this amendment be written in stone, so that it could never be changed. Later, when its sponsors abandoned the House version and substituted in its place the Senate Committee of Thirteen's somewhat less stringent formula, the idea that it would be unamendable persisted, most famously in Lincoln's inaugural address, which deemed the amendment "irrevocable."[25]

At work here was a pre–Civil War mindset that placed the Constitution on a pedestal. Americans sanctified the Constitution as holy writ, immaculate and eternal. So the prospective thirteenth amendment, in the eyes of its designers, would not change the Constitution but would instead spell out in so many words a point widely considered implicit in the Constitution. The cataclysm of Civil War partially eroded this originalist straitjacket and made it possible to see the Constitution as a "pliable text" that might be improved.[26] Modern constitutional authorities also lean toward the view that an "unamendable amendment" is an oxymoron. Under article 5 of the Constitution, they suggest, only two parts of the Constitution are off-limits to amendment: the provision that each state have two members of the Senate, and the provision that allowed slave importations from abroad to continue without interference for twenty years.[27]

The full committee endorsed the Adams amendment by a thumping twenty-one-to-three margin, with support that cut across sectional lines. Eleven of the sixteen Republicans voted for it, with only three opposed and two not present. Henry Adams, the son of Charles Francis Adams, explained in an anonymous newspaper article that his father had enabled Republicans to "set themselves right before the country" and show that they were not "enemies of the South." The proposed amendment would answer those who charged that Republicans were abolitionists in disguise, who would only "respect the Constitution until they should have the power to alter it." Tennessee's Nelson, like other Southerners, held out for a territorial compromise, but he had kind things to say about Adams's proposed constitutional amendment. It "must be regarded as removing the real and greatest apprehension which exists in the Southern mind." Republicans had disavowed any intention of attacking slavery in the states, and that ought to "allay the most alarming cause of distrust."[28]

The committee's actions divided Republicans. Many hard-liners opposed concessions. John A. Bingham complained to Joshua Giddings that the Committee of Thirty Three had been "made for compromise," even though its promoters attempted to shield their intentions. Bingham scorned the proposed "Constitutional Guarantee to slavery forever" and the plan "to admit New Mexico as a Slave State."[29] But Henry Adams affirmed his father's Republican bona fides and denied that there had been any "backing-down." Instead, he contended, Charles Francis Adams had moved adroitly to divide the South. He had reached out to "the strong party of Southern whigs in the border states who appeal to the republicans for a helping hand." They needed something "with which they may go before their constituents and resist secession." Otherwise, "they say that they are delivered up, bound hand and foot, to the democrats, without a hope of resisting the flood that is coming over them." Suddenly taking shape here was an entente cordiale between moderates North and South. As already noted, Seward got most members of the otherwise fractious Senate Committee of Thirteen to vote for a comparable proposal. Adams and Seward both hoped to stall the precipitous drive toward secession.[30]

But circumstances beyond anyone's control in late December and early January brought North and South to the brink of war. South Carolina's seceded on December 20, 1860. Six days later, under cover of darkness, Major Robert Anderson moved his small contingent of federal soldiers from Fort Moultrie, a site facing Charleston harbor that could not be defended if attacked from the mainland, to Fort Sumter, located on an artificial island a mile offshore. South Carolina commissioners arrived posthaste in Washington to demand that Anderson evacuate Sumter. Their ultimatum forced James Buchanan to make the most fateful decisions of his presidency. After reflecting for several days, he rebuffed the South Carolina commissioners and decided to try to hold Sumter. By so doing, he triggered an upheaval in his cabinet—several secession-tainted Southerners departed and were replaced by firm Unionists. In early January the beleaguered president and his new team attempted to reinforce Sumter, but the resupply ship, the *Star of the West*, turned back from the entrance to Charleston harbor at dawn on January 9, 1861, after being fired on. The events of late December and early January stirred belligerent patriotic outrage in the North and spiked efforts to craft a conciliatory response to the secession crisis.[31]

It appeared that the handiwork of the Committee of Thirty Three would go down in flames. A House Republican caucus on January 5 refused to support the committee's work or any other compromise proposal. No longer could a majority of the committee agree to anything, other than to allow Corwin to report to the full House on their deliberations. On Monday, January 14, two days after Seward's speech, he did so.[32]

Corwin began by reflecting on James Buchanan's annual message, issued in early December. There the president identified a culprit for the ills that beset the country. Even though the people of the North had no more right to interfere with slavery in the Southern states than with "similar institutions in Russia or in Brazil," he pontificated, their "incessant and violent agitation of the Slavery question" during the previous quarter century had deprived white Southerners of a "sense of security" in their homes and firesides. Knowing that slaves had acquired "vague notions of freedom" from the antislavery drumbeat, "many a matron throughout the South retires at night in dread of what may befall herself and her children before the morning." The fear of "servile insurrection" thus threatened to bring about disunion.[33]

To remedy the problem that had brought the country to such an impasse, Buchanan recommended that Northerners curb their "long-continued and intemperate" criticisms of slavery and respect the South's constitutional right to take slaves to territories and to reclaim fugitive slaves who had run away to the free states. Northern efforts to bar slavery from the territories or to ignore the Fugitive Slave Act "might have been endured by the South without danger to the Union" during quieter times, but the "immediate peril" required Northern concessions. "All for which the slave States have ever contended," Buchanan announced, "is to be let alone, and permitted to manage their domestic institutions in their own way." The president plainly insisted that people living in the free states had created the crisis and that it was their duty to reverse it.

Corwin considered Buchanan's indictment unconvincing. Hardly anyone in the free states intended to subvert Southern slavery. Any attempt to promote "domestic insurrection," he pointed out, would be "highly criminal" and subject to prosecution. But "the right of free discussion" must be preserved. The federal government ought not silence opinions that some found offensive, and the states needed to strike a fair balance that preserved "freedom of speech and of the press." Corwin also soft-pedaled other alleged grievances identified by the president. The Ohio congressman reasoned that Southern territorial claims had most salience in territories south of 36° 30′, the old Missouri Compromise line, which had become the New Mexico Territory as part of the Compromise of 1850. Its territorial legislature had voted in 1859 to establish slavery. The committee recommended admission of New Mexico into the Union as a slave state, so as to end the territorial controversy between North and South.[34]

Corwin explained that few Northerners opposed "the recovery of fugitives who really owe labor." But Northerners resented a "distasteful and offensive" provision of the Fugitive Slave Act that appeared to require any citizen to assist in the search for alleged fugitives. Northerners also suspected that that the Fugitive Slave Act had operated so as to "permit the seizure of persons who are free, and subject them to servitude contrary to both law and right."[35] Corwin explained that his committee wanted the law revised to remedy Northern complaints. It would exempt bystanders from any requirement that they act as enforcers, and it would recommend "a fair and impartial trial" for any alleged fugitive. To balance these two proposed concessions to Northern sensibilities, the committee urged that Northern state legislatures revisit their so-called personal liberty laws and remove provisions that would impair the rights of slaveholders to recover fugitives.

Corwin sharply demarcated between abolitionists and Republicans, and he accused Buchanan of deliberately blurring this key distinction. Some abolitionists rejected the Constitution. But their overall numbers were "so small, compared with the entire voting population of the free States," that they posed no real danger. Moreover, the "chief leaders and most talented orators" among abolitionists were "most strenuously opposed to the Republican Party in the late Presidential contest, and denounced it and its doctrines in bitter and unsparing terms." In no way did abolitionists represent "the great class of the Republican Party of the North and West."

Corwin did recognize, however, that Buchanan had identified the core fear that drove the secession movement—the belief held by many in the South that the North had "a secret design" to "accumulate political power" and ultimately use it to abolish slavery. Even though "preposterous" and without foundation, Corwin observed, "this prediction has been poured into the ears of excited multitudes from the mouths of popular orators and placed before their eyes in the pages of partisan presses, until in the Southern mind, it seems to have assumed the form of a plausible fact."

But Corwin was determined to "efface these false impressions" regarding the Republican Party and its agenda. The centerpiece of the Committee of Thirty Three's recommendations was the proposed constitutional amendment, designed to counteract Southern fears. The amendment, to bar any interference with slavery in the states where it existed, was the committee's most important rejoinder to Buchanan. Were it enacted, Corwin reasoned, the South could not legitimately demand "further security" for its rights.

Corwin paraded additional evidence that absolved Republicans of harboring hostile designs. When the national party "met in convention at Chicago" in May 1860, it adopted a platform that promised to uphold "the right of each State to order and control its domestic institutions according to its own judgment exclusively." These unmistakable code words showed that Republicans would not touch the slave system in the South. Finally, to show that their party stood as far apart from John Brown as it could, Republicans "denounce[d] the lawless invasion by armed force of the soil of any State or Territory, no matter under what pretext, as among the gravest of crimes."

Corwin did not, however, have the stage to himself. Two rock-ribbed Republicans, Cadwallader C. Washburn of Wisconsin and Mason W. Tappan of New Hampshire, drafted a minority report that rejected his suggestions. Because "the present discontent and hostility in the South" was "wholly without just cause," they specified that the Constitution needed to be "obeyed rather than amended." The solution to the troubles facing the country, Washburn and Tappan advised, lay in "efforts to preserve and protect the public property and enforce the laws, rather than in new guarantees for particular interests, or compromises, or concessions to unreasonable demands."[36]

The two hard-liners turned thumbs down on Corwin's proposed constitutional amendment. They opposed tampering with the Constitution because "no party in the Union proposes to interfere in any way with slavery in the

Origins of the Other Thirteenth Amendment

States, and the present dominant party expressly disclaims any such right or intention." Republicans would "faithfully abide" by this promise but would not offer "any greater guarantees of good faith than the present Constitution gives." Corwin's efforts to extract more would instead boomerang. The people of the North would reject the amendment—not because they "desire or intend to interfere with slavery, but because they will regard it as a humiliating requirement, proposing, as it does, that they shall enter into bonds for their good behavior, when they have neither committed nor meditated wrong." Were Congress to submit such an amendment, it would be a virtual acknowledgment "that there is danger of such interference." And when Northerners voted it down, the South would regard it as "a declaration of intention to interfere." The amendment would therefore "greatly add to the present hostile feeling."

Washburn and Tappan also opposed the amendment's "constitutional decree of perpetual bondage." They refused to tie the hands of future generations, the "millions yet unborn," and hold them hostage to the whims of a single state. The two Republicans mused presciently about an unknowable future in which "the vast majority North and South" might change their opinions. Neither they nor anyone else knew how imminently this change would come. Amid the mighty convulsion of a civil war that sent hundreds of thousands, both North and South, to their deaths, Northern majorities resolved to end the captivity of millions already born.

Several other minority reports were also filed. The most curious was written by a disgruntled Charles Francis Adams. He had played a key role in assembling the package of proposals advanced by Corwin. But Adams decided at the last minute that he no longer could countenance his handiwork. The sticking point for Adams had come a week before, on January 11, when the Committee of Thirty Three considered a resolution specifying that the "peaceful acquiescence in the election of a Chief Magistrate, accomplished in accordance with every legal and constitutional requirement, is a high and imperative duty of every citizen of the United States." Although some representatives from the slave states "cordially came forward" and supported this proposition, a larger number held back, on grounds that it would "do more harm than good." They decided "with their eyes open," Adams complained, that they would "violate and annul" the Constitution's "most fundamental" provisions. He gloomily concluded that the South would accept nothing less than constitutional recognition "of the obligation to protect and extend slavery," terms to which he would "never give his consent."[37]

Two days after making the case for the amendment and its related concil-

The Corwin Amendment

iatory package, Corwin conceded to Lincoln that the outlook was discouraging. He reflected on the difficulties he had encountered in trying to get the Committee of Thirty Three to reach agreement:

> If the states are no more harmonious in their feelings and opinions
> than these 33 representative men then, appal[l]ing as the idea is,
> we must dissolve and a long & bloody civil war *must* follow. I cannot
> comprehend the madness of the time. Southern men are theoretically
> crazy. Extreme Northern men are practical fools. The latter are re-
> ally quite as mad as the former. Treason is in the air around us *every*
> where. It goes by the name of Patriotism. Men in Congress boldly
> avow it, and the public offices are full of acknowledged secessionists.
> God alone I fear can help us. Four or five states are gone, others are
> driving before the gale. I have looked on this horrid picture till I have
> been able to gaze on it with perfect calmness.[38]

The next day Corwin sent a similarly frustrated letter to an old Virginia friend, Alexander H. H. Stuart, a colleague from the Fillmore cabinet. Corwin complained that Southerners were "acting on a stupendous mistake as to facts." They believed that "Northern people *hate* slavery, that they *hate them*, [and] want to deprive them of their property. All and each of these have no foundation in truth." He exaggerated. Some Northerners did hate slavery, though larger numbers were indifferent. But Corwin's lament was otherwise accurate. Few Northerners hated white Southerners, and hardly any proposed to take their slaves away.[39]

Stuart, the recipient of Corwin's letter, was exactly the sort of Southerner who was predisposed to bridge the North-South abyss. He lived in the Shenandoah Valley, a border South region where the hysteria that had swept the Deep South made little impact. Stuart's hometown of Staunton was the seat of Augusta County, long the banner Whig county in the state. He and his fellow Whigs saw no contradiction in their allegiances to state, region, and nation. They hoped that sensible leaders North and South would find ways to make common cause. They loved the Union and they dreaded war.[40]

Stuart had been doing his best to deflect the storm. A state senator, he had been amazed by the level of "madness" and "insanity" in Richmond in early January, as secessionists clamored to follow the Deep South's lead. He feared they might stampede the legislature. So Stuart worked to assemble a coalition of former Whigs and Douglas Democrats "to stay the storm." They agreed to an election for a state convention, but they attached conditions to guard against its hasty action and to assure proportionate representation for

Virginia's mountainous west, where secession was unpopular. Stuart and his allies wanted to avoid what had happened in the Deep South, where conventions had unilaterally removed states from the Union.[41]

By the winter of 1860–61, almost all former Whigs from the North had become Republicans, while those from the Upper South gravitated toward a grouping that called itself the Southern Opposition Party. Corwin and Stuart understood that they must enlist like-minded leaders from the free states and from the Upper South if the Deep South's startling course was to be contained and reversed. The impulse to reach out across sectional lines came naturally to former Whigs who had enjoyed ties of mutual respect and friendship before the partisan upheavals of the 1850s. Faced with imminent calamity, these former political allies, now estranged, realized they needed each other.[42]

PART III

Debating the Other
Thirteenth Amendment

Reaching across the Abyss

John Sherman was a rising Republican star. A prominent member of the U.S. House of Representatives before the age of forty, he was on the cusp of a long Senate career. He headed the powerful House Ways and Means Committee and had been the Republican candidate for Speaker just the year before.[1] Everyone knew Sherman was competent, but many found him cold—and that would ultimately thwart his presidential hopes. As his derisive nickname suggested, the "Ohio Icicle" would have failed the modern "beer test." But all this lay in the future. The big story in November 1860 was someone else's election to the presidency.

Sherman, who considered himself a "moderate conservative," hoped that the South would come to its senses after Abraham Lincoln's election. "You were long enough in Ohio and heard enough of the ideas of the Republican leaders," he pointed out to his soon-to-be-famous brother, William Tecumseh Sherman. "[You] know very well that we do not propose to interfere in the slightest degree with slavery in the States." [2]

These disavowals, contained in private correspondence, have the ring of authenticity. Whites in the Deep South refused, however, to believe them. It became an article of faith there that Republicans were abolitionists in disguise. By preventing the expansion of slavery, they would begin its slow strangulation—and they might even covertly support John Brown-type raids along the border. So South Carolina and the six other Deep South states decided to break up the Union rather than accept the results of the presidential election. By early January 1861, a grave crisis threatened to erupt into civil war.[3]

But the peace still held, and John Sherman wanted to keep it that way. So he must have squirmed as he read the belligerent pronouncements that filled his morning mail. Many of his home state correspondents implored the cautious Sherman to share their passion. They pronounced themselves *"stiff as iron"* and furious at traitors. "Stand square to the line and if war and blood must come let the blood guilt . . . rest upon those who brought the

John Sherman. "We do not propose to interfere in the slightest degree with slavery in the States." Sherman to William Tecumseh Sherman, Dec. 22, 1860, William T. Sherman Papers, Library of Congress. Library of Congress, Prints and Photographs Division, Brady-Handy Photograph Collection, LC-BH83- 2304.

country to this pass," one advised him. Northern men in the South had been whipped, tarred, feathered, and hanged, another enraged Buckeye blurted out. Had any foreign country done this to the United States, the result would be "war war war." Republicans must "stand by our colors," insisted a resident of Milan, Ohio; the only sure cure for King Cotton was "powder and lead." Repeatedly they beseeched Sherman to "stand firm" and show "back bone."[4]

Sherman also received many heavy-handed reminders of the political stakes involved. He was warned that no public man who "betrays the cause of Freedom and Humanity in the hour of need" had any political future. Any concessions would be "treason both to party and country." Just as compromise killed Henry Clay, Daniel Webster, and "the Old Whig Party," it could also kill the Republican Party and throw "thousands of voters in the North back into an abolition organization." The "present generation of politicians at Washington" would find that its "political graves are dug" if it were to "yield to the Lords of the Plantation now." New "Anti-Slavery parties" would separate from the "fossil Whigs" in each of the free states and thereby enable "the Democratic Party (so called)" to be "restored to power."[5]

Debating the Other Thirteenth Amendment

Sherman was conflicted. Unlike his constituents with itchy trigger fingers, he feared that war would make a bad situation far worse. He and a group of Republican moderates maintained "frequent and close communication" with fellow congressmen from the Upper South. What he and like-minded Republicans learned from them could not easily be reconciled with grass-roots sentiment in Ohio. Throughout the border slave states, including North Carolina and Tennessee, "a large class of true sincere Union men" deplored as much as any Northerner "the madness and wickedness of the disunionists." They appealed to Republicans "to give them aid and comfort and to strengthen their hands." Together they might yet "stay the flood of disunion which threatens to sweep over everything in resistless fury." The Upper South's Unionists persuaded Sherman that any use of force would be counterproductive. Instead he and they worked together to devise a plan that might alleviate the crisis peacefully.[6]

So Sherman was caught in the middle, and his speech to the House on Friday, January 18, 1861, reflected as much. In attempting to reconcile divergent perspectives, he insisted that the federal government occupied the moral high ground. It had done nothing whatever to endanger or coerce South Carolina. But the seceding states had repeatedly used extralegal force to seize federal installations and property: "The question is not whether the United States will coerce a State, but whether a State shall coerce the Government." South Carolina and the other seceding states also were coercing "the border slave States." The Deep South's "wild fanaticism" pressured the Upper South to take steps that would be unthinkable "in the light of calm and cool reason." Sherman appealed to the Upper South's representatives to resist the storm. "We must not allow the Government to crumble at our feet," he warned. The North would fight rather than accept disunion. But he eagerly preferred peace and conciliation to force and war, and he wanted antisecessionists in the Upper South to take the lead. "You can arrest this movement, and you alone can do it," he insisted. Do not allow your people, "under the smart of imaginary wrongs," to be "hurried into acts of madness."[7]

What would Sherman offer the Upper South? His speech centered on the two key proposals just discussed by the Committee of Thirty Three. First, in order to dispose of the divisive territorial issue, he would admit the New Mexico Territory into the Union as a state. Even though its population was "sparse" and its settlements were "remote from each other," it was the one remaining territory south of 36° 30′, the old Missouri Compromise line. It was "nominally" open to slavery though hardly any slaves lived there. After allowing the New Mexico Territory to become a state, he would "forego to the end of time the acquisition of a single foot of territory."[8]

Sherman also spoke out on behalf of the constitutional amendment, designed to reassure Southerners that federal power never could be used to attack slavery in the South. At first he was surprised to find the subject being discussed. He assumed it was "an axiom of American politics" that the federal government had no power to abolish slavery where it existed. But he had come to realize that many in the South actually believed "the oft-repeated assertion" that Republicans intended "to interfere with slavery in the States." He wanted "to convince the South that what has been so often stated . . . was not truly stated."[9]

A private and poignant exchange of letters with a former colleague reminded Sherman how grave the breach in North-South perceptions had become. Nathaniel Greene Foster, an "old line Whig" from Madison, Georgia, had run on the American Party ticket and served with Sherman in Congress from 1855 to 1857. They "sat side by side for a whole session," had "the highest regard for each other," and looked forward to the overthrow of the Democratic Party. Four years later, however, Foster was convinced Southern slaveholders would "gradually, but surely" be deprived of their property. He recognized that Republicans promised they would "not attack the institution in the states *directly*," but he accused them of planning "to arrive at the same result by *indirect* action." The people of Georgia would not "tamely submit to it" and would fight instead. "If we are to be destroyed we prefer not to go by inches."[10]

Sherman attempted to reassure Foster that he misunderstood the Republican Party, but the Georgian insisted that abolitionism was "stronger than you have been willing to let yourself believe" and that Sherman and other moderates would not be able to "hold the feeling of fanaticism in check." Foster was convinced that Republicans "had found it convenient . . . during the canvass" to suggest their admiration for John Brown. Carried by "the popular tide," they were ready to "wink" at impulses that ultimately would "set the slaves upon our women and children."[11]

Sherman thought Foster failed to make the essential distinction between attitudes and actions. The "people in the North" had a "fixed and immutable" belief that slavery was "a social, moral, and political evil," Sherman recognized, and this belief was "shared by the great body of the civilized world." But he and all other Republicans considered the South deluded for magnifying this "difference of opinion" into a deadly menace. Do not "flee from an apprehension," he implored Southerners. "Give the Republican Administration a fair chance." It would do nothing "to impair any constitutional right." [12]

Sherman stood with a cluster of congressmen from the North and Upper South—all of them former Whigs—who worked during January and February to counteract the secession movement. They knew they needed one another. But they also had to heed popular opinion in their home states. This chapter will introduce several of the major players and take account of the obstacles they faced. As we shall see, it was not easy to defend the middle ground at a time of fierce North-South polarization.

Sherman's speech set the stage for his eminent Ohio colleague Thomas Corwin, the central figure in the last chapter. On Monday, January 21, a week after he had reported for the Committee of Thirty Three, Corwin made his own case. He recalled that he had been a member of the House thirty years before, when South Carolina tried to exempt itself from acts of Congress that it considered unconstitutional. But South Carolina's attempted nullification of federal law "met with little sympathy" in other Southern states, and so that "unhappy difficulty" had been resolved. [13] Three decades later the situation was more ominous. As he spoke, the states of the Lower South were rapidly falling into line behind South Carolina, and soon they would attempt to organize a separate government, the Confederate States of America. This was a far more dangerous and immediate crisis than the one in 1832–33 or the one that elicited his 1847 oration.

Corwin implored white Southerners to reconsider. Point by point, he challenged the idea that any infringement of their rights had yet occurred— or that it might occur in the future if their states remained in the Union. The heart of the difficulty, he asserted, was the unfounded belief, repeated endlessly across the South, that the Republican Party menaced the slave system: "This is not inferred from anything which that party has avowed— not from any specific principles which it had adopted—but simply because you believe that, ultimately, the great Abolition party, which you always magnify in your imaginations fifty or one hundred times beyond its proper proportions, will obtain control of the Republican Party." Even though the Constitution gave Congress, the president, and the courts no more power over slavery in the states where it exists "than it gives them power to regulate the policy of the British empire in India," the idea had taken hold among the "masses of the South" that Republicans were determined "to interfere with slavery in the States." [14]

So what might yet be done? Corwin would not accept "the final destruction and overthrow of the best Government known among men." He set out, instead, to defend "the great experiment on this continent, which was intended to demonstrate that man was capable of self-government." He wanted to "remove unfounded prejudices," "explain unhappy misunderstandings," and overcome "apprehension of danger." As we have seen, the centerpiece of his eleventh-hour exercise in Union-saving was the constitutional amendment that Charles Francis Adams had introduced in the Committee of Thirty Three.

Corwin was "highly esteemed and much liked by all." But his speech on January 21 did not lend itself to his stock in trade—the "profusion of humorous sallies which so often make him the most entertaining of all speakers" and his ability to make listeners "roar with laughter or shout with enthusiasm." Instead, he rarely broke a smile. His "swarthy face" was "unillumined by a single spark of his accustomed humor, its expression grave and solicitous." Speaking with "nervous intensity," he implored his colleagues "to accept what he thought necessary for the salvation of his country." His words were received with "eager interest and respect." Many of his colleagues "deserted their seats" and gathered their chairs at the front of the chamber so that Corwin addressed them directly—they "listened to the old man as if spellbound, with tender veneration."[15]

Although the Deep South appeared deaf to their appeals, Sherman and Corwin counted on finding a more receptive audience in the Upper South. Two-thirds of white Southerners lived in the five slave states that bordered the free states, plus North Carolina, Tennessee, and Arkansas. If these eight states could be kept out of the secession vortex, the disunion movement might wither. Five days after Sherman's speech and two days after Corwin's, it became apparent that they had been heard.

The featureless, flat plains of West Tennessee seemed an unlikely locale to harbor a "Southern Black Republican." But his political opponents routinely hung this epithet—and worse—on Emerson Etheridge. Unlike many other Southern antisecessionists, the Tennessee congressman proclaimed unconditional loyalty to the Union. He ridiculed the disunion movement's central idea—that the Republican Party intended to interfere with slavery. Secessionists and Southern Rights supporters sputtered in frustration. Etheridge, they charged, had fallen into "the depths of disgrace and infamy." He appealed only to the "ignorant and blind lick-spittles" rather than to "the slaveholding and enlightened portion of the people."[16]

His critics concealed evidence that Etheridge had an attractive personality. A widower with two young daughters, he was just over forty. He stood

Emerson Etheridge. "I am speaking on a side that has few representatives on this floor. I am speaking on *the side of my country!*" *Congressional Globe*, 36:2 (23 Jan. 1861), A115, and as reported by "Sigma" (Ben Perley Poore), Jan. 23, 1861, in *Cincinnati Commercial*, Jan. 26, 1861. Library of Congress, Prints and Photographs Division, Brady-Handy Photograph Collection, LC-BH82- 4585 C.

tall with a face that projected "solid and manly qualities"—large hazel eyes, a "well developed broad forehead," straight brown hair that curled over his ears, and a dense beard. A "fine mellow voice" made him a compelling speaker. His young colleague Robert Hatton, newly elected to represent an adjacent district, quickly developed a fast friendship with Etheridge. "If he was a woman," Hatton gushed to his wife, Sophia Hatton, "you would be certain we were dead in love with each other. . . . We eat together, walk to and from the Capitol together, sit in the House together, room by each other, [and] are alike in politics, in religion, and our feelings and sympathies." Both stubbornly shunned alcohol and the other vices of Washington life.[17]

In 1860–61 close to two dozen members of the U.S. House of Representatives, including Etheridge and Hatton, were members of a political party that called itself the Southern Opposition. All were former Whigs, almost all from the Upper South. Tennessee had seven Opposition representatives, more than any other state. The Opposition bloc held the balance of power in the House, which was closely divided between Republicans and Democrats. Of most importance here, Opposition men opposed secession without exception. Their presence in Washington challenges simplistic stereotypes that depict the entire white South as eager to break up the Union.[18]

When Etheridge stood to address the House of Representatives on Wednesday, January 23, 1861, he charged that secessionists had fabricated a mass delusion: "Thousands believe honestly that Lincoln and his cohorts are coming down to apply the torch and the knife to the dwellings and people of the South." Etheridge condemned such baseless hysteria. Republicans posed no danger to the South, he insisted. They had renounced "any desire or any power to interfere with slavery in the States of this Union." He also scorned the idea that the South needed to expand slavery to the territories or that the North had defaulted on its obligation to return fugitive slaves. The evils that secessionists pretended to fear were flimsy or imaginary.[19]

At this juncture, "a thin, piping voice" demanded in a shrill tone—"I merely wish to know whether the gentleman is speaking on the side of the North or the South?" The interruption came from Shelton Leake, a Virginia disunionist. Etheridge immediately shot back: "I am speaking on a side that has few representatives on this floor. I am speaking on *the side of my country*!" A reporter for the *Cincinnati Commercial* described the retort as a "clincher"—"The noble, exalted tone and emphasis in which this was uttered, rang through the hall." It triggered "a shout of applause" from the audience in the galleries. Soon a groundswell developed in the free states to find a position in Lincoln's cabinet for Etheridge. His "unswerving patriotism" and his "sterling, practical qualities" stood out: "no better Southern man could be found."[20]

Etheridge opened the floodgates to a torrent of Southern Unionist oratory in late January and early February 1861. Few of his allies in Congress were quite so ready as he to give the Republican Party a clean bill of health, but they fully agreed that secession was a virulent epidemic that would sicken or kill its host. It threatened to ignite a civil war that would destroy slavery. Rammed through with hot haste, it confronted the Upper South with an outrageous fait accompli. Just as delegates from the Deep South were meeting in Montgomery, Alabama, to organize a separate Southern government, Southern antisecessionists in Washington were doing everything they could to thwart the Confederate cause.

John A. Gilmer of North Carolina pleaded with Republicans to stand with him against "this raging storm in the Southern States" and to reassure nervous white Southerners "of your purpose to deal justly and fairly with them." He reasoned that secessionists demanded "protection" for slavery in the territories, not because it was "really valuable to the South" or injurious

John A. Gilmer. "The Southern people do, whether justly or not, honestly believe that the Republican party . . . intend[s] to interfere with slavery where it exists in the States." *Congressional Globe*, 36:2 (Jan. 26, 1861), 581–82. Courtesy of the State Archives of North Carolina.

to the North, but rather in the hope that Republicans "will refuse it, and by your refusal, they hope the South will be inflamed to the extent of breaking up this Government." The most stringent territorial protection would be no more likely to create additional slave states, he insisted, than "the drying up of the Mississippi could be secured by act of Congress."[21]

Gilmer's views were notable for several reasons. Once a farm boy who grew up wearing homespun, he had become an accomplished lawyer and an increasingly formidable politician. His "full round face" and "laughing dark eyes" conveyed "an atmosphere of hope, confidence, and cheerfulness." He was selected in 1859 by the two dozen Southern Opposition representatives in the House to lead their party. After a bitter two-month deadlock, a bloc of moderate Republicans reached out to the Southern Opposition and thereby organized the House. This arrangement, which enabled Gilmer to chair an important committee, caused anguish and heartburn for Southern Democrats and Southern Rights absolutists. They feared that the Opposition would become more formidable if North-South tensions ebbed—and that a more permanent arrangement between the Opposition and the hated "Black Republicans" might evolve. And they suspected the worst of Gilmer.

Secessionist suspicions about Gilmer intensified in January 1861. As we have seen in chapter 5, William H. Seward and Thurlow Weed quietly persuaded Abraham Lincoln to offer Gilmer a cabinet seat. Lincoln had reservations about selecting any non-Republican, but he respected Gilmer, knew that he was an intense Unionist, and knew too that he had been a longtime

Whig. Having been elected president entirely with Northern votes, Lincoln recognized that including Gilmer in the cabinet might damp down Southern anxieties about Republican intentions and show that the new administration would be national, not sectional. For two months, the North Carolinian weighed Lincoln's offer. He hoped Republicans would offer the South a symbolic concession regarding slavery in the territories, and he eagerly sought reassurances that Lincoln would not use force against the seceding states. As rumors about the pending appointment leaked out, secessionists charged that Gilmer had made himself a "Black Republican" pawn and a traitor to his home region.[22]

When speaking to the House on Saturday, January 26, Gilmer embraced the constitutional amendment. Nobody stated so forcefully as he that the real issue at hand was "the question of slavery in the States." Everything else was "small and unimportant." In response to those Republicans who said they had no intention of touching slavery in the states and that no amendment was needed, he pointed out that leading Southerners incessantly charged otherwise, so that the Southern people, "whether justly or not," had become suspicious. The amendment would contradict these alarms "in the most positive and indubitable manner for all time to come." But he also contended that a territorial compromise was needed. The territories were an empty symbol that had been "magnified and misrepresented" by "ultra partisans" on both sides of the sectional divide. "Sensible gentlemen" North and South should "get together and settle it." He insisted that slavery had no future in the territories, so that Republicans "would lose nothing for your section or your party" by allowing it. Republicans should "consider well" the Crittenden Compromise, he suggested. Its promise to protect slavery in territories south of 36° 30′ could be disconnected "from territory hereafter to be acquired." But Gilmer was ready to accept other possibilities—an assurance that Congress would not legislate against slavery south of 36° 30′, or New Mexico statehood, as recommended by the Committee of Thirty Three, which showed "a feeling on the part of northern gentlemen" that he "had not expected." If the South could attempt to "make a slave State" out of the New Mexico Territory, it would have no cause for complaint.[23]

Gilmer's "honest appeal of a great heart" seemed to many of his listeners the "most effective" speech of the session. He pleaded with Republicans to avert the "butchery and destruction" of warfare by aiding "the Union men of the border states." When he finished, "dozens of Republicans and Southern Union men rushed forward to congratulate him," and "there was scarcely an eye in the house not filled with tears." Conciliatory Republicans told

Charles Francis Adams. "When the cry goes out that the ship is in danger of sinking, the first duty of every man on board . . . is to lend all the strength he has to the work of keeping her afloat." *Congressional Globe*, 36:2 (Jan. 31, 1861), A127. U.S. National Park Service, Adams National Historical Park.

newspaper reporters that "some compromise must be made to keep John A. Gilmer from being carried down by the secession tide."[24]

The appeals from Southern Unionists may have influenced Charles Francis Adams. Outraged by rule-or-ruin secessionist behavior, Adams was unwilling for a time to continue supporting the Committee of Thirty Three package that he originally had sponsored. But he reconsidered and started writing a speech. His son Henry Adams assisted him and predicted that it would challenge the "Hotspurs of the North." As he prepared, Charles Francis Adams "slept badly" for several nights, stressed by "anxiety and excitement." He obtained the floor on the last day of the month, Thursday, January 31—four years to the day before the House voted on a very different Thirteenth Amendment, as featured in Steven Spielberg's film *Lincoln*.[25]

Adams recognized that his stance might offend "many whose good opinion has ever been part of the sunlight of my existence." But he gave highest priority to the nation and its preservation. "When the cry goes out that the ship is in danger of sinking," he warned, "the first duty of every man on board . . . is to lend all the strength he has to the work of keeping her afloat."

Reaching across the Abyss

At stake was the fate of "the most magnificent example of self-government known to history."[26]

The South had been swept by "panic, pure panic," Adams observed. Many white Southerners, however, still hesitated to adopt "the irrevocable policy of disunion," and he was determined to reach out to them. Rather than "absolutely closing the door to reconciliation," as many of his fellow Republicans were inclined to do, he thought it wiser to heed the examples of Edmund Burke and William Pitt (Lord Chatham), who urged Britain to conciliate her disaffected American colonies in 1775. Had George III listened to Chatham's "words of wisdom," Adams observed, "he might have saved the brightest jewel of his crown." Instead he took the opposite course. "He rejected the olive branch. He insisted upon coercion. And what was the result? History records its verdict in favor of Chatham and against the king."[27]

When Adams reflected on history, people had to listen. He was, after all, more than just a representative from Massachusetts and the future ambassador to Britain. The son of John Quincy Adams and the grandson of John Adams, he brought to Washington a sense of perspective and gravitas often lacking in the rough-and-tumble world of national politics. Like his father and grandfather, Adams saw government as an essential constraint on the inherently turbulent and fractious nature of human societies. He therefore revered the Constitution. This solemn compact bound the nation together by guaranteeing the Southern states that slavery was secure within their borders while at the same time allowing the free states to distance themselves from it. And nothing was more important to him than preserving the Union. It was well known that Adams personally found slavery repugnant—he had been a leading "Conscience Whig" and the Free Soil Party's nominee for vice president in 1848. But he gave first priority to the Union.[28]

Adams's rock-solid antislavery credentials might have placed him alongside hard-line Republicans like his friend Massachusetts senator Charles Sumner, who opposed "any offer now, even of a peppercorn." But Adams saw the situation differently. He was especially concerned to counteract the idea that "any considerable number of men in the free States" wanted to interfere with slavery in the states where it existed. This was "an event which will never take place." He disagreed, however, with his many Republican colleagues who thought the "uneasiness" and "madness" of the South should be "neglected or ridiculed." When fears pervade "the bosoms of multitudes of men," he reasoned, an "imaginary evil grows up at once into a gigantic reality, and must be treated as such."[29]

To reassure white Southerners who worried that Republicans might at some point in the future have both the strength and the inclination to "initiate a plan of emancipation," Adams proposed enacting the constitutional amendment to safeguard slavery in the states. It would take away "no rights which the free States ever should attempt to use." Like all other Republicans, he hoped that white Southerners themselves would come to see that slavery retarded progress and economic development. At some point in the future, he predicted, they might take the "welcome" step of moving voluntarily toward emancipation.

Adams also boosted the other main part of the Committee of Thirty Three's proposal, the admission of the New Mexico Territory as a state. But he condemned Southern demands to protect slavery in territory "hereafter acquired." That condition, he reasoned, was deliberately contrived so that Republicans must reject it or dishonor themselves. To accept it would "disgrace," "degrade," and "humiliate us in the dust forever"—and "rather than this, let the heavens fall." As he spoke, his attentive audience was so silent "that you could have heard a pin drop."[30]

His family name and personal stature did not save Adams from harsh criticism—Sumner indeed thought his friend had "ruined himself." And while hard-line Republicans accused Adams of appeasing disunionists, Southern Rights supporters attacked him for rejecting the Crittenden Compromise. Those caught in the middle, however, commended Adams for having bravely tried to reach across the sectional divide and overwhelmed him with "a rush of congratulations" as he finished speaking. Tennessee congressman Thomas A. R. Nelson gave him "the very highest degree of credit" for making a peace offering "which may peril his popularity at home." George Prentice, editor of the *Louisville Journal*, likewise heralded Adams's "finished and masterly" speech—the "most significant" conciliatory overture any Republican had yet made.[31]

Adams spoke at a critical juncture in the secession winter. During the next week, two key Upper South states, Virginia and Tennessee, held votes regarding a state convention. Observers nervously awaited the Virginia vote, scheduled for Monday, February 4. Most of the state's large delegation in Congress, led by U.S. senators Robert M. T. Hunter and James Murray Mason, stated that the Union was irrevocably disrupted and endorsed Southern Rights candidates for the convention. But a groundswell of public opinion rejected secession. Voters east of the Blue Ridge, the most enslaved region in the Upper South, split almost evenly between Union and secession. West of the Blue Ridge, however, where whites far outnumbered slaves, secession was overwhelmed by a thunderous five-to-one margin. "Lord, how dumfounded are the secessionists here," crowed a Lexington Unionist. "A few days ago they were high up stairs and clamoring from the house tops. But 'such a getting down stairs, I never did see.'" Antisecession sentiment was most intense in Virginia's trans-Allegheny northwest, where fewer than 6,500 slaves were dwarfed by a white population that exceeded 250,000. "Would you," asked one northwesterner, "have us . . . act like madmen and cut our own throats merely to sustain you in a most unwarrantable rebellion?" Pro-Union delegates at the state convention would heavily outnumber prosecession ones.[32]

The returns from Virginia triggered a jubilant response in the free states. Northerners breathed a sigh of relief and jumped to the conclusion that the disunion movement had suffered a fatal reverse. Misled into thinking that the troubles facing the country would soon be over, an observer in Boston reported that the news from Virginia "sent a regular thrill through the city. The result was announced on Jamaica Pond when we were skating and the huge mass of people flocked together and cheered with one mind." Pennsylvania congressman Thaddeus Stevens, the South's most sharp-tongued critic, unleashed a stinging quip: "Well, well, well, old Virginia has tucked her tail between her legs and run, and thus ends the secession farce."[33]

Opponents of secession in the Upper South, elated by such robust evidence of popular support, displayed a new assertiveness after the Virginia vote. On Thursday, February 7, a key architect of the Committee of Thirty Three's package, Henry Winter Davis, spoke out. Wealthy, eloquent, and charismatic, the Opposition congressman from Baltimore occupied a unique position. As the one Southern representative who voted with Republicans to make William Pennington the Speaker of the House in early 1860, he was routinely lambasted by Southern Democrats as a "Black Republican." And indeed, once the war started he did gravitate to the Republican Party. But in early 1861, he was well positioned to search out common ground that Republicans and Southern Unionists might agree upon.[34]

Davis's bold speech attracted a huge throng, notwithstanding the worst storm of the winter. The "handsomest man in the House" packed the galleries, and the House floor was crowded with privileged onlookers, including senators and members of the just-gathered Peace Conference. As he stood to speak with his arms folded, Davis conveyed an "aristocratic" presence. His "studied attitude" bespoke self-confidence. His listeners were rewarded with a polished performance, quite unlike "the rude and ungraceful stump-oratory of most of our politicians." Although Southern Democrats tried at points to interrupt, Davis "carried the House and galleries along with him"

Debating the Other Thirteenth Amendment

Henry Winter Davis. "When the history of our great secession comes to be written, a century or two hence, the historian ought to make a parenthesis to describe Mr. Winter Davis." Henry Adams, "Letter from Washington," Feb. 7, 1861, in *Boston Advertiser*, Feb. 11, 1861, in Mark J. Stegmaier, *Henry Adams in the Secession Crisis: Dispatches to the* Boston Daily Advertiser, *December 1860–March 1861* (Baton Rouge: Louisiana State University Press, 2012), 198. Library of Congress, Prints and Photographs Division, Brady-Handy Photograph Collection, LC-DIG-cwpbh-01037.

and was rewarded with outbursts of "tumultuous applause." One reporter described its effects as "electrical." "When the history of our great secession comes to be written, a century or two hence," Henry Adams observed, the historian of the future would need to pay attention to "Mr. Winter Davis."[35]

Davis lamented that "perpetual and reiterated misrepresentation and exaggeration" had persuaded a great many ordinary Southerners that "the great body of the northern people" intended to do them harm and "destroy slavery." Southern electioneering techniques, he judged, were principally responsible for the situation. All too often, candidates for office in the South insinuated that their opponents had consorted with abolitionists. They deliberately ignored the obvious distinction between the Republican Party as a whole and the "small faction" of Northerners who rejected the constitutional restraints that all Republicans accepted. Davis explained that the constitutional amendment had been designed to counter such widespread misinformation, and he challenged his fellow Southerners to retrace their steps and work to "remove the impression that they have erroneously left upon their

Reaching across the Abyss

people's minds." If they did so, "there would be peace and quiet throughout the whole South within a month after they made the explanation."

Davis had little hope, however, of such a "natural, prompt, and honest remedy." The "course of debate in this House" persuaded him that "a revolutionary faction" had disguised itself "by being mingled in the ranks of a great political party." The "revolutionists" had been able to pursue their "treasonable purposes" because other Democrats had been afraid to call them out. But the constitutional amendment might yet erode the gross misimpression that "the northern people do contemplate disturbing slavery in the States." If that idea could be punctured, the revolutionists would lose most of their followers. Calling attention to the election that had just taken place in Virginia three days before, Davis boldly predicted that the package created by the Committee of Thirty Three—the constitutional amendment, along with the admission of New Mexico to the Union as a state—would kill the secession movement in the Upper South and "strip the enemies of the United States of all power for mischief."

Unlike most other Southern Unionists, Davis condemned the Crittenden Compromise. The same people who in 1854 insisted on repeal of the Missouri Compromise had done a somersault and announced that "this Union cannot endure" unless the Missouri line of 36° 30′ were reestablished and "all the region south, to Cape Horn" opened to slavery. "A more flagrant, inexplicable, unintelligible case of capricious inconsistency is unknown to history," Davis sarcastically observed. It would be "absolutely impossible," he predicted, to get majorities in either the House or the Senate to impose slavery "in any inch of territory where it does not already exist." The clamor for Crittenden's plan—which no Republican would touch—played directly into the hands of those who would destroy the Union.[36]

The day after Davis spoke, he was followed by Robert Hatton, who represented a Middle Tennessee district east of Nashville. Although only a freshman, the thirty-four-year-old impressed many observers as one of the Southern Opposition's rising stars. Slender and "rather tall," he had a high forehead and blue eyes set wide apart. His face appeared all the more long and angular because his head was topped by "a great quantity of thick brown hair" and he wore a sprawling chin beard. As we have seen, Hatton was close friends with his Tennessee colleague Etheridge.[37]

Hatton vehemently condemned the "disunionists of the cotton States," whose "reckless selfishness" and "utter disregard" of the border states made them "*practically* our enemies, as truly as are the most unprincipled fanatics in the North." The "chivalry of the cotton States" had launched a "disastrous

Robert Hatton. "The chivalry of the cotton States have kindly stepped forward . . . [to] counsel that we put in jeopardy our every material interest, and then—commit suicide!" *Congressional Globe*, 36:2 (Feb. 8, 1861), A172–73. Photograph by Mathew Brady, National Archives and Records Administration, 528692.

revolution" that placed the Upper South in grave danger. In appreciation, residents of the border states were to "put in jeopardy our every material interest, and then—commit suicide!" How, he bitterly inquired, shall "we of the border States ever be able to repay our Southern brethren for this unselfish and considerate advice?"[38]

Hatton eagerly commended the constitutional amendment. Too many leading Southerners had alleged that "the ultimate purpose of the Republican Party is, to destroy the institution of slavery in the States," and "a large portion of the Southern people" believed them. The constitutional amendment would put "this source of apprehension and irritation . . . forever at rest." But unlike Davis, Hatton also thought it important for Congress to split the difference regarding slavery in the territories. Politicians from "both sections of the country" had "so long and so angrily quarreled over it, that the people have gotten it into their heads that there is something vitally concerning them in it." In fact, there was "nothing in it" at all. He would simply divide the territories now belonging to the United States, so that the North could set the ground rules for territories above 36° 30′, while the South could do the same below the line. He did not touch "hereafter acquired."

On Saturday, February 9, the day after Hatton spoke in Washington, Tennessee voters soundly trounced secession. Unwilling to hazard the possibility that a state convention might fall into secessionist hands, they refused in a separate vote even to allow the convention to meet in the first place. The news from his home state delighted Hatton. "Excited and alarmed friends" had predicted that his congressional district would favor a convention and that a runaway convention might drive through a secession ordinance without referring it to the people. Suddenly that threat lifted. An enormous landslide in his home country produced a margin of more than ten to one for pro-Union candidates, and voters also opposed calling a convention by a margin that exceeded five to one. Hatton sent a joyful note to his friend, former governor William Bowen Campbell. "The consternation and dismay of the conspirators here, on the reception of the news of our election was the subject of universal observation and remark," he exulted. "The swords of the wicked and reckless revolutionists" had been "turned upon their own breasts." Campbell sent a comparably jubilant message back to his young protégé. "You have never seen such enthusiasm," he reported. "The Stars and stripes float every where and we will fight under no other banner."[39]

Following the Tennessee elections, rumors swirled about an agreement between conciliatory Republicans and Southern Unionists. Gilmer, Etheridge, and Thomas A. R. Nelson, the Tennessee representative to the Committee of Thirty Three, were reported to have said that if the North gave them "any basis on which to stand at home," their states could not be "dragged out of the Union" and they would "undertake themselves to crush out secession and rebellion all over the South." The *New York Times* editorialized exuberantly: "We have evidence now of a Union party in the Southern states. The government has friends, the Constitution has supporters there with whom to treat. Conciliation and compromise become now acts of friendly arrangement, instead of surrender to open and defiant enemies."[40]

The turn of events in early February appeared to vindicate the conciliatory approach that William H. Seward had devised. His regular visits to the Charles Francis Adams household, as observed by Adams's son Henry, the apprentice historian, reflected the mood of the moment. Henry Adams reported on February 8 to his brother in Boston that "the ancient Seward" was "in high spirits and chuckles himself hoarse with stories." Seward dismissed Sumner as "a damned fool" and led his listeners to believe that "we shall soon be afloat again"—the furor would ebb once Lincoln was inaugurated.

Debating the Other Thirteenth Amendment

"He says it's all right. We shall keep the border states, and in three months or thereabouts, if we hold off, the Unionists and Disunionists will have their hands on each other's throats in the cotton states. The storm is weathered."[41]

It wasn't all right and the storm wasn't weathered—as Seward knew better than anyone else. When visiting the Adams family, he exuded cheery optimism, and he certainly had reason to appear elated after the Virginia vote. Yet the problems facing the country were far from resolved. Blunting the secession drive in the Upper South was a huge accomplishment, but the dangers created by Deep South secession persisted and soon would intensify. Seward knew too that many who voted against secession in Virginia expected Republicans to offer explicit concessions regarding slavery in the territories. That was not about to happen. A majority of Republicans opposed any "backing down," either to appease Deep South secessionists or to reward Upper South antisecessionists.

Most opponents of secession in Virginia and Tennessee had qualified their allegiance to the Union. They expected the North to accept promptly the sort of territorial compromise that Republicans so far had spurned with near unanimity. And if Republicans were not disposed to compromise when the situation looked bleakest, they had even less motive to do so after hot air began to leak out of the secession balloon. The Washington correspondent for the *Springfield Republican* refused to celebrate. The North was ready to "concede something," but "not enough to bring back the cotton states," and "probably not enough to satisfy the border slave states." The border states kept demanding "no coercion"—none of the slave states in the Upper South was willing "to aid the federal government in executing the laws, even if a compromise were agreed to." Instead, they stood "between the government and the seceders" and threatened to join the exodus from the Union if force were used to prevent secession or the seizure of federal property.[42]

Seward had played an essential behind-the-scenes role in assuring Virginia Unionists that their concerns would be addressed. Once the election took place there on February 4, his contacts urged him to "come forward promptly with liberal concessions." James Barbour, a state legislator from Culpeper County, explained that antisecessionists had triumphed in his state only by assuring voters that the North soon would grant "constitutional guaranties of our slave property rights"—in other words, the right to hold slaves in federal territories. Without this, it was "as inevitable as fate" that Virginia would secede. Another of Seward's Virginia allies, whom he once promoted as a potential cabinet member, was Robert Eden Scott of Fauquier County. From a Republican perspective, however, Scott was an odd

Reaching across the Abyss

possibility. He demanded that the party scuttle the core idea in its Chicago platform—"that no more slave territory shall be acquired." Scott thought that an increasing slave population eventually would "demand more room"— and he considered it only "just" that the South "should have it." Comparable warnings came from Tennessee. His state's Union victory on February 9 was based on the belief that people in the North would "do us justice," wrote J. W. Merriam of Memphis. He declared that Tennessee would leave the Union unless "some fair basis of compromise" were adopted—that is, the Southern version of territorial rights.[43]

Even unconditional Southern Unionists wanted a territorial compromise. William Bowen Campbell, the former Tennessee governor and Robert Hatton's friend, feared that war might yet break out. But if Republicans embraced the Crittenden Compromise, the Cotton States would be "threwn entirely in the wrong." People in Tennessee would "have no sympathy" for them and would not fight on their behalf. J. R. Bailey, a Kentucky slaveholder who admired Henry Clay, "always looked hopefully forward" to a time when slavery would end. He refused to believe that there were "radical differences" that separated North and South. Instead, he explained to Seward, the difference was "more in words than in substance." But because "the masses" in the South had long been fed a diet that made no distinction between "freesoilism and abolitionism," Bailey doubted whether they could "unlearn in a few months the teaching of years." He therefore urged Seward to provide "something tangible" and to do so "speedily." "Cannot the Republicans so act in the present excited crisis as to give the Union men some ground to stand on," he pleaded. "Cannot *you* do something to give us a chance?"[44]

The Unfazed and the Alarmed

Jabez C. Woodman impatiently put words to paper as he sat at his desk. It was early December 1860. The deep chill of a New England winter had already enveloped Portland, Maine, where Woodman lived. But nothing could dissipate the heat in his message to William H. Seward. Newspaper reports suggested that the great New Yorker intended to appease the insolent slaveholders of the South, who threatened to disrupt the Union. Woodman would have none of it. A longtime antislavery activist, Woodman had been a leading Free Soiler. He had petitioned Congress in 1850 to bar slavery from the territories and to abolish slavery and the slave trade in the District of Columbia. Subsequently Woodman and others who shared his hatred of slavery found a political home in the Republican Party. He now spelled out the political arithmetic that forbade alienating the party's hard-core supporters. Republicans had swept the electoral vote of the North a month before, he reminded Seward, because of the *free soil principle*." The party's advantage in Maine and New Hampshire, along with several western states, depended on support from free soil Democrats. If Republicans sanctioned a territorial compromise or affirmed the validity of the Fugitive Slave Act, they would "throw away the ladder" that enabled the party to climb to victory. Moreover, Woodman added, the North had committed no wrong against the South. Instead, slaveholders had persistently undermined "the free principles of the constitution from 1790 to the present day."[1]

Woodman's letter reminds us that the constitutional amendment took shape amid deep disagreements among Republicans about what they and the country faced during the secession winter. Was the crisis genuine? Or had it been gotten up for effect—so that it might be turned off as readily as it had been turned on? And if the crisis was genuine, could or should Republicans do anything to ameliorate it? Much depended on how these questions were answered. This chapter will introduce several significant Republicans and explore the spectrum of their responses. It will become apparent that party leaders had to tailor their thinking to the demands of the Northern electorate, with New England and the New England exodus regions to the west bitterly suspicious of anything that might be characterized as backing down to the Slave Power. Those in the party who feared war and sought to conciliate the South faced a stiff challenge.

Elihu B. Washburne grew up in rural Maine. The state's hardscrabble interior is cut by several teeming rivers that tumble down from the mountains to the sea. His hometown, Livermore, is nestled in the Androscoggin Valley. Elihu was one of eleven children born to Israel and Martha Washburn, of whom ten lived to adulthood. His father enjoyed little success as a farmer or the proprietor of a general store, and the family always was "very, very poor." Maine's scanty agricultural frontier barely supported the pioneer farm families that flooded north from Massachusetts early in the nineteenth century, and the prospects for their many sons and daughters were, at best, uncertain. This was especially the case for families of modest means—the great majority. Yet three of the Washburn sons overcame the disadvantages of their humble origins and achieved political distinction. The eldest, Israel Washburn Jr., won a seat in Congress in 1850, served there for a decade, and was elected governor of Maine just before the outbreak of war. Two of his younger brothers also climbed the political ladder—after they had established themselves in the West. By the mid-1850s three Washburn brothers sat together in the House of Representatives—joining Israel were Elihu Washburne from Illinois (he added an additional letter "e" to the family patrimony) and Cadwallader C. Washburn from Wisconsin. Our focus here is Elihu, ultimately the most notable of the three and the one who left a trove of manuscripts.[2]

Washburne, born in 1816, became a printer's apprentice in his mid-teens and worked for the *Kennebec Journal*, published at the state capital, Augusta. He also managed to gain a legal education, capped by a year at Harvard Law School, where he earned a degree in 1840. The hard-driving, blunt, ambitious young man then headed west to Galena, a town on the Mississippi River in the northwestern corner of Illinois that retained French influences and had boomed because of nearby lead mining. His marriage there to Adele Gratiot connected him to an elite local family and helped open the door to a political career. Soon he called attention to his newfound status and prosperity by building a handsome Greek Revival house that still stands today.[3]

Washburne was elected to the House of Representatives in 1852 from a huge, fast-growing district in northernmost Illinois that stretched over 150 miles along the Wisconsin border from Lake Michigan west to the Mississippi. Whigs and Democrats competed closely in this district while Free

Soilers held the balance of power. Washburne, a Whig like his older brother Israel, initially won the seat by fewer than three hundred votes over an incumbent Democrat. During the campaign, Washburne rapidly backpedaled from his previous antiabolition stance. Few residents of Galena, in the center of the mining district, saw slavery as a moral problem, but the bulk of the district to the east was rapidly filling with New England Yankees. So Washburne became an outspoken opponent of the Fugitive Slave Act, and he avidly sought Free Soil support. Less honorably, he allowed his name to be printed surreptitiously as the candidate on some phony Free Soil ballots. By fair means and foul, he shrank the Free Soil vote and gained a narrow plurality victory.[4]

By 1854, amid the furor kindled by the Kansas-Nebraska Act, antislavery Whigs, free soil Democrats, and Free Soilers in northern Illinois united under the new Republican Party banner to give Washburne almost 70 percent of the November vote. Many former Democrats chose not to vote, out of apparent disgust with their party's stance on the Kansas issue. From this point forward, the district ceased to be competitive between the major parties and became instead one of the standout Republican districts in the country. But Washburne, having navigated the transition from Whig to Republican, knew that he could remain in office only so long as he could win Republican nominations. A potential rival attempted to upend him in 1854 by having the Republican district convention in August take a hard-line antislavery stance—it demanded repeal of the Fugitive Slave Act and the Kansas-Nebraska Act, abolishing slavery in the District of Columbia, and barring any new slave states from the Union. The opportunistic rival, Stephen A. Hurlbut, hoped that Washburne might be unwilling to adopt such advanced positions, but the incumbent fully accepted "all of the anti-slavery resolutions."[5]

Once the Republican Party formed, most of its candidates who ran for office in New England and New England exodus districts could count on robust margins in general elections. They had to worry, instead, about intraparty challengers. That meant paying close attention to the sensitivities of the most ideologically committed rank-and-file members of the party—those Republicans who saw slavery as an urgent moral problem. Often former Free Soilers, these upright men and women exercised influence beyond their numbers. They were positioned to make or break party nominees, and they used their power unhesitatingly.

Elihu Washburne's papers show that he commanded a loyal following among local antislavery absolutists who hated the "damnable institution."

The Unfazed and the Alarmed

Slavery was "worse than murder, adultery, theft, false-witness or covetous-ness; for it is the embodiment of these crimes," charged William Bradford Dodge, pastor of the Millburn Congregational Church and longtime head of the Lake County Anti-Slavery Society. "Who is so vile, mean, and criminal," he asked, "as the wretch who sells the fruit of his own body (a fair daughter) into hopeless prostitution?" Dodge and those who shared his religious zeal insisted that Republicans uphold "high moral principle" and work to remove all national support for slavery. He took the lead at local political meetings to undermine Washburne's potential rivals and to assure that the congress-man continued as the party's nominee.[6]

An outspoken egalitarian and abolitionist, Dodge moved to Illinois in 1844 from Salem, Massachusetts, where he had taught at Salem's Colored School and served as an official in the Salem Abolition Society. A student of his from Salem, Robert Morris, one of the first two African American lawyers in the United States, became a dedicated abolitionist and advocate for legal equality. "All that he was he owed to 'Master Dodge,'" Morris re-called. At a time when "the prejudice against color" in Massachusetts was "so strong," Dodge succeeded in getting his former pupils "treated justly, and even kindly." Dodge was among the rarest of the rare—a white man who genuinely believed in the equal worth and equal capability of black people. His most treasured possession was a piece of cloth sent him by an African chief—"for returning to him a kidnaped son who was sold into American Slavery." In December 1859, Dodge's church officially commended John Brown and lauded his efforts "peacefully to liberate the down-trodden slaves of Virginia" and to uphold "the doctrine of our fathers, that all men are cre-ated free and equal." The congregation also deplored Southern demands "to extend and perpetuate the atrocious system of slavery."[7]

Intraparty challenges, however, remained a problem for Washburne. Three rivals attempted to topple him in the summer of 1860. The exhausted incumbent reported to his wife that he had been "on the wing night and day" for three straight weeks as he attempted to deflect his opponents. He was aided by "devoted friends" who would have "fought or died for me almost." When the district's Republicans met at Rockford, Washburne initially failed by a few votes to secure renomination. Among them, the three other can-didates commanded a narrow majority, but they proved unable to combine their forces. Finally, to mollify his would-be successors, Washburne prom-ised to serve one last term in Congress. This was not a promise he would fulfill. Long before the next election, the Civil War intervened. Washburne, who had friendly relations both with Lincoln and Ulysses S. Grant, then claimed that he needed to remain on duty in Washington.[8]

When the Gulf States unexpectedly disrupted the Union following Lincoln's November election, Washburne's constituents were in no mood to appease Southern grievances. Instead they demanded that he "stand firm," not "back down one inch," and "yield not a hair." Republicans needed "to have *back bone*," wrote John Addams, the father of Jane Addams, who later would emerge as the pioneer of the settlement house movement and an inspiration to generations of women.[9] Another warned that any "proslavery compromise" would wreck the Republican Party and "send to their political graves" any who bent to the storm. Washburne's hard-line supporters, still angry about the Fugitive Slave Act, vowed that "the day of compromises" had passed. They demanded instead that Republicans honor their promise to work for the "ultimate extinction" of slavery.[10]

What motivated hard-line Republicans? In part they were infuriated by persistent reports that Northern businessmen and travelers in the South had been abused and even killed, and they suspected that news of many such outrages never reached the North. One reported the sad story of a local entrepreneur who had gone south to sell fruit trees, only to have his trees destroyed by a mob. Many Northerners considered such lawlessness an inevitable consequence of "the *pernicious and damnable* influences of the institution of slavery." So long as "the Rattlesnake Gentry of the South" were murdering "Northern men," another of Washburne's constituents cried out, nobody should offer concessions.[11]

Illinois Yankees also were determined to defend Northern values and institutions—their letters repeatedly affirmed the importance of "Free Schools, free speech, free press and *living* Christianity." One fifty-year-old resident volunteered his services to preserve the territories for "freemen." He would "sacrifice all that I have earned" and take his rifle in hand "to defend the liberty of person, liberty of the press and speech." If people in the free states caved in to Southern demands and allowed slavery to spread, "the more *terrible* will be the cost, in *blood* and *treasure*, in ridding ourselves of it."[12]

Washburne's correspondents were amazed by the claim "that we have been unjust to the South." Concessions might be appropriate, they reasoned, "if *we were* trespassing upon and invading the constitutional rights of the South." But the Republican Party carefully shaped its agenda so as to permit the slave states full authority within their jurisdictions. Even the most radical Republicans, who sought to end all federal responsibility for upholding

Elihu Washburne. "Shall we, the victors, surrender all we have fought and gained, because the vanquished are not pleased at being beaten? Who supposed they would be? The answer is simple. *We won't do it.*" R. H. McClellan to Elihu B. Washburne, Jan. 16, 1861, Elihu B. Washburne Papers, Library of Congress. Library of Congress, Prints and Photographs Division, Brady-Handy Photograph Collection, LC-BH83- 2249.

slavery, "never wanted to injure the south nor to interfere with *Slavery* in the states." To better explain the South's unreasonable behavior, some Republicans pointed to "wounded" Southern pride, coupled with the shock of suddenly finding their section "in a minority."[13]

Republicans struggled to understand why the Deep South appeared poised to pursue such a "suicidal" policy as secession. "Surely they are not such fools" as to think secession would be a remedy for their grievances, one reasoned; instead, it would bring about "the death of slavery." If secession led to war, another presciently predicted, "not a slave would tread North American Soil four years from now." Some observers therefore concluded that secession had to be seen as a high-stakes game of extortion, not a serious plan for action. It was designed to undermine the Republican Party and extract humiliating concessions. Many regarded secession as a deliberate effort to overturn the results of the presidential election. Shall the victors "surrender all we have fought and gained, because the vanquished are not pleased at being beaten? Who supposed they would be? The answer is simple. *We won't do it.*"[14]

Several of Washburne's constituents gave precedence to moral and humanitarian considerations. "Four millions of bondsmen have a rightfull interest in this question," declared one avowed abolitionist. Their claims "will not be ignored by Him who judgeth righteously." If the free men of the North were to compromise, "we shall hear the thunder tones of the Almighty—inquiring 'Where is thy brother.'" William B. Dodge likewise vowed that "the slave is my brother." He would "never cease to plead the cause of God's downtrodden poor" and remained confident that "God is with the slave!" Divine Providence was "working out their emancipation in deep, unfathomable counsels."[15]

But Northern hard-liners had a mixture of motives. If some gave priority to a "love of right and justice" and a sense of shared humanity with slaves, others insisted that they would not "work side by side with negro slaves" in the territories. They coupled their contempt for the South with a "hatred of niggers" and spurned any compromise that would "leave us in the condition little above slaves themselves." Antiblack sentiments did not lead necessarily to hard-line conclusions, however. R. H. McClellan of Galena was "sick of this nigger question" and content to let the slaveholders go, "with their niggers."[16]

The abolitionist wing of the party pushed back against antiblack ideas and those who would expel "the colored race from among us." "The colored man is despised because he has been enslaved," William B. Dodge insisted, "not because of any actual deficiency." If set free and given "equal privileges," he would "take good care of himself." Whenever given "opportunity to improve themselves," Dodge observed, blacks were "uniformly honest, truthtelling, industrious people."[17]

Many Republicans, notably those who viewed matters through a religious prism, predicted that secession might make slaves "more restive" and trigger a bloodbath. Like a dormant volcano that was "continually gathering force," the South could erupt "with terrible power," warned Dodge. Seeing their masters rise in rebellion "against the government of the U.S." might provoke slaves to make "some desperate effort to obtain their God-given rights." John James, a McHenry County "plough jogger," wrote as if he had just been rereading Harriet Beecher Stowe's famous novel. The "God of justice" had proclaimed "liberty to the captives." He would bring "a day of vengeance to the transgressors." Yet another predicted that "*famine* and *insurrection* in the South" would be "powerful auxiliaries in bringing back those States, to their senses, and to their allegiance."[18]

By late December and early January, amid Fort Sumter's first dramatic moment in the national spotlight, Washburne's mail revealed that many people were "absolutely frantic with rage" and "*dead set* against any and all concessions to the Pro-Slaveryites." The feeling among "reading and thinking Republicans" was described as "intense." One hothead threatened

The Unfazed and the Alarmed

to lynch any member of Congress who would "ignominiously surrender." Some Democrats who "three weeks since were loud against the Republicans" had changed their tune and become "the strongest" against secession. Any who voiced sympathies with the seceding states were denounced as "'tories'—under which they squirm, and have generally kept their mouths closed since."[19]

Washburne's correspondents repeatedly invoked the partisan imperative: "It is evident," wrote one, that "if the Republicans stand firm they will have large accessions from the Douglas party in this state." But were Republicans to compromise, "I fear we are lost and our ranks broken." We must "stand firm or the party is gone." Another contended that "God in Heaven" had gotten rid of the old Whig, Democratic, and American Parties because they had "bowed down to the Moloch of slavery." Washburne's brother-in-law, Charles L. Stephenson, judged in mid-January that no politician who dared to compromise Republican principles could "stand before the people a moment at this stage of the game." There was "a spirit abroad in the land that must be heeded and obeyed." People would "acquiesce in a reasonable fugitive slave law, granting to the South their full rights under the present Constitution and nothing more." Any further concession by Republicans would be "as fatal to them as a *snake bite*."[20]

Illinois Republicans were bewildered to read accusations in the *New York Tribune* and the *Chicago Tribune* that eminent party stalwarts such as Charles Francis Adams and William H. Seward dared to offer concessions to the South. Everyone honored John Quincy Adams as "the unflinching champion of Liberty." Did the son lack "the back bone of the old man, who stayed the whole pack of bloodhounds baying upon him"? And why did Seward, whose "every word" was long regarded as "the voice of God," now sound like Stephen A. Douglas by saying that Union mattered more than party? Any *"back down"* that involved *"vital principles"* would "lay us out 'colder than a wedge.'" Reports that Corwin was the Machiavellian mastermind behind the procompromise movement earned the Ohio veteran a cold response: "If you could hear the denunciations of Tom Corwin you would be astonished." But northern Illinois Republicans hesitated. Perhaps Adams had floated his New Mexico scheme only "for effect"? And perhaps the constitutional amendment was a clever ruse—after all, "who proposes to meddle" with slavery in the states? N. A. Vose of Waukegan, Illinois, gave Seward's speech high marks. "If I was a disunionist, I would say there was cats claws in all that soft fur." But Vose disliked the idea of amending the Constitution so as to prohibit any interference with slavery in the states. He would allow the states full power over slavery only so long as they could "*control and manage it without endangering the peace of the Union.*" If slavery became an insupportable "nuisance," he wanted Congress to have the power to abolish it.[21]

William B. Dodge, the Congregational minister in Millburn, insisted that slavery was utterly incompatible with American values. "Astonished" that Seward proposed "to put a perpetual guarantee of slavery into our uncorrupted Constitution," Dodge commended abolitionist Wendell Phillips for calling Seward to account. Unlike Phillips, however, Dodge turned a blind eye toward the ways in which the Founding Fathers had accommodated Southern slaveholders. Instead, Dodge placed the Constitution on a pedestal—it was "a sacred monument" to "our fathers wisdom and patriotism," and it should never include "a pledge to support the vilest oppression God ever suffered to degrade and curse humanity."

Dodge vowed that he wished slaveholders "no harm," but he thought they should be treated like disobedient children. This Old Testament patriarch had never given his own children a "sugar teat to stop their crying." Instead, he had given them "the rod." Dodge's providentialism made him welcome armed conflict—and he had plenty of company. If Southerners wanted to "dash their brains out," they should do so. They had "made the fire" and they must "quench it, or let it consume them." He would "let the caldron boil over"—God had given "wicked men the liberty to work out their own destruction." Republicans ought not remove "one stick of the fuel." If the South wished for war, "let them have it, till they are satisfied." The people in his region were "opposed to compromise of any sort." All they feared was "backing down."[22]

Others almost lightheartedly accepted the possibility of war. W. H. Baldwin was confident that no "long protracted war" could take place—sixty days "would be sufficient" to rout the secessionists. So too C. K. Williams cheerfully anticipated settling North-South issues "at the point of a bayonet" and thought "99 of every 100 Republicans" agreed with him. "If we must have a little fighting," John James decided, "let it come." E. G. Howe of Waukegan recognized that "the judicious men here dread war," but they dreaded even more any alteration of the Constitution to extend slavery. And that same thought echoed repeatedly. "Sooner than see slavery engrafted in the Constitution," Republicans in Mount Carroll would "prefer to see the Union scattered never more to be united."[23]

Under the circumstances, it mattered little what Washburne might have thought in private. His course was marked out by his constituents. When the constitutional amendment finally reached the House floor in late February, he and other stiff-backed men from the Upper North did their best to scuttle it. His brother Cadwallader Washburn had already tried to bury the amendment in committee, on grounds that the Constitution should be obeyed rather than amended. Washburne himself took the lead by tying the House in knots, demanding a vote on his brother's earlier proposal and repeatedly moving to adjourn in order to run out the clock. Because the amendment needed a two-thirds majority, the hard-liners very nearly succeeded in blocking it.[24]

A symbiotic relationship existed between grass-roots Republican opinion in the Upper North and the newspaper that circulated most widely through that region. The weekly edition of the *New York Tribune* had a circulation of almost three hundred thousand in early 1861, and its combative editor, Horace Greeley, estimated that a million people read each issue. The *Tribune* both reflected and helped to shape the thinking of a large segment of the Republican electorate. For many weeks, Greeley emblazoned an explicit rallying cry on the masthead of his newspaper:

NO COMPROMISE!
NO CONCESSIONS TO TRAITORS!
The Constitution as it is[25]

Hard-line Republicans who hated slavery looked to the *Tribune* as their Bible. "For the last three months," wrote the Massachusetts radical William S. Robinson, the *Tribune* had been "splendidly right." Its "grand and magnificent" stance had fearlessly challenged all compromises and compromisers.[26]

Every issue of the daily and weekly *Tribune* printed many letters from stiff-backed party loyalists who would not give an inch to Southern demands. "It rejoices me to know that there is one paper in the United States that has had the courage to come out boldly for the right," wrote a New Haven, Connecticut, reader: "*This is no time for compromise.*" So too Republicans "of the radical stamp" in Orleans County, in northwestern New York State, read the *Tribune* and "scorn[ed] all compromises which surrender principle or give *Slavery* the advantage over Freedom." A correspondent in Ashtabula County, Ohio—in the heart of Joshua Giddings's old district—praised the *Tribune* for standing up against politicians who stood ready to "perpetrate another outrage" that would "encourage and foster the great wrong of human Slavery." All "the genuine Republicans of Wisconsin," reported a reader in Madison, believed the "greatest danger" facing the country was "base and unholy compromises"; he praised the *Tribune* as "the greatest political power in America." The "firm and straightforward course of the *Tribune*" was said

Debating the Other Thirteenth Amendment

to be "universally commended" in eastern Iowa, where "not a weak back-bone, not a trembling knee, could be found." And a "lover of freedom" in Ann Arbor, Michigan, was confident that the *Tribune* spoke for majorities in "the whole North-West, who stand side by side with the patriots of New-York and New-England."[27]

Let us introduce another rising Republican star, Henry L. Dawes from Pittsfield, Massachusetts, situated astride the Housatonic River in west-ern Massachusetts between the Berkshire Hills and the higher peaks of the Taconic Range. Dawes came from a farm family in the Berkshires but had the drive to earn a degree from Yale College. For several years a teacher and a part-time editorial writer for newspapers, he soon shifted his focus to law and politics. He married Electa A. (Ella) Sanderson, whose father headed the academy in Ashfield, Massachusetts, where Dawes held his first job after college. Her letters reflect both principle and intelligence, traits that became even more apparent in the career of their notable daughter, Anna L. Dawes. After serving a number of terms as a Whig in the state legislature, Henry L. Dawes was elected to the U.S. House in 1856, when the Republican Party first competed in a presidential election. Slender and with a full beard that grayed as he aged, Dawes became a respected insider who would remain in the House for almost two decades. He was then promoted to fill Charles Sumner's Senate seat for the better part of another two decades. For our purposes here, Dawes invites attention because he, like Washburne, held onto his mail.[28]

The mood in western Massachusetts was similar to that in northern Il-linois. A hard-line constituency opposed any concessions to Southern seces-sionists. The Bay State, already the most ideologically antislavery state in the nation, became even more anti-Southern in reaction to the terrible beat-ing inflicted on Sumner in 1856 by Preston Brooks. Dawes revealed to his wife, Ella, in June 1860 that he and his colleagues were protecting Sumner from another assault. The Massachusetts senator, long incapacitated, had emerged from his protracted convalescence to deliver a ferocious oration that denounced "the madness for Slavery" and "the rage for its extension." Soon afterward uninvited visitors came to the door of Sumner's home in Washington and threatened to "cut his d—d throat." The root of the trouble, Dawes knew, was slavery's "damnable barbarism."[29]

Unlike Sumner, Dawes was not by temperament a hard-liner. He was more comfortable with political give-and-take. But that trait cost him. In August 1860, Massachusetts governor Nathaniel Banks attempted to make Dawes his successor in the state's top office. Sumner, however, suspected

Henry A. Dawes. "This is no time for flinching, receding from the high ground we have taken, yielding Principle, sacrificing truth & Justice & Right at the dictation of a few thousand insolent & enraged Slaveholders! No, No! A thousand times No!" P. K. Clark to Henry L. Dawes, Jan. 4, 1861, box 18, Henry L. Dawes Papers, Library of Congress. Photograph by Mathew Brady, National Archives and Records Administration, 526271.

the cabal might try to set him aside and countered with a bid "to weed out party leaders whose antislavery zeal was dubious." He roused his supporters on behalf of John A. Andrew, a longtime ally who fully measured up to Sumner's hard-line standards. When the state party met in convention in late August, Sumner's allies easily prevailed. Andrew, not Dawes, got the nomination that was tantamount to election.[30]

When Dawes arrived in Washington in early December 1860, a month after the election, he was appalled to find President Buchanan "giving aid and comfort to the Disunionists." Moreover, the uproar in the South left many Republicans baffled and even frightened. By the time Lincoln finally took office in March, Dawes feared, he might find "the Union dismembered, or a civil war, or perhaps both," with the Republican Party "split all to pieces." Ella Dawes shared his distress. Her blood boiled, she reported, to think that anyone would "yield" to secessionist bullying, but she was "pretty certain" that her husband would not "bow or bend to them." And he would not. Rather than agree to some "ignoble concession" that would only "postpone it for my children," he wanted to address the problem now. "If we can't live together except it be on terms of taking to our bosom the institution of slavery," then he would not care to live with the South for "another moment."[31]

Most of his constituents agreed. The "universal feeling of the Republicans, and nearly all the Democrats," one reported, was that the party "stand firm" against "compromises and concessions." Another judged that the core question was "whether *Freedom or Slavery* shall rule this nation." If Republicans "stand *firm* and prove *true* to their principles, God and the Right will prevail!" The pastor of a church beseeched Dawes not to sacrifice "truth and Justice and Right at the dictation of a few thousand insolent and *enraged Slaveholders*." It was "no time for flinching"—"No, No! A thousand times No!" What was needed was "*firmness* and *courage*."[32]

Dawes's private views were not as absolute as he felt obliged to display in public. He made a less ideologically charged assessment in a confidential letter to a political ally, but he admitted that he had no room for maneuver. Any deviation from a hard-line stance would raise "a rumpus in the extreme wing at home." He had been "flooded with letters that convince me of it," as did the editorials in local newspapers. And some of his colleagues in the Massachusetts delegation would be bound to pounce. If any part of the state's personal liberty law conflicted with "our Constitutional obligations," he confided, it should be repealed. But he was not about to say as much in public. That could be seen as yielding to "brazen faced treason." He "would not care to have others see" any evidence that he had misgivings. Another of his political cronies warned Dawes to "exercise extreme care what you put on paper . . . as well as to whom you write for the number of prudent *and judicious* men is very small."[33]

The initial Fort Sumter crisis in late December and early January roused many of Dawes's correspondents to a fever pitch. "Our country is sick, very sick," observed W. P. Porter. He advocated "considerable blood letting"— under the assumption that deluded South Carolinians would shed most of the blood. "Let them have say two months" of war on "a few well fought battle fields," and the survivors would realize how badly secession orators had misled them. Up among "the hills and mountains of New England," Porter insisted, there was "but one mind and one voice among the people." They demanded that "the Union *must and shall be preserved*," that "the laws must be enforced," and that "no compromises surrendering any thing fought for by the Republicans in the presidential canvass" would be tolerated. "Every inch of ground must be maintained"—any concessions that might have been offered "before the South assumed its present threatening attitude *must not now be made at all*." The prominent Amasa Walker, a longtime antislavery man but no fire-breathing radical, had never seen "the whole community so united as at this time. I meet nobody, old or young, rich or poor, radical or conservative, who expresses any wish to have any concessions made to the secessionists."[34]

The Unfazed and the Alarmed

Most Massachusetts citizens did accept that the slave states should enjoy "all the rights guaranteed to them by the Constitution." They could "have the institution of Slavery, and hug it to their bosom, if they will, though it is the greatest curse to themselves," reasoned P. K. Clark. But they could not force it on the free states or make it "a National Institution." Any such "nationalization of Oppression will subject us to the more awful displeasure of a Righteous God."[35]

At this juncture, Charles Francis Adams unsettled things among his Massachusetts colleagues by proposing an apparent concession. As we have seen above, he proposed that New Mexico enter the Union as a state and that the Constitution be amended to rule out any interference with slavery in the states where it existed. Even if he did not concede anywhere near enough ground to appease secessionists, his bold overture reverberated in the Bay State. A lively debate focused on the question of whether Adams had or had not compromised core Republican principles. Could he make the case that his proposals would help Union-loving men in the Upper South overcome their reckless secessionist adversaries in the Deep South?

One of Dawes's correspondents, D. W. Alford, reported that Adams had some support, so long as New Mexico would be "admitted at once, and come in as a free state." But many others were "almost as much averse to Mr. Adams' plan as to Mr. Crittenden's." They feared a "dishonorable surrender of principle." Nelson Clark took offense at "disgracefull" constitutional amendments that were to be "unalterable in all future time." The Constitution should be "obeyed" rather than changed "to appease the wrath of Traitors." If the Constitution were to be amended, advised F. E. Patrick, it should specify that no secession ever take place without consent of at least three-quarters of the states—that would be a "sine qua non."[36]

Dawes took aim at the constitutional amendment by writing a letter for his hometown newspaper, the *Berkshire Eagle*. He would not give slavery "rights and guarantees" that "the Democratic Party never dared to lisp in the days of its most abject subserviency to the slave power." He also castigated the amendment's minority veto provision—it gave preferential treatment to the slave states. Dawes's correspondents commended his "faithfulness to the cause in time of trial" and his opposition to Adams's "plan of gratuitous compromise." One wrote that Dawes's newspaper letter would, "like an electric battery," clear the heads of those who had been misled into supporting Adams. But others worried that Dawes had failed to provide "some plan of adjustment around which conservative Union men of the South can rally."[37]

Dawes also attempted to persuade two newspaper editors to oppose the

Adams package. One was his brother-in-law, Henry Chickering of Pittsfield, who edited the *Berkshire Eagle*. Chickering admitted that he had "overlooked, or at any rate not sufficiently examined," the part of the Adams proposition that related to amending the Constitution. And he was by no means the only one. From late December to late February, most people saw New Mexico statehood as the heart of the Adams package and paid less attention to the constitutional amendment. Chickering admitted that he did not think the amendment so "objectionable," but he politely deferred to Dawes, who was "in a position to understand it better" and had "doubtless given it vastly more consideration and close study."[38]

But Dawes encountered a determined skeptic in Samuel Bowles, editor of the *Springfield Republican*, not only the largest newspaper in western Massachusetts but one with a national readership. Bowles complained that hardliners in the Republican Party cared more "about getting Mr. Seward out of the Cabinet than anything else just now." Their behavior struck Bowles as wrongheaded. The New Yorker's presence in the cabinet was "a necessity" if the administration of the "simple Susan," Lincoln, were to enjoy any success. Bowles also contended that Republicans needed to do "*all they can afford to do*" to strengthen border state Unionists. The Adams propositions were not "concessions to traitors." Instead they made it possible for the Republican Party "to take a firm hold of the government."[39]

Bowles dared to advocate for conciliation even at the risk of offending his many hard-line readers. He contended that the constitutional amendment would not have been necessary had the Gulf States remained in the Union. But their secession created new anxieties in the border slave states, which faced the possibility of being substantially outnumbered in the Union so long as the Gulf States remained out. Bowles therefore accepted the amendment to reassure the Upper South's Unionists. They deserved assurances that the federal government never would interfere with slavery in their states.[40]

But Bowles did not try to persuade his longtime radical columnist, William S. Robinson, already mentioned in chapter 4, who wrote under the pen name "Warrington." Robinson lambasted "the ridiculous little constitutional amendment." The "most appropriate" comment on it, he decided, would be "the reply the fellow made" when told that a law had been passed forbidding him to marry his grandmother—"*Who in thunder wants to?*" Believing that "the border states are about as rotten as the cotton states," Robinson looked forward to the departure of all the slave states and the establishment of a smaller but entirely antislavery republic.[41]

Radical Republicans, who regarded any compromise as the worst thing that could possibly happen, occupied a strong position within the party. On the whole, they either believed war unlikely or assumed that any fighting that might occur would be quick and decisive. But others in the party—conservatives for lack of a better label—assessed the future differently. They were likely to be former Whigs. And they also were more likely to have maintained relations with former Whigs from the slave states. James Dixon, the U.S. senator from Connecticut, a conservative Republican and former Whig who had served two terms in the House during the 1840s, provided a telling case in point.

In early December, soon after Congress convened, Dixon wrote two insightful letters to Connecticut's Gideon Welles, the future cabinet member. Dixon gave short shrift to two contentious issues. He was confident that sensible people North and South could remove "obnoxious features" from the Fugitive Slave Act and modify various free-state personal liberty laws so as not to impair "our constitutional obligations to deliver up fugitives from service." Dixon also considered the matter of slavery in the states "easily adjusted" because "we claim no right to interfere with that and are willing of course to say so."

Much sooner than most Republicans, however, Dixon recognized that his section was on a collision course with the South. "*The difficulty,*" he lamented to Welles, "is in the territorial question. I do not now see how we can avoid splitting on that rock." The South would "press demands that our people will not agree to." It mattered not what "individual members of Congress might be willing to consent to." Unless their consent carried also "the consent of the people they represent," it would be worthless. Dixon knew that people in the free states would refuse to extend slavery to "the Southern regions which now or hereafter may be under our jurisdiction." The only real hope for the Union was to delay the impasse, use the interval to "strengthen the hands of the Union men" in the South, and hope for "returning reason." But the path ahead was strewn with danger. Although "all the Southern Union men" eagerly sought to "*gain time* by conciliatory measures," he did not expect the border states to stay with the Union if it became apparent that the Cotton States were "permanently separated." And he feared that an armed collision could occur, perhaps even before Lincoln's inauguration—"the ship is drifting fast upon the rocks." In the end he grimly discounted the likelihood of any peaceful accommodation. "Should the evil day come," he concluded, "we want a United North—and that, now, is about all I hope for."[42]

Another prominent worrier was Hamilton Fish, a former New York governor and U.S. senator who would emerge after the war as U. S. Grant's secretary of state. Fish's deepest allegiances were to the Whig Party, though he supported Lincoln in the 1860 election. The wealthy patrician—his mother was a Stuyvesant, and he was named for his parents' close friend Alexander Hamilton—was never in step with those who saw slavery as a pressing moral problem. He deplored "the useless, senseless, perpetual agitation of the slavery question."[43]

Fish's papers reveal that he, like Dixon, became deeply pessimistic about the situation by early December and looked to the future with "utmost apprehension." Fish believed that the North and South gravely "misapprehended" each other. He deplored the South's willful blindness to Northern reality—its insistence that William Lloyd Garrison, Wendell Phillips, and Joshua Giddings were the representative leaders in the free states, that John Brown was admired by more than "a few fanatics," and that the brutal assault on Charles Sumner required no apology. Southern grievances would be difficult to address, he feared, because the South could not point to any tangible way in which its rights had been violated. Slavery had no future "in *any part* of our Territories," so it made no practical difference whether it was either prohibited or protected there. And nothing in the Constitution forbade electing a president without Southern support. But Fish soon judged that "the movement at the South is, I think, beyond the control of those who originated it; they have succeeded in inflaming passions and in exciting alarms and hatreds which they cannot stay, and which are sweeping themselves along in this mad torrent which they have let loose."[44]

Under the circumstances, Fish decided that responsibility for defusing the crisis fell primarily to Republicans. "Great victors can afford great concessions," he reasoned, "and a great peace is rarely attained without them." He was especially inclined to reach out to Union men in Virginia and other border states and concede "almost all that they ask." Republicans were acting like mariners who "make no effort to save the ship." Their "suicidal" policy not only would lose them "the legitimate fruits of their victory" but would also lose the country itself, which would plunge into years of ruinous warfare. By contrast, Union-saving concessions would secure "the great result of the victory."[45]

Fish was struck by the contrast between public Republican bravado—to "concede nothing" and never "to back down"—and the more candid comments he heard when speaking confidentially or to a "trusted few." In private, reasonable Republicans let down their guard and wondered aloud whether "there cannot be some arrangement made." He commended James Dixon

The Unfazed and the Alarmed

for pointing out in a brief Senate speech that the neither secessionists nor hard-line Republicans were talking sensibly when each claimed to be part of a zero-sum game in which "freedom or slavery must now perish."[46]

Fish reached out to two former Senate colleagues, New York's William H. Seward and Maine's William Pitt Fessenden, to share his "painful solicitude for the future" and to see what they thought. Seward replied guardedly but in as candid a manner as anything else he wrote that winter, other than his confidential letters to Thurlow Weed. Nothing could be done, Seward admitted, to "hold back either South Carolina or any Gulf State." To make matters worse, Northern Democrats failed to understand "that secession is not merely a partisan game, now as heretofore." So they "stimulate and abet the treason, demanding humiliations of the Republicans which the Southern states confess to be useless, because too late." Seward hoped for a "reaction in favor of the Union in the Northern Democracy." He hoped too that the border slave states would begin to realize "that they are to be ruined by the licentiousness of the Gulf states if they go with them." But he worried that "fire eaters" might "provoke some violence or interference on our side." In short, Seward recognized that it would be impossible to regain the Deep South's allegiance in the foreseeable future, but he hoped that wise leadership in the North and the Union slave states might defuse the situation before it spiraled into civil war. What might young Henry Adams have made of this striking letter, so starkly in contrast to the jovial, upbeat Seward who frequented the Adams household?[47]

Seward could be said to have met Fish halfway—he acknowledged the seriousness of the crisis without indicating whether he fully shared Fish's forebodings. But Fessenden, who was close to Fish, seemed entirely unperturbed. As we have seen in chapter 4, Fessenden judged "the present condition of affairs any thing but alarming." He had "long been convinced that we can have no peace with the Slave power, until the utter folly of this long continued threat of disunion shall have been demonstrated by actual experiment." If Republicans yielded to Southern demands in the hope of preventing a bad situation from getting worse, he counseled, the basic "delusion" would remain and "break out in similar excesses" in the future. So the only right thing for Republicans to do was to do nothing. Southerners were held captive by "ignorance and pride" and needed to be made aware of "their own weakness." Only that realization would bring the cure, "speedy and certain."[48]

One of the Senate's most formidable Republicans thus discounted any serious possibility of war—a war that would soon kill one of his sons and maim another. What explains Fessenden's inability to grasp the likely consequences of his hard-line stance? His biographer, Robert J. Cook, emphasizes Fessenden's determination to reverse a series of unwarranted Slave Power victories during the 1840s and 1850s. He regarded the Republican Party as the proper instrument to redress the balance. After the party's landmark victory in November 1860, the stoic Yankee patriot would not give ground to what he regarded as empty threats.[49]

Like others who represented New England and its westward offshoots, Fessenden knew that many of his supporters were hard-liners. One of them, Woodbury Davis, considered it "absurd" to amend the Constitution—"the Southern *politicians* who are making all the trouble understand perfectly well that the Republicans *claim* no power to interfere with *slavery in the States*." To appease them would be "an act of folly." Proslavery bitter enders would not relinquish control "without a struggle"—and "the sooner it comes the better." Also among Fessenden's correspondents were those such as his abolitionist uncle, J. P. Fessenden, who had "taken the side of the oppressed against the oppressor" and viewed the crisis through a moral and religious prism. "Yield not" to slavery and "do your duty," the aging uncle beseeched his nephew. "The very *existence* of the Republican Party and the *safety* of the country" required "firmness of principle" and a refusal to "bow the knee to oppression and wrong."[50]

Fessenden regarded himself as far more than a rubber stamp for a hard-line constituency. But his constituents circumscribed his position and predisposed him to view the situation narrowly. For example, he privately held several Southern Unionists in high regard. He categorized both Tennessee's Emerson Etheridge and Maryland's Henry Winter Davis as "noble fellows." Their unconditional unionism constrained him from giving a rousing no-compromise speech to "keep up our friends at home." All that he could offer Etheridge and Davis, therefore, was "the benefit of *silence* when we can give nothing more." But Fessenden had a much lower estimate of the Upper South's many conditional unionists. They recognized secession's "folly and wickedness," he thought, but nevertheless hoped to exploit the situation to their own advantage and to break down the Republican Party. Unlike Dixon or Fish, Fessenden remained confident that the peace would hold—and that nothing would be gained and much lost if Republicans broke ranks and accepted any of the various Union-saving schemes.[51]

No Republican worked harder than Seward to defuse the crisis and conciliate Southerners who opposed secession. But anything he did to accommodate the South's purported Unionists raised suspicions among the

Upper North's hard-liners. R. W. McDade, a native of New York State, lived in Harvard, a northern Illinois town in Elihu Washburne's district. McDade hated to think that Seward would "back down" and "surrender" to the "*Slave Power.*" Any "compromises with traitors," he warned, would trigger the "complete annihilation" of the Republican Party. J. H. Fait, from Sheffield, Bureau County, Illinois—Owen Lovejoy's home county—noted with alarm that those locally who favored the Crittenden Compromise were not Republicans at all. Yet they now regarded Seward as an ally. The New York senator allegedly had stated that "Union is worth more than party," they claimed, but Fait wondered whether "we are to have Union at the expense of liberty." The South "had made us here in the north Blood hounds to catch their nigers"—"Now is this *Just*? Is it *fair*?" A former Liberty party member and Free Soiler from Bridgewater, Massachusetts, Fait was appalled that Seward stood ready to sacrifice Republican "principles" and "make the constitution more proslavery." He had "no language that was strong enough" to express his contempt for any who would think of "backing down after gaining a victory such as was achieved last fall."[52]

Henry Willis of Battle Creek, Michigan, bluntly demanded that Seward "stand firm to principle" and warned him against following a different course. Someone who had "stood up for freedom and Humanity" for a quarter century ought not now hobnob with "that arch traitor to Freedom, old Crittenden." If Seward "Betrayed the Confidence of Thousands who have looked to you as the Champion of Human Rights," they never would forgive him. Was he to end up like Daniel Webster, prostrated "before the Tyrants you so long opposed"? If Lincoln could not have "more firm and honest men in his Cabinett he had better at once Resign Go Home and Splitt more Rails."[53]

Because intense grass-roots Republican opposition ruled out territorial compromise, it opened the door, ironically, to what was billed as a lesser palliative: the constitutional amendment. This is not to say that hard-liners wanted the amendment—they certainly did not, and many condemned it. But with nothing else to show for their conciliatory efforts, Seward and Corwin came to see the amendment as a useful gesture. It would constitute a peace offering to the South's antisecessionists. And it just might cut through the mountains of misinformation that prevented Southerners from making a realistic assessment of the Republican Party.

9

The Amendment Assessed

Thaddeus Stevens took dead aim at James Buchanan. Their mutual disdain had a long history. Both Stevens and Buchanan resided in Lancaster, Pennsylvania, so that Stevens—of all people—represented the president in Congress. The Old Public Functionary was, in Stevens's estimate, "a man who, during his whole political life, has been the slave of slavery." Buchanan's annual message in December 1860, as we have seen, complained about "the long continued and intemperate interference of the northern people with the question of slavery in the Southern States." Buchanan's "atrocious calumnies," Stevens spat out, were "not worth a moment's consideration." The president "well knew that the anti-slavery party of the North never interfered, or claimed the right to interfere, or expressed a desire to intermeddle, with slavery in the States," Stevens complained. "Search the proceedings of their Legislatures, their conventions, and their party creeds, and you will find them always disclaiming the right or the intention to touch slavery in the States where it existed."[1]

Stevens was anathema in the South. His hatred of slavery was irrepressible, and his readiness to affirm the equal capabilities and worth of all people was a century or more ahead of its time. Stevens, an antislavery Whig, originally served in the House for two terms between 1849 and 1853. But he undermined his support among moderate and conservative Whigs by condemning the Compromise of 1850 and the Fugitive Slave Act, and so he failed to win renomination. He returned to Congress as a Republican in 1859 when he rode a wave of opposition to Buchanan's economic policies and the abortive effort to admit Kansas into the Union as a slave state. Unlike most other Republicans, Stevens eagerly tangled with proslavery Southerners and their Northern defenders. His sharp tongue and quick wit made him a formidable antagonist. Tommy Lee Jones's over-the-top filmed version of Stevens in Spielberg's *Lincoln* has earned the Great Commoner renewed public attention.[2]

Thaddeus Stevens. "The anti-slavery party of the North never interfered, or claimed the right to interfere, or expressed a desire to inter-meddle, with slavery in the States." *Congressional Globe*, 36:2 (Jan. 29, 1861), 621. Library of Congress, Prints and Photographs Division, Brady-Handy Photograph Collection, LC-BH83- 613.

When Stevens acknowledged the right of slaveholders to maintain the system in states where it existed, he spoke for his party. So did Owen Love-joy—along with Stevens, the other most pugnacious Republican hard-liner in the House of Representatives on the eve of war. Week after week and month after month, these two traded barbs with slavery's defenders. Each was a lightning rod, and each relished verbal combat. Lovejoy was the brother of the martyred newspaper editor Elijah Lovejoy, who died in 1837 defending his press against an antiabolition mob in Alton, Illinois. Two decades later, in 1855, Owen Lovejoy won a seat in the House. Nobody in Congress so epitomized the linkage between religious sensibilities and electoral politics. A Congregationalist minister, Lovejoy especially appealed to voters who saw slavery as a moral problem. But he also was a practical politician who carried his district by solid majorities and repeatedly won reelection. Bureau County, in north-central Illinois, Lovejoy's home, was dominated by New England emigrants. Abraham Lincoln once attended a large political rally there with him and marveled at the "great enthusiasm" the crowd displayed.[3]

Owen Lovejoy. "I am not in favor of abolishing slavery in the States where it exists by any act of Congress." *Congressional Globe*, 36:2 (Jan. 23, 1861), A86. Photograph by Mathew Brady, National Archives and Records Administration, 527168.

"It is said that this Republican Party is in favor of the abolition of slavery in the States," the Illinois congressman observed on January 23, 1861. No, he countered, "the Republican Party are in favor of no such thing."

"Well, but Lovejoy is," as I have heard it whispered around here. I merely wish to repeat—and I am willing to do so for the thousandth time, if it is necessary to disabuse the public mind—that I am not in favor of abolishing slavery in the States where it exists by any act of Congress. I never held to that doctrine, and never advocated it. If a bill were brought in here for that purpose to-day, I would not vote for it; because I do not think that the Constitution gives us the power to abolish it; and not because I do not wish to see it abolished, for God knows that I do. I want to see despotism abolished everywhere. I want to see slavery abolished in South Carolina; but it does not follow, therefore, that I would vote to have the Army and Navy go down there and abolish it. I want to see it abolished in the slave States; and if I were a native of Maryland, Virginia, Kentucky, Tennessee, or any of the slave States, I would vote to abolish it. Washington has said as much; and I hope there is nothing criminal in my now saying it. . . . But the Republican Party do not believe, there is not a man who voted for Lincoln who believes, that we have the constitutional power to abolish slavery in the States where it now exists.[4]

The Amendment Assessed

Anyone who attempts to understand the origins of the Civil War must recognize that Thaddeus Stevens and Owen Lovejoy specifically disavowed any attack on slavery in the slave states. They deplored slavery and hoped to see it ended, but they understood the Constitution to mean that white Southerners could continue to keep slaves in the states where slavery was established. Stevens and Lovejoy and all other Republicans opposed the expansion of slavery into new territories, but they believed that emancipation in Virginia, South Carolina, and Louisiana could come about only when white Southerners living in those states took action at the state level.

Stevens and Lovejoy both stood proudly among the party's radicals who wanted slavery "denationalized." So while they allowed that the slave states could manage slavery within their borders, they believed that Congress had the power to regulate or abolish it "where the law of no state operates." Stevens favored abolition in the District of Columbia but downplayed his stance in deference to the many Republicans who disagreed with him. He also considered the Fugitive Slave Act unconstitutional, but because the Supreme Court ruled otherwise he would not "resist its execution." Lovejoy went further. Asked whether he had engaged in "negro stealing," he boldly announced during a sensational speech to the House in February 1859 that he had assisted fugitives and would continue to do so. He wanted them to know that he lived "at Princeton, Illinois, three quarters of a mile east of the village," and he promised to aid each one who came to his door. His religious principles demanded that he take mercy on the "wanderer" and give "bread to the hungry and shelter to the houseless!"[5]

Of course, Stevens and Lovejoy sternly rejected all forms of compromise or concession. Believing that the South had no legitimate basis for its hysteria and its outrageous behavior, they insisted that the free states ought not appease the secession movement. Lovejoy contemptuously dismissed the idea that Republicans should "subjugate ourselves" like a "servile ox" and accept the "compromise collar." The "slave power" had a long history, he mourned, of extracting humiliating concessions from the North. "Compromise, or we will dissolve the Union," they threaten, "and then there will be found a Judas to betray, a Peter to deny, and a hired soldier to drive the nails, and the form of freedom is fastened, bleeding and quivering, to the accursed wood of compromise."[6]

I decided to write this book in the summer of 2010, when I happened across the early 1861 speeches by Stevens and Lovejoy. I had just finished a book on a tangentially related topic, in which I raised a cautionary flag about the way Lincoln so infatuated historians as to lead them to misunderstand the larger picture. I complained there that promoters of the Lincoln Legend had overplayed their hands. They depict a farsighted Lincoln who knew in advance what he wanted—and who stood ready to fight a war so that he could abolish slavery. "They downplay or ignore," I wrote, "his repeated assurances that he had no intention of interfering with slavery in the states where it already existed."[7]

This chapter will focus on the constitutional amendment's emergence as a hot potato during January and February 1861. For a time, it remained an afterthought. Republicans often dismissed it as "*useless*" or "superfluous" because they had "no desire to interfere with slavery in the South." The Southern states could "regulate their domestic affairs as they see fit."[8] Meanwhile, would-be Union-savers continued to think the vexing issue of slavery in the territories ought to be the center of attention. But Southern anxieties about the safety of slavery in the states fueled the territorial snarl. Even though slavery in the territories appeared to be the main stumbling block to sectional accord, the issue's eruptive force depended on a fear or dread among ordinary white Southerners that Republicans would somehow tamper with or undermine slavery where it existed. And that is exactly what the amendment addressed.

By February the amendment attracted more attention. It never won support from a majority of Republicans in Congress—and for those such as Stevens and Lovejoy it certainly remained "accursed"—but key Republican leaders and a fair number of other party members came to see its advantages. So a vigorous internal debate about its propriety unfolded. That debate occurred principally in the House of Representatives, where the report from its Committee of Thirty Three awaited action. But the debate preceded the action. Tom Corwin knew that he did not yet have a two-thirds majority, and so he heeded Seward's advice to "to put off a decision as long as he could" rather than bring the report to the House floor. To justify the delay, he pointed to the arrival in Washington, DC, of the so-called Peace Conference, a clever stratagem cooked up by Seward and some of his Virginia allies. "All action on the part of Congress has been suspended," the *Baltimore American* reported, "to await the deliberations of the Commissioners."[9]

In January the Virginia legislature invited all the states to send delegates to a special gathering in Washington, DC, timed to convene on the same date the legislature designated for the convention election, February 4. This prospective event enabled Virginians who opposed secession to argue that an overall settlement was within reach and that peaceful restoration of the Union remained possible. Soon dubbed the Peace Conference, the assemblage took over part of Willard's Hotel and remained in session for the next three and a half weeks. Its promoters heralded their handiwork as a legitimate sequel to the Constitutional Convention of 1787, but it failed to bring together all the discordant elements of the suddenly shattered Union. None of the seven seceding states participated—indeed, they met that same day in Montgomery, Alabama, to organize the government for a new nation, the Confederate States of America. Arkansas was an anomaly, the only slave state still in the Union that failed to attend the Peace Conference. The six New England states did send delegations, in part to keep an eye on proceedings that struck many Yankees as irregular and extralegal, but three hard-line northwestern states (Michigan, Wisconsin, and Minnesota) refused even to attend. Slow long-distance communications and transport with the Pacific Coast prevented Oregon or California from playing a role. Nevertheless, a substantial majority of states did send representatives, appointed by the legislature or the governor. The Upper South and the Lower North, where procompromise sentiment was strongest, were well positioned to craft a mutually agreeable outcome. Altogether fourteen free states and seven slave states sent 132 delegates to the conference, and a large majority of American citizens lived in states represented there. Throughout the month of February, it concealed its proceedings behind closed doors.[10]

The *New York Tribune* complained that the Virginia-inspired gathering was an "Old Gentlemen's Convention" dominated by "fossils" who were distinguished principally by their advanced age and political irrelevance. Nothing better reinforced this sneering stereotype than the unfortunate choice to preside over the gathering—the seventy-one-year-old former U.S. president, John Tyler. "Tall, white-haired, wearing a well-worn snuff-colored overcoat and thick buckskin gloves," Tyler impressed the Washington correspondent of the *Springfield Republican* as "some Rip Van Winkle just dug out of a past century." The one-time president's age was not his only handicap. Tyler was a Southern Rights particularist whose allegiance to the United States was suspect. He was "more cordially despised," one Northerner sourly reported, than anyone ever to reside in the White House.[11]

When the Peace Conference convened in early February, Union-saving moderates remained fixated by the presumed need for a territorial compromise. They worked to enact a modified version of the Crittenden Compromise that might attract more Northern support. A bare majority at the Peace Conference finally agreed, on February 27, to recommend a constitutional amendment that would prevent Congress or a territorial legislature from interfering with the rights of slaveholders in "present territory" south of

36° 30′. New territory could be acquired only with majority support from senators representing nonslaveholding states, plus a majority of those representing slaveholding states. Because the Crittenden version required territorial legislatures south of 36° 30′ to protect slavery (a more stringent matter than not interfering with slavery) and did not restrict the acquisition of new territory, the Peace Conference proposal involved a less assertive definition of supposed Southern Rights. By avoiding "protection" and "hereafter acquired," it watered down the two features of the Crittenden Compromise that Republicans found most objectionable. The Peace Conference proposal closely paralleled the stillborn Border State Plan, crafted by an ad hoc committee of House members in early January. But neither the Border State Plan nor the Peace Conference proposal could attract much Republican support. Moderate Republicans for the most part considered the report of the Committee of Thirty Three the most they could accept: the constitutional amendment securing slavery in the states, accompanied by statehood for New Mexico, the only U.S. territory south of 36° 30′. But the Peace Conference's retreat from the original Crittenden plan angered many Southern Democrats. They condemned the final package as a sellout and refused to support it. Notwithstanding the antisecession groundswell in Virginia, its Democratic-majority delegation and its counterpart from North Carolina rejected the final arrangement.[12]

The issue of slavery in the states was a subsidiary part of the Peace Conference proposal. Twelve states, principally from the Upper South and the Lower North, voted to include a provision that denied Congress the power "to regulate, abolish, or control" slavery in the states where it existed by law. Only seven states (five from New England) opposed this part of the package.[13] But some Peace Conference discussions suggested that the safety of slavery in the states was the real ghost in the room, even if everyone's fixation on the territories obscured it. Thomas Ruffin of North Carolina, a moderate Democrat, thought that the "true necessity that called us here" was the belief among white Southerners that the Republican Party and its new president "entertain views and designs hostile to our institutions." George W. Summers of Virginia, a leading pro-Union former Whig, likewise warned that Southern people were "apprehensive that their rights are in danger." Even though Virginia's voters had just rejected immediate secession, they remained "full of anxiety" and fearful that "the new administration has designs which it will carry into execution, fatal to their rights and interests." And James A. Seddon of Virginia, the most outspoken Southern Rights Democrat at the conference and the future Confederate secretary of war, indignantly condemned the "more heated zealots" among Republicans who would build "a cordon of free States" around the slave states—so that "in the end" slavery would be "extinguished altogether." For Seddon, there was "no difference between attacking slavery in the States and keeping it out of the territories." Echoing Calhoun, he announced that slavery's defenders had decided to draw a defensive line "around the citadel at a more remote point."[14]

The most extensive comments at the Peace Conference regarding slavery in states came from hard-line Republicans, who opposed a territorial compromise and pooh-poohed the supposed danger to slavery where it existed. David Dudley Field, a prominent attorney and legal scholar, had been a leading New York "Barnburner"—supporters of Martin Van Buren's Free Soil Party in 1848. Field insisted that the Republican Party "always repudiated all intention of interfering with slavery." He issued a blunt challenge to Southern delegates. "Have you told your people this? If you would explain it to them now, would they not be quieted? Do not reply that they *believe* we have such a purpose. Who is responsible for that belief? Have you not continually asserted before your people, notwithstanding every assurance we could give you to the contrary, that we are determined to interfere with your rights?"[15]

Amos Tuck of New Hampshire, also a former Free Soiler, pleaded with Southerners to recognize the specious nature of alarms that Republicans were "plotting the overthrow of slavery." Tuck insisted that there was "no disposition at the North to destroy slavery." Though "inflexibly and unalterably opposed" to allowing slavery to expand to the territories, the North was "willing to let slavery remain where it is." It was "a mistake and a pernicious error," Tuck charged, "for the South to believe that either party at the North proposes to raise any question relating to slavery within State limits. There is not a man at the North who could stand up long enough to fall down, if he should take such a position."[16]

Salmon P. Chase of Ohio, the most prominent Republican at the Peace Conference and soon to be appointed secretary of the treasury, corroborated Field and Tuck. As noted in chapter 2, Chase stood foremost in breathing life into the political antislavery movement. Lincoln's victory, Chase observed, was based on the idea of restricting slavery "within State limits" but "*not* war upon slavery within those limits." There was neither the desire nor the inclination on the part of "any considerable number" of people in the free states "to interfere with the institution of slavery within the States where it exists." Like Field, Chase challenged the Southern delegates at the Peace Conference to tell "your people that we of the free States have no purpose, and never had any purpose, to infringe the rights of the slave States, or of any citizen of the slave States." Hardly anyone in the free states, and certainly not members of the Republican Party, had "any wish or purpose to interfere with slavery in the States where it exists, or with any of your rights under the Constitution. You can say this with absolute truth, and with entire confidence."[17]

James Pollock, a Republican and a former governor of Pennsylvania, judged that "a few radical men at the North" had caused widespread apprehension in the slave states. So he decided to accept the Peace Conference compromise. In so doing, he set himself apart from most other Republicans. But Pollock's explanation for his action made it plain that he too considered Southern alarms groundless. He did "not believe for a moment" that there was any basis for the widespread Southern fear "that the Republican Party meditates unconditional interference with Southern rights." Nevertheless, he reasoned, the fear existed. "Acting upon it, several States have withdrawn from the Union. We must deal with it the best way we can. If we can satisfy our Southern brethren, in the name of peace let us do it." Pollock, who had "labored for the election of Mr. Lincoln" in his home state, insisted that hostility to slavery had not been the "leading idea" there during the 1860 campaign. Pennsylvania had other motivations for supporting Lincoln, he explained: "There was the repeal of the Missouri Compromise—ruinous discriminations in the Tariff—the corruption of the Government—the villainous conduct of its high officers; these and other considerations gave Mr. Lincoln more strength in Pennsylvania than the slavery question."[18]

Several days later, the more hard-line Pennsylvanian David Wilmot, author of the famous Wilmot Proviso and yet another Free Soiler, had an exchange with Pollock that generated additional discussion regarding slavery in the states. "Now all the North agrees there is no right under the Constitution to interfere with slavery where it exists," Wilmot reasoned—"no one has ever asserted such a right, or believed in it." He offered to join Pollock in a declaratory resolution to specify that the North had no right to touch slavery in the states. But Wilmot urged Pollock to reciprocate by supporting a comparable declaration against the alleged right of secession: "I now ask him to go with me, not against a mere shadow, but against what is the doctrine of a large portion of the people of the slave States." If the Constitution were to be amended to relieve an unjustified apprehension regarding the safety of slavery in the states, Wilmot thought it "high time that the Constitution was made unequivocal upon this subject of secession."[19]

During the weeks that the Peace Conference was in session, both the House and the Senate voted to organize new territorial governments—for

The Amendment Assessed

Colorado, Dakota, and Nevada. The departure of senators and representatives from the seceding states meant that Republicans held majorities in both houses. Past precedent suggested that Republicans would demand what Wilmot had championed for the past decade and a half: a specific restriction against slavery in the three new territories. But this did not happen. The three territorial bills were silent regarding slavery. What happened? Ohio's Ben Wade explained to the Senate that more than thirty thousand settlers now resided in the Pike's Peak region with "no law" and "no territorial government." In order to organize territorial governments there and in Dakota and Nevada, those who wanted slavery excluded reached some kind of informal agreement with those who wanted it included. Both sides "agreed that there should be nothing said about slavery in the territorial organization, one way or the other." Wade's account implied that the bills had been crafted to avoid a presidential veto.[20]

Wade downplayed the significance of the compromise that produced the three territorial bills. Historian David Potter observed, however, that their passage revealed a "profound irony." Disagreements about the territorial issue had "brought the country to the brink of war." Yet at the very moment when the Union was coming unhinged because Southerners objected to Republican plans to exclude slavery from all federal territories, those same Republicans agreed to organize three territorial governments with no such exclusion. In effect, Republicans quietly conceded that "popular sovereignty" would prevent slavery from spreading just as effectively as overt prohibition. One of Lincoln's friends recalled years later that the president-elect had been dismayed by the three territorial bills and the apparent readiness of many Republicans to accept Stephen A. Douglas's "popular sovereignty idea." Republicans also did not repeal the New Mexico territorial slave code, although they had the votes to do so and had tried to do so before the presidential election. These little-noticed developments reveal a great deal about the abstract aspects of the great crisis: Republicans contended for a territorial exclusion they did not need and chose not to exercise as they took power; Southerners contended for access to territories that were unsuited for slavery even if it was allowed or encouraged there.[21]

While the Peace Conference delegates labored, Republicans in the House of Representatives sorted through the possibilities. The party was divided. Several of its key leaders—Sherman, Corwin, and Adams—openly advocated the Committee of Thirty Three's package, but many backbenchers resisted. The Peace Conference remained in session, and as we have seen, Corwin thought it best to wait before bringing his proposals to the floor. The

Republican Party was in a holding pattern and would remain there until the last week of February, when the pace of activity suddenly intensified.

In the interim, House members jostled to have their say. They claimed hour-long segments, typically after the end of regular business in the late afternoon or evening, to make their views known. Most of these speakers were Republicans. The intended audiences for these performances were the voters back home in their districts. With "so many contestants for the floor, the struggle to obtain it is quite lively, though as much cannot be said of all the speeches," James E. Harvey dryly reported. Many were "carefully written out in advance" and delivered during "night sessions" to "empty benches."[22]

Be warned—the actors on the stage for the rest of the chapter are not familiar personalities. Stevens and Lovejoy remain memorable, but most House Republicans enjoyed little national visibility at the time and are forgotten today. Nevertheless, their earnest orations provide an excellent window into the spectrum of Republican ideas. Most Republicans who favored the constitutional amendment and New Mexico statehood came from the border North. On February 1, John W. Killinger, from Lebanon in south-central Pennsylvania, urged his party to reach out to "the loyal men of the South" in a "conciliatory spirit" and help them "break the back of secession." He emphasized the political perils that awaited Republicans if they obstinately opposed "all propositions for honorable compromise." A hard-line refusal to reach some kind of accommodation with Southern Unionists would "virtually disband the Republican organization in Pennsylvania, whatever may be its fate elsewhere." Proximity to the South also made the peril of war more tangible. New England and South Carolina might hurl defiance at each other, Killinger observed, but Pennsylvania had ample motive to avoid a conflict with the states on its border. The "middle states," acting together, should avoid playing "the part assigned to us" by the extremists on both sides. Those who would have to carry the muskets and provide "the battle-grounds" should first take the lead in trying to avert war. Killinger could not know how accurately he foretold the future—two gigantic armies were destined to clash near his district in 1863, at Gettysburg.[23]

When Virginia voters decisively rejected immediate secession on February 4, moderate Republicans responded enthusiastically. Benjamin F. Junkin, also from south-central Pennsylvania, spoke out three days later to welcome "the voice of the Old Dominion." Its "loyal Union men" had stood bravely by "the old flag," even though their loyalty was "pronounced treason by the mad revolutionists in their midst." Junkin, who represented the district centered around Carlisle, promised "to do all in my power to heal the

The Amendment Assessed

breach that now exists between the North and the South." That meant voting for the entire package proposed by the Committee of Thirty Three. He predicted that almost all Republicans would do so—it would be "cowardly" for them "to refuse this small boon to our brethren of the South." Republicans who rejected the package would be "marked as tending towards abolition." And if the Republican Party was for abolition, then he would be "the first to abandon and denounce it."

Junkin noted that the Republican Party's Chicago platform in 1860 opposed interference with slavery in the states. "If it is a good thing in a platform," he reasoned, "it will be a good thing in the Constitution." He did not see how Republicans could object "to taking a portion of that platform and incorporating it into the fundamental law of the land." He was equally outspoken regarding the Fugitive Slave Act. He judged that public opinion in Pennsylvania was overwhelmingly in favor of its enforcement, and he rejected the idea that an underground railroad operated in the state. The Republican Party did not support "negro-stealing." Junkin was outspokenly antiblack, and his overtly racist reasons for favoring the proposed thirteenth amendment will offend most readers today. His constituents disliked free negroes, he reported, and did not "in any manner associate with them." White Pennsylvanians opposed slavery in the territories because they did "not want to work alongside of slaves," and they dreaded a potential influx of freed slaves if emancipation were ever to take place. Junkin minimized the country's ideological divisions—white Southerners were "greatly in error" to think that the "freemen of the North" were hostile either to slaveholders or to slavery.[24]

Killinger and Junkin voiced sentiments that were widely shared in Pennsylvania, the largest and most important of the Lower North states that Republicans targeted in 1860. There the party "stressed economic self-interest, nativist principles, and hostility to the further spread of slavery, often in that order of emphasis," according to historian John F. Coleman. It opposed slavery extension because it would threaten economic opportunities for white workingmen and enhance Southern power "in national political councils." Coleman considered it misleading "to characterize such appeals as anti-slavery." Instead, "they asserted the interest of northern *whites* in preference to those of Southern *whites*" and frequently exhibited coarse racial prejudice.[25]

Albert G. Porter, from Indianapolis, Indiana, the state capital, likewise bid for conciliation. Speaking on February 19, he observed that flagrant "misrepresentation" and the "foulest deception" had created "a popular panic" in the South, as many there believed "their institutions are menaced, and that the party coming into power designs, in some sense, to put them under a yoke." The future governor advised Republicans to use "practical good sense" and demonstrate "a wise and firm moderation." So he eagerly championed the constitutional amendment. He knew that many of his fellow Republicans had "a great repugnance to amending the Constitution," but he thought it would "do no harm" because it simply would make explicit what already was implicit there. It would not "change or modify" the Constitution but would instead "prevent misconstruction of existing provisions." And it would strengthen the Union men in Virginia, Maryland, North Carolina, Kentucky, and Tennessee, who had struggled "bravely against odds." Porter's own family had Kentucky origins, and he had spent most of his childhood there. In his judgment, the interconnections between families along the border of the free and slave states had so far "stopped the conflagration" from spreading beyond the Deep South, and he hoped that the crisis might yet be peacefully surmounted.[26]

But Republicans from the Yankee North would have none of it. The heartland of the party stretched from New England through to the New England exodus regions of upstate New York, northern Ohio, and points west. Here *Uncle Tom's Cabin* had resonated most deeply, here the weekly *New York Tribune* circulated widely and was read by hundreds of thousands, here the Free Soil Party of 1848 demonstrated the potential of political antislavery, and here the anti-Nebraska insurgency of 1854 first crystallized to form the Republican Party.

Dozens of stiff-backed Republicans rose to counter what they saw as craven submission to Slave Power tyranny. Several examples will illustrate the arguments they employed. Sidney Edgerton from Akron, Ohio, in the heart of the militantly antislavery Western Reserve, spoke immediately after Charles Francis Adams on January 31. The one-time Free Soil partisan denied that the South had any legitimate grievances. Its rights had been "carefully secured" and "faithfully observed." The "cry of Southern wrongs" was a "subterfuge under which treason has sought to hide its wicked designs." Northern voters had "an unquestionable constitutional right" to elect Lincoln as president, "and for it we owe no apology." Although Lincoln differed with white Southerners on the subject of slavery, a majority of Americans—and a majority of "the civilized world"—agreed with him. If a minority could dictate "what shall be the peculiar views of a presidential candidate on the subject of slavery or any other subject, then we are slaves; and if we submit to such dictation, we ought to be slaves."[27]

The Amendment Assessed

Edgerton scoffed at the idea that the North should "compromise with slavery" and "give it new guarantees." Compromise would be "a sin, an outrage against humanity, and an insult to God"—a "crowing iniquity" and a "most ghastly atrocity." And even if compromise was desirable, this was "not the time to think of it." First, treason should be punished, "our plundered property restored, and the stars and stripes planted again upon every fortress in the land." In his view, the North had far more to complain about than the South. Unoffending Northern men in the South had been "scourged, branded, murdered," and denied legal redress. Why? Because "where slavery lives, liberty must die." He felt "humiliated and disgraced" by Southern lawlessness. If "guarantees are to be given," he asserted, "I demand them for freedom."

So what should be done? Unlike Adams, Edgerton would not touch the Constitution. It had been written to promote justice and secure liberty, and it ought not to be rewritten for opposite purposes. Rather than compromise with "despotism" and "barter away truth and right," he was ready to fight fire with fire: "if war must come, let it come." Peace was "not the first interest of a people." War, "fierce, bloody, and relentless," with "all its manifold horrors," was better than allowing "the sense of justice and humanity to die out of the hearts of the people." Edgerton closed with a prophecy and a warning: "The first blast of war will be the trumpet-signal of emancipation."

Emory B. Pottle represented the heart of the Burned-Over District, a region of western New York State where Yankees clustered and progressive causes incubated. His hometown of Naples stood at the southern end of Canandaigua Lake, in Ontario County. Speaking on January 25, he recognized that "slavery in the States is a matter belonging exclusively to you." In common with millions at home and abroad, he would welcome a time when "this subject of contention should no longer exist among us," but he was sworn to support the Constitution and had no sympathy with those "who would seek a realization of universal freedom over the ruins of that Constitution." He would "take the institutions of my country as I find them."[28]

Pottle, however, scorned the amendment. Southerners had created the crisis, he insisted, and only they could resolve it. If there were fears in the South, it was not the fault of the North—"the whole South is as hermetically sealed against the northern press as the Barbary States ever were," and Northern men had not been allowed to speak in the South.

No, gentlemen of the South, this was not our work, but your own.
In your eagerness to secure all the nonslaveholding votes in your

States, and prevent the spread of Republican principles there, you traduced us. Instead of telling, or allowing us to tell, frankly to your people what were our principles, and thereby showing that we were as loyal to the Constitution, and as true to the rights of the several States as any party that ever existed in the Republic, you denounced us as Black Republicans; as Abolitionists; as advocating social equality with the negroes, and the mixing of the races; as armed with fire and sword against the rights of the South, and only waiting success in the election of our President to march down to the Southern States and make the white man subordinate to the black.

He challenged Southern leaders to retrace their steps and admit that "the aims and object of the Republican Party have been misunderstood and misrepresented; that it has nothing to do with slavery in the States."

In Pottle's view, the Union could not be peacefully divided, and there was no middle ground. Either "the citizens of this Government must yield obedience to the Constitution, or the Government must compel that obedience." He warned Southerners not to deceive themselves by thinking they would have Northern allies if it came to war: "The North is to-day a unit—not *against you*, but *for the enforcement of the laws*." So Pottle, like Edgerton, warned that a terrible war could result—"it is no summer cloud that hangs over us to-day." He dismissed as bravado Southern boasts that they were ready to die bravely in battle: "Sirs, you do injustice to our common ancestry if you doubt that we can meet the shock of battle upon equal terms with you in this respect. Who doubts the courage of either section?" He hoped that the South would reconsider its rash course, but if it did not, and war resulted, then "all nice distinctions in regard to states rights would be lost sight of." If war came, he presciently predicted, Northerners would blame slavery for "destroying the Government, bankrupting our business, and slaughtering our people," and they would decide "to wipe out utterly and forever an institution which brings such evils upon us."

John Hutchins from Warren, Ohio, Joshua Giddings's successor in Congress, represented the Western Reserve district adjacent to Edgerton's. Hutchins spoke out on February 9 against any "new guarantees" for slavery. Anyone who voted for them would be guilty of "criminality and injustice." Kentucky senator John J. Crittenden's "atrocious propositions" were no compromise; they were a surrender. Faced with "the growing power of the free states," the South insisted on maintaining control of the federal government. And the price was even steeper—any Northerner hoping to appease slaveholders would have to sacrifice the free state's distinctive qualities—"destroy their free-school system; put down free speech; silence the press and pulpit; put a censorship upon their literature; . . . [and] eradicate from the breasts of their people the love of justice and the hatred of oppression."[29]

It should come as no surprise that Hutchins objected to the constitutional amendment. He had "never heard a Republican anywhere claim the right to interfere, by act of Congress, with the institution of slavery as it exists in the several States of this Union." He might support "a simple proposition" to this effect, "for I understand that to be the Constitution now." But Corwin had poisoned the matter for Hutchins by proposing to prevent the American people from amending the Constitution "on *one* subject," without the consent of all the states, when they were "at liberty to amend it on all other subjects." This was "against the spirit of the age."

Hutchins, like Pottle and Edgerton, was ready to fight—"this great crime must be put down as other crimes are put down. . . . Our forts must be recaptured, our stolen property recovered, the Constitution and laws must be obeyed. If that means coercion, then I am for *coercion*." Hutchins expected plenty of white Southern allies. He thought that "a large majority in the slave States" were "yet loyal to the Constitution" and that "a Union feeling in the States which have passed ordinances of secession . . . will yet put down rebellion there." He would "unite with all men who are for the integrity of the Union." He would not "adopt their views upon the slavery question," nor would he expect them to adopt his.

Edward Wade, the brother of Ohio's U.S. senator Ben Wade, represented the Cleveland district. Edward Wade once worked for the Liberty Party and was first elected to Congress in 1852 as a Free Soiler. In 1854 he signed the Appeal of the Independent Democrats, which spurred Northern opposition to the Kansas-Nebraska bill. He soon became a Republican. Seven years later, on February 19, 1861, Wade explained why he would not heed the appeals from border state Unionists. Some of these "noble-spirited men," he acknowledged, had contended against opponents who "might daunt the bravest, however great his pluck or courage." But the overall effect of their stance was to paralyze the federal government and hold it hostage. By insisting that any use of armed force would drive their states out of the Union, border state Unionists demanded, in effect, that the free states submit to "the insufferable arrogance of the Gulf States" and sacrifice "our acknowledged rights." They tell us "we must yield," or else "they will be compelled to go with the nullifiers and secessionists." And even though their requests sometimes were couched as if "asking a favor," often they were presented "in

Debating the Other Thirteenth Amendment

the most menacing spirit and language." To his mind, the border states had positioned themselves "as allies with the secessionists."[30]

Wade warned his "free State friends" that it would be political suicide to give in to entreaties or demands from "border State men." Northerners would not tolerate "new guarantees" for slavery. They would scuttle any amendment to the Constitution designed to make it more pleasing to slaveholders. "Where slavery is, it is yours," Wade contended, but "do not ask us to go beyond" those protections "which the Constitution and the laws agreeing with the Constitution" already gave to the South. Like Owen Lovejoy, Wade warned his fellow Republicans to withstand the "whip and spur," sure to be applied during the last days of the session, amid "whispering from the border States of unseen and undreamed-of dangers to the Union" and alarms about "horrors" that could only be averted "by concessions to slavery from the free States." The "slave power" had a history of finding Northern allies who were ready to barter "the interests of human liberty." While secessionists spouted "a tremendous cannonade of words," these supposed "border State friends of ours" would work to divide the Republican Party. "This kind of terrorism seems to have been reduced almost to a science."

Charles Sedgwick from Syracuse, in upstate New York, impressed Henry Adams as a "rigid Puritan" who might have sat in the Long Parliament and was "probably the most extreme man in the House on the slavery question." Charles Francis Adams had used history to buttress the case for conciliation; Sedgwick spurned any comparison between the situation facing the colonies in 1775 and the position of the South in 1861. Unlike the colonists, who contended for the "great principle" that "taxation should be accompanied in all cases by representation," secessionists had "no pretense whatever" that their rights had been infringed. Their states were "not only fully represented, but with more than equal representation"—a reference to the greater political clout given the slave states by the three-fifths clause. So their complaints were "groundless."

Accordingly, Sedgwick's February 7 speech rejected the Committee of Thirty Three's proposals. New Mexico statehood "would not settle the territorial question" because Southern malcontents demanded "nothing short of incorporating the Breckinridge platform and the Dred Scott decision into the Constitution." He likewise rejected the constitutional amendment "to pacify a mere imaginary fear for the future" and quell "apprehensions of events which will never take place." Nobody, he insisted, "claims the power which this amendment denies." Worse, the proposed amendment would make it "harder and more difficult" for any Southern state that might in the future try to emancipate slaves, because it allowed "the remotest State upon the Gulf" to forbid the federal government from assisting a state that wished to rid itself of slavery. Sedgwick bluntly condemned the slave system as a "disgrace" and a "calamity" that created an "irreconcilable difference" between North and South, and he feared that the Union would be weakened and crippled so long as the "black pall" remained. Daniel Webster had famously heralded "liberty and Union, now and forever, one and inseparable," but Sedgwick struck a different balance. He was so revolted by slavery that he countenanced allowing the slave states to depart: "We desire Union, but *we will have liberty.*" He considered compromise a greater evil than disunion, and he confided to his wife that he was "willing to have the slave states go." His flirtation with peaceable separation was not unique, but the outbreak of war in April ended all such tendencies among Northern hard-liners.[31]

The observant reader should discern, amid the simmering Yankee outrage at what was happening in the South, a persistent acknowledgment by hard-line Republicans that the Constitution prohibited any interference with slavery where it existed. And many other examples could be cited. Harrison Gray Otis Blake, from Ohio's Western Reserve, considered slavery "a reproach to the country throughout the civilized world," but he specified on January 25 that he had "never entertained, for a moment, the idea that we had any power or control over slavery in the States. I never saw any Republican who claimed any such power under the Constitution." John F. Farnsworth, who represented a northern Illinois district, bluntly acknowledged that "we of the North hate slavery" and regarded it as a "stain and a disgrace" and a "crime against humanity." But at the same time, he and his Republican colleagues embraced the Constitution and the Union and renounced any right "to legislate upon or to meddle with" slavery in the states where it existed. Republicans were committed to protecting slavery "from the assaults of the whole civilized world."[32]

In short, there was nothing extraordinary about the stances of Stevens and Lovejoy, with which this chapter began. They articulated a mainstream hard-line position. They would not touch slavery in the states where it existed. But they also would not, in Stevens's words, "show repentance for the election of Mr. Lincoln." People should be able "to choose whom they please President, without stirring up rebellion, and requiring humiliation, concessions, and compromises to appease the insurgents."[33]

Many hard-line Republicans warned the South that war would lead directly to emancipation, but only a very few of the most radical questioned the party's consensus view regarding the security of slavery in the states. Charles Sedgwick, as we have just seen, wanted the door to voluntary emancipation kept open, but he hardly expected prompt action. Daniel E. Somes, however, from Biddeford in southern coastal Maine, took an unusual tack on February 16 when he bluntly predicted that emancipation was "soon to come" and that sensible white Southerners would do better to allow it to happen in an orderly manner. Were the border states to adopt a system of gradual emancipation, then "the North will aid you in any reasonable endeavor to protect yourselves and your property, and the whole civilized world will applaud you in so humane an undertaking." But were the South to persist in its "treasonable designs," then "slavery in the States will date its downfall from the day the first act of treason was committed, and in a few years it will go out in blood."[34]

Somes lectured his fellow Republicans about the perils of a "vote for compromise"—"you sow, on soil now free, the seeds of whips, chains, theft, robbery, and murder. You vote to legalize the forcible separation of families . . . . You vote for the perpetuity of ignorance, and you vote for the overthrow of the freedom of speech and of the press. . . . You say to all traitors, go on with your robbery and treason." Seeing that Northerners would "make concessions, even to the sacrifice of our dearest principles," the South would discover that a threat to break up the government was an effective way to reverse the results of an election. Any Republicans who took the "fatal step" of compromising with the "slave power," Somes predicted, would be ruined, and whatever concessions they offered would prove to be barren. He warned Southerners "not to take the flimsy compromises which some few gentlemen on this side of the House would offer you." They did not represent the sentiments of the North, which would "repudiate any compromise, such as has been proposed, and the party that makes it." Like Charles Sedgwick, he concluded by deliberately recasting Daniel Webster's famous oration: "Let us have liberty and Union, if we can; but liberty without Union rather than Union without liberty."

Two Ohio Congressmen, James M. Ashley and John A. Bingham, went even further—they explicitly dissented from the near-universal Republican consensus regarding slavery in the states. Ashley, a pugnacious first-term firebrand from Toledo, was quick to speak and fiercely antislavery. Six feet tall, handsome, and "heavy-set," he had a commanding presence. A conspicuous mane of curly brown hair added to his visibility. The one-time Democrat had been radicalized by his party's pro-slavery drift. In 1854 he bolted to become a hard-line Republican. His political stance was undergirded by a deeply religious egalitarianism. Ashley's providential world view assured him that "an end to oppression and to slavery" was inevitable, and that, in the words of his favorite poet, John Greenleaf Whittier, "firm endurance wins at last." Like the Quaker Whittier, Ashley hoped slavery would end peacefully. But he warned that a wrathful God stood poised, "to-day as in the past," to "avenge the wrongs done to the least and weakest of His children" and to "bring destruction as a whirlwind upon the wrongdoer." Just as He had called forth the "mighty waters" to engulf the Pharaoh's "horse and chariot and rider," he would do the same to America's "slave barons."[35]

Ashley had made plain his differences with Republican orthodoxy during the 1856 presidential campaign. He strongly supported John C. Frémont, but distanced himself from the Pathfinder's constitutional views. Frémont "does not propose to interfere with slavery in the States where it now exists, but simply pledges himself to resist its spread into new Territories, nothing more, nothing less." By contrast, Ashley rejected the idea "that the Constitution of my country recognizes property in man." He opposed enslaving "any man or any race of men, however friendless or poor, whatever their race or color." Slavery could not "legally exist in this country, a single hour, under an honest interpretation of our national Constitution," he proclaimed. Ashley thus sided with the purists who believed in an antislavery Constitution, and he therefore differed "with my friends Garrison and Phillips." Neither Congress nor a state legislature "had the power to make a slave any more than to make a king."[36]

Ashley's speech on January 17, 1861, deplored all "deceptive compromises" to make slavery "constitutional and perpetual." Unlike Stevens and Lovejoy, however, he did not accept that slavery had a right to remain in the states where it existed. Ashley instead thought slavery should be banned "wherever the national jurisdiction extends." This may have sounded like William Jay and Salmon Chase, who would "denationalize" slavery. But Ashley's antislavery understanding of the Constitution gave his words a Delphic quality—did the "national jurisdiction" extend to the states? Emancipation was "the sentiment of all nations," Ashley insisted, "and we cannot resist it if we would." He also appeared unperturbed that the Southern revolution was "fast getting beyond the control of its authors." If war began, he predicted, "the doom of slavery" would be "inevitable." And once the first shots were fired, he demanded emancipation as a Union war aim. Eventually he drafted a constitutional amendment to settle the matter. He had talked about doing this as far back as 1856. He would become, as we shall see, the House manager for the actual Thirteenth Amendment in January 1865.[37]

Debating the Other Thirteenth Amendment

James M. Ashley. "I do not believe slavery can legally exist in this country, a single hour, under an honest interpretation of our national Constitution." Speech at Montpelier, Ohio, September 1856, in *Duplicate Copy of the Souvenir from the Afro-American League of Tennessee to Hon. James M. Ashley of Ohio*, ed. Benjamin W. Arnett (Philadelphia: A. M. E. Church, 1894), 623. Photograph by Mathew Brady, National Archives and Records Administration, 524418.

John A. Bingham, whom we already have encountered in chapter 3, delivered the most radical speech by any House Republican in early 1861. He had represented an east-central Ohio district since 1855. Bingham was described as "spare, and rather slight" with the "appearance of an austere, thoughtful man." His "brown, brilliant eyes" were "deeply set in his head." Although he might not at first "attract the attention of a casual observer," his "remarkable" power as a speaker set him apart. Bingham's voice—"sonorous, round, full and powerful"—and his gift for effective oral expression made him "one of the ablest debaters in the House." The formidable Ohio legislator was destined to become a powerful and influential player in the postwar era—as one of the three judges appointed to try Lincoln's assassins in 1865, and most especially as the author of the Fourteenth Amendment's hugely important first section in 1866.[38]

In early 1861, however, Bingham considered it his duty "not to amend the Constitution, but to maintain and uphold the Constitution." At the same time, he wanted to preserve "the inherent right of the people to alter or amend" the Constitution at some point in the future. The proposed amendment, he pointed out on January 22, created undeserved safeguards for slavery. It provided that "one class of States alone"—that is, the slave states—could "originate an amendment" having to do with slavery, and that a single

The Amendment Assessed

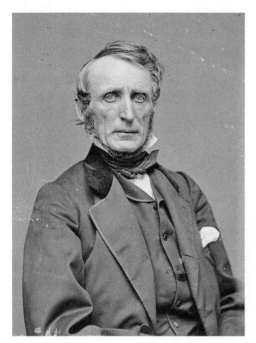

John A. Bingham. "Under the Constitution of the United States, this Government has power to interfere with slavery in the States . . . by emancipating the slaves in time of war." *Congressional Globe*, 36:2 (Jan. 22, 1861), A83. Photograph by Mathew Brady, National Archives and Records Administration, 526986.

slave state alone could block such an amendment. This would not be "in keeping with the genius of our institutions"[39]

Other Republicans besides Bingham demanded that the federal government "enforce the laws . . . put down rebellion . . . punish treason" and "recapture the forts, the arsenals, the arms, and the treasure of the United States." What set Bingham apart from his hard-line colleagues was his refusal to accept that "under the Constitution as it now is, the Government of the United States has no power *to interfere in any way* with slavery in the States." He warned, instead, that the amendment surrendered a power that the federal government should retain. He called attention to the argument once made by John Quincy Adams, who accepted that slavery was left to the "exclusive consideration and management" of the slave states during times of peace. But as we have seen, Adams contended that both the president and the commander of the army, in the event of war or insurrection, had "full power" to order "universal emancipation." And Bingham did not want that power compromised or surrendered.[40]

Bingham also based his case against "perpetual despotism" on "higher grounds." The amendment was a "written conspiracy against the liberties of four million men, and their descendants forever." It would "startle the civilized world." And the "twenty million freemen in the North" would rebuke

Debating the Other Thirteenth Amendment

it because it violated a "higher law" that was "obligatory alike on individual and collective man"—to uphold "the eternal verities of truth and justice." The outspoken Bingham concluded with an unmistakable salute to John Brown that must have jolted his Southern listeners and roused all their suspicions about the radical Republican agenda. He looked forward to a time when no state would "strangle men like felons on the gallows, because, in obedience to the Divine command, they remember those that are in bonds as bound with them."[41]

With the exceptions of Somes, Ashley, and Bingham, all Republicans forthrightly agreed that they could not touch slavery in the states where it existed. Several of the amendment's opponents such as Hutchins stated that they could accept a simple declarative resolution in its stead. James Wilson from Crawfordsville, Indiana, suggested that his colleagues might reaffirm a resolution enacted by the First Congress in 1790, which renounced any authority "to interfere in the emancipation of slaves, or the treatment of them." But Wilson was not willing "to bind the action of this Government, in all future time, in so preposterous and absurd a manner as is proposed by this amendment."[42] Another Indiana Republican, Charles Case, from Fort Wayne, agreed "that Congress had no right, under the Constitution, to interfere with the question of slavery in the States," and he too offered to support a resolution that said as much. But he considered the constitutional amendment "an insult to every northern man." Every other part of the Constitution could "stand or be changed by future generations." Why should slavery alone "have such extraordinary guarantees"?[43] Roscoe Conkling from upstate New York, not yet the strutting heavyweight he was to become after the war, saw the situation as did Wilson and Case. He would support a resolution to counter the "monstrous delusion" that Republicans planned to abolish slavery in the South. Even though Republicans opposed slavery, as did "the enlightened judgment of mankind," they recognized that the Southern states had the right to decide the matter for themselves. But Conkling ruled out the amendment: "Let us keep the Constitution as it is."[44]

Aware that a majority of House Republicans could not accept the amendment, conciliatory Republican managers picked up on the purported willingness among some naysayers in their caucus to accept a simple resolution as a lesser palliative. They suddenly moved on Monday morning, February 11, to compel a snap vote on a motion by George W. Palmer of upstate New York, which specified that "neither Congress, nor the people or governments of the non-slaveholding States, have the right to legislate upon or interfere with slavery in any of the slaveholding States in the Union." This

The Amendment Assessed

passed the House unanimously. The 161 voting in its favor included many of the most hard-line Republicans—Lovejoy, Bingham, Blake, Hutchins, and three-quarters of the others who opposed forming the Committee of Thirty Three.[45] Only a few—notably Ashley, Stevens, Edgerton, Somes, and New Hampshire's Mason W. Tappan—may have tacitly registered their displeasure by not voting.[46]

But the amendment's supporters did not give up. They continued to think it important. They were also eager to offer an alternative to the modified territorial compromise that the ad hoc Peace Conference was about to propose. After a long, circuitous railroad trip from Springfield, Lincoln finally arrived in Washington on Saturday morning, February 23, just as the Peace Conference was limping toward an agreement. The next evening, Sunday, February 24, he met with the amendment's manager, Tom Corwin. If something was to be done, it had to happen soon—the congressional session would end and the presidential inauguration would take place in little more than a week, on Monday, March 4.[47]

PART IV

The Abortive Launch

10

Congress Acts

Their train plunged through the late winter darkness. After secretly leaving Harrisburg, Pennsylvania, the small traveling party of three headed east to Philadelphia. There they were escorted to sleeping berths at the back of the night train headed south. They arrived in Baltimore after 3:00 A.M. Horses dragged the train's cars through the empty streets that connected between two depots. This was accomplished without incident. Just as the sky brightened on Saturday morning, February 23, 1861, the train reached Washington, DC, and the three surreptitious passengers from the end of the train emerged on the platform. One was the crack detective Allan Pinkerton. The second was a tall, burly, heavily armed bodyguard, Ward Hill Lamon. The third was President-Elect Abraham Lincoln. The trio had stayed incognito during the overnight journey to guard against a threatened assassination plot in Baltimore. Hardly anyone in Washington knew that Lincoln would be aboard this train, but Elihu Washburne got wind of the secret plan and was at the depot to greet his home-state ally.[1]

Lincoln arrived in the capital just nine days before his scheduled inauguration. Nobody ever before had prepared to wield power amid such tension and danger. Secession and the threat of war created an unprecedented impasse. From the moment Lincoln stepped off the train, he was beset by conflicting opinions about the propriety of offering concessions to the South. Hard-line Republicans hated the idea of "backing down." They suspected that New York senator William H. Seward would betray the party by supporting an unseemly compromise. But conciliatory Republicans judged it imperative to hold the Upper South in the Union. To assure that Lincoln take office and have the opportunity to show that he was no enemy of the South, they would try to accommodate the pro-Union leadership emerging in Virginia, Kentucky, North Carolina, and Tennessee. Republican divisions were made even more acute by the presence in Washington of the Peace Conference—the ad hoc gathering called by Virginia, with behind-the-scenes support from Seward, that had attracted representatives from most states still in the Union.

Its promoters looked to the Peace Conference to come up with a plan that might arrest the secession movement in the Upper South and even bring back the seceded states. But Seward, though relieved that the Upper South rejected immediate secession, knew that the "agony and panic" continued in "all its fierceness." He had no hope that anything useful would emerge from the Peace Conference. And he feared that Lincoln did not adequately comprehend the challenges facing him. A few days before the president-elect appeared, Charles Francis Adams noted in his diary that Seward "seemed to be more discouraged than I had yet seen him."[2]

By the time Lincoln reached Washington, as we saw in the previous chapter, the Peace Conference was on the verge of approving a territorial compromise, albeit one shorn of the poisonous provisions—protecting slavery in territory south of 36° 30′, now held or "hereafter acquired"—that made the Crittenden Compromise totally unacceptable to Republicans. Yet the watered-down Peace Conference version was, for most Republicans, no more palatable. Lincoln must have been dog-tired; he had subjected himself to a grueling blur of receptions and speechmaking across the free states for most of two weeks, capped by the previous night's anxious trip. But however much he might have wished otherwise, he could hardly avoid the Peace Conference. He was staying at Willard's, the same hotel where its meetings were held and where its members also were lodged. So he made himself available for a reception with Peace Conference delegates the very evening he arrived, Saturday, February 23, and he exchanged pleasantries with many of them. "He paid special attention to the Southern delegates," historian Michael Burlingame notes, but he diplomatically deflected discussions of substance.[3]

Republicans who disliked any concession and preferred to do nothing found themselves on the defensive as the Peace Conference's pending territorial compromise emerged. Instead, the idea began to take hold that the party should get behind an alternative. Lincoln, who played some kind of supportive role in December when the idea of a constitutional amendment first surfaced, met privately with Corwin on Sunday evening, February 24, and gave him the go-ahead. Lincoln and Corwin agreed, historian Roy Franklin Nichols concluded, that a revised version of the amendment agreed to by the Committee of Thirty Three "would be their olive branch, and they expected their party to back the move." It also may be conjectured that Seward played a role. The New York senator stayed close to Lincoln all weekend and entertained him at home for the better part of Sunday after-

The Abortive Launch

noon. Seward had both the motive and the opportunity to encourage the president-elect to get behind the amendment that the Senate's Committee of Thirteen had approved in December.[4]

The Committee of Thirty Three's original version read as follows: "No amendment of this Constitution having for its object any interference within the States with the relation between their citizens and those described in section second of the first article of the Constitution as 'all other persons,' shall originate with any state that does not recognize the relation within its own limits, or shall be valid without the assent of every one of the States composing the Union."[5] However inelegant the prose, its intent was plain. No free state could initiate an amendment to the Constitution that might interfere with slavery in the states where it existed, and any such amendment would have to be ratified by all the states, not just the three-quarters constitutional majority. John A. Bingham may have hated it, but Corwin, Adams, Davis, and others all defended this version in their speeches to the House in late January and February.

On February 26, however, Corwin announced that he wished to offer substitute language for the original, after having consulted with a majority of committee members who were "friendly" to it. Asserting that it was "vital" and of "utmost importance" to give priority to the amendment, Corwin resurrected the exact language that Seward proposed in December: "No amendment shall be made to the Constitution which will authorize or give to Congress the power to abolish or interfere, within any State, with the domestic institutions thereof, including that of persons held to labor or service by the laws of said State."[6] Seward's version sidestepped any award of special status for the slave states, particularly the idea that any one slave state might wield veto powers. Its minimalist language simply prohibited any future amendment to the Constitution that empowered Congress to abolish or interfere with slavery in the states. Even if enacted, it was potentially as subject to future amendment or repeal as any other part of the Constitution. Two months before, all five Republicans on the Senate's Committee of Thirteen had accepted Seward's version, and it also had gained support from six of the committee's other eight members. Corwin did not explain why he preferred the substitute, but his motives may be inferred. He judged that he could not get two-thirds majorities in Congress for the more absolutist language. Working with Lincoln's tacit approval, Corwin decided he could attract more Republican votes by using Seward's handiwork.

Corwin, who was "not a veteran parliamentarian for nothing," battled on Tuesday, February 26, and Wednesday, February 27, to replace his original amendment with Seward's. His motion spurred "a wild scene of confusion and filibustering" as "rigid anti-compromisers" attempted to paralyze the House. Charles Francis Adams raged in his diary against his Republican colleagues' "ill-tempered" behavior and "fiery remarks." Speaker William Pennington of New Jersey, "never distinguished for clear-headedness," was judged by one reporter to have "lost control at the helm" and had to give way to J. Morrison Harris of Maryland, who presided for the remainder of the first day. Test votes amid the filibuster suggested that Corwin enjoyed close to a two-thirds majority. Doggedly he and his supporters overcame delaying tactics and voted down various substitute proposals—the Crittenden Compromise, restoration of the Missouri line, and a call for a national convention. They also bottled up the hard-line rejoinder that condemned "compromises or concessions to unreasonable demands" and stated that the existing Constitution needed to be "obeyed rather than amended." When the Peace Conference narrowly adopted its watered-down territorial compromise on Wednesday morning, it may have aided the amendment's Republican promoters. They could then reiterate to their party colleagues that Corwin offered a sensible alternative, better than having to choose between the Peace Conference plan and nothing at all.[7]

Finally, late on Wednesday afternoon, February 27, the House voted 120–61 to replace the original version of the amendment with the Seward version. The margin was tantalizingly close to the two-thirds needed. But just moments later, when Corwin tried to get the House to adopt the revised amendment, he could not get the required two-thirds. The final tally stood at 120–71. So it appeared that the amendment was dead. Its supporters, with their backs against the wall, were forced to try some high-wire maneuvers. They moved to reconsider the vote and then adjourned the House by a wafer-thin margin, 92–90.[8] An intense overnight push to change the result then followed. Charles Francis Adams privately deplored the "remarkable exhibition of folly." A united Republican vote "would have carried with it the proof of a conciliatory spirit," he wrote in his diary, but the actual result "leaves an implication at least of a desire to keep open the chance of direct interference at some favorable moment hereafter."[9]

The House reconvened the next morning, Thursday, February 28, aware that a showdown vote soon would take place. Throngs of visitors were on the floor. "Great confusion prevailed in the hall," the *Congressional Globe* soberly reported, "and the Speaker was unable, after repeated efforts, to restore order." One of Corwin's supporters blamed the difficulties on "strangers," who were "here to bolster up the Red Republican part of the House."

The outspoken hard-liner Owen Lovejoy of Illinois retorted by blaming delegates from the recently completed Peace Conference—they were "busy-bodies" who had "no business upon this floor." Two last-minute speakers, David Kilgore of Indiana and Benjamin Stanton of Ohio, pleaded with their "Republican friends" to recognize "the importance of the vote which we soon will be called upon to give." Both asserted that the constitutional amendment simply reaffirmed what "the most ultra men" in the party had long declared they had "no power to do and no disposition to do." Its defeat, however, would send an ominous message to the Union slave states. With seven slave states having seceded, the eight remaining slave states were "entitled to additional guarantees." In the future, as more western free states joined the Union and as border slave states such as Delaware became free states, the Union slave states might fear that emancipation would be forced upon them. Even though Republicans were "sincere" and "in earnest" when disavowing any interest in tampering with slavery in the states, they could not "answer for the progress of public opinion" in the future.[10]

Kilgore and Stanton made the strongest possible case for the amendment. Once visualized as a means of bringing the Deep South to its senses by undercutting the key rationale for secession, it was expected to perform a different function by the time the House vote took place. The *Washington National Republican* explained that "the slave States adhering to the Union" needed new security. Because the free states would be close to having the power "to amend the Constitution by a three-fourths vote" if the Deep South remained out of the Union, the nonseceding states in the Upper South had a legitimate claim to new constitutional guarantees. The influential *Springfield Republican* likewise reprinted and commended a substantial excerpt from Stanton's speech. Its Washington correspondent depicted the amendment as a responsible overture to the "loyal and patriotic" men of the Upper South, who had been left "a defenseless minority in Congress" by the "disloyal and traitorous" behavior of the Deep South.[11]

Kilgore also reminded Republicans that the amendment was "reported to have been drawn up" by the "very skillful hand" of their "distinguished leader"—that is, Seward—whom "a large majority of those who voted against it yesterday were in favor of elevating to the Presidency in preference to the gentleman who has been elected." Kilgore's point, of course, was that Seward had been the presidential candidate of choice for most hard-liners less than a year before. Stanton likewise noted that Seward and the other Republicans on the Senate Committee of Thirteen had unanimously accepted this same amendment in late December.[12]

Congress Acts

The vote proved to be a tense cliffhanger. When it finally became apparent that the amendment had just carried, 133–65, the result was greeted with "loud and prolonged applause, both on the floor and in the galleries."[13] The "moderate Republicans" had shown their "good faith," the *Cincinnati Commercial* editorialized, and attempted to overcome the "pervading popular delusion in the South" by passing "the Seward amendment which Corwin substituted for his own." They affirmed "what everybody assents to except perhaps Mr. Lysander Spooner and a few abolitionists." A correspondent for the *Springfield Republican* chimed in. The House vote challenged the "misapprehensions" and "misrepresentation" that underlay secession. It enabled "the brave and devoted men of the border states" to stand up against "the Southern enemies of the Union." The amendment would "disarm these enemies" by taking away "their best weapon of attack"—the spurious claim that Republicans intended "to abolish slavery in the states." But "stiff and uncompromising Republicans" such as William S. Robinson continued to scorn "the ridiculous little constitutional amendment." It prohibited something that was not going to happen in any case. Its only redeeming quality was that it demanded a far smaller price in "decency and self-respect" than the Crittenden Compromise and other measures that would have diluted Republican opposition to slavery in the territories.[14]

The House vote deserves close assessment (see table). By a margin of seventeen votes, sixty-three to forty-six, House Republicans remained unreconciled to the amendment. On the other hand, the Republican minority was just large enough to push the amendment over the top because it gained nearly unanimous support from Upper South representatives of both parties (Democratic and Opposition) and from Northern Democrats.

The amendment was least acceptable to Republicans from the Upper North—New England and the New England exodus states to the northwest. A deeply held religious and ideological distaste for slavery was most apparent in Greater New England, where the Free Soil insurgency of the late 1840s severely eroded allegiances to the Whig and Democratic Parties and where the Republican Party first coalesced in 1854. Three out of four New England Republicans—twenty-one of twenty-eight—voted against the amendment, as did ten of fourteen from the Northwest, defined to include northern Illinois. In aggregate, Republicans in these Yankee strongholds rejected the amendment, thirty-one to eleven.

By contrast, the amendment enjoyed robust support among Republicans who represented three Lower North states—New Jersey, Pennsylvania, and Indiana. The Republican Party had not taken hold in these states as readily

House Republican Votes for and against the Other Thirteenth Amendment

	For	Against	Not Voting
New England			
Connecticut	0	4	0
Maine	2	3	1
Massachusetts	3	8	0
New Hampshire	0	3	0
Rhode Island	1	1	0
Vermont	1	2	0
TOTAL	7	21	1
Upper North			
New York	9	16	1
Ohio	6	9	0
TOTAL	15	25	1
Northwest			
Illinois	1	3	0
Iowa	0	1	1
Kansas	0	1	0
Michigan	1	3	0
Minnesota	2	0	0
Wisconsin	0	2	0
TOTAL	4	10	1
Lower North			
Indiana	4	3	0
New Jersey	2	0	1
Pennsylvania	14	4	2
TOTAL	20	7	3
GRAND TOTAL	46	63	5

Source: Congressional Globe, 36th Cong., 2d Sess., February 28, 1861, p. 1285.

Notes to New England: Maine: Freeman Morse and Ezra French switched from "against" on February 27 to "for" on February 28; John J. Perry switched from "against" on February 27 to "not voting" on February 28.

Notes to Upper North: New York: Martin Butterfield switched from "against" on February 27 to "for" on February 28; James A. Graham switched from "against" on February 27 to "not voting" on February 28; George W. Palmer did not vote on February 27 but voted "for" on February 28. Ohio: Thomas Theaker did not vote on February 27 but voted "for" on February 28; John Sherman was paired for the amendment on February 27 and voted for it on February 28.

Notes to Northwest: Iowa: Samuel R. Curtis was paired against the amendment on February 27 and 28. Minnesota: Cyrus Aldrich switched from "against" on February 27 to "for" on February 28.

Notes to Lower North: Indiana: David Kilgore switched from "against" on February 27 to "for" on February 28. New Jersey: John L. N. Stratton did not vote on February 27 but voted "for" on February 28; Speaker of the House William Pennington, as was the custom, did not vote on either day but was understood to favor the amendment. Pennsylvania: John Covode switched from "against" on February 27 to "not voting" on February 28; William Millward did not vote on either day.

as in the Upper North. None had substantial pockets of previous Free Soil activity, and none had been carried by John C. Frémont in 1856. As late as 1858, when members of the still-sitting House had been elected, those in Pennsylvania and New Jersey ran on the ticket of the "People's Party" and thereby disdained the Republican label. By a twenty-to-seven margin, Republicans in these two states and in Indiana favored the amendment. Thaddeus Stevens was not the typical House member from the Lower North.

Ohio was caught between conflicting tendencies. Parts of northern Ohio—the Western Reserve—reflected more intense New England influences than any part of the West and therefore spurned the amendment. As we have seen, many of the most outspoken radicals in Congress represented northeastern Ohio. But Ohio also was home to Corwin, the amendment's formidable manager, along with the powerful John Sherman, who was about to be promoted to the U.S. Senate and who voted for the amendment despite the hard-line orientation of his northwestern Ohio district (he was paired in favor on February 27). Adding to the complexity of the Ohio situation was the no-holds-barred battle to gain dominance in Lincoln's cabinet, which pitted forces allied with Ohio's Salmon P. Chase against those of New York's William H. Seward. For some House members, the vote on the amendment was in effect a proxy vote on the Chase-Seward struggle, with the advantage in Ohio to the home-state Chase, who opposed the amendment. In the end Ohio's Republicans rejected the amendment, nine to six. Corwin and Sherman enlisted only four other colleagues, each of whom like Corwin represented a central or southern part of the state.[15]

The situation in New York State, in many ways comparable to Ohio, was even more complicated. The Yorker region—New York City and the Hudson Valley—coexisted uneasily with the upstate Yankee heartland along the Erie Canal, to which New England emigrants had swarmed during the earlier part of the century. Differing cultural outlooks and economic priorities separated Yorker from Yankee. Ideological antislavery had deep roots in Yankee New York, especially in the Burned-Over District amid the Finger Lakes, where the fires of reform enthusiasm often blazed.[16] Upstate New York was a key Republican hearth, and its representatives had reason to heed their strong-willed constituents. Nevertheless, the amendment's architect was William H. Seward from Auburn, long the eloquent voice of his adopted home region. Seward was assisted by his right-hand man, Albany editor Thurlow Weed, and by Buffalo congressman Elbridge G. Spaulding, both of whom did their best to win support for the amendment in the New York delegation. The result, to make a long story short, was a better showing for Seward than might otherwise have been expected even though the amendment failed decisively among New York Republicans, sixteen to nine. The proamendment push in New York produced several unlikely converts. Home-state allegiance, vis-à-vis the Seward-Chase tussle, also played a role. On balance, the upstate region's New England orientation ultimately decided the matter, but Seward and his friends extracted just enough New York support to secure the amendment's ever-so-narrow overall victory.

The vote on February 28 should be compared with the prior day's vote. Fewer than twenty-four hours after the amendment's apparent defeat, its promoters managed to get twelve Republicans to vote differently—either by switching their vote, by absenting themselves after first having voted against the amendment, or by voting for it on February 28 after not voting the day before. These twelve Republicans who changed their votes are of particular interest. Be warned once again: few of the individuals mentioned in the next several paragraphs were known outside their districts and none are remembered today. But sometimes the study of history requires detective work, and the reader must patiently sift the details.[17]

Half the Maine delegation voted differently on February 28 than it had on February 27, as two Republicans switched and one absented himself. The three involved had not been renominated and were finishing their terms in Congress; therefore, they were under less pressure to bend to the anticompromise preferences of their constituents. Freeman Morse, from the shipbuilding city of Bath, had served two terms in Congress. A person of some stature, he headed the House Naval Affairs Committee. Morse received a plum diplomatic appointment several weeks later—as U.S. consul to London. Like Morse, Ezra French, from nearby Damariscotta, also switched his vote. French, who had served a single term in Congress, was appointed second auditor of the treasury in August 1861, a post he held until his death almost two decades later. John J. Perry, from Oxford, had harshly criticized the amendment when speaking in January: "The existence in the Southern States of groundless fears, engendered by willful falsehood, is no reason for a change in the Constitution." But Perry, who edited the *Oxford Democrat* and was a well-known Democrat turned Republican, did not vote on Thursday after opposing the amendment on Wednesday.[18]

Three other Republicans who voted differently came from upstate New York—Martin Butterfield from Palmyra, east of Rochester in Wayne County; James A. Graham from Delhi in Delaware County, southwest of Albany; and George W. Palmer, who hailed from Plattsburgh far to the north. Butterfield switched; Graham voted "no" on Wednesday and then did not vote on

Thursday; Palmer did not vote on the Wednesday but voted for the amendment on Thursday. Like Freeman Morse from Maine, Palmer soon received a diplomatic appointment, as U.S. consul to Crete. Palmer had pestered Thurlow Weed all winter for an appointive office.[19] The three New Yorkers, like their three counterparts in Maine, each were at the end of their terms.

One other Republican with a changed vote landed an attractive post. Thomas C. Theaker, from Bridgeport, Ohio, across the river from Wheeling, Virginia, had lost his attempt to win a second term in Congress. He withheld his vote on February 27 and then voted for the amendment on February 28. He received an appointment to the U.S. Patent Office's Board of Appeals and would subsequently become commissioner of the Patent Office for several years after the war.

David Kilgore, whom the amendment's managers selected to speak on February 28, switched his vote from February 27 to favor the amendment. The Kentucky-born Kilgore was a mainstream Republican with Whig and American Party antecedents. He lived in Yorktown, Indiana, northeast of Indianapolis. Of all the districts in the state, the one he represented was least likely to countenance such deviation from antislavery orthodoxy. Its residents included a substantial Quaker element, centered in Wayne County. In 1858 Kilgore barely survived a challenge for the Republican nomination from George W. Julian, who earlier held the seat as a Free Soiler and whom we already have encountered in chapter 3 because of his correspondence with abolitionists. Two years later, Kilgore stepped aside and Julian reclaimed the seat. So Kilgore was finishing his two terms in Congress and apparently decided to vote his convictions rather than his district. He would not again hold elective office.[20]

Three other House members who would remain in Congress voted differently on February 28. John Covode, from Westmoreland County, Pennsylvania, voted against the amendment on February 27 but did not vote the next day. He announced immediately after the second vote that he was paired with William Millward of Philadelphia, one of only two Republicans who had missed both votes. Officially Millward favored the amendment and Covode did not. But Covode, who presented himself as a hard-line Republican, had not paired his vote with the absent Millward on February 27. Covode, who recently had headed the well-publicized investigation of the Buchanan administration's misdeeds, had ample motive to help party leaders Corwin and Sherman. Because the influential former Anti-Mason and multiterm Pennsylvanian did not represent a strongly antislavery constituency, he was well positioned to make a strategic switch between February 27 and 28.[21]

Two others who would remain in Congress for an additional term also changed positions between the two votes. Cyrus Aldrich, who held an at-large seat from Minnesota, represented a frontier region that was less invested in North-South issues. By switching his vote from "no" to "yes" on February 28, he aligned with Minnesota's other at-large House member, William Windom, who stood on the cusp of a prominent career. John L. N. Stratton, from Mount Holly, New Jersey, represented a marginal district that went Democratic in 1862. The other two New Jersey Republicans already favored the amendment, and Stratton may simply have missed the vote on February 27. Or he may have hesitated to offend the sensibilities of Quakers in his West Jersey district.[22]

The three Maine men, the three New Yorkers, and Theaker either received patronage appointments, or voted with same-state colleagues who got something. On the face of it, there is reason to suspect that some kind of quid pro quo might have been involved. The person who was positioned to wield the requisite influence was Seward, likely working through his right-hand man, Thurlow Weed, who was in Washington the last week of February. As the incoming secretary of state, Seward could deliver diplomatic appointments. Home-state ties should have enabled Weed to talk frankly with Seward's three upstate colleagues.

If this line of speculation has merit, then a great irony is involved. Four years and one war later, in January 1865, Seward once again masterminded passage of a very different Thirteenth Amendment—the one that actually abolished slavery!—a tale now fixed in popular memory by Steven Spielberg's *Lincoln*. The 1865 amendment also faced an uphill fight to collect the requisite two-thirds House majority. But Seward and Weed put shoulder to the wheel and used some of the same practical techniques that appear to have rescued the earlier amendment in 1861.[23]

House passage of the amendment elicited reactions in the press. The *New York Tribune*, as we have seen, spurned all compromise. Its editor, Horace Greeley, made it his mission to prevent any Republican backsliding. If people in the free states stood firm and refused to appease secessionists, he predicted, the furor would cease. The Union would endure without compromise and without war. An element of personal vitriol helped to fuel the *Tribune*'s combative stance. Greeley had once been close to Seward and Weed, but he and they had fallen out. The year before, Greeley took pleasure in thwarting Seward's quest for the Republican presidential nomination; Weed returned the favor in February 1861 when he blocked Greeley's bid to succeed Seward in the Senate.[24]

Congress Acts

The *Tribune* took a sour view of the amendment. It contended that any gesture of "mistaken magnanimity," no matter how inconsequential, would have "fatal consequences" because it would appear to confess that "the North is in the wrong." Greeley breathed a sigh of relief when the amendment failed to secure the needed two-thirds vote on Wednesday, February 27. But when the House reversed itself the next day, the *Tribune* glossed over the unexpected turn of events. Its Washington correspondents did not try to explain how the 133–65 vote had been secured or why its passage generated "uproarious applause" on the House floor and in the galleries. They lamely conceded that "the proposition itself is hardly objectionable" and blandly announced that it "only asserts what has never been denied, that Congress has no power to interfere with the domestic institutions of the States." Seward supported "Mr. Corwin's programme" as a way "to win time," the *Tribune* surmised, but its Senate prospects were "very doubtful." [25]

Over the next several days, the *Tribune* tried to accommodate itself to the unpleasant new reality. Greeley would not touch the embarrassment on his editorial page, but he enlisted several reporters, led by James Shepherd Pike, to put a brave face on the situation. Pike decided the amendment involved "no surrender of principle" and no "surrender of Republican doctrine on the Slavery question." It would reassure "those in the Slave States who really apprehend mischievous consequences to their institutions from an undue growth of the Anti-Slavery sentiment in the North." The day after Lincoln accepted the amendment in his inaugural address, the *Tribune* implied that the new president had helped to orchestrate its passage; the votes were there to defeat it "if there had been any such disposition." [26]

The *New York Herald* brought a perspective quite unlike that of Greeley's *Tribune*. The *Herald* had a daily circulation of eighty thousand, the largest in the world. It offered its readers a more extensive newspaper than any other (often twelve pages rather than eight), without the one-day-per-week sabbatarian blackout conventional in the business—it published every day of the week, including Sundays. Edited by the flamboyant James Gordon Bennett, the *Herald* tended to take a Democratic slant, and it enjoyed more readership in the South than any other Northern newspaper. But during the secession winter it posted the capable, young Henry Villard in Springfield, Illinois, where he provided some of the best-informed reportage regarding the president-elect, Abraham Lincoln. [27]

The *Herald* adopted an outspokenly procompromise editorial stance in late 1860 and early 1861. It warned incessantly that the Union could be resurrected only if the Crittenden Compromise were swiftly adopted, and it

depicted the Republican Party—especially its "Greeley, Garrison, and Giddings" wing—as the chief obstacle to enacting this essential palliative. Bennett loved to challenge his crosstown rival, the *Tribune*'s Horace Greeley,
who hated all compromise; their rivalry sold newspapers. But the *Herald*
was influential: its stance appealed to Northern Democrats and Southern
Unionists, and it stoked the apparent surge of support for compromise
among merchants in the three big Northeastern cities—Philadelphia, Boston, and New York.[28]

Because Bennett was fixated by the purported merits of the Crittenden
Compromise or its watered-down version adopted by the Peace Conference,
the *Herald* never had anything good to say editorially about the proposed
constitutional amendment. It was a "fond folly to imagine that the border
States could be pacified by such puerile legislation," the *Herald* huffed. "Not
one slaveholding state will be satisfied with so paltry a sop." A "sneaking
adaptation of the Chicago platform to new music," the amendment was
designed "to humbug the South" and "to accomplish abolitionist objects,
under a plausible disguise." Unless Republicans adopted "more enlarged
views" and embraced "broad measures of conciliation," the border states
would conclude that "their just demands" were to be "slighted." The "inevitable result" would be "a blaze of secession feeling" in the Upper South that
would unite all the slave states in a separate confederacy.[29]

Even as the *Herald* editorially dismissed the amendment, however, its
news coverage followed a different tack. The *Herald* reporter at the Capitol
on February 28 noted that the House vote "produced tremendous applause
on the floor and in the galleries" and inspired hope for "a final and satisfac-
tory adjustment." The amendment's supporters were "in high spirits now"
because they saw the vote as a rebuke to the "abolition element" of the Republican Party and an indication that Lincoln intended to reach across party
lines. By approving the amendment, the House showed "what direction the
wind blows in administration circles."[30]

At 10:30 P.M. that same evening, a demonstrative crowd, supported by
the marine band, gathered at Willard's Hotel, on the corner of Pennsylvania
Avenue and Fourteenth Street, to call out Lincoln. The band played "Hail to
the Chief," to which the president-elect responded graciously by promising
to overcome all current "misunderstanding." He looked forward to convincing Southerners "that we regard you as in all things being our equals—in all
things entitled to the same respect and to the same treatment that we claim
for ourselves—[cries of "Good," and applause]—that we are in no wise disposed, if it were in our power, to oppress you or deprive you of any of your

rights under the Constitution of the United States, or even narrowly to split hairs with you in regard to these rights [long and prolonged cheering], but are determined to give you, so far as lies in our hands, all your rights under the Constitution, not grudgingly, but fully and fairly. [cries of "Good" and applause.]"[31]

The crowd then proceeded to Tom Corwin's residence, on G Street between Fourteenth and Fifteenth Streets. Here the band struck up "the favorite, patriotic air of 'Hail Columbia,'" to which Corwin responded amid "vociferous cheering." He emphasized that the House vote assured each state that it could "mold its own domestic institutions according to its own ideas of policy and propriety," and he predicted that "the developments of to-day, accompanied by such as we shall be happy to see in the course of a few weeks," should dispel much current misapprehension. He assured his listeners that Lincoln intended to uphold "the Constitution and the institutions of this country," and he urged that the new president and his ideas receive "a liberal and fair consideration."[32]

The "immense throng" then headed to Seward's home, on F Street between Thirteenth and Fourteenth Streets. But he was still attending a dinner party. So they "took up the line of march" to the quarters of Hannibal Hamlin, on Pennsylvania Avenue near Third Street. Amid "loud and prolonged cheering," the incoming vice president expressed confidence that North and South soon would "understand each other better" and that Republicans had no desire to "encroach upon the rights of their neighbors." The applause at this point, the *Herald* reported, "was so enthusiastic and continuous that that it was some time before Mr. Hamlin was enabled to resume."[33]

By giving priority to the constitutional amendment, Corwin effectively abandoned the other parts of the Committee of Thirty Three's proposals. The next day the House voted on the much-discussed issue of New Mexico statehood. That measure needed only a majority vote, but it failed ignominiously, 71–115. Charles Francis Adams noted in his diary that Kentucky senator John J. Crittenden wanted to derail the New Mexico bill because it would have the effect of creating an additional free state. Others shared this view. The *St. Louis Democrat* had a New Mexico correspondent who reported that the territory "would slough off her infamous slave code at an early day and enter the Union a free state." Slavery in New Mexico was "a very stunted exotic" confined to a few "federal officeholders." The region had "no actual slave interest." Corwin, Adams, and a sprinkling of other conciliatory Republicans voted for New Mexico statehood, as did many of the

Southern Opposition, but Republicans broke heavily against the bill after finding that it, unlike the constitutional amendment, would not command solid support from Southerners who remained in Congress.[34]

The House then turned to the often-charged issue of revising the Fugitive Slave Act. The Committee of Thirty Three proposed to relieve bystanders from having to assist in capturing fugitives and to accord alleged fugitives a jury trial. But the jury trial segment was unpalatable to many Republicans because it specified that the trial would take place in the state from which the alleged fugitive fled, a jurisdiction where he or she had no right to testify in court. Seward and his Republican colleagues on the Committee of Thirteen had rejected just such a stipulation in December. Many House Republicans had no interest in making less offensive a law they considered inherently offensive, and many Southerners disliked taking any steps to appease Northern antislavery sentiment. Nevertheless, the committee proposal to revise the law did pass narrowly, 92–83. It attracted a crazy-quilt pattern of support that cut across party and sectional lines. But the fugitive slave issue was not the rock on which the Union was about to split, and the House's action never was taken up in the Senate. The House then rejected decisively, 47–126, a proposal to strengthen the power of governors to demand rendition of fugitives from justice who fled from one state to another. Few Republicans supported this measure.[35]

The constitutional amendment, as passed by the House, thus became the most tangible reassurance that conciliatory Republicans extended to Southern Unionists. The Republican Party would not touch the watered-down version of the Crittenden Compromise encompassed in the Peace Conference agreement. And insiders knew by this point that Seward's and Weed's Southerner-in-the-cabinet possibility had evaporated—North Carolina's John A. Gilmer, unable to obtain assurances that Lincoln would follow a peace policy and fearful that hard-liners would dominate the cabinet, decided that he could not accept the offer that would have made him secretary of the navy.[36]

But the amendment had only cleared an initial hurdle. Before it could go to the states, it needed a two-thirds majority in the Senate, with time fast running out. So a high-stakes drama played out in the Senate during the weekend before Monday's scheduled presidential inauguration. As we have previewed in the Prologue, the Senate wrangled over the House-passed amendment—the "bread pill"—from midmorning on Saturday, March 2, until shortly before dawn on Monday, March 4. After a long, all-day session on Saturday, the Senate adjourned at 1:00 A.M. on Sunday. It then reconvened at 7:00 P.M. for a most unusual Sunday evening session, and it sat continuously until 7:00 A.M. on Monday.[37]

A reporter for *Harper's Weekly*, who patiently listened to the two marathon sessions, penned a lively account of the Senate's struggles over the amendment. He noted that its chances appeared poor because a majority of Republicans thought that it "smacked of compromise." At the same time, secession-leaning Democrats from the Upper South feared that it would "strengthen the Union sentiment in their States" though they dared not vote against it. The unlikely duo of Charles Sumner and Virginia's James Murray Mason collaborated to drag it down by "proposing a multiplicity of amendments, and consuming time by debate and divisions by ayes and noes." Sumner, who had taken years to recover from the terrible beating inflicted on him by Preston Brooks in May 1856, was the most vehemently anti-Southern and anticompromise member of the Senate. The "haughty" Mason was "embittered by his Secessionist tendencies, which are not shared by the people of his State. He sees himself toppling over from the height of political power to insignificant obscurity. He dies hard."[38]

"Against this combination of Republicans and secessionists," the *Harper's Weekly* reporter continued, "stood Senator Stephen A. Douglas, of Illinois." He "entered the lists on Saturday morning with the air of a man who is going to fight in earnest. And even in such bodies as the United States Senate pluck is apt to tell." Douglas found himself in the odd position of championing a measure that had originated among conciliatory Republicans and that failed to address the ostensible core issue fueling North-South controversy—slavery in the territories. And by reaching out to Republicans as he did here, Douglas also scuttled an accusation that had been one of the staples in his partisan arsenal. Especially when debating Lincoln in their celebrated 1858 Senate contest, he had been adamant that Republicans were dangerous abolitionists in disguise. But Douglas set aside old partisan posturing because he feared war, and he much preferred getting something that might save the peace rather than nothing at all. To get something, however, he had to run a gauntlet of hair-raising obstacles.

Conciliatory Republicans designated one of their number to defend the amendment—Edward Baker of Oregon, who had just taken his Senate seat in December. A British-born immigrant and a celebrated orator, Baker had already made his mark in Illinois, where he became close friends with Lincoln. Both were ardent Whigs, both were elected to the U.S. House—and

Lincoln named his second son Edward Baker Lincoln. So it hardly is far-fetched to suspect that when Baker spoke on March 2 and 3, he voiced sentiments that Lincoln shared. The amendment alone would not resolve the crisis facing the country, Baker observed, but it was "one step towards it." Its passage would not reward traitors or bend to threats. Instead it would "sustain good Union men" in states that had already rejected secession— Virginia, North Carolina, Tennessee, and Kentucky. It was an "olive branch" that would give "the Union-loving men of the South something to strengthen them against the men that hate the Union." The amendment would also enable Republicans to answer the "untrue and unfounded" accusations "so often made, and so powerfully made, that we really do, in our secret hearts, intend to interfere with slavery in the States." Republicans would "make a great mistake" if they did not vote for the amendment.[39]

Baker challenged his Republican colleagues to recognize what they were up against. "I am very sure there is no right of secession," he observed, "but I am equally sure there is the fact of secession." The rebels had seized forts, written a constitution, organized a government, selected a president, "and, whether right or wrong, they have an ardent and determined population to support them." But the amendment would put secessionists in the wrong by showing that their core complaint was groundless. If war nevertheless started—"God forbid!"—supporters of the Union would need the largest possible coalition. "You cannot coerce fifteen States," Baker reasoned, but it might be possible to coerce seven. Should the Gulf States continue to resist federal authority, he wanted "ten, twenty, or thirty thousand" Tennessee riflemen on his side, not shooting at him.[40] Baker was all too prescient—just months later he became one of the war's first prominent battlefield casualties, gunned down by Confederate soldiers from Mississippi and Virginia at the Ball's Bluff debacle in October 1861.

Douglas refused to wither during the all-night session that dragged from Sunday evening into Monday morning. Alert and relentless, he turned aside calls for a recess, properly fearful that delay would prove fatal to the amendment. The *Harper's Weekly* reporter, who sat observing through the night, gained a high estimate of the Illinois senator's stamina and ability: "Not a sign of impatience escaped him even during the most wearisome of the long speeches which consumed the precious hours of the waning session. But the instant the floor was vacant he pressed his point. To personal attacks, and they were many, his sole reply was—Let us vote."[41] Many senators slept at their desks or on sofas, while those still awake looked "jaded," but Douglas persisted "with bull dog tenacity." The Little Giant used his last reserves. He would be dead even before Baker, not on the battlefield but in reality just as much a victim of the war he tried so earnestly to prevent.

The hours dragged on. Finally, around 5:00 A.M. on Monday, only seven hours before inauguration ceremonies were to begin, supporters of the amendment buried a hard-line Republican declaration that the Constitution required no change or improvement—that it should be "obeyed rather than amended." This went down twenty-five to thirteen. But the fate of the amendment remained uncertain. Two additional test votes suggested that supporters of the amendment would fall slightly short of the two-thirds majority required because a baker's dozen of Republicans stood ready to vote against it.[42]

Finally, just before 5:20 A.M., the showdown moment arrived. The amendment passed twenty-four to twelve, exactly two-thirds. All twelve votes opposed were cast by Republicans. But eight crucial votes in favor also came from Republicans. In addition to Baker, the amendment's Republican supporters included both Iowa senators, James W. Grimes and James Harlan, and both Connecticut senators, James Dixon and Lafayette S. Foster. The other three were Henry B. Anthony of Rhode Island, New Jersey's John C. Ten Eyck, and Lot M. Morrill of Maine. Six of the Senate's twenty-six Republicans failed to vote, evidence in part that the final tally took place at an outrageous hour. But it was conspicuous that William Pitt Fessenden of Maine, who voted with the majority of the party in several test votes only minutes before and who plainly was present on the Senate floor, did not vote one way or the other.[43]

The actions of the two Maine senators are of particular interest. Morrill, whose tenure as governor ended in early January, had been appointed later that month by his successor, Israel Washburn, to the Senate seat vacated by Hannibal Hamlin, the incoming vice president. Shortly before the decisive vote took place, Morrill spoke out against the "bread pill." It would, he complained, subvert the Constitution and change its "whole spirit." Those who had "industriously misrepresented" Republicans should "tell the South precisely the truth"—that "no party in the North entertains any purpose of a crusade against slavery in the slave States." The amendment was "not necessary," Morrill insisted, and "of course I shall vote against it."[44] Just a few hours later, however, he reversed himself and enabled the amendment to pass. Something beyond what met the eye was motivating the Maine delegation.

Fessenden's stance almost certainly must be understood in the context

The Abortive Launch

William Pitt Fessenden. "Mr. Senator Fessenden is exceedingly anxious that Hon. Freeman H. Morse shall be consul to London."—Abraham Lincoln. Memorandum in the Lincoln Papers, ca. Mar. 15, 1861, in *The Collected Words of Abraham Lincoln*, 4:284. Library of Congress, Prints and Photographs Division, Brady-Handy Photograph Collection, LC-DIG-cwpbh-02087.

of his drive to secure a significant appointive office for his friend Freeman Morse, whose House term was ending. A client of Fessenden's in the hierarchy of the Maine Republican Party, Morse aspired to win either the patronage-rich position of collector of customs for the port of Portland or else a diplomatic post. At stake for Fessenden was the need to "confirm his own political influence to Republicans in Maine."[45] Seward told him confidentially that he could have for himself any position abroad that he desired, but Fessenden preferred the Senate. So he threw his substantial influence behind Morse's bid to become the American consul in London. Fessenden assured Lincoln that the appointment would be "highly regarded and approved by the people of Maine." Aware that Fessenden was "exceedingly anxious" that Morse go to London, Lincoln complied.[46]

Could Morrill's vote and Fessenden's strategic nonvote have been connected to the switched votes by the three Maine Republicans in the House on February 28? The circumstantial evidence is formidable. Fessenden knew that Seward and Lincoln wanted the amendment to pass. On the merits, he plainly disagreed. He privately deplored Seward's efforts to defuse the crisis and valued his own reputation as "the most determined adversary of compromise in the ranks of the Republican party."[47] But in the end, what apparently most mattered for Fessenden was the chance to reward a loyal lieutenant and to demonstrate that he had an inside track with the new Republican administration. He may well have calculated—correctly, it would appear—that his nonvote could be hidden amid the excitement of inauguration day. Certainly either Morrill or Fessenden could have tipped the balance the other way in the Senate just as their Maine colleagues could have done in the House. Without the key votes from Maine, the amendment would have been defeated.

New York's William H. Seward, who initially drafted the amendment in December, appeared in the Senate the evening of March 3 but did not remain during the early hours of March 4. He faced an impossible dilemma as he tried to satisfy antisecession Southerners *and* mainstream Republicans. He had rejected the Crittenden Compromise and then he again disappointed his Southern friends by voting to set aside the Peace Conference package, a toned-down version of Crittenden's plan. Instead, as historian Russell McClintock has noted, Seward and the hard-line Illinois Republican Lyman Trumbull teamed up to call for a national constitutional convention. By stating that a national convention would be preferable to the Peace Conference plan, Seward attempted to smooth over the festering divisions within the Republican Party, even at the price of absorbing many harsh words from Virginia. He was in the midst of an intense effort to persuade Lincoln to write a more conciliatory inaugural address, and he did not wish to become a lightning rod for any more intraparty recrimination. He was also eager to provide cover for Lincoln, who had quietly agreed to assist Corwin and the amendment's promoters. But I think that McClintock reads the situation too much at face value in saying that Seward's support for a national convention meant that he had become indifferent to the constitutional amendment. I would suggest instead that Seward's seeming disappearance from the stage reflected the extreme sensitivity of his situation, caught in a tense standoff between conciliatory and hard-line Republicans as both jousted for Lincoln's favor. Seward continued to see the amendment as a useful palliative just as when he first drafted it. His motives were different than Fessenden's, but the effects of their nonvotes were identical. So long as only twelve Republicans voted against the amendment, it could squeeze through.[48]

Other pieces of circumstantial evidence suggest that Seward remained committed to the amendment. We have surveyed the intriguing patterns of last-minute vote changes and subsequent diplomatic appointments. We also should consider the unusual alliance across party lines that brought Seward and Douglas together in early March. As McClintock has shown better than anyone else, both were determined to try to prevent a military confrontation with the seceded states, and both hoped to strengthen pro-Union sentiment in the Upper South. Seward left the hard legislative work on the amendment to Douglas, who relished such a challenge. The Little Giant kept mentioning throughout the memorable all-night session on March 3–4 that the amendment was the only game left in town, and Seward surely agreed. At one point Douglas asserted directly that he had Seward's support—during the lead-up to the final vote one Democrat declared that he could not participate because he was paired with Seward, but Douglas firmly interjected to set him straight: "He is with you on this question."[49]

The acrimony generated by the struggle to shape Lincoln's cabinet and the dilemma of dealing with the seceded states shattered the solid front of five Republicans who had supported the amendment when it first emerged from the Committee of Thirteen in late December. Only one of the five— James Grimes from Iowa—voted for the amendment in March. As we just have noticed, Seward was conspicuously absent from the overnight proceedings, and so, less conspicuously, was Vermont's Jacob Collamer. Both absences should be seen, however, through the same lens—helpful to the proamendment forces because they deprived Republicans of two votes at a time when a majority of party members on the floor voted against the amendment. The other two Republicans on the Committee of Thirteen— James Doolittle of Wisconsin and Ohio's Ben Wade—voted against the amendment. Their reversals suggest that a "yes" vote had become harder for Republicans who represented New England exodus states where people read the weekly *New York Tribune*.

Douglas taunted Wade for his inconsistency—Wade and his Republican colleagues should vote for the "bread pill," as they had in December, he contended, to show that "the danger was imaginary." If they refused to do so, Douglas warned, they would show that the danger was real. Wade lamely explained that the proposed amendment had been "sprung" on him by his Republican colleagues in December, that he "had nothing to do with getting it up," and that he soon realized after a "moment's reflection" that he should not have voted for it. Had Wade, Douglas wondered, been "acting in bad faith" and "trying to cheat the committee"? Wade was reduced to saying that the Constitution had "no defect in it," so there was no need to amend it. He likewise opposed giving "bread pills" to patients who willfully pretended to be afflicted by nonexistent diseases.[50]

Lincoln undoubtedly worked behind the scenes to get the amendment passed. For years, and most especially during his 1858 Senate campaign with Douglas, he denied that he was an abolitionist; he "would not interfere with slavery where it existed." He reiterated that point during the secession crisis. According to Henry Villard, a top reporter for the *New York Herald*, Lincoln promised one visiting Southerner in December 1860 that "slave property would be as secure from encroachments" once he became president "as it had been under Mr. Buchanan." He repeated that vow in February—he would "protect slavery in the States where it exists."[51]

Ready to accept constitutional language that was consistent with his reassurances, Lincoln reached a meeting of the minds with Corwin on Sunday evening, February 24.[52] On Wednesday evening, February 27, when the fate of the amendment hung in the balance after it had failed to get the requisite margin in the House just hours earlier, Lincoln met with five Southern Union delegates from the just-completed Peace Conference. He continued to reject the modified territorial compromise the Peace Conference had narrowly approved that morning, but he did indicate to his visitors, as they sat in a semicircle, the lanky Lincoln with "his elbows upon his knees," that he was "willing to give a constitutional guarantee that slavery should not be molested in any way directly or indirectly in the States."[53] James E. Harvey, the well-informed insider who wrote for several newspapers, reported on March 3 that it was "well known that Mr. Lincoln advised his Republican friends in the Senate" to vote for the constitutional amendment. And young Henry Adams, who closely observed the situation in Congress in early 1861, recalled shortly afterward that the amendment survived because of "some careful manipulation, as well as the direct influence of the new President."[54]

Perhaps the strongest evidence that Lincoln wanted the amendment involves the seemingly unrelated matter just discussed—the votes of Maine's House and Senate members. His soon-to-be vice president, Hannibal Hamlin, had vacated his Senate seat in mid-January to avoid taking any stance that "might be interpreted as foreshadowing the policy of Mr. Lincoln."[55] Would five of Maine's eight representatives and senators have voted the way they did on such a significant matter as the constitutional amendment without some quiet say-so from Hamlin?—and would Hamlin have done this without Lincoln's approval? Neither strikes me as possible. Hamlin was especially well positioned to influence the vote of Lot Morrill, his successor in the Senate; both came from the Democratic wing of Maine's Republican Party. So did House member John J. Perry, a "lifelong friend" of Hamlin's."[56] Another straw in the wind, as we have seen, was the boisterous crowd, accompanied by the marine band, that serenaded Lincoln, Corwin, and Hamlin on the evening of February 28 just after the amendment passed the House. For the crowd to have visited Hamlin and cheered him in such lusty fashion, its leaders must have considered him one of the amendment's friends.[57]

No lively crowds or brass bands heralded the Senate's eleventh-hour action on the amendment. Crowds and bands would indeed assemble in Washington that day, but they were there for the inauguration. And this was an inauguration like no other. Seven states had already declared their independence and organized a separate government rather than tolerate the first president ever elected without support from any slave state. The amendment would not be the main story featured in the newspapers on March 4 or March 5. The Senate's action came far too late to make the Monday papers, and so much else happened on Monday that the story of the amendment's passage would struggle for a mention on Tuesday. If you wanted to conceal evidence that anything had happened, you could not have chosen a better moment than 5:20 A.M. on March 4.

11

The President Speaks

Smoke smoldered amid the charred ruins of Richmond as the tall visitor wearing a distinctive stovepipe hat stepped from his boat at the waterfront. Newly freed slaves recognized him first—and they flocked to thank him for their liberation. The encounter was both fitting and miraculous. It was Tuesday, April 4, 1865. Abraham Lincoln had been staying at Union head-quarters, downriver at City Point, awaiting a military breakthrough. He rushed to the fallen city to see whether a Confederate surrender might be within reach. Both that day and the next, he conferred with several promi-nent Southerners.

But nobody with official status remained in Richmond to meet with Lin-coln. The Confederate government had evacuated the capital of its crum-bling nation on Sunday night, April 2, with orders that soldiers set fire to bridges, warehouses, and the armory. The logic was to impede the advance of the Union army and to deny it useful supplies. The fires, however, blazed out of control and consumed much of the city's commercial center. The massive Gallego Flour Mills, among the world's largest, were consumed. Not until the next day, Monday, April 3, when Union soldiers arrived, were the fires brought under control. Thomas Jefferson's state capitol building, designed to resemble a Roman temple, survived the inferno because it was screened from the city by a pleasant wooded hillside that remains today. But the view from the capitol's front portico was one of desolation.[1]

As Lincoln tried to end the enormous convulsion that had dominated his presidency, he reflected back on the situation four years before when he first took office. In hopes of "arresting the secession movement" and avoid-ing war, he explained to one of his visitors, he passed word to "his friends in Congress" on the "last night of the session" in early March 1861, just before his inauguration, that they should pass the resolution "proposing an amend-ment to the Constitution prohibiting Congress from any interference with the institution of slavery in the slaveholding states."[2]

At first glance, the source for this alleged recollection seems improbable.

Duff Green, the aging Jacksonian turned Calhounite, had a political pedigree almost antithetical to Lincoln's. Green's enthusiasm for territorial expansion might also have distanced him from Lincoln. And the Civil War placed them on opposite sides—the Kentucky-born Green was a Georgia railroad builder when the Union disintegrated. But the two had become acquainted in the late 1840s at the Washington boardinghouse run by Ann Sprigg, and Green was connected by marriage to Lincoln. In 1849, Lincoln had asked Green to help him win an appointive office from Zachary Taylor. A decade later in December 1860, as noted in chapter 5, Green's tie to Lincoln remained well-enough known to insiders that James Buchanan dispatched him to Springfield to try to persuade Lincoln to support the Crittenden Compromise.[3]

Green and Lincoln next met in Richmond on April 5, 1865, during Lincoln's visit to the just-surrendered Confederate capital. Green sought the interview, and the evidence suggests that Lincoln welcomed the opportunity to talk with a Southern elder and an old friend. Although the prospect of Confederate defeat and emancipation apparently distressed Green, he recalled one year later that Lincoln received him "with great kindness." During this conversation, Lincoln reminded Green that in 1861 he had supported the constitutional amendment forbidding interference with slavery and had done his best to avert war.[4]

Green's version of his talk with Lincoln garbled some points of detail— Green thought the amendment had unanimously passed both houses of Congress on March 3, whereas it had barely squeezed through the House on February 28 and the Senate on March 4.[5] But Green's report of the conversation appears authentic. As we have seen, the Senate certainly did pass a prospective thirteenth amendment at the very last moment, just hours before Lincoln's inauguration, and the House had done likewise a few days earlier. We also have surveyed the evidence that suggests Lincoln was active behind the scenes in promoting the amendment during the week before the inauguration.

Any question about Lincoln's position on the amendment was resolved when he delivered his inaugural address. Standing at the east front of the Capitol shortly after 1:30 P.M. on March 4, 1861, a windy but "gloriously bright" early spring day, he pointedly denied that he or the Republican Party intended to "interfere with the institution of slavery in the States where it exists." He had neither the "lawful right" nor the "inclination" to do so. Lincoln then noted that Congress had just passed a constitutional amendment to address the matter. Because he considered "such a provision to now be implied constitutional law," he had "no objection to its being made express, and irre-

The President Speaks

vocable." In short, the man who would later be known as the Great Emancipator first came to power having just accepted a constitutional amendment
designed to prevent any attack on slavery in the states where it existed.[6]

Two members of the audience listened with special interest to Lincoln's
words. Stephen A. Douglas had just forfeited a night's sleep, but he summoned the energy to "make his association with the new President as conspicuous as possible," historian Roy Franklin Nichols wrote. Douglas "crowded
hard upon Lincoln's heels" as they walked from the Capitol building to the
wooden platform erected over the steps of the East Portico, stood close to the
new president as he spoke, and at several points seconded the conciliatory
parts of the message "*sotto voce*"—"Good!" "That's so." "*No coercion!*" Douglas
knew that peace hung by a thread; he was more than willing to set aside a
quarter century of partisan rivalry to move Lincoln away from a military confrontation with the nascent Confederacy.[7] Charles Francis Adams also stood
amid the outdoor throng listening to Lincoln. When the new president gave
the amendment his explicit imprimatur, the usually modest Adams basked in
the moment—"Of all people I had the greatest occasion to be gratified, as the
amendment . . . which goes by my name has thus been fully justified." Douglas
considered the danger of civil war grave and imminent—in retrospect, of
course, we know that the hardheaded Little Giant understood the ghastly
situation perfectly—but Adams persuaded himself that calamity already had
been averted. Feeling "serene and clear and confident," the Massachusetts
diarist dared to hope that "the crisis of the slave question" would soon pass
off with no more "confusion and disorder." He doubted that he ever again
would have a comparable opportunity "to benefit my country."[8]

Lincoln's inaugural address walked a fine line. On the one hand, he rejected secession as invalid. He regarded the Union as both "perpetual" and
"unbroken," and he interpreted his oath to mean that he was president of
all thirty-four states. On the other hand, the inaugural promised to seek "a
peaceful solution of the national troubles." He urged "calm thought and reflection" and implored disaffected Southerners to reconsider their course.
"We are not enemies, but friends," his memorable peroration concluded.
"We must not be enemies." Some evidence suggests that Lincoln understood
long before March 4 that the outrageous action of the Deep South states
had set in motion a dilemma that was bound to lead to an armed collision,
but I agree with historian Michael Burlingame, who makes a compelling
case that Lincoln, immediately after the inauguration, "could breathe a sigh
of relief and look forward to a peaceable solution to the secession crisis."[9]
He had reason to think that he had gone the extra mile to extend an olive

branch to white Southerners, even at the risk of alienating more radical Republicans. In addition to endorsing the constitutional amendment, his inaugural address insisted that he would heed the fugitive slave clause of the Constitution. By so doing, he demonstrated that he had no agenda, overt or covert, to menace slavery in the states. One additional circumstance also suggests that the new president hardly expected to fight secessionists in the foreseeable future—he had just appointed Simon Cameron as secretary of war even though many regarded the Pennsylvanian as incompetent or corrupt, or both. In short, the Duff Green interview rings true: Lincoln hoped to preserve the peace rather than fight a war when he first took office. Lincoln's iconic Second Inaugural, a month before his conversation with Green, asserted the same point—his first inaugural had been "devoted altogether to *saving* the Union without war."[10]

To understand Lincoln's position, we should look at the contrasting views of those few Americans who "yearned for a conflict" against the South and slavery and who flatly refused to accept slavery in the states. Frederick Douglass, the great African American abolitionist, condemned Lincoln's promise to maintain slavery where it existed. Douglass had long faulted the Republican Party for its refusal to interfere with slavery. The inaugural address fulfilled Douglass's "worst fears." It was "wholly discreditable" and evidence of "cowardly baseness," he wrote, for Lincoln to take office by "prostrating himself" before the "slave-holding oligarchy." Douglass "wanted the old Union destroyed," writes his biographer David Blight. Throughout the secession winter, he flayed the conciliators for proposing to accommodate "tyrants and traitors." Disunion "might mean war and untold suffering," Douglass recognized, but he "dreamed of witnessing the power of the federal government mobilized to crush slavery." A declaration of war against "slavery and slaveholders" could bring about a new Union that would bring equal citizenship to all.[11]

What we see here, in chrysalis, is the way growing majorities of Americans at the start of the twenty-first century now understand what happened 150 years ago. Since the Civil Rights Movement of the 1960s, an "emancipationist memory of the war" has gained ground and largely supplanted a "reconciliationist vision" that obscured what the war had been about in the first place. The conventional wisdom of the early twentieth century—a hundred years ago—erased slavery as a cause of the war, validated the white South's Lost Cause mythology, and tacitly accepted that black Americans must remain a people apart unable to share the opportunities that other Americans took for granted. But the ongoing quest for racial justice in America in the past half century has rekindled an understanding of Civil War–era history that sees the situation as Douglass did.[12]

Once the war began in earnest, it followed the trajectory that Frederick Douglass anticipated. He could see ahead better than his contemporaries. He therefore deserves stature as an American prophet who understood the events of his own lifetime in ways that make sense to Americans today. But our new sensibilities, which give deserved priority to emancipation and racial justice, do not provide a good guide for understanding the political situation in the winter before the war began, when Northern moderates struggled to maintain the peace and conciliate the disaffected white South. Racial justice and emancipation were not part of the mainstream agenda—or Lincoln's agenda—even though he and his fellow Republicans disliked slavery and hoped that it would eventually disappear. This book provides a reminder of the distance we have come—and the distance that we still must go.

For a short interval after Lincoln took office, it appeared that the middle might hold. On March 6, Stephen A. Douglas took the floor of the Senate to defend Lincoln's inaugural as a "peace-offering rather than a war message." He commended it as "a much more conservative document" than he had expected, and he concluded that "the Administration stands pledged by the inaugural to a peaceful solution of all our difficulties." Two pro-Union congressmen from East Tennessee, T. A. R. Nelson and Horace Maynard, reached a similar conclusion after meeting privately with Lincoln the evening of March 7. They asked Lincoln "how his inaugural was to be understood," whereupon Lincoln assured them *"that it meant peace"* and promised to do all that he could to "avoid a collision." One of the congressmen professed to be "quite satisfied with the assurances of the President."[13]

The constitutional amendment played a prominent part in the thinking of those who anticipated a peaceful resolution of the crisis. The *Springfield Republican* editorialized on March 5 that the amendment was "a solemn re-assurance on a point vital to the South." Even though it was beyond dispute that "the federal government has no right or authority to interfere with slavery in the states," many Southerners feared otherwise. This leading proponent of a conciliatory Republican viewpoint contended that the amendment, in tandem with the inaugural address, would strengthen the reaction in the South "in favor of the Union." Douglas, who was convinced that the Union could not be preserved by war or "cemented by blood," heralded Lincoln's willingness to accept the amendment just approved by Congress. By so doing, Lincoln had "sunk the partisan in the patriot." Douglas disavowed "any political sympathy" with the Lincoln administration." He rejected its stance on several "great principles." But on the core matter of finding a peaceful resolution to the crisis and "preventing any future difficulties" by amending the Constitution, Douglas was ready to clasp hands with Lincoln—"I am with him."[14]

To be sure, Douglas and most Upper South Unionists would have welcomed a territorial compromise, either Crittenden's or the Peace Conference plan. They had to fend off those such as Virginia senator James Murray Mason, who scornfully charged that Republicans were as committed as ever to barring slavery from the territories and that Lincoln had not compromised any previous Republican position by accepting the constitutional amendment. But Tennessee's T. A. R. Nelson saw the situation differently. By establishing three western territories (Colorado, Dakota, and Nevada) without restrictions on slavery and assembling two-thirds majorities in favor of the amendment, Congress had removed "the only real ground of apprehension in the slave States." So likewise, Tennessee's Andrew Johnson announced that passage of the three territorial bills and the constitutional amendment enabled him "to go before the people of the South and defy disunion." North Carolina's John A. Gilmer thought that Congress had helped to restore a "plain common sense view of things" by enacting "a perpetual guaranty against Congressional interference with Slavery in the States" and the "territorial organization without the Wilmot Proviso." With such tangible evidence of Northern conservatism, he asked, "what more does any reasonable Southern man expect or desire?"[15]

The framers of the constitutional amendment hoped to counter the hysteria in the white South and to contain, and ultimately reverse, the secession movement. That project necessarily would take time, certainly many months, more likely years. In the interim, however, the seven-state Confederacy's assertion of sovereignty raised difficult questions that had the potential to come to a violent head far sooner. One location in particular had threatened for more than two months to trigger armed conflict. As we have already noticed, a small contingent of U.S. soldiers under the command of Major Robert Anderson occupied Fort Sumter, located on an artificial island a mile offshore at the mouth of Charleston harbor. With every other military installation in the harbor under Confederate control, secessionists worked systematically during January and February to build up artillery reinforcements that menaced Sumter. The *Star of the West*'s failed resupply mission in early January left the fort ever more vulnerable; its food supplies were dwindling, and it had not received additional arms.

The Sumter dilemma landed in Lincoln's lap the moment he took office.

The President Speaks

Anderson reported that he had only six weeks of provisions to feed his men, and the general-in-chief of the U.S. Army, Winfield Scott, calculated that twenty-five thousand troops and a naval fleet would be needed to hold the fort. Scott's advice pointed toward abandoning the outpost because nothing resembling the necessary force could be gathered on such short notice. But Lincoln's inaugural had promised to "hold, occupy, and possess the property, and places belonging to the government," and he well knew that Sumter had become a powerful symbol of Northern commitment to hold the Union together. The last thing the new president wanted was to begin his term by giving up Sumter. But he also wanted to keep the peace. Sumter had the potential to ignite an armed conflict—and if shooting started there, the Confederates were all but certain to crush the small Union force.[16]

In defending Lincoln's peaceful intentions, Douglas tiptoed around Sumter, the greatest immediate threat to peace. Taking advantage of inside information apparently leaked to him by Seward, Douglas breezily revealed that Anderson's forces were low on food and that "all military men" considered the outpost impossible to reinforce. The Illinois senator asserted that the logic of Lincoln's inaugural "pledged" him to "abandon the fort and withdraw the troops" if that "should be necessary to a peaceful solution of the national troubles." He and Seward set the stage for a prompt decision to evacuate Sumter at a time when it might still be blamed on the outgoing Buchanan administration. They hoped to avert an armed collision and confine secession to the Lower South.[17]

Southern Unionists did their utmost to show that Sumter was too dangerous to hold. Their most candid and emphatic statement came in a series of four letters written to Seward by John A. Gilmer during the week after the inauguration. Called home at the end of the congressional session by "the extreme and dangerous illness of a member of my family," Gilmer begged Seward to "weigh well the suggestions which I make to you." His plea was based on an up-to-date assessment of the fast-changing political balance in the Upper South, where secessionist fortunes had fallen into steep decline. Disunionists had been defeated at the polls in state after state—most recently in his home state of North Carolina—and their "only hope" was to shed blood. "The seceders in the border states and throughout the South ardently desire some collision of arms," Gilmer reported. To rekindle the momentum of their stalled revolution, they would "give a kingdom for a fight."[18]

Gilmer warned that any fighting in the near future would play into the hands of secessionists and unite the South. Anxieties about federal interference with slavery had become closely tied to the supposed threat of "coercion"—that is, any use of federal force against the seceding states. So long as war remained a threat, the constitutional amendment could not have a tranquilizing effect. "The only thing now that gives the secessionists the advantage of the conservatives," Gilmer explained to Seward, as we have seen in chapter 4, "is the cry of coercion—that the whipping of a slave state is the whipping of slavery." The Union men in the Upper South would be "swept away in a torrent of madness" if a collision occurred. But if the administration relinquished Sumter and demonstrated its peaceful intentions, it would choke off the secession impulse in the Upper South.

Of course Gilmer well knew that Sumter confronted the administration with a cruel quandary. The fort was a supremely visible symbol of the federal government's unwillingness to acquiesce in secession. Giving it up would stir keen disappointment in the free states, and it would especially enrage many of Lincoln's most ardent hard-line supporters. How then did Gilmer reconcile his undoubted long-run hopes for reunion with his short-term advice against challenging the secessionists? His answer hinged on the assumption that the Deep South could not maintain its independence without the manpower and resources of the Upper South. The administration should give first priority to keeping secession confined to the Deep South, and that meant abstaining from force. Gilmer envisioned a process that might require two years to achieve results. The actual experience of "going out into the cold for a while" would create strains in the Deep South and erode the novelty of independence. At the same time, "Union Conservative men" would solidify their control in the Upper South. Eventually they would "unite cordially with the free states" to pressure the Deep South. In short, time was on the side of the Union; the Confederate enterprise would wither once it became plain that majorities of white Southerners opposed secession.

Hoping to forestall any momentum toward secession in the Virginia Convention, Seward sent word privately to the leader of Union forces there, George W. Summers—that the administration intended to remove its men from Sumter. Summers reported that the news had "acted like a charm" and given the Unionists "great strength." Without revealing his source of information, he announced to the convention that "a pacific policy has been wisely determined on at Washington, and that the troops in Fort Sumter are now or will soon be withdrawn." Seward also leaked the story to the newspapers, which featured it prominently. Eager to forestall any attack, he also made sure that Confederate authorities in Montgomery received the same news. The evidence is plain that Seward jumped the gun, confident that he could persuade the reluctant new president.[19]

The President Speaks

Seward's bold gambit temporarily quieted the crisis, but he could not redeem his promises. Only one person could do that, and Lincoln was dissatisfied with his choices. By holding Sumter, the federal government showed that it would not tolerate secession indefinitely; simply giving it up, historian Russell McClintock writes, "would signal the surrender of federal authority in the seceded states and a de facto acknowledgement of disunion." Might there yet be some way to hold Sumter? Or would trying to hold it necessarily start a war? Above all, was peace a prerequisite to restoring the Union? Seward and his Southern Unionist allies believed that peace was indeed essential to preventing secession in the Upper South and that any use of force could undermine the Union advantage there. War, they feared, would irrevocably shatter the Union. By their lights, time was on the side of the Union if war could be prevented. But Lincoln had reason to worry that time was not on the side of the Union. The Deep South's separation was becoming more permanent every day with no evidence of any disposition to reconsider. Lincoln feared that the hands-off policy favored by Seward would make the Deep South's independence irrevocable. So he was open to other ideas.[20]

In the end, of course, Lincoln decided to try to hold Sumter. He concluded that peaceful reunion was impossible, and he was ready to gamble that the Union could be forcibly reunited. He gave the Confederates fair warning that he would try to send food to the beleaguered outpost and would make no effort to send in additional weapons or ammunition if the food could be landed. But he had ample reason to suspect that the Confederates would use force to thwart the resupply mission and likely seize control of Sumter. They, however, would have to fire the first shot, and the actual decision to commence hostilities would have to be theirs, not his.[21]

The outbreak of war in April 1861 forever eclipsed the House and Senate's last-minute approval of the would-be thirteenth amendment—and Lincoln's explicit acceptance of it. During 1862 the war became an inconclusive bloodbath on a scale that nobody could previously have imagined. Many thousands of enslaved people fled their masters, sought protection from the Union army, and stood ready to fight. Growing numbers of free state residents, and undoubted majorities of Republicans, abandoned the idea that war could restore "the old Union as it was." Instead, they resolved to build a new Union without slavery. Only by eliminating the source of the war could the future be secured. So it was that the real Thirteenth Amendment enacted in 1865 absolutely reversed the original version and ended the slave system that the other thirteenth amendment of 1861 was designed to safeguard.

The Abortive Launch

12

The Ratification Fizzle

Abraham Lincoln and William H. Seward each put in grueling long days during the weeks after the inauguration. The explosive situation in the South competed for attention with a myriad of other weighty matters and time-consuming details. Crowds swarmed the corridors at the "Executive Mansion," as the White House then was called. "The throng of office-seekers is something absolutely fearful," wrote Lincoln's assistant John Hay. "They come at daybreak and still are coming at midnight."[1] The new administration also had to demonstrate to other countries that the United States remained ready to protect its national interests notwithstanding its internal problems. Nevertheless, both the president and his secretary of state took time in mid-March to countersign individual messages to the governors of all thirty-four states, including the seceded states. They thereby provided official notice that a prospective constitutional amendment had passed both houses of Congress by the requisite two-thirds majorities and that it awaited action by the states. Three of these documents have recently come to light—one to Florida, one to California, and one to North Carolina.[2]

By the time Lincoln and Seward dispatched these messages, they had many other things on their minds. As sketched in the previous chapter, one day after the Senate approved the would-be thirteenth amendment, Lincoln received word from Major Robert Anderson that the Union outpost at Fort Sumter would soon run short of food. General-in-Chief Winfield Scott then reported that the outpost no longer could be held without twenty-five thousand men supported by a naval fleet—a far larger force than could be assembled. This news fell like a thunderclap.

For the next month-plus, Sumter became the whole focus of attention. Lincoln and Seward were locked in an urgent disagreement about Southern policy. Seward tried, and ultimately failed, to persuade Lincoln that it was too dangerous to hold Sumter. Instead, Seward contended, Lincoln should cut his losses, withdraw Anderson, and thereby provide breathing room for antisecessionists in the Upper South. But Lincoln demurred. Besieged for weeks by applicants for federal jobs as he tried to address the excruciating Sumter dilemma, he finally decided that he could not relinquish the outpost. He knew, however, that Sumter almost certainly would be attacked by the seceded states. And what might happen then? If war broke out, would he lose the Upper South as Seward had warned? Trying to answer these questions might cause a migraine—and it did. As the crisis came to a head in late March, Lincoln "keeled over with a sick headache" and spent a fretful night without sleep. He later stated that "all the troubles and anxieties of his life" had not matched what he encountered in March and early April. The unexpected challenges during his first weeks in office were, Lincoln recalled, "so great that could I have anticipated them, I would not have believed it possible to have survived them."[3]

The Sumter issue shunted aside the would-be thirteenth amendment. Discussion continued to rage about conciliating the slave states that had resisted the initial secession surge, but the focus of discussion could no longer be the long-run future of slavery. Instead, the focus narrowed to the immediate short term and the sputtering fuse at Sumter. Unlike the amendment, Sumter was right here and right now. Seward waged his last-ditch fight almost singlehandedly. The amendment's two other principal Republican promoters had to turn their attention elsewhere. Lincoln tabbed both Corwin and Adams to head abroad on key diplomatic assignments—Corwin to Mexico and Adams to England (the Adams appointment was Seward's doing).

But somewhat like a chicken that continues momentarily to stagger about after being decapitated, the amendment initially showed signs of life. As the first prospective constitutional amendment to win two-thirds majorities in both houses of Congress for more than half a century, it attracted notice from both the outgoing and the incoming president—even though neither had any official role to play in the amending process. Late in the morning on his last day in office, just before the ceremonies took place to inaugurate his successor, James Buchanan signed a copy of the amendment that just had passed the Senate. And shortly afterward, as we have seen, Lincoln used his inaugural address to chime in circumspectly.

During the critical first weeks of the Lincoln administration, the amendment gained favorable notice in the Upper South. The pro-Union *Raleigh Register* asserted that it "effectually spikes the guns" of secessionists, who kept warning that Republicans would abolish slavery in border slave states that remained in the Union. The amendment, passed by a Republican Congress and approved by Lincoln in his inaugural address, showed conclusively otherwise. William G. Brownlow's *Knoxville Whig* likewise saw the amendment as a decisive answer to concerns that three-quarters of the states might in the future "alter and amend the Constitution" and empower Congress "to abolish slavery in the States." Instead, the amendment prohibited any such interference and attempted, "so far as it can be accomplished," to make the ban "perpetual." L. A. W., the Washington correspondent for the *Louisville Journal*, wrote that the amendment "will go far toward satisfying the South," while the newspaper's editor, George D. Prentice, blasted allegations that Northerners favored "abolishing slavery everywhere." Instead, by organizing three territorial governments with no restriction against slavery and by passing the amendment, Republicans had backed away from their hard-line dogmas and stood up for "peace and reconciliation." Congressman T. A. R. Nelson of East Tennessee thought that the amendment would "remove the only real ground of apprehension in the Slave States." He relished the irony—"it blows the irrepressible conflict doctrine moon-high," and it did so with "the sanction of the author of that doctrine himself," that is, Seward.[4]

By contrast, the amendment disappeared beneath the radar in the North during March. Only here and there did it become something of a political football, seized upon by Democrats. For example, the *Portland Eastern Argus*, a major Democratic newspaper, heralded the amendment for beginning "the good work of reconciliation" and urged its ratification by the Maine legislature "as soon as it shall be officially communicated." Because the amendment would indicate "a friendly spirit and purpose on the part of the free states," Union men in the slave States regarded its adoption "as of very great importance." But the *Eastern Argus* complained that Maine's Republicans were sitting on their hands, unwilling to aid "our Southern friends." They refused to "come forward like men and sustain the administration in this matter." The *Eastern Argus* appeared unaware of an exquisite irony—a majority of Maine's Republicans in Congress had surreptitiously facilitated the amendment's passage.[5]

Some members of the Kentucky legislature were so eager to endorse the amendment that they moved initially to ratify both the Adams version (which had been dropped) and the Seward version (which had been approved by Congress). Its Kentucky supporters tempered their enthusiasm by observing that the amendment did not "secure to the slave States all the rights to which they are justly entitled" and therefore could not be considered a comprehensive "adjustment of existing difficulties." But they quickly pivoted to accept the half loaf—the amendment would "remove one cause of apprehended danger" while also evincing "a disposition on the part of the people of the North to make some advances towards a reconciliation with their Southern brethren."[6]

Kentucky's state senate unanimously approved the amendment on April 1, but Southern Rights Democrats in the lower house dragged their feet and attempted initially to adjourn the special legislative session without acting on it. They received encouragement from former vice president John C. Breckinridge, who recently had replaced Crittenden in the U.S. Senate and who spoke to the legislature the next day. Arguing that the seceded states would accept nothing less than the Crittenden Compromise—including its "hereafter acquired" clause—Breckinridge dismissed lesser measures such as the amendment and urged the legislature to issue an ultimatum to Congress and the free states. The *Louisville Journal* denounced Breckinridge's stance as a thinly veiled subterfuge to remove Kentucky from the Union by insisting on terms that the North never would accept.[7]

Breckinridge's allies created a smokescreen of reasons for disdaining the amendment. They charged that Congress had no authority to ratify it because seven states were unrepresented there. They also dismissed the value of the amendment because the Republican Party had never "claimed the power to interfere with slavery in the States." But Curtis F. Burnam, a legislator from Madison County in eastern Kentucky, sharply rebutted the amendment's critics. He showed that Congress had acted legally, with far more than a quorum present. And he insisted that "wily" Southern Rights politicians had persistently "indoctrinated" the Southern people to think that Republicans threatened slavery. Burnham considered it "amazing that gentlemen should now ignore the existence of a fact which, prior to the late Presidential election, had been spread broadcast over the land." He condemned secessionists for refusing to recognize the amendment's "assurance of permanent security to slavery in the States" and for pretending instead that "no spirit of concession has ever been evinced by the North."[8]

Finally, as the legislative session ended and just before ominous reports about the possibility of fighting at Sumter began to appear in the newspapers, Southern Rights Democrats in the lower house climbed off their high horse and accepted the amendment. Kentucky thereby became the first state to ratify it.[9]

No other state ratified before war broke out, but two free states followed during the weeks to come, a period of intense war fever and preparation but little actual combat. The Ohio senate took up the amendment in mid-April just as electrifying war news swept across the land. On April 16, the senate voted twenty-one to thirteen to consider what one newspaper designated as "the Seward-Corwin amendment" but then voted eighteen to seventeen to refer it to the committee on Federal Relations. All those who wanted to delay the amendment, among them future U.S. president James Garfield, who represented Portage County in the Western Reserve, voted to send it to committee. The very next day, however, the committee on Federal Relations recommended its adoption. Once again, the amendment's opponents tried to sidetrack it, but they lost on another close vote, eighteen to seventeen. During the ensuing debate, several Republicans, among them John Q. Smith from southwestern Ohio, complained that the amendment had become futile—even if "passed by every free State, it would be received in the South with sneers." Other Republicans agreed that the amendment simply affirmed the obvious—"no one supposes Congress has the power here disclaimed"— and it would not "do any good." But in order to satisfy popular sentiment and avoid being "misconstrued," they set aside their "own feelings" and agreed to vote for ratification. "Let it not be said this war is to abolish slavery in the States," resolved George Harsh from Stark County. It was instead a war "to redress the wrongs and insults to our flag and to punish traitors." The Senate thereupon voted to ratify the amendment, twenty-seven to eight, with only the most hard-line Republicans, including Garfield, opposed. It may be suspected that Corwin still wielded influence in his home state.[10]

The Ohio house did not consider the amendment until a month later, on May 13, the last evening of its session. By that point, most Republicans opposed it. Alvin C. Voris, who represented part of northeastern Ohio's Western Reserve, and whose fine wartime letters to his wife have been published as a book, complained that "the very people whom it was intended to conciliate, are in arms against us."[11] Samuel E. Browne from southwestern Ohio explained that he had favored the amendment when it first was introduced, but he no longer could accept concessions to men "now with arms in their hands, to make war upon us." Tobias A. Plants, a lawyer, newspaper publisher, and future Republican congressman from Pomeroy, a county seat in southern Ohio, found the amendment both unnecessary and ineffectual. "All the world knows," he pointed out, that Republicans "without exception" considered slavery "a purely *local* institution, limited to the *States* which maintain it, and over which Congress has no control whatever." He also observed, however, that no "sane man" believed that the amendment would "bring back the revolted states to their allegiance." But Ohio Democrats took a different view. Newton A. Devore from southwestern Ohio thought that everyone "who had promised not to interfere with the institutions of the South" should vote for the amendment. And George W. Andrews from western Ohio announced that he was going into the army at the head of a regiment, "but it was not against slavery that *he* was going to fight." After a bruising debate, the house narrowly accepted the amendment, forty-seven to forty-two. A few persistently conciliatory Republicans voted with Democrats to create the final margin. But after the vote was cast, the amendment's opponents attempted to scuttle it on grounds that a majority of the house's members had not voted for it—some were absent as the session ended. The speaker of the house, Richard C. Parsons from Cleveland, ruled with the amendment's opponents, but his decision was reversed, forty-five to forty-two, and so the amendment was ratified.[12]

Three years later, however, on March 31, 1864, the Ohio legislature rescinded its ratification. At the beginning of the war, there was substantial if far from unanimous Northern willingness to accept that the war was being waged to restore the Union, with slavery kept intact. By the latter part of the war, however, public opinion in the free states had shifted, and Republicans with near unanimity insisted that the war must end the slave system. The passionate antislavery advocate James Ashley pronounced a telling retrospective on his state's 1861 actions. Deliberately echoing Whittier's scathing dismissal of Daniel Webster, Ashley wished that he could have "walk[ed] backward with averted gaze" to cover the "political nakedness" of his beloved Ohio, after its legislature "committed the indefensible folly of ratifying the pro-slavery amendment of the committee of thirty-three, and thus officially consented to its becoming part of our national Constitution."[13]

One other free state, Rhode Island, also gave the amendment a thumbs-up at the end of May 1861. That outcome came about after Rhode Island held a state election during the brief interval between the inauguration and the outbreak of the war. In that election, a hybrid Constitutional Union ticket that included a mixture of Douglas Democrats and Conservative Republicans challenged Rhode Island's two Republican incumbents in the U.S. House, Christopher Robinson and William D. Brayton. Both Robinson and Brayton were considered hard-liners, although Robinson, unlike Brayton, "finally gave way under the tremendous Union pressure brought to bear upon him, and voted for the Corwin amendment." Their Constitutional Union challengers, William P. Sheffield, a conservative Republican, and George H. Browne, a Douglas Democrat, positioned themselves as friends of the amendment and a conciliatory Southern policy. Browne, a former member of the Peace Conference, endorsed Lincoln's inaugural "to the marrow"—thereby distancing himself from Brayton regarding the amendment.[14]

The Abortive Launch

The two challengers were elected in early April just before the showdown at Sumter. That election set the stage for the Rhode Island legislature's ratification of the amendment. On May 31 in the state senate, it was "read and passed," apparently unanimously. That same afternoon it was taken up and approved by a convincing forty-three to eighteen margin in the lower house. Its opponents there tried but failed to postpone its consideration until the following January. Most Republican legislators apparently considered it prudent to accept the amendment. But the state's major newspapers continued to snipe at each other. The pro-Republican *Providence Daily Journal* insisted that the amendment would only have been relevant before the outbreak of military hostilities and that "a measure of so much importance" ought not now be adopted. But its Democratic rival, the *Providence Evening Press*, commended the state for having "done her duty" and warned that if other free states rejected the amendment, they would "play into the hands of the rebel leaders." Any suspicion that the war was to be fought for abolition would "convert honest Union men of the South into unwilling rebels."[15]

In Rhode Island, as in Ohio, three years of warfare generated second thoughts about the amendment. On February 8, 1864, Henry B. Anthony, U.S. senator from Rhode Island, moved to repeal its approval by Congress, just three years before. Anthony recalled that he had voted for the amendment in early 1861 to rebut "the misrepresentation of demagogues" and to "avert the evils of civil war." But those whom "it was intended to conciliate" instead rebelled under a "false pretext" to prevent a Republican administration "from doing what it solemnly avowed it had no purpose of doing." Even had the pretext been true, "there was abundant remedy by peaceful means and within the Constitution" to prevent any interference with slavery in the states. What secession triggered instead was an enormous war that "advanced public opinion to a point which it would not have attained in scores of peaceful years." No longer would it be proper to provide "new guarantees" for slavery or to reaffirm "the old ones." Instead, "the true policy now is to strike at slavery"—the "primal cause, the sustaining power of the rebellion"—and to amend the Constitution accordingly. "What the Republican Party could not do, what no election could do, what no peaceable movement would have been likely to accomplish in many years, slavery has done of itself and to itself," Anthony concluded. "It has sealed its own doom; it has made its existence incompatible with the safety of the Republic, with the continuation of the Union. It has committed suicide." The U.S. Senate soon approved a radically different Thirteenth Amendment, and the House followed suit in January 1865. Anthony knew which way the wind was blowing.[16]

The Ratification Fizzle

Indiana did not ratify the amendment because Republicans controlled the legislature in 1861–62, and those who had no use for Corwin's handiwork prevented its consideration. But the question of slavery in the states was addressed during a special legislative session in late April and May 1861. On April 30, the state senate resolved unanimously that the state's men and resources would not be used "in any aggression upon the institution of slavery or any constitutional right belonging to any of the States." A month later, however, after General Benjamin Butler had won permission to protect "contrabands" at Fortress Monroe in Virginia, Indiana's same state senate became snarled by another proposed statement. It was universally agreed that the war was being waged to "crush out rebellion," restore the Union, and maintain the Constitution. But would Indiana also explicitly disavow "any sectional, political, or anti-slavery purpose"? John F. Miller, a Republican from the South Bend district, opposed any concession designed "to appease the wrath of rebels," who falsely claimed that the war was being waged to destroy slavery. There was not "a Union man within the borders of the United States" who wanted "to abolish slavery by force of arms," Miller insisted. But George K. Steele, a Republican moderate from the west-central part of the state, disagreed with Miller and the "great majority" of his "political friends." Steele favored the resolution because it "gives the lie" to accusations that the war was being fought to destroy slavery, and it would help Union men in Kentucky who were desperately contending against the false claims made by secessionists. In the end, the resolution to forswear any "anti-slavery purpose" was tabled by the margin of a single vote, twenty-one to twenty.[17]

One last flurry of ratifications followed in early 1862. By that point much had changed. The Battle of Bull Run, on July 21, 1861, ended the phony war phase and initiated a huge buildup of military forces on both sides. In November 1861, Lincoln quietly floated a trial balloon toward Delaware, the least enslaved slave state. Might its slaveholders accept a system of gradual emancipation, with compensation? A majority of Delaware's slaveholders spurned the overture.[18] Two additional border slave states made it plain that they too preferred to hold fast to slavery when, in close succession, they ratified the constitutional amendment—Maryland, on January 10, 1862, and the so-called government of Virginia, meeting in Wheeling, on February 13, 1862.

Maryland acted amid growing signs that slavery's hold was becoming tenuous. Governor Augustus Bradford demanded in his inaugural address in early January 1862 that the Union war effort adhere strictly to the policy Lincoln avowed in his inaugural address—that there be no interference with slavery in the states where it existed. But he complained that a "desperate minority" of Republicans, eager to transform the war into an abolition crusade, threatened to "inflict upon the cause of the Union the severest blow it has yet encountered." Bradford's forebodings soon became tangible. By mid-February, the U.S. Senate started considering legislation to abolish slavery in the District of Columbia, which prompted Maryland's legislators to complain that "the agitation of this subject is calculated to disturb the relation of master and slave within this state."[19]

Both houses of the Maryland legislature eagerly ratified the amendment on the same day, January 10, without dissent. But the unanimous facade concealed an anxious undercurrent. Two members of the legislature beseeched their colleagues to offer a more substantive olive branch in hopes that Confederates might awaken to see the wisdom of returning to the Union. Lewis P. Firey, a state senator from Washington County in western Maryland, thought that Congress should enact the Crittenden Compromise and offer to readmit the seceded states "upon their original footing of equality and right" if they would lay down their arms. A member of the House of Delegates, Thomas S. Alexander of Baltimore, likewise feared that "unrelenting war" and "complete subjugation of the Rebels" would not restore the Union. It would, instead, lead to a military occupation of conquered territory. Alarmed by indications that the federal government no longer remained bound by Lincoln's inaugural promise to respect slavery in the states, Alexander urged a renewed statement of conservative war aims in order to "induce the Rebels to see that by returning again to their allegiance their rights would be respected."[20]

Alexander hoped to heed the example of "the celebrated Burke," who called for concessions to disaffected Americans in the 1770s. But his colleague Reverdy Johnson of Baltimore County, the former and future U.S. senator, rejected "any similarity between the present time and the days of '76" and saw no basis for the Burkean parallel. The South had been amply represented in the federal government, had suffered no wrongs, and had no real grievances. He thought it improper "to conciliate with these men." Better, Johnson thought, to heed Andrew Jackson's example when confronted by South Carolina's nullification in 1832—"crush it out."[21]

Proslavery forces held the upper hand in Wheeling in early 1862, but they did face opposition. One member of the legislature's lower house, Joseph Snider of Monongalia County, contended that "peace propositions" such as the constitutional amendment had no place so long as the war continued. "When it was held out to the rebel States as an olive branch of peace," Snider recalled, "they spit upon it" and said "if you would give them a blank sheet of paper they would not write the terms of compromise upon it." He would not "truckle to these traitors." They had "forfeited all their rights but the right of the halter about their necks." Only after "the rebellion was crushed and wiped out" would he accept the amendment. George McC. Porter of Hancock, the northernmost county in the panhandle above Wheeling, likewise noted that he would "willingly" have voted for the amendment before the "rebellion" started, but no more. Moreover, Porter warned that the amendment made "no allowance for a change of ideas, or for what may occur in a hundred years." Sounding very much like hard-line Republicans in Congress just a year before, Porter advised his colleagues not to "preclude yourselves forever from changing the Constitution." The amendment would "divide the friends of the country upon the question of slavery" and would "only produce irritation." Notwithstanding Snider's and Porter's objections, the House voted twenty-six to five to approve the amendment on January 24, and the Senate concurred three weeks afterward, on February 13.[22]

By the winter of 1861–62, a constitutional convention was meeting in Wheeling, as was the purported Virginia legislature. The convention was drawing up the framework for what would emerge as the separate state of West Virginia. This process required popular ratification of a new state constitution plus permission from the legislature to divide the state. It also required an act of Congress, which posed a high hurdle. There was a growing sense by early 1862 that the Republican majority in Congress would not accept an additional slave state. In short, the only way to secure a new state was to make it a free state. One northwesterner from Fairmont, identified only as "A Virginian," insisted that "the people want a free state and have for years." If given a chance to vote, they would reject "the old curse" and "pronounce for *Free State* in thunder tones." Gordon Battelle, a Methodist minister and leader of the Free State forces at the convention, defended gradual emancipation on grounds both of "principle" and "expediency." He condemned the slave system as wrong and unjust even though ameliorated by "humane" slaveholders who "resisted the temptations to avarice and power." Ending slavery would liberate free white labor and promote "real and genuine prosperity." Battelle also rebutted the claim that emancipation would hinder "our Union brethren" in Kentucky and Tennessee. But instead, at the behest of James H. Brown of Kanawha, "the strongest anti-free State man in the Convention," the clause calling for gradual emancipation was tabled by a single vote, twenty-four to twenty-three, and then deleted. Brown did accept language that barred additional slaves from being brought into the new state, but he vigilantly protected the prerogatives of western Virginia slaveholders, who were concentrated in his home region of the Kanawha Valley, where slave labor was a mainstay in the saltworks. To the distress of the *Wheeling Intelligencer*, Brown's "Eastern Virginia" mindset carried the day.[23]

New state promoters who wanted that state to be a free state feared that the convention had made a fatal mistake. Even though the constitution overall had the potential to be "the best one our people ever have had," the *Wheeling Intelligencer* editorialized, there was an "imminent risk that the whole new state project will fall to the ground." Congress would likely reject "a miserable little nigger state, with just enough slavery among us to degrade the white labor already here and repel it from abroad." And if the war ended soon—as was widely anticipated in the overconfident early months of 1862—the chance to create a new state might then be lost. "We shall see ourselves in all probability mocked like Tantalus, and all our hopes passing away right under our lips without our being able to realize one of them." Of course the war did not end soon. So even though Congress indeed wanted West Virginia to become a free state and came close to demanding that it abolish slavery immediately, a compromise based on gradual emancipation finally was agreed upon. The Wheeling government accepted the quid pro quo and thereby gained admission to the Union as the separate state of West Virginia.[24]

One final ratification followed immediately on the heels of Maryland's and Virginia's actions. The day after the vote in Wheeling, that is, on February 14, 1862, a constitutional convention in Illinois also approved the amendment. The Illinois state legislature had decided in January 1861 that the upcoming year would be a good time to hold a constitutional convention, and it established ground rules to elect delegates in November—striking evidence that war remained unexpected in the free states at the very moment when secession was sweeping the Deep South. By November, a facade of wartime unity produced bipartisan tickets in many Republican districts while Democrats continued to dominate in "Egypt" (southern Illinois), as had long been the case. The result was a constitutional convention with a large Democratic majority. Soon after it convened, the convention took up the would-be thirteenth amendment. Republicans complained that ratification would be superfluous because the federal government never would interfere with slavery, but they focused on jurisdictional concerns. They charged that the convention would usurp the prerogatives of the state legislature by acting on the amendment. They also contended that the convention did not meet the standard specified in the U.S. Constitution for ratifying constitutional amendments because it had been called only to propose amendments to the state constitution. The *Chicago Tribune* bitterly complained that the "mob at Springfield" was "an illegal body." But convention Democrats prevailed and ratified the would-be thirteenth amendment, thirty-nine to twenty-three. In the end, the convention's principal work—a new state constitution—was narrowly defeated by popular referendum in June 1862 as rural Republican counties in northern Illinois opposed the constitution by margins that paralleled Lincoln's 1860 victory. But separate referenda on three antiblack propositions (to bar negroes and mulattoes from the state and to deny them voting rights) carried by top-heavy majorities.[25]

The upshot was a muddle. Did the convention have authority to ratify the amendment? Did the popular referendum against the constitution invalidate the convention's ratification of the amendment? And what force did the antiblack provisions have after winning popular approval even as the new constitution itself went down to defeat? It is probable that the constitutional amendment still enjoyed majority support in Illinois in early 1862. Sustained hard fighting had not yet begun—though it would soon—and majorities of white citizens still could not imagine interfering with slavery in states where it existed. Except in a number of antislavery counties in the northern part of the state, Illinois whites refused even to allow that African Americans had the right to live among them. But in the months ahead, growing numbers of whites in Illinois and throughout the free states, horrified by the ghastly bloodbaths of 1862, concluded that slavery would always endanger the Union if it were allowed to persist. Ultimately, this sentiment led in 1865 to the real Thirteenth Amendment, which abolished slavery. Every free state would ratify that amendment.[26]

Illinois's irregular action ended the ratification fizzle. The would-be amendment thereupon slipped into permanent obscurity. Only infrequently do specialists, notably constitutional historian David Kyvig, even mention it. He rejects the idea that its framers "were simply going through motions they knew to be hopeless," and he sees the amendment as something that might have had a "great impact" if ratified. But under the circumstances, he judges, it was "too pallid a symbol of reassurance" to quiet secession's mad momentum. Nevertheless, he and other experts on constitutional law believe that the amendment is only "dormant," not dead. Were enough other states to ratify it, the other thirteenth amendment could still become part of the Constitution and negate the actual Thirteenth Amendment.[27] But don't hold your breath.

The Abortive Launch

Epilogue One

James M. Ashley and the Thirteenth Amendment

Abraham Lincoln issued the Preliminary Emancipation Proclamation on September 22, 1862. Just three weeks later, the state of Ohio held congressional elections. This was not a propitious moment for the Republican Party—which had rechristened itself the Union Party. During the summer of 1862, the war had gone badly. Ghastly fighting both east and west showed that the Confederacy could survive punishing losses and regroup to take the offensive. As Confederate armies rampaged through Kentucky, just across the Ohio River, voters in the Buckeye State headed to the polls. Many loyal Republicans in the army were unable to cast absentee ballots. The result was a Union-Republican nightmare. All but five of Ohio's nineteen seats in the U.S. House were won by Democrats, who condemned Lincoln's management of the war and railed against emancipation. Any interference with slavery, Democrats trumpeted, would be self-destructive and sure to make white Southerners fight even harder. Lincoln, they sneered, had capitulated to Republican radicals, whose crazed schemes would make disunion permanent.

But one outspoken Ohio radical survived. James M. Ashley of Toledo believed that slavery caused the war and that the Union military effort would languish until the war's root cause was attacked. Well before the center of gravity in the Republican Party was willing to enlarge Union war aims to include emancipation, Ashley pushed a militant antislavery agenda. His ideas were more in tune with northeastern Ohio's Western Reserve. But Ashley's district in the northwestern corner of the state was no more than marginally Republican, and the incumbent was in danger. His victory came about only because he had two opponents. Conservative Toledo Republicans rallied around a prominent ex-Whig, Morrison R. Waite, the future Chief Justice of the U.S. Supreme Court. In two of the district's eight counties, Waite collected almost all the votes cast against Ashley. But a Democratic candidate, Edward L. Phelps, did the same in three other counties. Ashley won fewer than 40 percent of the ballots cast, and his opponents together outpolled him by four thousand votes. His plurality victory nevertheless was impressive. Assailed from both sides as a dangerous, deluded visionary, Ashley prevailed. "Considering the nature of the contest, and the powerful influences against which he had to contend," wrote one local newspaper, "the election of Mr. Ashley is the greatest triumph, personal and political, ever achieved by a public man in this section of Ohio."[1]

Just over two years later, Union prospects were far brighter. Confederate armies maintained a bare stalemate outside Richmond and Petersburg but were coming unhinged everywhere else. Lincoln had secured reelection. The president greeted the returning session of Congress in December 1864 with a plea to push ahead on Ashley's signature idea—a constitutional amendment to abolish slavery. The election had shown, Lincoln observed, that an amendment now was "the will of the majority." It was the right means to secure the agreed-upon "common end"—the perpetuity of the Union. The battle, everyone knew, would be fought in the U.S. House. The Senate had approved the amendment overwhelmingly in April 1864. But Republican margins in the House were slender—its representatives had been elected in the grim autumn of 1862—and the House fell well short of a two-thirds majority when it voted in June 1864. Did the amendment have a chance in the lame-duck session?[2]

It did. The House acted, the requisite number of states ratified, and the Thirteenth Amendment to the Constitution, which abolished slavery throughout the United States, took effect in late 1865. Steven Spielberg's film *Lincoln* dramatized the pivotal juncture leading to its enactment—the House vote on January 31, 1865. Suddenly this off-the-beaten-path story has become a salient part of public consciousness. Many millions have watched Daniel Day-Lewis's Oscar-winning performance, and a fair fraction have had their curiosity whetted enough to read more. The book they first turn to is likely the one touted as the basis for the movie—Doris Kearns Goodwin's *Team of Rivals: The Political Genius of Abraham Lincoln*. There they find that she does indeed provide a number of quoted conversations used verbatim by Tony Kushner, Spielberg's screenwriter. But they find too that Goodwin devotes only five pages of a huge book to the specific topic.[3]

A little more browsing reveals that others besides Goodwin have written comparable summations of the nail-biting drama leading up to House passage of the amendment—the major recent biographies of Lincoln and Seward by Michael Burlingame and Walter Stahr, respectively, plus the most widely read single volume on the war years by James M. McPherson. Of these, Burlingame's account delves most deeply into the behind-the-scenes

Epilogue One

tale of how the requisite two-thirds House majority was secured. Anyone seeking a concise synopsis of the matter should turn first to Burlingame rather than to Goodwin.[4]

But the attentive reader will also learn that other studies must be consulted. When the eminent Lincoln scholar James G. Randall died in 1953, he left behind the half-written manuscript for the fourth and final volume of his life's work, *Lincoln the President*—and he specified that the then-young scholar Richard N. Current should complete the job. Using an entire chapter near the end of the book to detail the story of the Thirteenth Amendment, Current noted that "the great majority of those who had been slaves in early 1861 remained in bondage at the start of 1865." Lincoln wanted to change that. Concerned to guarantee that all wartime emancipation initiatives receive constitutional sanction, the president was deeply invested in securing the amendment's passage. Current provided several glimpses of the lobbying campaign to secure the necessary House votes, but he did not dwell on the matter.[5]

In 1963, LaWanda Cox and John H. Cox tapped into heretofore unavailable sources—the voluminous papers of William H. Seward—to provide a fuller account than ever before available of behind-the-scenes maneuvers leading up to the House vote on January 31, 1865. The Coxes showed that Seward gathered an "extraordinary lobby" to secure passage of the amendment. It was led by the shadowy W. N. Bilbo of Nashville, Tennessee, and it included three none-too-savory New Yorkers: Robert W. Latham, George O. Jones, and Richard Schell. Bilbo and his lieutenants "played a critically important role" in convincing wavering Democrats either to vote for the amendment or to absent themselves. Their persuasive techniques included the plausible case that the Democratic Party sooner could rebuild itself if it let go of slavery. But tangible inducements also played a role—promises of appointments, and even hard cash. In the end, a pivotal combination of Democrats and border state Unionists allowed the amendment to pass.[6]

In 2001, Michael Vorenberg provided a full, modern study of how the Thirteenth Amendment came to be enacted. Its penultimate chapter, "The King's Cure," focuses on the dramatic finale in the House. It superseded all previous assessments. Vorenberg not only extends the cast of characters involved in lobbying but also shows that two rival lobbying groups competed against each other. Lincoln and Seward hoped to reunite the Republican Party, which suffered bitter divisions in the summer of 1864. Some radicals such as Henry Winter Davis, convinced that the constitutional amendment could never be passed, contended that "Congress had the power to abolish slavery by statute." Lincoln, who insisted that permanent emancipation required a constitutional amendment, countered with a pocket veto of their Wade-Davis bill. Passing the amendment would close the breach that divided radicals from the administration and party moderates. Lincoln and Seward also left the door open to potential Democratic converts in the hope that a reunited Republican Party could be enlarged into "a permanent Union party."[7]

Vorenberg also demonstrates, however, that Seward's archrivals, the Blair family of Maryland and Missouri, hoped that passage of the amendment would rupture the Republican Party. Lincoln's former postmaster general Montgomery Blair, his brother Francis Preston Blair Jr., and their father, Francis Preston Blair Sr., abhorred all thought of racial equality. Once the amendment was enacted, the Blairs calculated, radical Republicans would launch a campaign for black rights that was sure to boomerang and repel the great majority of white Americans. A new party composed of Democrats and non-radical Republicans might then emerge, and it would look for leadership to former Democrats in the Republican Party—in particular, to the Blair family.[8]

Vorenberg identifies the Thirteenth Amendment as a watershed in constitutional thought. Until 1865, tradition and precedent dictated that the Constitution should endure unchanged. But the enormous cataclysm of war showed that the Constitution had failed to perform its key function: "to hold the states of this Union together." Growing numbers of Northerners began to question narrow originalism and to see the Constitution as a "pliable text" that might be improved. Instead of regarding the Founding Fathers as all-knowing and the 1787 Constitution as sacrosanct, they complained about "the danger of Constitution-worship." Some blamed the "long-dead framers" for having allowed "the cause of the war, slavery, to survive." It became possible to think of rewriting the Constitution in ways "rejected or unimagined by the framers." But the amendment's mainstream supporters carefully shielded their efforts from accusations that they harbored a radical agenda. They contended, instead, that it offered "a conservative form of change." They rejected more far-reaching definitions of equality and shunted into the background vigorous African American efforts to couple the end of slavery with a real commitment to equal rights. The freedom they established was only vaguely defined—an "absence of chattel slavery but less than absolute equality."[9]

Vorenberg also provides a deft account of the lobbying campaign on behalf of the amendment in January 1865. Despite long-standing speculation that illicit means were used to persuade fence-sitters, he doubts whether votes were bought or sold. He acknowledges "some" corruption, but he absolves Lincoln of any direct role in deal-making. Did the president proclaim that he was "clothed with immense power" and order his supporters point-blank "to procure those votes"? Tony Kushner, Spielberg's screenwriter, grabbed at these decades-later recollections, but Vorenberg does not think Lincoln expressed himself in such overinflated ways. Nor do I. Nonetheless, Vorenberg does emphasize Lincoln's active role in the ratification campaign. He and those working at his behest persuaded a number of Democrats and border state Unionists to accept the amendment as a necessary first step toward sectional reconciliation as well as an opportune catalyst for postwar partisan reorganization. The amendment's new supporters had a mixture of motives and cared little about racial justice. They recognized, instead, that it no longer made political sense to remain tied to the decaying carcass of a slave system that had been fatally unhinged by the war. The vote was "the crowning moment of their careers" for many House members because it meant that disagreements about slavery would never again cause a hideous war.[10]

Leonard L. Richards's history of the Thirteenth Amendment's enactment, published in 2015, nicely complements and supplements Vorenberg's book. Richards centers his narrative on Ohio congressman James M. Ashley, whom we have encountered in chapter 9 and at the start of this epilogue. As soon as fighting began, Ashley was determined to make emancipation a Union war aim. In the winter of 1861–62, he contended that the seceding states had forfeited whatever constitutional protection they might earlier have enjoyed. They should instead, once conquered, be governed as territories. It was a mainstream Republican position, Ashley knew, that Congress had the power to end slavery in the territories. In addition, Ashley bid to confiscate rebel property and distribute it to loyal Southerners, without regard to color. These overtures were too radical for the moment, but they were indicative of things to come.[11]

Two years later, in the winter of 1863–64, much had changed. Emancipation had indeed become a Union war aim, and Abraham Lincoln had used his powers as commander-in-chief of the army to order the freedom of slaves in the Confederate South. Increasing numbers of black soldiers were enlisted in the Union army. But despite Lincoln's Emancipation Proclamation, most slaves remained enslaved, either behind Confederate lines or in the Union slave states. Ashley wanted to make emancipation universal and irrevocable and to base it on more than the extraordinary wartime exercise of executive power. So he proposed a double-barreled assault on the hated "slave barons." First, he submitted language for a thirteenth amendment that would be the polar opposite of the one Congress had approved in early 1861. It would abolish slavery and "involuntary servitude" everywhere in the United States. That would include pro-Union regions of the South, such as Kentucky, which were exempted from the Emancipation Proclamation. Ashley coupled this with a proposal to organize new state governments in the rebel states as they became subject to Union military authority. He would enfranchise "all loyal male citizens"—and that meant ex-slaves. And he would bar from voting and office holding all who had fought for the rebels or held office in a rebel state. In his mind, stern reconstruction measures were concomitant with ending slavery.[12]

During 1864, as we have seen, the amendment gained momentum. It was approved by the Senate in April, and it earned a strong boost in Lincoln's annual message to the lame-duck session of Congress, which convened in December. The president had not taken a clear proamendment stance when it was before the Senate and House earlier in the year. But he contended that November's election results assured the amendment's House passage when the new session of Congress gathered one year hence. So, he reasoned, why not now?—and "the sooner the better." Lincoln had reason to prefer quick action. Union military prospects appeared bright, but the Confederacy had rebounded before. Military setbacks always hobbled the administration's political leverage. Alternatively, the war might end with a Union victory that would undercut a key rationale for getting rid of slavery. Nobody at the time could foresee the future. And we know, with hindsight, that Lincoln had only months to live.[13]

The amendment's pivotal arena remained the House, and there Ashley took the lead. "Slavery has forced this terrible civil war upon us," he insisted, and the time had come for a return to first principles. The "great and good men" who formed the Constitution knew that "a majority in a republic cannot rightfully enslave the minority." They desired "the speedy abolition of slavery" and expected that it soon "would cease to exist." In Ashley's view, the Constitution had been "grossly perverted" and "persistently violated." "Trading politicians" for the past thirty years had disgraced themselves, "first by apologizing for, then justifying, and at last openly defending slavery as a right guaranteed by the national Constitution." Had they done otherwise, and instead followed the lead of those who wrote the Constitution, "we should have had no such desolating war as we have in this country to-day."[14]

Ashley also insisted that "the eyes of the wise and good in all civilized nations are upon us." He framed the Civil War as a decisive test of liberal nationalism. Those who rebelled against the Union wanted a government "administered exclusively by a privileged class, a slaveholding aristocracy, in which capital shall own the laborer." But the "earnest, uncompromising anti-slavery men of this country," though "few in numbers," had enlisted the "almighty power and force of truth" and had "educated the nation" to embrace "universal emancipation." That had "changed the tone and sentiment of the masses in Europe towards the North" and ended fears of European intervention to aid the rebels. "Man's capacity for self-government is on trial before the world," he insisted, "and we must conquer or the verdict will be against democratic government and in favor of privilege and despotism everywhere."[15]

Richards emphasizes Ashley's tactical dexterity. He stood for equal rights, but he knew the amendment could not pass without support from a significant increment of those who abhorred his broader egalitarian agenda and who indeed hoped to destroy the egalitarian wing of the Republican Party. He carefully counted noses and worked behind the scenes to influence a number of lame ducks. The Ohio congressman collaborated closely with Lincoln and Secretary of State Seward to entice a key bloc of the amendment's former opponents—border state Unionists and Democrats—either to switch their stance or to absent themselves from the key vote. Ashley's role, even if marginalized in Spielberg's *Lincoln*, was absolutely central. Long before the president got behind the amendment, Ashley laid the groundwork and forced the issue to public attention. "The passage of the Thirteenth Amendment," concludes Ashley's biographer, Robert F. Horowitz, "owes more to him than to any other man."[16]

Ashley's victory was momentous. He believed that the amendment reenacted original principles and followed through on what the Founders always intended. He also believed that it potentially opened the door to dramatic new definitions of citizenship and rights. And therein lay a problem. Many who voted for his amendment did not share his vision of a transformed social order. Mainstream Republicans in late 1864 and early 1865 did want equality before the law but not equal voting rights. Conservatives from varying political backgrounds starkly opposed any hint of equality. They calculated instead that slavery should end but that former slaves should remain a dependent underclass without citizen rights. Ultimately, Ashley's victory was bittersweet. Moderate Republicans did subsequently move in his direction when confronted by President Andrew Johnson's neo-Confederate apostasy. But Ashley's hopes for a national postwar commitment to equal

Epilogue One

political and economic rights would not be realized. The Ohio firebrand always stood far in advance of his party. He lost his House seat in 1868 after trying unsuccessfully to remove Ohio's strictures against black voting.[17]

By the 1890s the aging Ashley was largely forgotten. But he continued to be held in high regard by African Americans, who faced a tragic and outrageous spiral of disfranchisement, legalized Jim Crow, and lynching. On Emancipation Day, September 22, 1893, a committee from the African Methodist Episcopal Church held a ceremony at the World's Fair in Chicago to present Ashley with an edited "souvenir" volume of his compiled orations and speeches. The chief editor, Benjamin W. Arnett, recalled sitting in the gallery of the House of Representatives on January 31, 1865, to witness "the last great parliamentary battle between Freedom and Slavery." He saluted Ashley's unforgettable leadership in "the cause of universal freedom."[18]

FROM THE PERSPECTIVE OF A century and a half later, the abolition of slavery and the enactment of the Thirteenth Amendment appear to be such overwhelming necessities that we find it difficult to imagine a time when anyone might have judged otherwise. It seems to Americans of the early twenty-first century more than strange that there had been a surprisingly comparable effort, only four years earlier, to amend the Constitution to make slavery more secure. This sense of strangeness, this distance from a remote era, is no modern invention. Once the war ended and slavery with it, the participants themselves found it difficult to recapture accurately their outlook in the years leading up to the war.

Henry Wilson provides a striking case in point. A prominent Massachusetts senator from the mid-1850s, he became vice president of the United States in 1873 and died while in office in 1875. During his last years Wilson undertook a massive, three-volume history of the Civil War era. He wrote there that Republicans before the war had been less than candid when they promised not to interfere with slavery where it already existed. Unhappy "to share in the work of oppression," they looked forward to slavery's "complete extinction" and confidently expected that "the system would soon yield to the potent influences of reform and pass away." Those who were committed to slavery suspected correctly that Republicans harbored an "ulterior purpose" and that they "must have an object far beyond the prevention of slavery in a Territory where it can never exist." In exposing such Republican "inconsistency," Wilson went far toward validating secessionist fears.[19]

In part, Wilson's recollections reflected his own outlook, which was far more ideologically antislavery than the average Republican's. Born into abject poverty and hired out as an indentured servant during his adolescence, Wilson resented all aristocratic advantage and pretense. He was drawn to the abolitionist petition campaigns of the 1830s, and he maintained respectful ties to several prominent abolitionists, notably Theodore Parker and Lydia Maria Child. Because he found the Whig Party a blunt instrument for advancing reform causes, he became a tireless champion of Free Soil coalition politics from the late 1840s to the mid-1850s. Without Wilson's practical skills, Charles Sumner could not have been elevated to the U.S. Senate.[20]

Before the war, however, Wilson carefully respected the limits set forward by William Jay in the 1830s and maintained thereafter by antislavery political leaders such as Salmon P. Chase. Wilson's maiden speech to the U.S. Senate, in February 1855, specified that he and the people of Massachusetts were "unalterably opposed" to slavery and "in favor of all practicable efforts for its entire abolition." But at the same time, "we do not propose to interfere with slavery in the States. We believe that slavery in the States is a local institution—that we are not responsible for its existence, and that we have no legal authority to interfere with it in any way whatever." He did call, however, for ending slavery "wherever we are morally or legally responsible for its existence"—in the District of Columbia and in the territories. And because states were responsible for the extradition of fugitives, not the federal government, he favored the "immediate and unconditional repeal" of the "inhuman and unconstitutional" Fugitive Slave Act. All of this echoed the views of Jay and Chase, who wanted slavery "denationalized." Once the federal government was "relieved from" responsibility for slavery, Wilson predicted, Southerners who were opposed to its existence would "get rid of it in their States in no distant day." In this manner, Wilson predicted, slavery would be "peacefully abolished."[21]

When the Republican Party coalesced in 1856, Wilson became its vigorous champion. He vigilantly deflected accusations that it had any hidden abolition agenda. To be sure, his position on the District of Columbia and fugitives put him outside the emerging Republican consensus of the late 1850s, as did his confidence that white Southerners might abandon slavery at "no distant day." But he was a team player, not an ideological hairsplitter. As we have seen in chapter 3, Wilson carefully distinguished between Republicans and abolitionists. No Republican, he insisted, ever stated that Congress had any power "to abolish slavery in the slaveholding States." Republicans cherished the Union and believed that "the Constitution as it is should be preserved." He denounced Democrats for perpetrating the false idea that Republicans endangered slavery. He privately considered John

Epilogue One

Brown a "damned old fool" and regarded his attack on Harper's Ferry as "insane." Wilson's final major speech before the start of the war denounced the Crittenden Compromise as a "complete surrender" to the "dark spirit of slavery," but he absolved Massachusetts and the free states from intending "to interfere directly or indirectly with slavery in the States."[22] So Wilson's postwar recollections provide a misleading version of his prewar stance.

There were many Wilsons. Before the war, almost all Republicans specified that slavery in the states lay beyond their reach. The prophetic exceptions—notably James M. Ashley and John A. Bingham—were few and far between. Subsequently, Republicans found it awkward to acknowledge the constraints on their prewar antislavery stance. Even if the mother of imagined historical memory wasn't outright necessity, the cautious constitutional opponents of slavery typically remembered themselves as having stood taller before the war than they actually did. Lydia Maria Child, the outspoken abolitionist, noted in 1864 that "new anti-slavery friends are becoming as plentiful as roses in June." They often told her they had "always been anti-slavery." She did not "contradict the assertion," she observed tongue-in-cheek. "I merely marvel at their power of keeping it a secret so long."[23]

Lincoln deserves the last word. He found slavery distasteful and painful. But he also thought that the slave states had a constitutional right to maintain the system. During his first debate with Stephen A. Douglas in August 1858, Lincoln fended off accusations that he was an abolitionist. "I have no purpose, directly or indirectly, to interfere with the institution of slavery in the States where it exists," he insisted. "I believe I have no lawful right to do so, and I have no inclination to do so." He repeated this passage verbatim in his inaugural address on March 4, 1861. He thought that the "ultimate extinction" of slavery would come about only when whites in the slaveholding states wanted it to come about. And that would take time—he hardly expected it to occur "in less than a hundred years at the least."[24]

The great convulsion of civil war brought emancipation far sooner than anyone could have predicted. In October 1864, Lincoln was visited by Sojourner Truth, the legendary black preacher, feminist, and abolitionist. She commended him for being the only president who had done anything for her people. Lincoln countered that he was "the only one who ever had such opportunity." He then tersely summarized what made the difference: "Had our friends in the South behaved themselves, I could have done nothing whatever."[25]

Epilogue One

Epilogue Two

John A. Bingham and the Fourteenth Amendment

In 1947, U.S. Supreme Court Justice Hugo Black wrote a memorable dissent in *Adamson v. California* (332 U.S. 46, 68–123). The Alabama-born Black was already establishing himself as a champion of civil liberties on what presently would become known as the Warren Court. Black insisted that the Fourteenth Amendment required the various states to strictly heed the Bill of Rights—the first eight amendments to the U.S. Constitution. His stance was destined to define a position that the court would largely adopt in succeeding decades.

Black studied the Fourteenth Amendment's history. He concluded that its framers intended to hold the states to the same standards that the Bill of Rights imposed on the federal government. In so doing, he resurrected from history's scrap heap Ohio's John A. Bingham, who turned out to have been the driving force behind the crucial first section of the Fourteenth Amendment. A member of the Joint Committee on Reconstruction, Bingham wrote the words that conferred national and state citizenship on "all persons born or naturalized in the United States"—and that barred states from passing laws that would "abridge the privileges or immunities of citizens of the United States," or "deprive any person of life, liberty, or property without due process of law," or deny any person "the equal protection of the laws."[1]

Several years after Black's dissent, Jacobus tenBroek published *The Antislavery Origins of the Fourteenth Amendment.* This pathbreaking study demonstrated that the intellectual framework undergirding the amendment had been constructed before the Civil War by slavery's most resolute opponents. They dared to imagine a Constitution that no longer upheld slavery but instead required equal rights for all. Amplifying Black, tenBroek concluded that Bingham, more than any other individual, combined "the various strands of abolitionist constitutional development" to create the Fourteenth Amendment's first section.[2]

Until recently, however, there had not been an adequate biography of

Bingham. This lacuna has now been filled by Gerard N. Magliocca. He dubs Bingham the "Founding Son"—the man who repaired the flawed work of the Founding Fathers and made equal citizen rights part of the Constitution. Without Bingham, writes Magliocca, "there would have been no Fourteenth Amendment as we know it." His handiwork has become the most important part of the Constitution. Bingham also coined that now-common phrase the "Bill of Rights."[3]

We have already encountered Bingham in chapters 3 and 9, where it was apparent that he dared to stand apart. His views about race and slavery were incubated in the stern context of the Associate Presbyterian Church, often called "Seceders" because they rejected "mainline Presbyterianism." This denomination's small Franklin College, which closed almost a century ago, became "the fountain-head of the abolition sentiment of eastern Ohio." There Bingham met and befriended a fellow student, Titus Basfield, a former slave who had endured ghastly hardships. Unlike most future leaders of the Republican Party, Bingham regarded African Americans as "his social and political equals."[4]

First elected to the House of Representatives in 1854, following passage of the Kansas-Nebraska Act, the lawyer-politician Bingham quickly emerged as a leading Republican radical. He championed "the absolute equality of all" and insisted that no "word of caste" polluted the Constitution's "great charter of our rights." He saw the war as proof positive of slavery's iniquity, and he resolved to work for a postwar constitutional settlement that removed all doubt regarding equal citizen rights. He wanted a Constitution that assured the equal protection of the laws to "any human being who behaves himself . . . no matter whence he comes, or how poor, how weak, how simple—no matter how friendless."[5]

Bingham's biographer, Magliocca, and his fellow legal scholar, Garrett Epps, have now established that the visionary Ohio congressman sought and secured "an amendment that was almost breathtaking in its breadth and ambition." The Fourteenth Amendment, Epps writes, brought about "by far the most sweeping and complex change ever made in the original Constitution." Indeed, Epps contends that the 1787 Constitution "died at Fort Sumter" and that the architects of the new "second Constitution," who attempted to repair the flawed work of the Founders, should be considered the "second founders." For Bingham, it was a matter of assuring that the Constitution be understood as, in his view, it was always intended. No state ever had the right, he insisted, to deny any person "the equal protection of the laws or to abridge the privileges and immunities of any citizen of the Republic."[6]

Epilogue Two

Bingham's insistence that the Fourteenth Amendment take priority created an odd anomaly in the pioneering modern studies of Reconstruction that appeared during the 1960s and early 1970s. In the eyes of historians Eric McKitrick and Michael Les Benedict, Bingham was a "conservative" who obstructed the Republican Reconstruction agenda. Magliocca and Epps reject this interpretation. Bingham's focus in 1866 and 1867 was rewriting the Constitution. When he deviated tactically from the Republican consensus—in being willing to delay equal voting rights and in opposing the Civil Rights Bill of 1866—he did so because he saw the amendment as the essential centerpiece of Reconstruction. He wanted civil rights incorporated into the Constitution before it became a legislative matter, and he subsequently accepted equal voting rights as a means to secure the amendment's ratification.[7]

Magliocca notes that Americans remember selectively. They honor the political achievements of the Founding Fathers but have little curiosity about the military history of the Revolution. By contrast, armchair generals continue to refight the battles of the Civil War, but they disdain political history. Except for Lincoln, the political leaders of his era are "largely unknown."[8] This may be especially the case for those who championed equal citizen rights. For almost a century, their work was written off as a fool's errand.

Eventually that would change. During the several decades following Justice Black's 1947 dissent, the Supreme Court moved on a broad front to expand the so-called doctrine of incorporation—that is, the requirement that states adhere to the Bill of Rights. This revolution in jurisprudence breathed life into the Civil Rights Movement. The NAACP Legal Defense Fund's formidable attorney Thurgood Marshall, assisted by historians Alfred Kelly and John Hope Franklin, addressed the question of whether the framers of the Fourteenth Amendment intended to abolish school segregation, in the arguments leading to *Brown v. Board of Education* (347 U.S. 483). Although the answer to that specific question was ambiguous, Marshall took an expansive view of the equal protection clause and contended that Congress had a right "to stop the states from making distinctions in law between people."[9]

Bingham's handiwork assured that the Civil Rights Movement of the 1950s and 1960s had far stronger constitutional foundations than the pre–Civil War abolition movement. Imaginative visionaries led by Alvan Stewart tried to make the case for an antislavery Constitution during the 1830s and 1840s, but they persuaded few outside their own circle. For Lincoln and the Republican Party, state laws upholding slavery were legitimate, and the power of the federal government could not legally be used against slavehold-

Epilogue Two

ers. Nelson Mandela and South Africa's antiapartheid movement of the late twentieth century faced the same dilemma—not only did they challenge deeply discriminatory social and economic practices; they also challenged fundamental law.

Had John A. Bingham lived to see the consequences of his labors, the "father of the Fourteenth Amendment" would have been gratified. In the 1950s and 1960s, those who challenged American apartheid faced an uphill task, to be sure. But thanks to the vision of Bingham and his 1866 allies, the U.S. Constitution provided a potential bulwark. Long ignored, twisted, and misinterpreted, the first section of the Fourteenth Amendment moved to center stage a century after it first was written. President John F. Kennedy's watershed speech of June 11, 1963, identified a "moral issue" that was "as old as the Scriptures" and "as clear as the American Constitution"—the question of whether "all Americans are to be afforded equal rights and equal opportunities." Three months later, on August 28, 1963, Martin Luther King Jr. stood at the foot of the Lincoln Memorial and faced a huge throng. He too emphasized the "sacred obligation" inherent in "the magnificent words of the Constitution and the Declaration of Independence." With soaring rhetoric, he preached about his dream, a dream that was "deeply rooted in the American dream." King's unforgettable plea that his fellow citizens live up to the requirements of their Constitution elevated him, in the words of his biographer Taylor Branch, to status as a "new founding father," the one who made it a moral imperative that the constitutional transformation of the Civil War era be heeded.[10]

Words on paper, however necessary, are far from sufficient. Both in the 1860s and the 1960s, ordinary people, at great risk to themselves, stood up to challenge the status quo. From the very start of the war, slaves started undermining slavery with their feet. Anywhere the Union army advanced into the South, slaves flocked to Union lines. Sometimes they were received decently, and sometimes they were treated disgracefully. On the whole, the Union Army welcomed able-bodied laborers but had little use for children or dependents. It certainly did not see itself as a social welfare organization. Many Union soldiers were as contemptuous of slaves as they were of the slaveholders who had caused all the trouble in the first place.[11]

What ultimately drove emancipation was commonsense calculation. Slaves did much of the work in the South and thereby enabled a large portion of Southern white men to fight. Reducing the amount of slave labor in the South made it harder to keep Confederate armies in the field and to keep them supplied. Slaves who enlisted in the Union Army, once that became possible, effected the most decisive transfer of assets. That always was the reason Lincoln offered to justify emancipation—it gave the Union more soldiers, and at the same time it diminished the Confederate workforce. Slaves themselves thereby did much to transform a war originally fought to restore "the old Union as it was" into a revolutionary war to create a new slave-free Union.[12]

It made a big difference that slaves had white allies. Outright abolitionists, plus hard-line Republicans who saw slavery as a moral problem, created a political constituency that grew in size and leverage. Their numbers before the war were modest. But during wartime, mainstream white Northerners increasingly grasped the logic and the justice of emancipation. If the rebels fought for slavery, then the one sure way to avert future rebellions was to end slavery.

The parallels to the Freedom Movement of the 1960s are substantial. Few African Americans in the mid-twentieth-century Deep South could register to vote, and the humiliations of racial segregation were strongly entrenched behind a bulwark of state and local laws, coupled with repressive violence. By 1962, the movement appeared stalled and the *Brown* decision a dead letter. The Jim Crow system withstood the lunch counter sit-ins in 1960, the Freedom Rides in 1961, and the mass campaign in Albany, Georgia, in 1962. Here and there across the rural and small-town South, black demonstrators were routinely beaten and jailed. Most such incidents were small-scale and ignored in the national press.[13]

Birmingham, Alabama, Taylor Branch writes, was "the toughest bastion of racism in the South." The decision to inaugurate a protest movement there in 1963 initially appeared foolhardy. Along with many others, Martin Luther King was arrested and imprisoned. He surreptitiously composed his "Letter from Birmingham Jail," but the *New York Times* was not interested. The letter languished, unread. Then, everything changed. The children in the streets, the dogs, the fire hoses—these finally "broke through people's emotional barriers, not only in the United States but around the world." By then television sets were ubiquitous in American homes and fast spreading across the globe. The whole world was watching Birmingham's "nonviolent Bastille Day." Suddenly King's Letter from Birmingham Jail went viral. Soon Kennedy had to get off the fence and speak directly about civil rights as no American president ever had done before. His successor, Lyndon B. Johnson, grabbed the unique moment to shepherd the Civil Rights Bill of 1964 and the Voting Rights Act of 1965 into law.[14]

Unexpected circumstances temporarily moved racial justice from the periphery to the center of the public arena both in the 1860s and the 1960s. As with American slavery, American racism had become an international liability. White Northerners who hated slavery had their counterparts a century later. High-quality political leadership, an essential ingredient, stepped forward at both key moments to take advantage of new opportunities. But without the initiative and courage of ordinary black Americans — slaves in the 1860s and black Southerners in the 1960s — nothing would have changed.

Alas, in both instances, we are bound to reflect back and wonder how much really changed and how much remained the same. The constitutional amendments of the 1860s failed to overcome the malign legacy of American slavery, and the breakthrough legislation of the 1960s could not rectify all accumulated injustices. Racial inequality was and is a national scandal, not just a Southern shortcoming. Nevertheless, the promise of equality lives and the struggles continue.

Bibliographical Postscript

The other thirteenth amendment lurks hidden in the shadows of Civil War-era historiography. The idea that Abraham Lincoln ever accepted giving slavery in the states explicit constitutional sanction is so counterintuitive that it cannot be part of popular memory. The amendment is an especially awkward topic today when celebrations of the Great Emancipator's life and leadership attract ever larger audiences. This bibliographical essay will review how historians have—and have not—come to grips with the amendment. What emerges is a case study of the way that popular yearning for a history that Americans can feel good about works at cross-purposes to understanding what actually happened. When myth and history collide, myth holds the advantage.

The first person to write in detail about the other thirteenth amendment was James G. Blaine, as towering a figure in the latter nineteenth century as he is forgotten today. He would not become a member of Congress until 1863, but his memoir, *Twenty Years of Congress*, published in two volumes during the mid-1880s, showed that he knew a great deal about what had happened behind closed doors at the national Capitol two years before, in early 1861. At that time, Blaine lived in Augusta, Maine, where he was speaker of the state's house of representatives. He wore multiple hats when he wrote in the 1880s—as historian, as custodian of the Republican Party's legacy, and as presidential aspirant. His strictures against the amendment ultimately reflected his partisan outlook.

Blaine's hindsight shaped his perspective. In his view, "the compromising course of the majority in each branch of Congress" during the secession winter reflected a "misjudgment." Efforts to "allay the excitement" in the slave states by offering "new concessions" were "well meant" but conveyed the wrong message. The apparent evidence of Northern irresolution and "timidity" emboldened Southern leaders to think they could organize their new confederacy "without resistance" and thereby "dissolve the Union without war."[1]

Blaine took aim at the most innocuous Northern concessions. By voting to organize the new territories of Dakota, Colorado, and Nevada without prohibiting slavery, he contended, Republicans in the House and Senate made "an extraordinary change of position." In so doing they abandoned their party's founding issue—stopping slavery in the Kansas Territory after repeal of the Missouri Compromise. Their 1861 stance likewise shortchanged the long struggle by "anti-slavery Whigs and Free-Soilers" to enact the Wilmot Proviso. In effect, Blaine charged, Republicans belatedly embraced the position championed by the oft-criticized Daniel Webster in 1850—that Northerners need not prohibit slavery in the West because climate and rainfall would achieve the same result. Republicans likewise conceded a key point to their tenacious antagonist Stephen A. Douglas, who was "justified in his boast that, after all the bitter agitation which followed the passage of the Kansas-Nebraska Bill, the Republicans adopted its principle and practically applied its provisions in the first Territory which they had the power to organize."[2]

Blaine sharply faulted the work of the House Committee of Thirty Three and took particular exception to the constitutional amendment proposed by Charles Francis Adams. "No Southern man," Blaine huffed, "had ever submitted so extreme a proposition." By offering unprecedented safeguards for slavery where it existed, Adams got the worst of both worlds—he "tended only to lower the tone of Northern opinion without in the least degree appeasing the wrath of the South."[3]

Adams correctly withdrew his support for the amendment in mid-January, Blaine thought, after Southern members of the committee refused to affirm that "peaceful acquiescence" in the results of a presidential election was "the paramount duty of every good citizen of the United States." But when Adams reversed course once again on January 31 to speak out in favor of the amendment and the rest of the committee report, he "humiliated the North." Blaine lauded the two hard-line Republicans, Cadwallader C. Washburn of Wisconsin and Mason W. Tappan of New Hampshire, who refused to go along and issued a bluntly worded minority report that declared the South had no just cause for its rash actions; they demanded that the Constitution be "obeyed rather than amended."[4]

With the eye of an experienced parliamentarian (he had become Speaker of the U.S. House from 1869 to 1875), Blaine dissected the amendment's tumultuous course in Congress during the last week of the session. He noted that Thomas Corwin inserted substitute language that pared away the minority veto even while it preserved the core idea of safeguarding slavery in the states against interference; by so doing, he attracted just enough Republican votes in the House to accomplish his purposes. Blaine disparaged the outcome by noting that some of the votes in favor of the amendment were cast by members "who soon after proceeded to join the Rebellion." They were assisted by some of "the weightiest Republican leaders" in the Senate, among them William H. Seward and William Pitt Fessenden, who withheld their votes, so "it may be presumed that they consented to the passage of the amendment." As discussed in chapter 10, Blaine provided something close to a smoking gun regarding the Maine delegation's pattern of vote-switching and vote-withholding, which had been concealed in plain sight for a quarter century.[5]

Why did Lincoln endorse the amendment in his inaugural address? Blaine surmised—correctly in my opinion—that the new president came into office still hopeful for an "amicable adjustment." He believed that secessionists "could be brought to see that Union was better than war" and that slavery "would be imperiled by a resort to arms." Lincoln "had faith in the sober second-thought." He also hoped a "mild and conciliatory policy" might hold Virginia, North Carolina, and Tennessee in the Union. And he likely shared the widespread view that war would destroy "the last hope for restoration of the Union."[6]

Blaine closed his discussion of the other constitutional amendment by celebrating "the rapid revolution of public sentiment" that occurred during wartime. "Whoever reads the thirteenth amendment to the Constitution as it now stands," he wrote, will be startled to compare it "with the one which was proposed by the Thirty-sixth Congress." What happened in 1861 offered "useful lessons" about the potentially irresponsible conduct "of public men in times of high excitement."[7]

Blaine came close to second-guessing Lincoln, but the immense ten-volume Lincoln biography penned by his two wartime secretaries, John G. Nicolay and John Hay, leaned the other way. Working closely with Lincoln's son, Robert Todd Lincoln, they always gave Lincoln the benefit of the doubt.[8] Nicolay and Hay depicted the amendment as "a measure of adjustment that might have restored harmony to the country." But it was doomed because the Cotton States were controlled by "a conspiracy bent upon rebellion as its prime and ultimate object." Nicolay and Hay noted how Corwin moved away at the last minute from the language drafted by his Committee of Thirty Three, they summarized the story of its passage by the House and Senate, they pointed out that Buchanan approved it "only an hour or two before the inauguration of his successor," and they included Lincoln's inaugural words. "But nothing came of it," Nicolay and Hay concluded. "The South gave no response to the overture for peace, and in the North it was lost sight of amid the overshadowing events that immediately preceded the outbreak of hostilities."[9]

James Ford Rhodes also saw the amendment as potentially useful, even if ineffectual. His extensive history of the wartime era depicted the amendment as a matter of "the highest importance" because it directly addressed "the question on whom rests the blame for the Civil War." Approved by both houses of Congress and accepted by the incoming president, it represented a promise by the North to the South—"we will forever respect your peculiar institution in the States where it now exists." But, Rhodes concluded, "it was not considered a sufficient concession by Virginia, North Carolina, and Tennessee, and it had no effect whatever on the States which constituted the Southern Confederacy."[10]

The modern era of historical writing about the immediate months and weeks preceding the war began in 1942 with young David Potter's classic first book, *Lincoln and His Party in the Secession Crisis*. Potter considered the would-be thirteenth amendment a subsidiary stopgap, rushed through only after Congress failed to enact meaningful compromise. He pointed out that the amendment, ostensibly offered by Charles Francis Adams, was in fact orchestrated by Seward as part of a campaign to divide the South and buy time so that Lincoln could be peacefully inaugurated. Potter suggested that the amendment and the related measure to admit New Mexico as a state had little intrinsic significance and that its authors were "indifferent" to the substance of what they proposed. But Potter also shared the estimate of young Henry Adams—that Seward played his hand brilliantly during the secession winter and engaged in "a fight which might go down to history as one of the wonders of statesmanship."[11]

Kenneth Stampp, by contrast, writing shortly after Potter, depicted Seward and Adams as deceitful manipulators. The constitutional amendment, their "sole achievement," was a "complete fiasco" because "the only slavery compromise that had a chance of satisfying Southerners was Crittenden's." Seward's and Adams's "real purpose" was "not to save the Union by compromise but to gain some strategic advantage over the secessionists." Stampp and Potter interpreted the same basic information quite differently. Stampp saw no "statesmanship." For him, all "conciliatory gestures" were deceptive, devious, and fraudulent. His antislavery allegiances always manifest, he despised the idea of amending the Constitution to safeguard slavery in the states. He was bound to look askance at any who contemplated such retrograde action. In effect, Stampp resurrected the frame of interpretation articulated by Blaine in the late nineteenth century.[12]

Allan Nevins wrote a desultory account of Union-saving efforts in the Committee of Thirteen and the Committee of Thirty Three, but he painted with a broad brush and left many loose ends. His most specific segment detailed the "bold proposal" for New Mexico statehood advanced by Charles Francis Adams and Henry Winter Davis "apparently with some aid from Seward." Nevins applauded the "adroit" offer to create an illusory slave state that was certain to become a free state. It demonstrated that the South's real motive for demanding slavery in the territories was "hereafter acquired"—its hope of acquiring a Caribbean slave empire. His single cryptic paragraph on the constitutional amendment stated that this "most important" of the House proposals potentially "chained the country in dealing with slavery inside the States." Nevins found that the amendment enjoyed significant Republican support. But he gave the matter no more than cursory attention, and he did not touch its passage by the Senate.[13]

Roy Franklin Nichols's 1948 masterwork, *The Disruption of American Democracy*, dissected the collapse of the Southern-oriented Democratic Party during James Buchanan's troubled tenure as president. His assiduous research showed what was going through the minds of key insiders, especially the heavyweight Southerners who ran the U.S. Senate. His final eight chapters—140 pages—approached the grave postelection crisis from the vantage points of Jefferson Davis, Judah Benjamin, and Robert M. T. Hunter. Only by immediately adopting the Crittenden Compromise, they insisted, could disunion be averted. They scorned lesser measures, and so did Nichols. The Committee of Thirty Three, he wrote, recommended a "hodgepodge" of "miscellaneous resolutions." The Peace Conference "had labored and had brought forth a mouse." Nichols included a full account of how the House and Senate passed the prospective constitutional amendment. He saw it as a last-minute expedient that assumed significance only after other compromise proposals languished. He admired the parliamentary skill exhibited by Thomas Corwin and Stephen A. Douglas in securing its eleventh-hour passage—"Corwin was not a veteran parliamentarian for nothing" while Douglas brought characteristic energy to the "thankless task" of setting aside the Peace Conference proposal and giving priority instead to the amendment. But Nichols judged that little could be expected from the amendment they "had worked with such diligence to save." Too little and too late, it "was not likely to mend matters much."[14]

Patrick M. Sowle wrote a doctoral dissertation in 1963 that focused on three leading "conciliatory Republicans"—Seward, Adams, and Thurlow Weed. An industrious young scholar, Sowle took advantage of access to the papers of his three key principals to challenge significantly the better-known books by Potter and

Stampp. Sowle faulted Potter for downplaying the "bitter feuding" between conciliatory and hard-line Republican factions, and he thought that Potter overstated Lincoln's ability to rally the party "behind his ideas about the crisis." Sowle also faulted Stampp for exaggerating the readiness of Republicans for war. But Sowle's segments on the would-be thirteenth amendment are cursory. He knew that the amendment emerged as a pivotal issue during the last week of the congressional session. He doubted, however, that Lincoln had any interest in it, and he was unaware that two differing versions of the amendment were under discussion.[15]

A journal article by R. Alton Lee, "The Corwin Amendment in the Secession Crisis," published in 1961, also called attention to Corwin's efforts on behalf of the would-be thirteenth amendment. Lee correctly noted that the amendment, both then and since, was overshadowed by Crittenden's proposed compromise and the work of the Washington Peace Conference. The amendment's last-minute passage was "prompted by the necessity of holding the border states in the Union." On the basis of circumstantial evidence, Lee surmised that Lincoln had promoted the amendment from the start in order to deflect demands for a compromise on the territorial issue—a view that has since received strong endorsement from William J. Cooper, Michael F. Holt, and Phillip Magness. Together with Nichols, Lee provided the most detailed account until now of the amendment's passage in the House and Senate.[16]

A 1977 journal article by Norman Graebner, "Thomas Corwin and the Sectional Crisis," offered less than Nichols or Lee about the actual passage of the amendment by Congress. He focused instead on the work of the Committee of Thirty Three in December and January. Graebner emphasized Corwin's distance from the Republican mainstream. A "reluctant Republican" who hoped to "convince Southerners that the Whig tradition lived on in the Republican Party," Corwin actually favored a territorial compromise such as the restoration of the Missouri line. The constitutional amendment was a "futile" fallback, doomed to irrelevance because "Corwin's voice was never that of the Republican Party." Graebner had a point—Corwin, like Seward, would have been open to restoration of the Missouri Compromise, which said nothing one way or the other about territory south of 36° 30′. But Lincoln and the Republican Party generally were not prepared to make such an offer even though the party had first arisen to protest repeal of the Missouri Compromise. So Corwin (and Seward) played the cards they were dealt as best they could. A majority of Republicans did not want the amendment, but Lincoln accepted it, and it became the centerpiece of his administration's policy toward the Union slave states during the key interval in late February and early March 1861.[17]

When David Potter died in 1971, he left an unfinished draft of his masterwork, *The Impending Crisis, 1848–1861*. It appeared five years later, completed and edited by Don E. Fehrenbacher. Its penultimate chapter, "Winter Crisis," included the arresting assertion that the territorial issue by early 1861 had become an empty sideshow that was "largely exhausted," whereas the constitutional amendment, by contrast, could have been "an appallingly greater concession to the South." This striking sentence reversed Potter's earlier dismissal of the amendment. And it informs every page of this study.[18] The overall editors of the New American Nation

Series, in which Potter's great book appeared, reported that Fehrenbacher wrote the last two chapters. But at many points in those last two chapters, both the ideas and the pattern of word usage appear more characteristic of Potter than of Fehrenbacher. Potter used memorable words and phrases such as "appallingly," "admirable felicity," "irresolute," and "eruptive," but none of these appear in Fehrenbacher's own final book, which is available for electronic searching.[19]

Contemporary historians who write about the secession crisis have not taken into account Potter's valedictory assessment. They are aware of the prospective thirteenth amendment, but they usually depict it as marginal and secondary—as indeed it appeared at the time. Its passage by Congress was a "small action," writes Maury Klein, and few "expected anything from it." He views the amendment as an inadequate "pacifier," a footnote to the failed efforts to enact a more substantive compromise. Because majorities of Republicans in both the House and Senate opposed it, the party overall "stood fast against compromise."[20]

Many historians today eagerly display themselves as proemancipation and pro-Lincoln. Accordingly they find it challenging to explain Lincoln's position on the would-be thirteenth amendment. In some instances they simply ignore it. This is what Harold Holzer chose to do in *Lincoln President-Elect*, an otherwise minute and admiring account of Lincoln's life from the presidential election through to the inauguration. Holzer briefly dismisses the amendment—it was "toothless" and "tepid," a "last-gasp effort." But he doesn't touch the evidence that Lincoln played a concealed role in securing its passage. And Holzer pointedly ignores the key passage in Lincoln's inaugural address, where the new president announced that he could accept it.[21] Brian Dirck's study *Lincoln and the Constitution* likewise is entirely silent regarding the would-be thirteenth amendment notwithstanding a title that would appear to invite serious consideration of the subject.[22]

Doris Kearns Goodwin's beautifully written and widely read 2005 book, *Team of Rivals*, focuses on the interactions of Lincoln, Seward, and Salmon P. Chase. Her subtitle, *The Political Genius of Abraham Lincoln*, plainly indicates her overall view. Goodwin suggests that Lincoln might not have wanted to mention the amendment in his inaugural but that he substantially rewrote the document at Seward's behest. Readers are left with the impression that Lincoln bent over backwards to accommodate his soon-to-be secretary of state and that this episode did not measure up to the new president's otherwise high standards.[23]

Adam Goodheart gained wide notice for his book *1861: The Civil War Awakening*, which focuses on Northern attitudes between the autumn months of 1860 and the early summer of 1861. His core idea is that white Northerners, having long blinded themselves to the obvious, awoke to take on the task at hand. They finally grasped that emancipation was necessary. Thus, it was "a war against slavery, even before it began." Goodheart therefore has difficulty explaining Lincoln's professed readiness to accept the amendment. He surmises that this part of the inaugural address was composed in an apparent fit of absentmindedness. For good reason, Goodheart observes, the first inaugural is not "quoted much today."[24]

The most sustained effort to depict Lincoln as a radical emancipationist throughout his presidency—and indeed long before—was written by James Oakes, who, like Goodheart, exudes confidence that "the destruction of slavery was inscribed in the Republican electoral victory in November of 1860." In *Freedom National: The Destruction of Slavery in the United States, 1861–1865*, Oakes contends that Lincoln and the Republican Party were committed not only to banning slavery in the territories but also to "abolishing it in Washington," repealing "the despised Fugitive Slave Act," and "admitting no new slave states into the Union." They hoped to bring about abolition sooner rather than later. Lincoln also suspected, Oakes maintains, that slavery could not be abolished peacefully. By the time of his inauguration, he and "virtually all Republicans" understood that "secession meant war and war meant immediate emancipation."[25]

Here with a vengeance is history written from the heart—history as we might like it to have been. But the interpretation Oakes presents cannot stand scrutiny. In his famous senatorial debate with Stephen A. Douglas at Freeport, Illinois, on August 27, 1858, and repeatedly thereafter, Lincoln specifically disavowed every advanced position that Oakes attributes to him. Responding to questions from Douglas, who was attempting to paint him as an abolitionist, Lincoln vowed that he had never advocated "the unconditional repeal of the fugitive slave law." He would not bar additional slave states from joining the Union. And he was not "pledged to the abolition of slavery in the District of Columbia." Douglas persisted by showing that Elihu Washburne, an ally of Lincoln's who represented the Freeport district in Congress, had run on a platform in 1854 that included all the heresies that Lincoln just disavowed. Lincoln then wrote privately to Washburne and hoped that he might qualify his position regarding the admission of slave states—but if he could not do so, "burn this without answering it."[26]

In 1859 and 1860, Lincoln continued to deflect accusations that he or the Republican Party embraced radical or abolitionist ideas, and he reined in those in the party who had a more expansive antislavery agenda than territorial restriction. Repeatedly he cautioned other Republicans against "tilting against the Fugitive Slave law." That would "utterly overwhelm us in Illinois with the charge of enmity to the constitution itself." He ghost-wrote a document to emphasize that he would consider emancipation in Washington, DC, only if it were approved by a majority of residents there and done gradually, with compensation to slaveholders.[27]

Oakes calls attention to an oft-reprinted article from the *Chicago Daily Democrat*, edited by "Long John" Wentworth, which "spelled out in dramatic detail what would happen to the slave states should Republicans triumph at the polls." Wentworth sneered, just before the November 1860 election, that the South could keep its "barbarous system of slavery" but could no longer expand it to new territories. Surrounded by "a cordon of Free States, as with a wall of fire," slavery would "gradually die out." But there are problems with this piece of "dramatic detail." Oakes never mentions that Wentworth was prone to outbursts that made mainstream Republicans consider him an irresponsible loose cannon. Indeed, some of Lincoln's supporters feared that Wentworth was a wolf in sheep's clothing who deliberately published radical editorials that made Lincoln appear to be an "ultra abolitionist." Just after the election, Wentworth threatened to hang any of the "cowardly" and insolent "slave oligarchy" who dared to try their "little game of secession." Widely reprinted and commented upon in the South, this bit of over-the-top taunting became such an embarrassment that Lincoln felt obliged to shoot it down. "Were the character of the *Chicago Democrat* understood in the South as well as it is here in Illinois," announced the *Illinois State Journal*, the Springfield newspaper widely presumed to speak for the president-elect, "Mr. Lincoln would not be held responsible for such sensational articles. . . . It is hardly necessary for us to say, from what we know of Mr. Lincoln, that its insulting tone in no manner reflects his feelings or sentiments."[28]

Oakes makes light of the time frame Wentworth mentioned—that the child already was born "who will live to see the emancipation of the last slave on the American Continent." In other words, emancipation might be completed around 1950. Lincoln himself once likewise speculated during his debates with Douglas that the ultimate extinction of slavery would require "a hundred years at the least"—but Oakes writes that Lincoln reversed himself "in the very next breath." That is incorrect: Lincoln immediately moved to a different topic. However much they differed regarding anti-Southern grandstanding, neither Wentworth nor Lincoln contemplated that slavery might end in the foreseeable future—and their views were shared by the overwhelming majority of Republicans. Goodheart and Oakes believe that people in the free states eagerly welcomed an abolition war even before the first exchange of shots at Fort Sumter. A few unrepresentative outliers did so, but the generalization cannot be sustained.[29]

Oakes offers only the most cursory mention of the would-be constitutional amendment. A "pointless" and "meaningless" reiteration of the position that anti-slavery politicians long had articulated, the amendment "changed nothing." Lincoln's endorsement of it was strictly "pro forma." Republicans intended to strangle slavery and to do so sooner rather than later, Oakes insists, while Southerners correctly recognized that they were gravely imperiled. He mentions that "a number of congressional Republicans" voted against the amendment, but he is unaware that Republicans divided sharply on the matter, with majorities in both houses opposed to the supposed "empty gesture" and Lincoln siding with the pro-amendment minority. Finally, Oakes ignores the evidence that Lincoln and most other Republicans in early March wanted to preserve the peace. They hoped that the fever in the South might start to break once it became apparent that Southern rights in the Union were unchanged from what they had been before.[30]

Oakes has collected glowing endorsements.[31] A useful corrective may be found, however, in Robert J. Cook's biography of William Pitt Fessenden, a notable U.S. senator from Maine. Although the political antislavery movement elevated Fessenden to power, he was neither an abolitionist nor someone with strong humanitarian sensibilities. He thought that the South exercised disproportionate power in the nation. As discussed in chapters 4 and 8, he welcomed the showdown that followed Lincoln's election, and he was confident that the disunion movement would crumble if Republicans refused to compromise. He did not expect a war, and he certainly had no agenda for uprooting the slave system in the states where it existed. His biographer considers the influential Fessenden a representative Republican whose "centrist" views typified the party.[32]

Bibliographical Postscript

Russell McClintock provides the most reliable guide to the overall situation in late 1860 and early 1861, as may be seen by my reliance on his work throughout this book. He tersely summarizes the divergent perspectives of the two key principals. Seward knew that Southern Unionism was precarious. Even though "Upper South unionists denied that the Republican threat to slavery was severe or imminent enough to justify immediate secession," they demanded Republican concessions. But Lincoln knew that any reversal of Republican policy would destroy the party, and he "did not understand why repeated assurances that the North had neither authority nor inclination to interfere with slavery were not enough to satisfy the South." McClintock offers a conventional view of the amendment, which he pronounces "a relatively harmless gesture" that had little effect. He notes that the package created by the House Committee of Thirty Three—the proposed constitutional amendment plus New Mexico statehood—was initially overshadowed by the Senate Committee of Thirteen's well-publicized deadlock and by Northern indignation at South Carolina's attack on the *Star of the West* in Charleston harbor. Although conciliatory Republicans thereafter became more amenable to making overtures to border state Unionists, the party remained paralyzed by conflicting impulses of conciliation and firmness. Some Republicans contended that the paramount matter was to keep the Upper South in the Union while others said that any Northern concessions would appease traitors. "Seward's constitutional amendment" was the one concession to run the gauntlet and win approval because it did not touch Republican opposition to slavery expansion and because Republicans all along "denied the federal government's right to interfere with slavery in the states."[33]

Michael Burlingame's two-volume epic, *Abraham Lincoln: A Life*, is the most comprehensive modern biography available. Burlingame thinks that Lincoln supported the amendment as "a sop to the Sewardites and to public opinion in the Upper South and the Border States." Lincoln took the position he did knowing that "the amendment had little chance of being adopted by three-quarters of the states." Burlingame also floats the possibility that Lincoln accepted the amendment only inadvertently and that Seward somehow tricked him into commending it in his inaugural address. Here Burlingame relies on the authority of John A. Bingham, the Ohio radical who looms large in this book. It is apparent why Lincoln might have wanted Bingham to think something along these lines—the future Father of the Fourteenth Amendment adamantly opposed countenancing slavery in the Constitution. But Bingham's 1886 recollection—a full quarter century after the event—cannot easily be squared with available evidence from February and March 1861. Lincoln was never haphazard in his use of words, and Burlingame himself correctly surmises that Lincoln covertly aided the moderate Republicans who were attempting to get the amendment passed. Burlingame also writes—and I agree with him—that Lincoln anticipated a peaceful resolution to the secession crisis when he delivered his inaugural address. If so, the amendment cannot be dismissed as an empty gesture.[34]

Eric Foner wisely cautions that "we should not see Lincoln's career as a straight line leading to emancipation."[35] In his compelling and widely read book *The Fiery Trial*, Foner recognizes that the constitutional amendment was more than just "a minor concession" and that it angered many hard-line Republicans. But Foner judges that the South correctly understood Lincoln—that he was unwilling to retreat from "the central issue of the controversy," his insistence that slavery was wrong and ought not to be allowed to expand. Accordingly "many Southerners did not view Lincoln's inaugural address as conciliatory." And Foner notes that an even more thoroughgoing concession "would not have brought back the seven seceded states." The Crittenden Compromise "would have strengthened the hand of Unionists in the Upper South" but would have done nothing to resolve the crisis. Most so-called Unionists "were prepared to secede rather than see force used against the Confederacy even if the latter struck the first blow." Foner implies that Lincoln was posturing when he commended the amendment. He knew that it would have no effect, but he used it to put the blame for the coming war where it belonged.[36]

The principal difficulty with Foner's formulation is his confidence that things were bound to turn out exactly as they did. From the perspective of early March 1861, however, the future was inscrutable. Considerable evidence suggests that Lincoln hoped to preserve the peace at the moment he took office—a view shared by both David Potter and Michael Burlingame—and that Lincoln hoped that his reassurances might find an audience among reasonable Southerners.[37] Historians need to keep in mind that history is "understood backwards"—as if viewed through a rearview mirror—even though it must be "lived forwards." Hindsight strips away history's "cliff-hanging excitement" and its ability to surprise.[38] By knowing what happened, we impose on ourselves a kind of tunnel vision, in which the course of history is predetermined and the more astute actors at the time understand what is coming.

Mark Stegmaier provides a carefully annotated collection of dispatches written anonymously by young Henry Adams during the secession winter for the *Boston Advertiser*. Adams was moonlighting from his regular job as secretary for his father, Charles Francis Adams, a key promoter of the constitutional amendment. Henry Adams used his ringside seat in Washington to explicate the conciliatory overtures developed by his father and Seward. The collection acquires added weight because Henry Adams already had keen historical sensibilities; he knew that he was witnessing scenes that would engage the attention of historians "a century or two hence." Stegmaier's welcome book complements a related published chapter of private family letters in which Henry Adams candidly enlightened his brother, Charles Francis Adams Jr., about the unfolding drama.[39]

Building on David Potter's insights, Don H. Doyle demonstrates that the American Civil War occurred at a critical moment in the worldwide history of liberal nationalism. So long as Union leaders rejected emancipation, Europeans found it impossible to accept American claims that the war was being waged for some higher purpose. Lincoln's explicit embrace of the would-be thirteenth amendment "demoralized friends of freedom around the world." Doyle shows how the subsequent enlargement of Union war aims restored the stature of the United States as an exemplar of democratic nationalism and carried great weight in the battle for European public opinion. James Ashley certainly would have agreed.[40]

William J. Cooper separates himself from modern secession crisis historiography, especially the pro-Lincoln version. Deploring the incoming president's unwillingness to accept a Union-saving compromise, he contends that the crisis might have been resolved peacefully in December had Lincoln reached out promptly to Jefferson Davis and accepted the Crittenden plan. Lincoln's refusal to do so marked him, in Cooper's eyes, as "a partisan's partisan, not the leader of a country." In my view, Cooper's bold challenge to conventional wisdom falls short even though based on deep research in relevant primary sources. Had Lincoln done what Cooper wanted, he would have destroyed the Republican Party. And it is far from clear whether, by so doing, he could have arrested the secession movement in the Deep South. Davis was no longer leading there but was instead rushing desperately to catch up. Because Cooper thinks the Deep South could have been deterred only by a rapid offer of the Crittenden Compromise, he cannot see comparable merit in the Border State Plan or the constitutional amendment, which were designed to hold the Upper South. In his view they were too little and too late to be effective, and the amendment did not even touch the territorial issue. Cooper notwithstanding, the most spectacular leadership failure in 1860–61 was not Lincoln's. The leading men in the Deep South have a far better claim to that dubious distinction. They set in motion a panic they could not control. Never in American history did political leaders make such a disastrous miscalculation.[41]

One self-described historian, Thomas J. DiLorenzo, ought not be considered among the scholars already mentioned. His polemic, *Lincoln Unmasked: What You're Not Supposed to Know about Dishonest Abe*, contends that Lincoln only pretended to dislike slavery. DiLorenzo attempts to show, instead, that Lincoln had proslavery and racist motives for trying to weaken Northern state personal liberty laws and for accepting the constitutional amendment. Indeed, he depicts Lincoln as the master manipulator who hatched the amendment scheme. At the same time, DiLorenzo writes, Lincoln cynically used the territorial issue to goad white Southerners to fight. Lincoln's motive throughout, as DiLorenzo sees it, was to establish Northern economic supremacy. He shed oceans of blood and destroyed the old prewar Constitution to accomplish his objectives. Does DiLorenzo believe what he writes? I have no idea. But I do know that his work has as much relation to history as astrology does to astronomy, or scientology to science.[42]

As noted in Epilogue One, Michael Vorenberg wrote the first full book about ratifying the actual Thirteenth Amendment that did become part of the Constitution in 1865—the amendment that abolished slavery. But he begins by examining the situation that prevailed in the antebellum era, when most Americans believed that "Congress could not abolish slavery in the states." During the secession crisis, Vorenberg writes, a flurry of proposed amendments, among them Seward's, offered even greater protections to the South and slavery than had been part of the original Constitution. By specifically affirming what was already generally assumed, Seward hoped to "put an end to secessionist propaganda that Republicans planned to abolish slavery." House and Senate passage of Seward's amendment marked "the first legislative success of the embryonic Lincoln administration," Vorenberg states. But he has nothing good to say about this ironic "success." It was "an expedient tool to preserve the loyalty of the upper South and to breed Unionism in the deep

South." Even though Lincoln gave the amendment a "lukewarm" endorsement in his inaugural address, Vorenberg judges that the president and other Republicans had been "unnerved" to have supported it in the first place. More than a century before, James G. Blaine made the same criticism.[43]

Leonard L. Richards wrote the other full book on the Thirteenth Amendment, as also discussed in Epilogue One. Richards both complements and supplements Vorenberg's account. Richards surmises—correctly in my opinion—that Lincoln and Thurlow Weed put the other thirteenth amendment in motion when they consulted in Springfield in December 1860. Richards also explains why Corwin decided at the last minute to go for Seward's version of the amendment rather than the one proposed to the House by Charles Francis Adams. Like Vorenberg, Richards is appalled that both houses of Congress approved the amendment. Borrowing Franklin D. Roosevelt's memorable phrase, Richards surmises that the hero of his book, Ohio congressman James Ashley, thought the day the Senate voted "should live in infamy." This is doubtless true. Ashley retrospectively stated that no more "shameless exhibition on the part of a civilized people can be found in history." But there is a great irony involved. If March 4, 1861, was a day of infamy, it also was the great day that every Republican eagerly anticipated—not least Ashley—when Abraham Lincoln first took his oath of office. The paradoxical confluence of these two events lies at the heart of this book.[44]

Afterword

I explained in chapter 9 that this book originated when I stumbled across Thaddeus Stevens's early 1861 speech, in which he explained that "the anti-slavery party of the North never interfered, or claimed the right to interfere, or expressed a desire to intermeddle, with . . . slavery in the States where it existed." A little more browsing revealed that Owen Lovejoy agreed. "If a bill were brought in here for that purpose to-day," he stated, "I would not vote for it; because I do not think that the Constitution gives us the power to abolish it; and not because I do not wish to see it abolished, for God knows that I do."

If the two most outspokenly antislavery members of the House of Representatives considered slavery in the states beyond reach, it calls into question the whole logic of secession. Were those who tried to break up the Union fleeing a deadly menace? Or were they overreacting to a shadow—and in the process creating what soon became a deadly menace? Stevens and Lovejoy believed that they could not touch slavery during peacetime, but wartime soon became another story entirely. By forfeiting the protection of the Constitution, the slaveholders left themselves uniquely vulnerable.

At this point, I decided to learn more about the history of the so-called Corwin Amendment, the eleventh-hour effort to add reassuring (for slaveholders) words to the Constitution. Suddenly concocted in late 1860, as we have seen, the prospective amendment briefly seemed to offer a way to blunt the secession impulse and reverse the slide toward war. The incoming president, later to become the Great Emancipator, even accepted it in his inaugural address. I soon found that the story of the amendment had fallen between the cracks, that William H. Seward was at least as much its mastermind as Thomas Corwin, that neither would have acted without the tacit acquiescence of the president-elect, and that much could be learned about the broader crisis by bringing the amendment into sharp focus. Even though it was almost universally assumed that slavery in the states could not be disturbed, the amendment was controversial. Hard-line Republicans such as Stevens and Lovejoy spurned it. They recognized that slavery in the states could not be legislated away, but they saw no reason to amend the Constitution to that effect. They considered any seeming concession to the South humiliating and inadmissible.

The political crisis that led to civil war has long intrigued me. During the wild five-month ride between Abraham Lincoln's election as president in November 1860 and the fall of Fort Sumter in April 1861, all previous political arrangements and taken-for-granteds suddenly became obsolete, and the unimaginable became the new reality. Nothing at all comparable had ever before occurred. The European powers watched smugly and waited for the upstart colossus across the ocean to crumble. I always have tried to understand the crisis on its own terms, to learn what the participants at the time thought they were doing, and to discover how they expected the situation to play out. By so doing, I have set myself apart from those historians who emphasize moral imperatives and celebrate the roles played by abolitionists and hard-line Republicans. I too honor those individuals who gave priority to the core principles of the New Testament and the Declaration of Independence. But I worry that historians shortchange the big picture when they play favorites. We cannot understand the most calamitous political breakdown in American history merely by commending those historical actors whose ideas square with modern sensibilities.

Students in two sections of my seminar on Abraham Lincoln at The College of New Jersey wrestled with a rough draft of this book in 2013 and offered me many useful suggestions for its revision. I greatly appreciate the work of Alyssa Anderson, Kimberly Costanzo, Eric Discepolo, Jonathan Dowler, Samantha Falvey, Rebecca Flores, Benito Gonzalez, Diane Iannacone, Ashley Isola, Jessica Lessner, Alexa Logush, Dylan Lynch, Alexandra Marshall, Nicole Mascetti, Katherine Miller, Paul Mitchell, Caroline Nucatola, Stephanie Pappas, Kathryn Picardo, John Potestivo, Nicole Prozzo, Chelsea Sandmeyer, Leilani Saunders, Nicholas Schade, Steven Thompson, and Caitlin Wiesner. Both they and I enjoyed the refreshing role reversal—as the teacher's draft chapters were subjected to the withering critical scrutiny of twenty-eight hardworking apprentices. This book is dedicated to them and to the thousands of other TSC and TCNJ students who brightened my life during the past four decades. Special thanks to Bruce Eelman, Rob Cook, and Holly Kent, whose accomplishments and friendship so validate my work as a teacher. Many others leap to mind, notwithstanding the passage of time—Corlis Holman, Stephanie Steinberg, Jennifer Fleming, Colleen McDermott, Ann Marie Nicolosi, Dave O'Neill, Danielle Sabato Burke, Ryan Christiansen, Maria Tomasetti, Matt DeBlock, Caitlin Dearing, Lauren Wells, Bill Rosselli, Vidya Subramanian, Julie Sears, Josh Luger, Kevin Caprice, Aaron Harmaty, Joanna Oliver, the many spirited students who enrolled in Modern World History in spring 2005, the high-octane cohort who arrived to study the Coming of the Civil War in fall 2012, and my last two classes in spring 2014. The College of New Jersey awarded me a sabbatical semester to complete the research for this book and to write its initial draft. Cynthia Paces, who so ably chairs the History Department, has always gone the extra mile for me. The college's interlibrary loan specialist, Elizabeth Maziarz, tracked down many essential sources.

Someone from a different generation entirely contributed significantly to this book. Frank Maloy Anderson (1871–1961), a pioneering professional historian, was a relentless researcher. For many years he painstakingly compiled and organized thousands of notes from which he planned to build a multivolume history of the secession crisis, prospectively entitled "The Two Hundred Days of 1860–1861." Alas, the book never got written. Anderson's son instead willed the collection of notes to the Library of Congress. They function today as a marvelously specific road map. Anderson has posthumously guided my own research and led me to many pertinent manuscript and newspaper collections. While at the Library of Congress, I have benefited especially from the assistance of Jeffrey M. Flannery and his staff in the Manuscript Division. The Library of Congress also has created digital images for thousands of Civil War-era photographs, especially its Brady-Handy Collection. Assisted also by Wikimedia Commons, scholars now have unrestricted access to a priceless archive of photographs from more than a century and a half ago when this striking new technology had just burst onto the scene.

285

Several colleagues read and commented on papers I presented at panels of the Society for Historians of the Early American Republic in July 2011, the Abraham Lincoln Institute Symposium in March 2012, and the Society of Civil War Historians in June 2012. I thank Kristen Oertel, Michael Burlingame, Stephen Maizlish, Frank Towers, Rachel Shelden, and Matthew Mason for reacting to early versions of what I had to say about the other thirteenth amendment and for helping me visualize how these ideas might be structured in a book. Philip Magness kindly allowed me to use some of his research about ratifying the amendment. Gregory Peek generously shared his deep knowledge of Indiana politics. Mark Stegmaier will not agree with every word here, but I know that our conversations and his diligent research have made this a better book. Russell McClintock critiqued my earlier papers and has influenced me in myriad ways. Clay Risen, editor of the *New York Times* Disunion blog, gave me a crash course about writing for a wider public. Several of my Disunion essays reappear here in revised form with the permission of the *Times*. Clay also hit upon the "other thirteenth amendment" sobriquet before my students and I did.

Charles Dew and Jonathan Earle read the manuscript version of this book's penultimate draft for the University of North Carolina Press. They affirmed that the topic was a worthy one and showed me how to pull the final version into shape. I am fortunate indeed to have had such expert readers. UNC Press called all hands on deck to get this volume into print. Jad Adkins, Dino Battista, Kim Bryant, Michael Donatelli, Laura Dooley, Rebecca Evans, Chuck Grench, Gina Mahalek, Jay Mazzocchi, John Sherer, Mark Simpson-Vos, and Iza Wojciechowska have led this memorable team effort. UNC Press has also allowed me to extract a few passages from my 1989 book, *Reluctant Confederates: Upper South Unionists in the Secession Crisis*.

Loving support from Betsy Crofts, Anita Verna Crofts, Sarah Crofts, and Tori (the best cat in the world) is a great gift. Without it, I could not write. Betsy waded through my prose during the weeks before the final version went into the mail, and she repeatedly found that I think faster than I type. So her eagle editorial eye in spotting omitted words must be included on the long list of her abundant virtues. I am staring at a computer screen amid mid-September warmth at the farmhouse on Quaker Ridge. Summer lingers but autumn impends. I have tried to understand and explain history for over half a century.

Daniel W. Crofts
Casco, Maine
September 17, 2015

Afterword

Notes

Abbreviations

AEJ   *Albany Evening Journal*

CF Adams Diary
    Charles Francis Adams Diary, Massachusetts Historical Society

CG, 36:2 (Jan. 12, 1861), 341–44
    Congressional Globe, 36th Cong., 2d Sess. (Jan. 12, 1861), 341–44

Crofts, *Reluctant Confederates*
    Daniel W. Crofts, *Reluctant Confederates: Upper South Unionists in the Secession Crisis* (Chapel Hill: University of North Carolina Press, 1989)

CWAL Roy P. Basler, ed., *The Collected Works of Abraham Lincoln*, 9 vols. (New Brunswick, NJ: Rutgers University Press, 1953–55)

Freehling, *Road*
    William W. Freehling, *The Road to Disunion*, vol. 1, *Secessionists at Bay, 1776–1854*; vol. 2, *Secessionists Triumphant, 1854–1861* (New York: Oxford University Press, 1990, 2007)

LC   Library of Congress

Lincoln Papers
    The Robert Todd Lincoln Collection of the Papers of Abraham Lincoln, Library of Congress

McClintock, *Lincoln and the Decision for War*
    Russell McClintock, *Lincoln and the Decision for War: The Northern Response to Secession* (Chapel Hill: University of North Carolina Press, 2008)

Nichols, *Disruption*
    Roy Franklin Nichols, *The Disruption of American Democracy* (New York: Macmillan, 1948)

NY Herald
    New York Herald

NY Times
    New York Times

NY Tribune
>New York Tribune

Potter, *Impending Crisis*
>David M. Potter, *The Impending Crisis, 1846–1861*, completed and edited by Don E. Fehrenbacher (New York: Harper and Row, 1976)

Potter, *Lincoln and His Party*
>David M. Potter, *Lincoln and His Party in the Secession Crisis* (New Haven, CT: Yale University Press, 1942, 1962; the 1962 edition is reprinted with introduction by Daniel W. Crofts [Baton Rouge: Louisiana State University Press, 1995])

Seward Papers
>William Henry Seward Papers, University of Rochester

Weed Papers
>Thurlow Weed Papers, University of Rochester

Prologue

1. The "legislative day" of Saturday, March 2, remained in effect as the Senate went into marathon session on Sunday evening and Monday morning, March 3 and 4. All entries in the *Congressional Globe* on March 2, 3, and 4 are dated March 2.

2. *CG*, 36:2 (Mar. 2, 1861), 1400; Alvy L. King, *Louis T. Wigfall: Southern Fire-Eater* (Baton Rouge: Louisiana State University Press, 1970), 110–11; H. L. Trefousse, *Benjamin Franklin Wade: Radical Republican from Ohio* (New York: Twayne, 1963), 141–43, nickname on 64.

3. *CG*, 36:2 (Mar. 2, 1861), 1387–89, 1391; Robert W. Young, *Senator James Murray Mason: Defender of the Old South* (Knoxville: University of Tennessee Press, 1998), xii, 104–5.

4. *CG*, 36:2 (Mar. 2, 1861), 1387–89, 1395; Robert W. Johannsen, *Stephen A. Douglas* (New York: Oxford University Press, 1973), 4–5, 498–99, 659–60, 836–39.

5. *CG*, 36:2 (Mar. 2, 1861), 1391.

6. Crofts, *Reluctant Confederates*, 257–59; McClintock, *Lincoln and the Decision for War*, 209–12; John A. Gilmer to Stephen A. Douglas, Mar. 8, 10, 1861, Douglas Papers, University of Chicago. So far as I know, Gilmer initiated the "bread pills" analogy—"The South is deranged, and only needs a few bread pills, to cure their madness." Gilmer to Thurlow Weed, Jan. 12, 1861, Weed Papers.

7. *CG*, 36:2 (Mar. 2, 1861), 1400.

8. Walter Stahr, *Seward: Lincoln's Indispensable Man* (New York: Simon and Schuster, 2012), 239–45; Crofts, *Reluctant Confederates*, 254; McClintock, *Lincoln and the Decision for War*, 194–99; *CG*, 36:2 (Mar. 2, 1861), 1360.

9. "Two Nights in the Senate," *Harper's Weekly*, Mar. 16, 1861, 162; The *New York Herald* specified on March 5 that the vote took place just before 5:20 A.M. This is likely accurate. Other sources place it anywhere between 4:30 and 6:30 A.M. It appears that some reporters assigned to cover the Senate may not have been awake

when the crucial vote took place. On the rebuilding of the U.S. Capitol in the latter 1850s and early 1860s, see Guy Gugliotta, *Freedom's Cap: The United States Capitol and the Coming of the Civil War* (New York: Hill and Wang, 2012).

10. Abraham Lincoln, First Inaugural Address, Mar. 4, 1861, *CWAL*, 4:270–71.

11. Abraham Lincoln, Second Inaugural Address, Mar. 4, 1865, *CWAL*, 289 8:332–33.

12. The ideas in this paragraph have multiple origins. See especially Freehling, *Road*; J. Mills Thornton III, *Politics and Power in a Slave Society: Alabama, 1800–1860* (Baton Rouge: Louisiana State University Press, 1978); and William L. Barney, "Rush to Disaster: Secession and the Slaves' Revenge," in Robert J. Cook, William L. Barney, and Elizabeth R. Varon, *Secession Winter: When the Union Fell Apart* (Baltimore: Johns Hopkins University Press, 2013), 10–33.

13. Crofts, *Reluctant Confederates*.

14. Michael Burlingame and John R. Turner Ettlinger, eds., *Inside Lincoln's White House: The Complete Civil War Diary of John Hay* (Carbondale: Southern Illinois University Press, 1997), 41 (Sept. 24, 1862).

15. *CG*, 36:2 (Feb. 28, 1861), 1284. Confusion regarding the word "slavery" and the matter of irrevocability may also have its roots in the incorrect assumption that the prospective thirteenth amendment passed by Congress in late February and early March 1861 read the same way as a related part of the so-called Crittenden Compromise. A copy of the Crittenden Compromise may be consulted in the *CG*, 36:2 (Feb. 27, 1861), 1260–61. The prospective thirteenth amendment appeared to preclude future congressional action against slavery. Nevertheless, it would have remained subject to repeal. Half a century later, in 1919, national prohibition was enacted by the Eighteenth Amendment but then rescinded when the Twenty-First Amendment repealed the Eighteenth in 1933. Article 5 of the Constitution prohibits only two types of amendment—interfering with the importation of slaves before 1808 and depriving any state of equal representation in the U.S. Senate.

16. Nichols, *Disruption*, 475–82, see also 481; Potter, *Impending Crisis*, 552–53. See the Bibliographical Postscript for confirmation that Potter rather than Fehrenbacher wrote this key sentence.

17. Nichols would have rejected my animal categories. His ultimate verdict on the prospective thirteenth amendment of 1861 was that "after great labor the Congress had brought forth a mouse that scurried around for only a few moments, scarcely noticed." Nichols, *Blueprints for Leviathan: American Style* (New York: Atheneum, 1963), 173.

18. David Lowenthal, *The Past Is a Foreign Country* (Cambridge: Cambridge University Press, 1985), xix, 343, 348.

19. David W. Blight, *Race and Reunion: The Civil War in American Memory* (Cambridge, MA: Harvard University Press, 2001), 231, 236–37; Abraham Lincoln to Joshua Speed, Aug. 24, 1855, *CWAL*, 2:320.

20. Harold Holzer, *Lincoln President-Elect: Abraham Lincoln and the Great Secession Winter, 1860–1861* (New York: Simon and Schuster, 2008).

21. Between November and March, patronage requests and recommendations for and against the appointment of various persons dominated Lincoln's incoming

mail and far outnumbered messages that directly addressed North-South issues or secession.

22. James Oakes, *Freedom National: The Destruction of Slavery in the United States, 1861–1865* (New York: W. W. Norton, 2013), 49–54; James Oakes, *The Scorpion's Sting: Antislavery and the Coming of the Civil War* (New York: W. W. Norton, 2014); Adam Goodheart, *1861: The Civil War Awakening* (New York: Alfred A. Knopf, 2011), 19.

23. McClintock, *Lincoln and the Decision for War*, 1; Gary W. Gallagher, *The Union War* (Cambridge, MA: Harvard University Press, 2011).

24. The ideas in this paragraph reflect in part the keen insights of chapters 7 and 8 in Michael F. Holt, *The Political Crisis of the 1850s* (New York: Wiley, 1978), 183–259.

25. My line of thought here owes much to Edward L. Ayers. See his book *In the Presence of Mine Enemies: War in the Heart of America, 1859–1863* (New York: W. W. Norton, 2003), xx, and his essay "Worrying about the Civil War," in *Moral Problems in American Life: New Perspectives on Cultural History*, ed. Karen Halttunen and Lewis Perry (Ithaca, NY: Cornell University Press, 1999), 145–66, reprinted in Edward L. Ayers, *What Caused the Civil War? Reflections on the South and Southern History* (New York: W. W. Norton, 2005), 103–30. See also Daniel W. Crofts, *A Secession Crisis Enigma: William Henry Hurlbert and "The Diary of a Public Man"* (Baton Rouge: Louisiana State University Press, 2010), 190–91.

26. Lowenthal, *Past Is a Foreign Country*.

Chapter 1

1. William Jay to Elizur Wright, Apr. 13, 1838 (draft), John Jay Papers, Columbia University Rare Books and Manuscript Library (hereafter Jay Papers).

2. William Jay, *Miscellaneous Writings on Slavery* (Boston: John P. Jewett, 1853), 353–59; Bayard Tuckerman, *William Jay, and the Constitutional Movement for the Abolition of Slavery* (New York: Dodd, Mead, 1893), 86–91, 96. Jay is the subject of a brief modern biography: Stephen P. Budney, *William Jay: Abolitionist and Anticolonialist* (Westport, CT: Praeger, 2005). Unlike other prominent abolitionists, however, Jay has no entry in the *Dictionary of American Biography*. Bertram Wyatt-Brown wrote in 1969 that Jay is a "much-neglected figure," and that remains true today. Bertram Wyatt-Brown, *Lewis Tappan and the Evangelical War against Slavery* (Cleveland, OH: Press of Case Western Reserve University, 1969), xiii.

3. Jay, *Miscellaneous Writings on Slavery*, 217.

4. Ibid., 218–20; Brian D. Humes et al., "The Representation of the Antebellum South in the House of Representatives: Measuring the Impact of the Three-Fifths Clause," in *Party, Process, and Political Change in Congress: New Perspectives on the History of Congress*, ed. David Brady and Mathew D. McCubbins (Stanford, CA: Stanford University Press, 2002), 452–66.

5. Max Farrand, *The Records of the Federal Convention of 1787*, 3 vols. (New Haven, CT: Yale University Press, 1911), 2:221–23 (Madison's notes, Aug. 8, 1787).

6. Garrett Epps, *Democracy Reborn: The Fourteenth Amendment and the Fight for Equal Rights in Post–Civil War America* (New York: Henry Holt, 2006), 3; Walter Stahr, *John Jay: Founding Father* (London: Bloomsbury Academic, 2005); Edgar J. McManus, *History of Negro Slavery in New York* (Syracuse, NY: Syracuse University Press, 1966); Don E. Fehrenbacher, *The Slaveholding Republic: An Account of the United States Government's Relations to Slavery*, ed. Ward McAfee (New York: Oxford University Press, 2001), 93.

7. Tuckerman, *William Jay*, 29–38.

8. Ibid., 43–52.

9. Jay, *Miscellaneous Writings on Slavery*, 342–51.

10. John C. Calhoun, "Further Remarks in Debate of His Fifth Resolution," in *The Papers of John C. Calhoun*, ed. Clyde N. Wilson et al., 28 vols. (Columbia: University of South Carolina Press, 1959–2003), 14:80–86; *CG*, 25:2 (Dec. 18, 27, 1837, Jan. 3, 1838), 38, 55, 73.

11. Tuckerman, *William Jay*, 8–9, 53–62, 105–6, 158; Robert H. Abzug, *Passionate Liberator: Theodore Dwight Weld and the Dilemma of Reform* (New York: Oxford University Press, 1980), 123–52.

12. Jay, *Miscellaneous Writings on Slavery*, 359–63.

13. Jay to Abel Libolt, Dec. 14, 1838 (draft), Jay Papers; *Constitution of the American Anti-Slavery Society*, in *Constitution of the Anti-Slavery Society* (Boston: Isaac Knapp, 1838), 11, available online through openlibrary.org at http://archive.org/stream/constitutionofan00amer#page/n1/mode/2up. The call for abolition "without expatriation" meant that freed slaves should not be banished from the United States, as proposed by the American Colonization Society (ACS). The AA-SS insisted that the ACS pandered to white racial prejudices and that its approach would never end slavery. For robust overviews of the circumstances leading to the founding of the AA-SS, see James Brewer Stewart, *Holy Warriors: The Abolitionists and American Slavery* (New York: Hill and Wang, 1976), 50–56; and Wyatt-Brown, *Tappan*, 103–9. For an informed reconsideration of the colonization movement, with renewed emphasis on its antislavery motivation, see Beverly C. Tomek, *Colonization and Its Discontents: Emancipation, Emigration, and Antislavery in Antebellum Pennsylvania* (New York: New York University Press, 2012).

14. Jacobus tenBroek, *Equal under Law* (New York: Collier Books, 1965), originally published as *The Antislavery Origins of the Fourteenth Amendment* (Berkeley: University of California Press, 1951), 33.

15. Tuckerman, *William Jay*, 39–43.

16. William M. Wiecek, *The Sources of Antislavery Constitutionalism in America, 1760-1848* (Ithaca, NY: Cornell University Press, 1977), 15–16, 172–201.

17. *Constitution of the Anti-Slavery Society*, 9, 11; Tuckerman, *William Jay*, xi–xii, 69–73.

18. Tuckerman, *William Jay*, 86–91, 96; Jay to Ellis Gray Loring, Mar. 5, 1838 (draft), Jay Papers.

19. TenBroek, *Equal under Law*, 66–69; Alvan Stewart, "A Constitutional Argument on the Subject of Slavery," in tenBroek, *Equal under Law*, 281–95; Luther Rawson Marsh, ed., *Writings and Speeches of Alvan Stewart on Slavery* (New York:

A. B. Burdick, 1860); Frederick J. Blue, "A Self-Sharpening Plough: Alvan Stewart's Challenge to Slavery," in *No Taint of Compromise: Crusaders in Antislavery Politics* (Baton Rouge: Louisiana State University Press, 2005), 15–36, esp. 18, 20–21, 30–33; Wiecek, *Sources of Antislavery Constitutionalism*, 16, 249–75; Jay to Wright, Nov. 13, 1838 (copy), Jay Papers.

20. TenBroek, *Equal under Law*, 69–72; Budney, *William Jay*, 41–44, 60–62.

21. TenBroek, *Equal under Law*, 72–115; Frederick J. Blue, "Free Men, Free Soil, and Free Homes: Jane Swisshelm's Search," in *No Taint of Compromise*, 143–46; William Goodell, *American Constitutional Law, in Its Bearing upon American Slavery*, 2nd ed. (Utica, NY: Lawson and Chaplin, 1846; reprint ed., Freeport, NY: Books for Libraries Press, 1971), 101–2, 133.

22. Marsh, *Writings and Speeches of Stewart*, 142–44; tenBroek, *Equal under Law*, 84–85; Aileen Kraditor, *Means and Ends in American Abolitionism: Garrison and His Critics on Strategy and Tactics, 1834–1850* (New York: Pantheon, 1969), 195.

23. Tuckerman, *William Jay*, 52–53, 86–97; William Jay, *Inquiry into the Character and Tendencies of the American Colonization and American Anti-Slavery Societies*, 4th ed. (New York: R. G. Williams for the American Anti-Slavery Society, 1837), 163–65; Jay to Loring, Mar. 5, 29, 1838 (drafts), Jay to Wright, Apr. 13, 1838 (draft), Nov. 13, 1838 (copy), Jay to Libolt, Jan. 28, 1839 (draft), Jay Papers.

24. Garrison quoted in Kraditor, *Means and Ends in American Abolitionism*, 196–97; James Brewer Stewart, *Wendell Phillips: Liberty's Hero* (Baton Rouge: Louisiana State University Press, 1986), 123–24. Wendell Phillips, *The Constitution, a Pro-Slavery Compact; or, Selections from the Madison Papers*, 2nd ed. (New York: American Anti-Slavery Society, 1845), v–vi; Wiecek, *Sources of Antislavery Constitutionalism*, 16–17, 228–48; Paul Finkelman, "Making a Covenant with Death: Slavery and the Constitutional Convention," The Cleveland Civil War Round Table, http://clevelandcivilwarroundtable.com/articles/society/slavery_founders.htm.

25. Tuckerman, *William Jay*, 52–53, 86–97, 132. Two recent monographs complicate the conventional view of Garrison just summarized. Bruce Laurie focuses on Massachusetts to depict "the passion of antislavery activists for political engagement." Garrison's broad "distrust of politics" never was absolute. He opportunistically allowed himself wiggle room when other abolitionists delved into electoral politics. Laurie provides a detailed study of the interactions among abolitionists, labor reformers, temperance supporters, blacks, and nativists in Garrison's home state, where abolition sentiment was more widespread than anywhere else and where the Liberty and Free Soil Parties established a vigorous presence. Bruce Laurie, *Beyond Garrison: Antislavery and Social Reform* (New York: Cambridge University Press, 2005), 9, 45–46. W. Caleb McDaniel's sprightly study situates the famed abolition leader in the context of international reform politics. McDaniel concludes that Garrison and his allies were "politically savvy, intellectually sophisticated liberal reformers." They knew that the Atlantic world was convulsed by the struggle that pitted democracy against aristocracy and monarchy, and they saw that the American political system never could become healthy and democratic until

cleansed and purified. It was hypocrisy to hold up the United States as an exemplar for the world, the Garrisonians insisted, so long as it was corrupted by slavery and caste prejudice. Their use of "extra-parliamentary tactics" was thus strategic, not holier-than-thou. W. Caleb McDaniel, *The Problem of Democracy in the Age of Slavery: Garrisonian Abolitionists and Transatlantic Reform* (Baton Rouge: Louisiana State University Press, 2013), 15. But for my purposes here, Garrison plainly understood the Constitution in ways that differed from both Jay and Stewart. Jay, too, saw a flawed Constitution, but unlike Garrison, he attempted to work within its constraints. Stewart's and Garrison's views of the Constitution were polar opposites, however much they shared a prophetic utopianism.

26. Eric Foner, *The Fiery Trial: Abraham Lincoln and American Slavery* (New York: W. W. Norton, 2010), xix.

27. Wiecek, *Sources of Antislavery Constitutionalism*, 16–17, 202–27. The best single source on the rise of antislavery politics is Richard H. Sewell, *Ballots for Freedom: Antislavery Politics in the United States, 1837–1860* (New York: Oxford University Press, 1976), though the author might not accept the emphasis in this paragraph regarding the limitations that Republicans imposed on themselves. The most incisive assessment of the position of the Republican Party in 1860 is chapter 7 in Michael F. Holt, *The Political Crisis of the 1850s* (New York: Wiley, 1978), 183–218.

28. Wiecek, *Sources of Antislavery Constitutionalism*, 213–17; Sewell, *Ballots for Freedom*; Eric Foner, *Free Soil, Free Labor, Free Men: The Ideology of the Republican Party before the Civil War* (New York: Oxford University Press, 1970); Michael J. McManus, *Political Abolitionism in Wisconsin, 1840–1861* (Kent, OH: Kent State University Press, 1998). For one Republican among many who considered himself "an abolitionist pure and simple," see Samuel Drummond Porter to William H. Seward, Dec. 5, 1860, Seward Papers.

29. William Jay to John Jay, Sept. 13, 1848, Jay Papers; Tuckerman, *William Jay*, 107–57.

30. Tuckerman, *William Jay*, 149–51, 157; William Jay to John Jay, June 7, Sept. 2, 1856, William Jay to Maria Banyer, June 21, 1856, Jay Papers.

31. Tuckerman, *William Jay*, 157; Frederick Douglass, "Eulogy of William Jay," May 12, 1859, in *The Frederick Douglass Papers*, ed. John Blassingame, *Series One: Speeches, Debates, and Interviews*, vol. 3, *1855–63* (New Haven, CT: Yale University Press, 1983), 249–76, quotations on 252–53, 258–59, 265. Douglass glossed over Jay's earlier fears that the abolition movement would suffer if blacks played too prominent a role in it. On Jay's racial views, which became more liberal between the 1830s and 1850s, see Budney, *William Jay*, 39–40, 128; and Wyatt-Brown, *Tappan*, 179.

Chapter 2

1. *CG*, 25:3 (Feb. 13, 1839), 180–81; James Brewer Stewart, "Joshua R. Giddings, Antislavery Violence, and the Politics of Congressional Honor," in *Abolitionist Politics and the Coming of the Civil War* (Amherst: University of Massachusetts Press, 2008), 120–24.

2. James Brewer Stewart, *Joshua R. Giddings and the Tactics of Radical Politics* (Cleveland, OH: Press of Case Western Reserve University, 1970), 43–49, quotations on 44–45; see also the biography by his son-in-law, George W. Julian, *The Life of Joshua R. Giddings* (Chicago: A. C. McClurg, 1892).

3. Potter, *Impending Crisis*, 44–47.

4. Frederick J. Blue, "A Self-Sharpening Plough: Alvan Stewart's Challenge to Slavery," in *No Taint of Compromise: Crusaders in Antislavery Politics* (Baton Rouge: Louisiana State University Press, 2005), 21–30; Luther Rawson Marsh, ed., *Writings and Speeches of Alvan Stewart on Slavery* (New York: A. B. Burdick, 1860), 195–218.

5. *Register of Debates*, 24th Cong., 1st sess. (Feb. 8, 1836), A768–69; Freehling, *Road*, 1:327–36.

6. *CG*, 24:1 (May 25, 1836), 498–99. Leonard L. Richards, *The Life and Times of Congressman John Quincy Adams* (New York: Oxford University Press, 1986), 118–25.

7. *Register of Debates*, 24th Cong., 1st sess. (May 25, 1836), 4040, 4046–47.

8. *CG*, 27:2 (Apr. 15, 1842), 429.

9. Stewart, *Giddings*, 39–40, 67–74; Corey Brooks, "Stoking the 'Abolition Fire in the Capitol': Liberty Party Lobbying and Antislavery in Congress," *Journal of the Early Republic* 33 (2013): 523–48.

10. Stewart, *Giddings*, 103–9; Richards, *Adams*, 171–82, quotation on 182.

11. *CG*, 29:1 (Jan. 5, 1846), A72–74; Richards, *Adams*, 182–85.

12. Stewart, *Giddings*, 110–14; *CG*, 29:1 (Jan. 5, 1846), A72–74.

13. The standard study of the subject, Donald F. Warner, *The Idea of Continental Union: Agitation for the Annexation of Canada in the United States, 1849–1893* (Lexington: University of Kentucky Press, 1960), skirts the pre–Civil War enthusiasm for Canada shared by some Northern opponents of slavery. See Walter G. Sharrow, "William Henry Seward and the Basis for American Empire, 1850–1860," *Pacific Historical Review* 36 (1967): 325–42; and Howard I. Kushner, "Visions of the Northwest Coast: Gwin and Seward in the 1850's," *Western Historical Quarterly* 4 (1973): 295–306.

14. Stewart, *Giddings*, 110–18; Richards, *Adams*, 185–97; Jonathan H. Earle, *Jacksonian Antislavery and the Politics of Free Soil, 1824–1854* (Chapel Hill: University of North Carolina Press, 2004), 123–43.

15. John Niven, *Salmon P. Chase: A Biography* (New York: Oxford University Press, 1995), 79.

16. Salmon P. Chase to Joshua R. Giddings, Feb. 15, 1842, Chase to Gerrit Smith, May 14, 1842, Chase to Henry B. Stanton and Elizur Wright, Sept. 23, 1842, in *The Salmon P. Chase Papers*, vol. 2, *Correspondence, 1823–1857*, ed. John Niven (Kent, OH: Kent State University Press, 1996), 87–89, 96–99, 119–20; Niven, *Chase*, 76–83.

17. Chase to Smith, May 14, 1842, in Niven, *Chase Papers*, 2:96–99; Niven, *Chase*, 88; Earle, *Jacksonian Antislavery*, 144–62.

18. Stanley Harrold, *Gamaliel Bailey and Antislavery Union* (Kent, OH: Kent State University Press, 1986), 64–66; Stephen P. Budney, *William Jay: Abolition-*

ist and Anticolonialist (Westport, CT: Praeger, 2005), 73–76; Gamaliel Bailey to James G. Birney, Mar. 31, 1843, in *Letters of James Gillespie Birney, 1831–1857*, ed. Dwight L. Dumond, 2 vols. (Washington, DC: American Historical Association, 1938), 2:727.

19. Donald Bruce Johnson and Kirk Harold Porter, eds., *National Party Platforms, 1840–1972* (Urbana: University of Illinois Press, 1973), 4–8; Chase to Lewis Tappan, Feb. 15, Sept. 12, 1843, in Niven, *Chase Papers*, 2:101–5; Frederick J. Blue, *The Free Soilers: Third Party Politics, 1848–54* (Urbana: University of Illinois Press, 1973), 1–15; Harrold, *Bailey*, 66, 109–14.

20. Frederick J. Blue, *Salmon P. Chase: A Life in Politics* (Kent, OH: Kent State University Press, 1987), 61–68; Niven, *Chase*, 99–113.

21. Johnson and Porter, *National Party Platforms*, 13–14; Blue, *Free Soilers*, 74–75, 293–94; Niven, *Chase*, 90, 109–10; Joel Silbey, *Party over Section: The Rough and Ready Presidential Election of 1848* (Lawrence: University Press of Kansas, 2009), 77, 164–66.

22. Blue, *Free Soilers*, 141–51; Silbey, *Party over Section*, 142–45; Earle, *Jacksonian Antislavery*, 163–80.

23. Chase to Charles Sumner, Nov. 27, 1848, in Niven, *Chase Papers*, 2:195–99; Stephen E. Maizlish, *The Triumph of Sectionalism: The Transformation of Ohio Politics, 1844–1856* (Kent, OH: Kent State University Press, 1983), 99–120.

24. On the complex Ohio situation that enabled Chase to claim a Senate seat, see Niven, *Chase*, 114–23; Blue, *Chase*, 68–79; and Maizlish, *Triumph of Sectionalism*, 121–46. Sumner's route to the Senate is detailed in David Donald, *Charles Sumner and the Coming of the Civil War* (New York: Alfred A. Knopf, 1960), 183–204. The New Hampshire situation may be traced in Richard H. Sewell, *John P. Hale and the Politics of Abolition* (Cambridge, MA: Harvard University Press, 1965), 49–67; and Earle, *Jacksonian Antislavery*, 78–102.

25. Blue, *Free Soilers*, 137, 188–96.

26. *CG*, 31:1 (Mar. 26–27, 1850), A468–80, quotations on 468–69, 478; Niven, *Chase*, 137–38; Harrold, *Bailey*, 130.

27. *CG*, 31:1 (Feb. 15, 19, May 14, 1850), A222, A178–79, A574.

28. *CG*, 31:1 (Feb. 20, 1850), A141–43.

29. *CG*, 31:1 (Feb. 27, 1850), A198–201. Doubtless deliberately, Toombs linked antislavery politicians to Garrison.

30. Donald, *Sumner and Civil War*, 37, 192.

31. Sumner to Wendell Phillips, Feb. 4, 1845, in Irving H. Bartlett, ed., "New Light on Wendell Phillips: The Community of Reform, 1840–1880," *Perspectives in American History* 12 (1979): 138.

32. *CG*, 32:1 (Aug. 26, 1852), A1102–13.

33. Donald, *Sumner and Civil War*, 227–37; *CG*, 32:1 (Aug. 26, 1852), A1102–13, 1120.

34. *CG*, 32:1 (Aug. 26, 1852), A1114–18.

35. Ibid., A1120–21, 1125.

36. Blue, *Free Soilers*, 232–68.

37. Michael F. Holt, *The Political Crisis of the 1850s* (New York: Wiley, 1978);

Edward L. Ayers, *What Caused the Civil War? Reflections on the South and Southern History* (New York: W. W. Norton, 2005), 138–42; Daniel W. Crofts, "Communication Breakdown," *NY Times,* Disunion (blog), May 21, 2011, http://opinionator.blogs.nytimes.com/2011/05/21/communication-breakdown/.

38. *CG*, 33:1 (Jan. 30, 1854), 275–81. Hale was out of the Senate between 1853 and 1855.

39. *CG*, 33:1 (May 25, 1854), A769.

40. Ibid., A764–65; H. L. Trefousse, *Benjamin Franklin Wade: Radical Republican from Ohio* (New York: Twayne, 1963), 91.

41. Ronald P. Formisano, *The Birth of Mass Political Parties: Michigan, 1827–1861* (Princeton, NJ: Princeton University Press, 1970), 242–43, 254–55; Michael J. McManus, *Political Abolitionism in Wisconsin, 1840–1861* (Kent, OH: Kent State University Press, 1998), 39–40, 91–93, 173–82.

42. William E. Gienapp, *The Origins of the Republican Party, 1852–1856* (New York: Oxford University Press, 1987), 113, 116–17, 122–24; George W. Julian, *Speeches on Political Questions* (New York: Hurd and Houghton, 1872), 128–31.

43. Jonathan H. Earle estimates that a quarter of the emerging Republican Party electorate had Democratic antecedents and that Democrats had an even larger presence at the leadership level. Earle, *Jacksonian Antislavery*, 195–96.

44. Allan Nevins, *Ordeal of the Union: A House Dividing, 1852–1857* (New York: Charles Scribner's Sons, 1947), 118–59.

45. Potter, *Impending Crisis*, 238–39.

46. Michael F. Holt, *The Rise and Fall of the American Whig Party: Jacksonian Politics and the Onset of the Civil War* (New York: Oxford University Press, 1999), 825–35.

47. Gienapp, *Origins of the Republican Party*, 45; Holt, *Rise and Fall of the American Whig Party*, 837.

48. Gienapp, *Origins of the Republican Party*, 45, 98.

49. Holt, *Rise and Fall of the American Whig Party*, 836–908, quotation on 837.

50. Gienapp, *Origins of the Republican Party*, 273–304, quotation on 301. Only in Saint Louis and Delaware did the Republican Party enjoy any significant support in the slave states.

51. *CG*, 33:2 (Feb. 23, 1855), A241; Chase to Theodore Parker, July 17, 1856, in Niven, *Chase Papers*, 2:444–46.

52. Donald Bruce Johnson and Kirk Harold Porter, eds., *National Party Platforms, 1840–1972* (Urbana: University of Illinois Press, 1973), 27–28. Gienapp, *Origins of the Republican Party*, 335–38, emphasized the "strong antislavery principles" in the platform.

53. Gienapp, *Origins of the Republican Party*, 341–43.

54. Potter, *Impending Crisis*, 262–63; Nevins, *Ordeal of the Union*, 497–500.

55. Allan Nevins, *Frémont: Pathmarker of the West* (New York: Appleton-Century, 1939), 440–52.

56. Gienapp, *Origins of the Republican Party*, 413–48.

57. Stewart, *Giddings*, 240–41; Niven, *Chase*, 153–90; Donald, *Sumner and Civil War*, 238–347.

Chapter 3

1. *NY Herald*, Dec. 3, 1856; Michael F. Holt, *Franklin Pierce* (New York: Times Books, 2010).

2. *CG*, 34:3 (Dec. 2, 1856), A1–3.

3. *NY Times*, Dec. 3, 1856; *NY Herald*, Dec. 4, 1856; Elizabeth Brown Pryor, *Reading the Man: A Portrait of Robert E. Lee through His Private Letters* (New York: Viking, 2007), 269. It was widely suspected that the actual author of Pierce's message was his attorney general, Caleb Cushing. Given the "limited range" of Pierce's vision, Henry Wilson sneered, the message was more likely written by "learned" and industrious Cushing. *CG*, 34:3 (Dec. 19, 1856), A63. John M. Belohlavek, *Broken Glass: Caleb Cushing and the Shattering of the Union* (Kent, OH: Kent State University Press, 2005), 281, accepts that Cushing "apparently penned" Pierce's "last-ditch, caustic attack."

4. William E. Gienapp, *The Origins of the Republican Party, 1852–1856* (New York: Oxford University Press, 1987), 413–448.

5. Here Brown paraphrased a letter that Henry Wilson had written to abolitionist Wendell Phillips, on June 20, 1855, which urged all "friends of freedom" to overcome their differences and pull together—"Let us remember that more than three millions of bondsmen, groaning under nameless woes, demand that we shall cease to reproach each other, and that we labor for their deliverance." *CG*, 34:3 (Dec. 11, 1856), 106.

6. As we shall see, Brown paraphrased Seward's speech in Cleveland in October 1848, when he stated that "slavery can be limited to its present bounds, it can be ameliorated, it *can* be and *must* be abolished and you and I can and must do it." See George E. Baker, ed., *The Works of William H. Seward*, 3 vols. (New York: Redfield, 1853), 3:291–302.

7. *CG*, 34:3 (Dec. 2, 1856), 11–16.

8. Ibid.; *NY Herald*, Dec. 4, 1856.

9. *CG*, 34:3 (Dec. 11, 1856), 85–91.

10. Ibid., 91.

11. *CG*, 34:3 (Dec. 4, 11, 1856), 28–29, 89. William H. Hurlbert, "The Political Crisis in the United States," *Edinburgh Review* 104 (1856): 561–97, quotations on 566, 592, 596; see Daniel W. Crofts, *A Secession Crisis Enigma: William Henry Hurlbert and "The Diary of a Public Man"* (Baton Rouge: Louisiana State University Press, 2010), 50. Butler discovered that Hurlbert was a native South Carolinian who had been "educated at the North." Louisiana senator Judah Benjamin, who knew Hurlbert, mentioned that he lived in New York City.

12. *CG*, 34:3 (Dec. 2, 11, 1856), 10–12, 96–97.

13. *CG*, 34:3 (Dec. 2, 19, 1856), 13–14, A64–66; Richard H. Abbott, *Cobbler in Congress: The Life of Henry Wilson, 1812–1875* (Lexington: University Press of Kentucky, 1972), 89; Lysander Spooner, *The Unconstitutionality of Slavery* (Boston: Bela Marsh, 1860). The best source on Gerrit Smith's Radical Abolition Party is John Stauffer, *The Black Hearts of Men: Radical Abolitionists and the Transformation of Race* (Cambridge, MA: Harvard University Press, 2002), 8–44.

14. *CG*, 34:3 (Dec. 19, 1856), A64–66.

15. *NY Herald*, Dec. 4, 1856.

16. *CG*, 34:3 (Dec. 4, 19, 1856), 28–29, A64–65; Abbott, *Cobbler in Congress*, 88–90.

17. *CG*, 34:3 (Dec. 11, 19, 1856), A66.

18. *CG*, 34:3 (Dec. 2, 1856), 15–17.

19. *CG*, 34:3 (Dec. 4, 1856), 30–35; Robert J. Cook, *Civil War Senator: William Pitt Fessenden and the Fight to Save the American Republic* (Baton Rouge: Louisiana State University Press, 2011), 103–4.

20. *CG*, 34:3 (Dec. 8, 1856), 53–56.

21. Ibid.

22. *CG*, 36:1 (Jan. 20, 1860), 548.

23. *CG*, 34:3 (Dec. 10, 1856), A34–35.

24. *CG*, 34:3 (Dec. 11, 1856), 105. As noted in chapter 2, Giddings had warned about the possibility of bloodshed in January 1846 when he called for the United States to go to war with Britain in order to acquire Oregon. Such a war, he hoped, "must prove the death of slavery." James Brewer Stewart, *Joshua R. Giddings and the Tactics of Radical Politics* (Cleveland, OH: Press of Case Western Reserve University, 1970), 112–13.

25. *CG*, 34:3 (Dec. 10, 1856), 78–79.

26. Joshua R. Giddings to Laura Ann Giddings, Dec. 7, 1856, Giddings-Julian Papers, LC; Stewart, *Giddings*, 247–51, 259–60; *CG*, 34:3 (Dec. 16, 1856), A46.

27. *CG*, 34:3 (Dec. 16, 1856), A45–48.

28. William Goodell to George W. Julian, June 18, 1857, Giddings-Julian Papers.

29. Julian to Thomas Wentworth Higginson (draft), Oct. 24, 1857, Giddings-Julian Papers; George W. Julian, *Speeches on Political Questions* (New York: Hurd and Houghton, 1872), 126–53.

30. Julian, *Speeches*, 127–28, 153; Patrick W. Riddleberger, *George Washington Julian: Radical Republican* (Indianapolis: Indiana History Bureau, 1966), 52. For a good brief overview of Julian's political career, see Frederick J. Blue, "George Washington Julian: Free Soiler—Republican," in *No Taint of Compromise: Crusaders in Antislavery Politics* (Baton Rouge: Louisiana State University Press, 2005), 161–83.

31. James L. Huston, *The Panic of 1857 and the Coming of the Civil War* (Baton Rouge: Louisiana State University Press, 1987).

32. Salmon P. Chase to Charles Sumner, May 1, 1857, in *The Salmon P. Chase Papers*, vol. 2, *Correspondence, 1823–1857*, ed. John Niven (Kent, OH: Kent State University Press, 1996), 449; Chase to Gerrit Smith, Mar. 30, 1858, Chase to Sumner, Sept. 10, 1859, in *The Salmon P. Chase Papers*, vol. 3, *Correspondence, 1858–March 1863*, ed. John Niven (Kent, OH: Kent State University Press, 1996), 9, 18–19.

33. David Herbert Donald, *Lincoln* (New York: Simon and Schuster, 1995), 162–95, esp. 194–95; Michael Burlingame, *Abraham Lincoln: A Life*, 2 vols. (Baltimore: Johns Hopkins University Press, 2008), 1:363–435; Don E. Fehrenbacher, *Prelude to Greatness: Lincoln in the 1850's* (Stanford, CA: Stanford University Press, 1962), 19–47, 161; William C. Harris, *Lincoln's Rise to the Presidency* (Lawrence: Uni-

versity Press of Kansas, 2007), 58–83; Daniel W. Crofts, "Lincoln the Politician, 1854–56," in *A Companion to Abraham Lincoln*, ed. Michael Green (Malden, MA: Wiley-Blackwell, forthcoming).

34. Abraham Lincoln to Joshua Speed, Aug. 24, 1855, *CWAL*, 2:320.

35. Chase to Lincoln, June 13, 1859, in Niven, *Chase Papers*, 3:14–15; Lincoln to Chase, June 20, 1859, *CWAL*, 3:386.

36. Allan Nevins, *Ordeal of the Union: A House Dividing, 1852-1857*, vol. 2 (New York: Charles Scribner's Sons, 1947), 142. For a classic short summation of the famed 1858 campaign, see Potter, *Impending Crisis*, chap. 13, "Lincoln, Douglas, and the Implications of Slavery," 328–55.

37. Lincoln's first debate with Douglas at Ottawa, IL, Aug. 21, 1858, *CWAL*, 3:14.

38. Lincoln to George Robertson, Aug. 15, 1855, *CWAL*, 2:317–18. See Burlingame, *Abraham Lincoln*, 1:409. Alyssa Anderson, a student at The College of New Jersey, first showed me that this key letter deserved close attention. Lincoln wrote to Robertson just a week before his similarly candid comment to Joshua Speed about fugitive slaves. Robertson, whose name surfaced during the secession crisis as a possible appointee for Lincoln's cabinet (see C. F. Mitchell to Lyman Trumbull, Dec. 10, 1860, Lyman Trumbull Papers, LC), became one of the many propertied Kentuckians who, in the end, clung to slavery. In 1862 he sued to recover an alleged fugitive who sought protection from Union soldiers. The case landed on Lincoln's desk and persisted long after the war. Robertson won a judgment against the offending Union officer in 1871, but in 1873 Congress voted to cover the costs of the settlement. See Lincoln to Robertson, Nov. 26, 1862, *CWAL*, 5:512–14; and William C. Harris, *Lincoln and the Border States: Preserving the Union* (Lawrence: University Press of Kansas, 2011), 210–11.

39. Abraham Lincoln, speech at Peoria, IL, Oct. 16, 1854, speech at Chicago, July 10, 1858, debates with Douglas at Ottawa, Jonesboro, and Galesburg, IL, Aug. 21, Sept. 15, Oct. 7, 1858, *CWAL*, 2:255, 500, 3:11, 22, 34–35, 105, 226, 233.

40. Lincoln, speeches at Springfield and Peoria, IL, Oct. 4, 16, 1854, *CWAL*, 2:245, 255, 272.

41. Lincoln, speeches at Ottawa, Charleston, Quincy, and Alton, IL, Aug. 21, Sept. 18, Oct. 13, 15, 1858, *CWAL*, 3:16, 181, 277, 311.

42. Brian Dirck, *Lincoln and the Constitution* (Carbondale: Southern Illinois University Press, 2012), 26, 30.

43. Lincoln, speech at Quincy, IL, Oct. 13, 1858, *CWAL*, 3:276.

44. James Oakes, *Freedom National: The Destruction of Slavery in the United States, 1861-1865* (New York: W. W. Norton, 2013), 1–2, 5, 45–48; James Oakes, *The Scorpion's Sting: Antislavery and the Coming of the Civil War* (New York: W. W. Norton, 2014), 22–50; Adam Goodheart, *1861: The Civil War Awakening* (New York: Alfred A. Knopf, 2011), For a more sustained critique of Oakes and Goodheart, see the Bibliographical Postscript.

45. *CG*, 34:3 (Dec. 2, 1856), 12; Walter Stahr, *Seward: Lincoln's Indispensable Man* (New York: Simon and Schuster, 2012), 153–60, 176–81.

46. Baker, *Works of Seward*, 3:291–302, quotation on 301–2; Frederick W. Seward, *William H. Seward*, 3 vols. (New York: Derby and Miller, 1891), 2:85–87;

Stahr, *Seward*, 112; Doris Kearns Goodwin, *Team of Rivals: The Political Genius of Abraham Lincoln* (New York: Simon and Schuster, 2006), 132–34.

47. Stahr, *Seward*, 174–75; Frederic Bancroft, *The Life of William H. Seward*, 2 vols. (New York: Harper and Brothers, 1899–1900), 1:458–65; *CG*, 34:3 (Dec. 11, 1856), 105.

48. *CG*, 36:1 (Jan. 4, 1860), A54.

49. Abraham Lincoln, "Address at Cooper Institute, New York City," Feb. 27, 1860, *CWAL*, 3:538.

50. Donald Bruce Johnson and Kirk Harold Porter, eds., *National Party Platforms, 1840–1972* (Urbana: University of Illinois Press, 1973), 31–33.

51. Stewart, *Giddings*, 271–73; Johnson and Porter, *National Party Platforms*, 31–33.

52. Michael S. Green, *Lincoln and the Election of 1860* (Carbondale: Southern Illinois University Press, 2011), provides a well-informed modern overview.

53. Lincoln to John B. Fry, Aug. 15, 1860, *CWAL*, 4:95.

54. Nichols, *Disruption*, 46–47, 348–49.

55. In 1848, the Free Soil presidential ticket ran as follows in Bingham's district: Columbiana, 15.9 percent; Carroll, 10.8 percent; Harrison, 14.4 percent; Jefferson, 9.4 percent. Data from the *Weekly Ohio State Journal* (Columbus), Nov. 29, 1848.

56. Gerard N. Magliocca, *American Founding Son: John Bingham and the Invention of the Fourteenth Amendment* (New York: New York University Press, 2013), 39–65; C. Russell Riggs, "The *Ante-Bellum* Career of John A. Bingham: A Case Study in the Coming of the Civil War" (Ph.D. diss., New York University, 1958), 121, 265n. Bingham served in the House from 1855 to 1863 but was defeated for reelection in 1862 as Republicans suffered heavy losses amid wartime discouragement. He regained the seat in the 1864 election and continued in office from December 1865 until March 1873.

57. Magliocca, *American Founding Son*, 42–46, 56, 64; Jacobus tenBroek, *Equal under Law* (New York: Collier Books, 1965), originally published as *The Antislavery Origins of the Fourteenth Amendment* (Berkeley: University of California Press, 1951), 145–48; Garrett Epps, *Democracy Reborn: The Fourteenth Amendment and the Fight for Equal Rights in Post–Civil War America* (New York: Henry Holt, 2006), 164–72, 225–27. See Epilogue 2.

58. *CG*, 34:1 (Mar. 6, 1856), A124.

59. *CG*, 34:2 (Jan. 13, 1857), A135–40, quotations on 136, 140; Stewart, *Giddings*, 46–49.

60. *CG*, 35:2 (Feb. 11, 1859), 981–85. Other Republicans, such as Indiana's Charles Case, agreed that Oregon had transgressed "the common rights of humanity" but decided to vote for statehood under its proposed antislavery constitution, rather than allow it to "remain under the corrupting influence of this rotten Administration." Ibid., 981. The next day the House narrowly voted, 114–103, to admit Oregon. Alexander Stephens of Georgia delivered an eloquent case for its admission. *CG*, 35:2 (Feb. 12, 1859), A121–25. An awkward coalition opposed admission. It included some more ideological Republicans who shared Bingham's concerns, plus a number of Southerners—those who opposed admitting additional states

with antislavery constitutions and those former Whigs who suspected that Oregon would become a Democratic state. Ibid., 1011.

61. *CG*, 36:1 (Apr. 24, 1860), 1836–40.

62. Magliocca, *American Founding Son*, 42; Stewart, *Giddings*, 237, 262; Riggs, "Career of Bingham," 140–43. Giddings and Lincoln had been messmates at Mrs. Sprigg's boardinghouse, where Giddings had boarded for more than a decade. But the 1848 campaign strained relations there between Free Soilers such as Giddings and those who remained loyal Whigs such as Lincoln. In December 1850, Giddings moved to new quarters, which he shared with a circle of "first rate free-soilers," including his future son-in-law, George W. Julian. Stewart, *Giddings*, 167–68, 195.

63. Bingham to Giddings, Jan. 14, 1861, Joshua R. Giddings Papers, Ohio Historical Society, copy in Seward Papers. See Magliocca, *American Founding Son*, 72–73; Riggs, "Career of Bingham," 326–28; and Erving E. Beauregard, *Bingham of the Hills: Politician and Diplomat Extraordinary* (New York: Peter Lang, 1989), 54–55.

Chapter 4

1. Robert S. Holt to Joseph Holt, Nov. 9, 1860, Joseph Holt Papers, LC.

2. Robert S. Holt to Joseph Holt, Nov. 20, 1860, Holt Papers; see Elizabeth D. Leonard, *Lincoln's Forgotten Ally: Judge Advocate General Joseph Holt of Kentucky* (Chapel Hill: University of North Carolina Press, 2011), 38–40; Daniel W. Crofts, "Joseph Holt, James Buchanan, and the Secession Crisis," in *James Buchanan and the Coming of the Civil War*, ed. John W. Quist and Michael J. Birkner (Gainesville: University Press of Florida, 2013), 208–36; and Daniel W. Crofts, "Union Man," *NY Times*, Disunion (blog), May 30, 2011, http://opinionator.blogs.nytimes.com/2011/05/30/union-man/.

3. In the winter of 1860–61, before the war started, people differentiated between the "Gulf States" or the "Cotton States" from South Carolina west to Texas, where secession first took hold, and the so-called Border States, which initially opposed Southern independence. Today's frequent juxtaposition of the "Lower South" and the "Upper South" was not common terminology in the nineteenth century. The Confederate States of America ultimately included the seven Gulf or Cotton States and four Border States because the Upper South fractured after the war started. The pro-Confederate Upper South (Virginia, North Carolina, Tennessee, and Arkansas) went one way, the pro-Union Upper South (Delaware, Maryland, Kentucky, Missouri, and the future state of West Virginia) the other. J. William Harris reports that the term "Deep South" first was used in the 1930s. J. William Harris, *Deep Souths: Delta, Piedmont, and Sea Island Society in the Age of Segregation* (Baltimore: John Hopkins University Press, 2001), 1, 369n1. I shall use the terms "Deep South," "Cotton States," "Gulf States," and "Lower South" interchangeably. I refer to the "Upper South" or "Border States" as all eight slave states that remained in the Union at the time of Lincoln's inauguration. A third of white Southerners lived in the Lower South, a third in the soon-to-be seceding states of the Upper South, and a third in the non-seceding Border States. But all of this is too

neat and clean—significant numbers of Union supporters remained trapped be-hind Confederate lines, especially in East Tennessee, while pro-Confederate minor-ities in Maryland, Kentucky, and Missouri were unreconciled to Union authority.

4. *NY Herald*, Jan. 14, 1861 (Galveston correspondent, Dec. 23, 1860); Nichols, *Disruption*, 410. For a comparable recent assessment of the psychic turmoil in the Deep South, see William L. Barney, "Rush to Disaster: Secession and the Slaves' Revenge," in Robert J. Cook, William L. Barney, and Elizabeth R. Varon, *Secession Winter: When the Union Fell Apart* (Baltimore: Johns Hopkins University Press, 2013), 10–33.

5. *Mississippi Democrat Extra* (Columbus), account of proceedings held at Co-lumbus, MS, on Nov. 19, 1860, in Beverly Matthews to Caleb Cushing, Nov. 22, 1860, Caleb Cushing Papers, LC. The resolutions were slightly qualified: secession would follow unless the "non-slaveholding States" immediately repealed "all their odious, offensive and unconstitutional legislation" that obstructed "the rendition of fugitives from labor" and instead offered "positive security for our domestic peace and property rights in the Union."

6. James H. Hill to Lyman Trumbull, Nov. 23, 1860, William L. Hodge to Trum-bull, Nov. 23, 1860, Lyman Trumbull Papers, LC. Wendell Phillips was the peerless Garrisonian orator.

7. William M. Clark to Lewis Thompson, Jan. 10, 1861, Lewis Thompson Papers, Southern Historical Collection, University of North Carolina; *NY Times*, Dec. 7, 1860 (report from Montgomery, AL, Nov. 29, 1860).

8. Freehling, *Road*, 2:345–498.

9. Ulrich B. Phillips, ed., *The Correspondence of Robert Toombs, Alexander H. Stephens, and Howell Cobb*, Annual Report of the American Historical Association for the Year 1911, 2 vols. (Washington, DC: American Historical Association, 1913), 2:505–17, quotations on 508, 514–15. See Nichols, *Disruption*, 349–50, on how white Southern elites feared a potential loss of political power.

10. *CG*, 36:2 (Dec. 11, 1860), 49.

11. William W. Freehling and Craig M. Simpson, eds., *Secession Debated: Geor-gia's Showdown in 1860* (New York: Oxford University Press, 1992), 40, 46–47; James Oakes, *The Scorpion's Sting: Antislavery and the Coming of the Civil War* (New York: W. W. Norton, 2014). William H. Seward once predicted that slavery would suffer the self-inflicted fate of the scorpion, but the source he cites, a speech published in the *New York Times* on Oct. 15, 1855, does not include any such lan-guage. *Scorpion's Sting*, 36, 180n14.

12. *CG*, 36:2 (Dec. 10, 1860), 33.

13. *Lancaster Daily Evening Express*, Jan. 17, 1861, in *Northern Editorials on Secession*, ed. Howard Cecil Perkins, 2 vols. (New York: D. Appleton-Century for the American Historical Association, 1942), 2:1045.

14. William P. Fessenden to Hamilton Fish, Dec. 15, 1860, container 47, Hamil-ton Fish Papers, LC.

15. *CG*, 36:2 (Jan. 10, 1861), 312–16.

16. *CG*, 36:2 (Jan. 29, 1861), 629–32, quotations on 630–31. Van Wyck's blunt talk offended proslavery rowdies. Three would-be assassins fell on him one night

several weeks later. Miraculously, he fought them off, suffering a severe gash on one hand. Adam Goodheart, "Guns, Blood and Congress," *NY Times*, Disunion (blog), Mar. 16, 2011, http://opinionator.blogs.nytimes.com/2011/03/16/guns-blood-and-congress/.

17. *AEJ*, Jan. 9, 17, 28, Feb. 2, 1861; Crofts, *Reluctant Confederates*, 220.

18. *AEJ*, Nov. 30, 1860.

19. *AEJ*, Nov. 30, Dec. 17, 1860; Patrick M. Sowle, "The Conciliatory Republicans during the Winter of Secession" (Ph.D. diss., Duke University, 1963), 18–21. Sowle's pioneering work, which should have become a book, is still well worth reading. He first pinpointed Seward's and Weed's almost immediate awareness that a grave crisis impended. But Sowle exaggerated the strength of conciliation sentiment in the Republican Party and minimized the intense opposition to any "backing down" in the Republican heartland of the Upper North—New England and the New England exodus areas to the west.

20. Preston King to Thurlow Weed, Feb. 1, 1861, Weed Papers; Sowle, "Conciliatory Republicans," 34–36, 58–59, 164–68; Potter, *Lincoln and His Party*, 68–74, 81–88; Crofts, *Reluctant Confederates*, 219.

21. William B. Campbell to A. C. Beard, Mar. 15, 1861, copy, Campbell Family Papers, Duke University.

22. Samuel Smith Nicholas, "South Carolina, Disunion, and a Mississippi Valley Confederacy," partially reprinted in *AEJ*, Jan. 28, 1861; also in Samuel Smith Nicholas, *Conservative Essays, Legal and Political* (Philadelphia: J. B. Lippincott, 1863), 145–59.

23. How does Arkansas fit? Those who referred to the "Border States" generally had seven states in mind, not eight. Because Arkansas included a substantial cotton-growing region directly across the river from Mississippi, it often was considered part of the Lower South. But the Arkansas upcountry initially rejected secession. Only after the outbreak of war did Arkansas join the Confederacy, along with Virginia, North Carolina, and Tennessee. See note 3, above, and James M. Woods, *Rebellion and Realignment: Arkansas's Road to Secession* (Fayetteville: University of Arkansas Press, 1987).

24. *CG*, 36:2 (Feb. 6, 7, 1861), A167, A199; Crofts, *Reluctant Confederates*, 126–27, 334–40.

25. *Brownlow's Knoxville Whig*, Jan. 17, 1861, also weekly edition, Jan. 19, 1861.

26. Ibid.; see Robert Tracy McKenzie, "Contesting Secession: Parson Brownlow and the Rhetoric of Pro-Slavery Unionism, 1860–1861," *Civil War History* 48 (2002): 301–6.

27. Lincoln to George Robertson, Aug. 15, 1855, *CWAL*, 2:317–18.

28. "Warrington," Dec. 20, 1860, in *Springfield Republican*, Dec. 22, 1860. On Robinson, see Bruce Laurie, *Beyond Garrison: Antislavery and Social Reform* (New York: Cambridge University Press, 2005), 164–68.

29. George W. Julian, *The Life of Joshua R. Giddings* (Chicago: A. C. McClurg, 1892), 377–83; Joshua Giddings to George W. Julian, Feb. 22, 1861, Giddings-Julian Papers, LC.

30. William Herndon to Trumbull, Dec. 21, 1860, Jan. 27, Feb. 9, 1861, Trum-

bull Papers; Herndon to Charles Sumner, Dec. 10, 1860, Charles Sumner Papers, Houghton Library, Harvard University. In the letter to Sumner, Herndon underlined the words "dead"—once, twice, and then three times.

31. *Springfield Republican*, Dec. 12, 1860; James Brewer Stewart, *Joshua R. Giddings and the Tactics of Radical Politics* (Cleveland. OH: Press of Case Western Reserve University, 1970), 247–51, 259–60; David Donald, *Lincoln's Herndon: A Biography* (New York: Alfred A. Knopf, 1948), 135, 141, 132–33, 131.

32. Two books call attention to the international context. Andre M. Fleche explores "the competing nationalist ideologies both sides developed as they presented their cases to each other and to the world." *The Revolution of 1861: The American Civil War in the Age of Nationalist Conflict* (Chapel Hill: University of North Carolina Press, 2012), 3. Don H. Doyle likewise situates the American Civil War amid the era of "nationalist independence movements." *The Cause of All Nations: An International History of the American Civil War* (New York: Basic Books, 2014), 29. The most thought-provoking assessment of Confederate claims to nationality remains David M. Potter, "The Historian's Use of Nationalism and Vice Versa," in *The South and the Sectional Conflict* (Baton Rouge: Louisiana State University Press, 1968), 34–83, esp. 60–83.

33. *AEJ*, Jan. 18, 1861.

34. John A. Gilmer to William H. Seward, Mar. 7, 8, 9, 12, Apr. 12, 1861, Seward Papers, reprinted in Frederic Bancroft, *The Life of William H. Seward*, 2 vols. (New York: Harper and Brothers, 1899–1900), 2:545–49. For a qualified defense of the stance taken by Southern Unionists, see Crofts, *Reluctant Confederates*, 104–29, 353–60.

35. Nelson D. Lankford, *Cry Havoc! The Crooked Road to Civil War, 1861* (New York: Viking, 2007), 6, 235–36; Crofts, *Reluctant Confederates*, 194; Potter, *Lincoln and His Party*, Preface to the 1962 edition in the 1995 edition, xlix.

36. Potter, *Impending Crisis*, 490n16; *NY Times*, Dec. 7, 1860, Jan. 24, 26, 1861 (reports from Montgomery, AL, Nov. 29, 1860, Jan. 15, 19, 1861).

37. *New York Daily News*, Jan. 9, 1861, in Perkins, *Northern Editorials on Secession*, 1:298–300.

38. Marcellus Emery to Caleb Cushing, Jan. 30, 1861, Cushing Papers; *Bangor Daily Union*, Jan. 14, 22, 24, 1861.

39. *NY Herald*, Feb. 16, 17 (Washington Correspondent, Feb. 15, 1861), 18, 19, 23, 1861.

40. *CG*, 36:2 (Jan. 16, 1861), 416–18.

41. *CG*, 36:2 (Jan. 14, 16, 1861), 367–72, 410–11, 418–21; *NY Times*, Jan. 17, 1861; McClernand to the *Peoria Blade*, Jan. 22, 1861, in *Chicago Tribune*, Feb. 21, 1861.

42. *CG*, 36:2 (Jan. 14, 1861), 374.

43. *New York World*, Jan. 12, 1861.

44. Eric Foner, *Politics and Ideology in the Age of the Civil War* (New York: Oxford University Press, 1980), 50; Eric Foner, *Free Soil, Free Labor, Free Men: The Ideology of the Republican Party before the Civil War* (New York: Oxford University Press, 1970), 36–39, 313–16; Kenneth M. Stampp, *And the War Came: The North and the Secession Crisis, 1860–61* (Baton Rouge: Louisiana State University Press,

1950), 1–3, 170–76; William J. Cooper, *We Have the War upon Us: The Onset of the Civil War, November 1860–April 1861* (New York: Alfred A. Knopf, 2012), 3–7, 66–81, 102–12, 148.

45. Potter, *Lincoln and His Party.* 9–19, quotations on 16, 18; Potter, *Impending Crisis,* 484, 531–32, 553.

46. Michael F. Holt, *The Political Crisis of the 1850s* (New York: Wiley, 1979), 8, 216; William E. Gienapp, *The Origins of the Republican Party, 1852–1856* (New York: Oxford University Press, 1987), 191–92, 357–65, quotations on 191, 359, 361–62; McClintock, *Lincoln and the Decision for War,* 25–27.

47. Freehling salutes Potter's *Impending Crisis* as "my favorite synthesis of the late antebellum period" and notes that its influence pervades his own writing "in ways I cannot trace, much less fully acknowledge." Freehling, *Road,* 1:617n1, 2: 367–68. Freehling also echoes Roy Franklin Nichols on how elite white Southerners distrusted nonslaveholders. Nichols, *Disruption,* 349–50.

48. Edward L. Ayers, *In the Presence of Mine Enemies: War in the Heart of America, 1859–1863* (New York: W. W. Norton, 2003), 83–84, 428n54; Edward L. Ayers, *What Caused the Civil War? Reflections on the South and Southern History* (New York: W. W. Norton, 2005), 128.

Chapter 5

1. Potter, *Lincoln and His Party,* 164–70; Walter Stahr, *Seward: Lincoln's Indispensable Man* (New York: Simon and Schuster, 2012), 215–17. It may have been fortuitous that Weed and Seward found themselves on the same train. Seward had written to Weed earlier that same morning, eager to learn "how and where I can meet you." William H. Seward to Thurlow Weed, Dec. 22, 1860, Weed Papers.

2. William E. Gienapp, *The Origins of the Republican Party 1852–1856* (New York: Oxford University Press, 1987), 308–11, 339–43.

3. *AEJ,* Nov. 30, 1860; Stahr, *Seward,* 211; McClintock, *Lincoln and the Decision for War,* 72, 294n28.

4. George P. Morgan to Weed, Dec. 4, 1860, Weed Papers; Crofts, *Reluctant Confederates,* 219–20; Henry Adams to Charles Francis Adams Jr., Dec. 9, 1860, Jan. 26, 1861, Adams Family Papers, Massachusetts Historical Society (microfilm edition), in *The Letters of Henry Adams,* ed. J. C. Levenson et al., 6 vols. (Cambridge, MA: Belknap Press of Harvard University Press, 1982–88), 2:204–5, 225.

5. *AEJ,* Dec. 17, 27, 1860; Crofts, *Reluctant Confederates,* 217–19; Mark J. Stegmaier, "'An Imaginary Negro in an Impossible Place?' The Issue of New Mexico Statehood in the Secession Crisis, 1860–1861," *New Mexico Historical Review* 84 (2009): 263–90.

6. *AEJ,* Dec. 1, 17, 1860.

7. Harriet A. Weed, ed., *Autobiography of Thurlow Weed* (Boston: Houghton, Mifflin, 1884), 602–14.

8. Abraham Lincoln to Lyman Trumbull, Dec. 10, 1860, Lincoln to William Kellogg, Dec. 11, 1860, Lincoln to Elihu B. Washburne, Dec. 13, 1860, Lincoln to John A. Gilmer, Dec. 15, 1860, *CWAL,* 4:149–53.

9. Abraham Lincoln, "Resolutions Drawn up for Republican Members of the Committee of Thirteen," Dec. 20, 1860, *CWAL*, 4:156–57; Frederic Bancroft, *The Life of William H. Seward*, 2 vols. (New York: Harper and Brothers, 1899–1900), 2:10.

10. Thomas D. Morris, *Free Men All: The Personal Liberty Laws of the North, 1780–1861* (Baltimore: Johns Hopkins University Press, 1974), 203–8.

11. Christopher Childers, *The Failure of Popular Sovereignty: Slavery, Manifest Destiny, and the Radicalization of Southern Politics* (Lawrence: University Press of Kansas, 2012), 11–15.

12. Crofts, *Reluctant Confederates*, 95–100.

13. Seward to Lincoln, Dec. 16, 1860, Lincoln Papers; Crofts, *Reluctant Confederates*, 221–22, 227–28; Weed, *Autobiography*, 602–14.

14. Potter, *Lincoln and His Party*, 170.

15. Stahr, *Seward*, 178.

16. Carl Schurz, *The Reminiscences of Carl Schurz, 1852–1863* (London: John Murray, 1909), 221–22, called to my attention by Michael Burlingame's review of Stahr, *Seward*, in the *Wall Street Journal*, Sept. 12, 2012, and in Michael Burlingame, *Abraham Lincoln: A Life*, 2 vols. (Baltimore: Johns Hopkins University Press, 2008), 1:655.

17. Stahr, *Seward*, 209.

18. Samuel Bowles, editor of the influential *Springfield* (MA) *Republican*, designated Lincoln a "simple Susan" in a private letter to Massachusetts congressman Henry Dawes. Bowles to Dawes, Feb. 26, 1861, box 18, Henry L. Dawes Papers, LC; Charles Francis Adams Jr. to Frederic Bancroft, Oct. 11, 1911, copy, Allan Nevins Papers, Columbia University, quoted in Burlingame, *Abraham Lincoln*, 2:98.

19. Henry Adams to Charles Francis Adams Jr., Dec. 9, 1860, in Levenson, *Letters of Henry Adams*, 1:204–5; Israel Washburn to Seward, Dec. 19, 1860, Seward Papers.

20. Potter, *Lincoln and His Party*, 156–87, "agent" on 163, 169.

21. McClintock, *Lincoln and the Decision for War*, 144–48, 170–75, quotations on 144, 170.

22. *NY Times*, Dec. 24, 1860.

23. George Ellis Baker, ed., *The Works of William H. Seward*, 5 vols. (Boston: Houghton, Mifflin, 1884), 4:416–20; Potter, *Lincoln and His Party*, 16.

24. Freehling, *Road*, 2:345–498.

25. William J. Cooper, *We Have the War upon Us: The Onset of the Civil War, November 1860–April 1861* (New York: Alfred A. Knopf, 2012), 48; Ulrich B. Phillips, ed., *The Correspondence of Robert Toombs, Alexander H. Stephens, and Howell Cobb*, Annual Report of the American Historical Association for the Year 1911, 2 vols. (Washington, DC: American Historical Association, 1913), 2:505–17, esp. 508, 514–15; Robert S. Holt to Joseph Holt, Nov. 20, 1860, Joseph Holt Papers, LC; *Charlotte Bulletin*, quoted in *North Carolina Whig*, Jan. 29, 1861, in Joseph Carlyle Sitterson, *The Secession Movement in North Carolina* (Chapel Hill: University of North Carolina Press, 1939), 200–201.

26. Lincoln to Gilmer, Dec. 15, 1860, *CWAL*, 4:151–53; William P. Fessenden to Hamilton Fish, Dec. 15, 1860, container 47, Hamilton Fish Papers, LC.

27. 36th Cong., 2d Sess., Rep. Com. No. 288, *Journal of the Committee of Thirteen*, in *Index to the Reports of the Committees of the Senate of the United States for the Second Session of the Thirty-Sixth Congress* (Washington, DC: George W. Bowman, 1861), 1–19.

28. Potter, *Lincoln and His Party*, 173–76; Mark J. Stegmaier, *Henry Adams in the Secession Crisis: Dispatches to the* Boston Daily Advertiser, *December 1860–March 1861* (Baton Rouge: Louisiana State University Press, 2012), 58–61; *Journal of the Committee of Thirteen*, 10–11; Bancroft, *Seward*, 2:10; Lincoln, "Resolutions Drawn up for Republican Members of the Committee of Thirteen," Dec. 20, 1860, *CWAL*, 4:156–57. The jury trial overture collapsed because Republicans wanted the trial in the state where the alleged fugitive was recaptured. When Southerners and Democrats voted that the trial should take place in the state from which the alleged fugitive fled, Republicans refused to go along. *Journal of the Committee of Thirteen*, 7–8, 11; Seward to Lincoln, Dec. 26, 1860, Lincoln Papers, with a copy in Frederick W. Seward, *Seward at Washington, as Senator and Secretary of State: A Memoir of His Life, with Selections from His Letters*, 2 vols. (New York: Derby and Miller, 1891), 2:484–85.

29. James E. Harvey to Weed, Dec. 24, 1860, Weed Papers—but the letter is misdated; it plainly was written on December 25 to describe events known to have taken place the previous day. See Crofts, *Reluctant Confederates*, 220; and Crofts, "James E. Harvey and the Secession Crisis," *Pennsylvania Magazine of History and Biography* 103 (1979): 177–95. Harvey wore several hats; one among them was his role as telegrapher for the *New York Tribune*.

30. Stegmaier, *Henry Adams in the Secession Crisis*, 58–63; Bancroft, *Seward*, 2:29; Crofts, *Reluctant Confederates*, 219.

31. Seward to Lincoln, Dec. 26, 1860, Lincoln Papers. Lincoln and the five Senate Republicans agreed to reject the territorial compromise at the heart of the Crittenden proposal. They also distanced themselves from Northern personal liberty laws. And they wanted to revise the Fugitive Slave Act so as to make its operation less obnoxious in the free states. But they did not see eye to eye. The senators demurred from Lincoln's idea that "the fugitive slave clause of the Constitution ought to be enforced by a law of Congress." Any such language threatened to "divide our friends," Seward noted, a portion of whom were "unwilling to give up their old opinion, that the duty of executing the constitutional provisions, concerning fugitives from service, belongs to the states, and not at all to Congress." In other words, hardline "freedom national" Republicans rejected the idea that the federal government had a responsibility to recapture fugitives. The Republican senators also ignored Lincoln's suggestion that Congress explicitly reiterate Andrew Jackson's demand "that the Federal Union must be preserved."

32. Cooper, *We Have the War upon Us*, 68, 107–8, 285n74, 291n55. Cooper credits historian Michael F. Holt for persuading him regarding Lincoln's "unwritten guidance." Cooper and Holt follow R. Alton Lee, "The Corwin Amendment in the Secession Crisis," *Ohio Historical Quarterly* 70 (1961): 11–17, esp. 15–17; and George Fort Milton, *The Eve of Conflict: Stephen A. Douglas and the Needless War* (Boston: Houghton Mifflin, 1934), 527. These views have been strongly

affirmed by Phillip Magness, "Abraham Lincoln and the Corwin Amendment," History News Network (blog), June 20, 2014, http://historynewsnetwork.org/blog/153391. Cooper and Holt rely on inference and conjecture. They argue that Lincoln did not want a written record of his role in framing the amendment even though he did write down for Weed several other sensitive items that he hoped Senate Republicans would support. Cooper suggests that Lincoln soon rejected his supposed handiwork because "he wanted no public identification with a measure that might upset the hard-liners." Cooper, *We Have the War upon Us*, 68, 107–8, 285n74, 291n55. Historians Mark Stegmaier and David Potter, by contrast, are not impressed with the case that Lincoln initiated the amendment. Stegmaier believes that Grimes and the other Republicans on the Committee of Thirteen devised the amendment even before Seward returned—and before they had heard from Lincoln. Stegmaier also thinks that Seward acted independently of Lincoln. Stegmaier, *Henry Adams in the Secession Crisis*, 58–63. Potter emphasized that Lincoln's written memorandum did not mention the amendment and that the Republicans on the Committee of Thirteen "did not act in very literal conformity" with the written suggestions Lincoln did make. Potter, *Lincoln and His Party*, 173–75.

33. Seward to Lincoln, Dec. 26, 1860, Lincoln Papers.

34. *CG*, 36:2 (Dec. 27, 1860), 195–201.

35. *CG*, 36:2 (Dec. 17, 1860), 99–103.

36. *Journal of the Committee of Thirteen*, 1, 10–11.

37. Henry Adams to Charles Francis Adams Jr., Jan. 8, 1861, Levenson, *Letters of Henry Adams*, 1:218–20; the letter refers both to Seward and to Charles Francis Adams, and it hints that Seward provided the elder Adams with discouraging information.

38. Stahr, *Seward*, 222–23; Salmon P. Chase to Seward, Jan. 10, 1861, James W. Grimes to Seward, Jan. 12, 1861, Seward Papers,.

39. Robert Vincent Remini, *Daniel Webster: The Man and His Time* (New York: W. W. Norton, 1997), 27, 662–81.

40. Hyatt H. Waggoner, ed., *The Poetical Works of Whittier* (Boston: Houghton Mifflin, 1975), 186–87.

41. "Independent" (James E. Harvey), Jan. 13, 1861, in *Philadelphia North American*, Jan. 14, 1861; Guy Gugliotta, *Freedom's Cap: The United States Capitol and the Coming of the Civil War* (New York: Hill and Wang, 2012).

42. *CG*, 35:1 (Mar. 3, 1858), 939–42.

43. "Independent" (Harvey), Jan. 13, 1861, in *Philadelphia North American*, Jan. 14, 1861.

44. *CG*, 36:2 (Jan. 12, 1861), 341–44.

45. *AEJ*, Jan. 9, 1861; Gilmer to Weed, Jan. 12, 17, 1861, Weed Papers; Crofts, *Reluctant Confederates*, 220–29; Potter, *Lincoln and His Party*, 280–85, 295–96; Patrick M. Sowle, "The Conciliatory Republicans during the Winter of Secession" (Ph.D. diss., Duke University, 1963).

46. Charles Sumner to Salmon P. Chase, Jan. 19, 1861, Salmon P. Chase Papers, LC; Thaddeus Stevens to Chase, Feb. 3, 1861, in *The Selected Papers of Thaddeus Stevens*, ed. Beverly Wilson Palmer and Holly Byers Ochoa, 2 vols. (Pittsburgh:

University of Pittsburgh Press, 1997–98), 1:200; *NY Times*, Jan. 22,1861; Frances Seward to William Seward, Jan. 19, 1861, Seward Papers; Crofts, *Reluctant Confederates*, 237; Stahr, *Seward*, 225–26.

47. Waggoner, *Poetical Works of Whittier*, 332.

48. Henry Adams, "The Great Secession Winter of 1860–61," in *The Great Secession Winter of 1860-61 and Other Essays*, ed. George Hochfield (New York: Sagamore, 1958), 29.

Chapter 6

1. Josiah Morrow, ed., *Life and Speeches of Thomas Corwin: Orator, Lawyer, and Statesman* (Cincinnati, OH: W. H. Anderson, 1896), 83, 305; *CG*, 29:2 (Feb. 11, 1847), A211–18. There is no modern biography of Corwin.

2. Morrow, *Life and Speeches of Corwin*, 313; Michael A. Morrison, "'New Territory versus No Territory': The Whig Party and the Politics of Western Expansion, 1846–1848," *Western Historical Quarterly* 23 (1992): 45–46; Stephen E. Maizlish, *The Triumph of Sectionalism: The Transformation of Ohio Politics, 1844–1856* (Kent, OH: Kent State University Press, 1983), 63–67, 84–90.

3. Carl Schurz, *The Reminiscences of Carl Schurz*, vol. 2, *1852-1863* (New York: McClure, 1907), 214–15.

4. Michael F. Holt, *The Rise and Fall of the American Whig Party: Jacksonian Politics and the Onset of the Civil War* (New York: Oxford University Press, 1999), 265–67.

5. *CG*, 36:1 (Jan. 23–24, 1860), A134–50; Morrow, *Life and Speeches of Corwin*, 385–456.

6. Abraham Lincoln to John J. Crittenden and Thomas Corwin, Sept. 2, 1850, *CWAL*, 2:93.

7. Lincoln, speech at Columbus, Ohio, Sept. 16, 1859, *CWAL*, 3:400–401.

8. Corwin to Lincoln, Sept. 25, Oct. 17, 1859, Lincoln Papers. Lincoln's letters to Corwin do not survive, but other things he wrote at the time reflect the same viewpoint—that fifty thousand former Democrats in Illinois would vote Republican only if the party nominated someone with unmistakable antislavery credentials, not an old Whig on an innocuous platform. See Lincoln to Nathan Sargent, June 23, 1859, *CWAL*, 3:387–88.

9. Waddy Thompson to Corwin, Oct. 16, 1860, William L. Hodge to Corwin, Oct. 18, 1860, copies enclosed in Corwin to Lincoln, Oct. 28, 1860, Lincoln Papers.

10. Corwin to Lincoln, Oct. 28, Nov. 4, 1860, Lincoln Papers.

11. S. W. Spencer to Corwin, Oct. 29, 1860, Corwin to Lincoln, Nov. 4, 1860, Lincoln Papers.

12. Lincoln, "Eulogy on Henry Clay," July 6, 1852, Lincoln to George Robertson, Aug. 15, 1855, *CWAL*, 2:125–26, 317–18; William J. Cooper, *We Have the War upon Us: The Onset of the Civil War, November 1860–April 1861* (New York: Alfred A. Knopf, 2012), 72–73.

13. Morrow, *Life and Speeches of Corwin*, 312–13.

14. *CG*, 36:2 (Dec. 4, 1860), 6–7; *New York World*, Dec. 10, 1860; *NY Tribune*,

Dec. 14, 1860; *CG*, 36:2, *Journal of the Committee of Thirty-Three*, H.R. Rep. No. 31, 1–2. The *Committee of Thirty-Three Report* is separate.

15. Corwin to Lincoln, Dec. 10, 11, 1860, John A. Gilmer to Lincoln, Dec. 10, 1860, Lincoln Papers.

16. Corwin to Lincoln, Dec. 10, 11, 1860, Lincoln Papers; Crofts, *Reluctant Confederates*, 221–24.

17. Corwin to Lincoln, Dec. 10, 11, 1860, Gilmer to Lincoln, Dec. 10, 1860, Lincoln Papers.

18. Lincoln to Lyman Trumbull, Dec. 10, 1860, Lincoln to William Kellogg, Dec. 11, 1860, Lincoln to Elihu B. Washburne, Dec. 13, 1860, Lincoln to Gilmer, Dec. 15, 1860, Lincoln to Alexander Stephens, Dec. 22, 1860, *CWAL*, 4:149–53, 160.

19. Corwin to Lincoln, Dec. 24, 1860, Lincoln Papers.

20. *Journal of the Committee of Thirty-Three*, 36th Cong., 2d Sess., H.R. Rep. No. 31, Dec. 21, 1860, 14–15.

21. Henry Winter Davis to David Davis [September 1860], Lincoln Papers, the source for the next two paragraphs.

22. *NY Tribune*, Dec. 13, 1860 (special dispatch from Washington, Dec. 12, 1860).

23. Martin B. Duberman, *Charles Francis Adams, 1807-1886* (Stanford, CA: Stanford University Press, 1961), esp. 223–57.

24. *Journal of the Committee of Thirty-Three*, Dec. 28, 1860, 19.

25. Lincoln, First Inaugural Address, Mar. 4, 1861, *CWAL*, 4:270.

26. Michael Vorenberg, *Final Freedom: The Civil War, the Abolition of Slavery, and the Thirteenth Amendment* (Cambridge: Cambridge University Press, 2001), 192.

27. The would-be thirteenth amendment prompted a learned essay about the impossibility of enacting "unamendable" amendments to the Constitution. See A. Christopher Bryant, "Stopping Time: The Pro-Slavery and 'Irrevocable' Thirteenth Amendment," *Harvard Journal of Law and Public Policy* 26 (2003): 501–50.

28. Potter, *Lincoln and His Party*, 291–96; Mark J. Stegmaier, *Henry Adams in the Secession Crisis: Dispatches to the* Boston Daily Advertiser, *December 1860– March 1861* (Baton Rouge: Louisiana State University Press, 2102), 49–51; *Journal of the Committee of Thirty-Three*, Dec. 21, 28, 1860, 14–15, 19. The Journal is preceded by Corwin's own report, "Disturbed Condition of the Country." It is followed by the minority report of C. C. Washburn and Mason W. Tappan; see pp. 5–6 for their opposition to the Adams amendment. The next minority report from the South (Taylor, Phelps, Rust, Whiteley, Winslow) approved of the amendment but considered it insufficient. "But standing alone as it does, we cannot regard it as likely to contribute in any material degree to the settlement of the existing troubles." See pp. 15–16 of this minority report. T. A. R. Nelson's comments are on pp. 5–6 of his minority report. Adams had his own minority report. The *Committee of Thirty-Three Report* (H.R. Rep. No. 31) is separate.

29. Bingham to Giddings, Jan. 14, 1861, Joshua R. Giddings Papers, Ohio Historical Society, copy in Seward Papers.

30. Stegmaier, *Henry Adams in the Secession Crisis*, 49–63.

31. Kenneth M. Stampp, *And the War Came: The North and the Secession Crisis, 1860–61* (Baton Rouge: Louisiana State University Press, 1950), 83–98; Maury Klein, *Days of Defiance: Sumter, Secession, and the Coming of the Civil War* (New York: Random House, 1997), 190–97.

32. *Journal of the Committee of Thirty-Three*, 32–40; Potter, *Lincoln and His Party*, 297–99; Norman A. Graebner, "Thomas Corwin and the Sectional Crisis," *Ohio History* 86 (1977): 243–44; CF Adams Diary, Jan. 5, 14, 1861.

33. John Bassett Moore, ed., *The Works of James Buchanan, Comprising His Speeches, State Papers, and Private Correspondence*, 12 vols. (Philadelphia: J. B. Lippincott, 1908), 11:7–43; *NY Times*, Dec. 5, 1860.

34. Thomas Corwin, "Disturbed Condition of the Country," Jan. 14, 1861, H.R. Rep. No. 31; *NY Times*, Jan. 17, 1861; *NY Herald*, Jan. 19, 1861. The two newspaper versions of Corwin's report contain slight differences in wording.

35. Solomon's Northup's *Twelve Years a Slave* (Baton Rouge: Louisiana State University Press, 1968), the classic account of how a free black man from the North was kidnapped and sent South as a slave, is now widely known because it was made into a film in 2013. See also Julie Winch, "Philadelphia and the Other Underground Railroad," *Pennsylvania Magazine of History and Biography* 111 (1987): 3–26.

36. C. C. Washburn and Mason W. Tappan, "Disturbed Condition of the Country," Minority Report, H.R. Rep. No. 31.

37. Charles Francis Adams, "Disturbed Condition of the Country," Minority Report, H.R. Rep. No. 31.

38. Corwin to Lincoln, Jan. 16, 1861, Lincoln Papers.

39. Corwin to Stuart, Jan. 17, 1861, Alexander H. H. Stuart Papers, University of Virginia.

40. Edward L. Ayers, *In the Presence of Mine Enemies: War in the Heart of America, 1859–1863* (New York: W. W. Norton, 2003), 44–46, 50–52.

41. Crofts, *Reluctant Confederates*, 57, 137–39. The convention would be apportioned on the "white basis," the standard used for the House of Delegates, rather than the "mixed basis" used for the Virginia Senate, which took into account slave property as well as white population.

42. Daniel W. Crofts, "The Southern Opposition and the Crisis of the Union," in *A Political Nation: New Directions in Mid-Nineteenth-Century American Political History*, ed. Gary W. Gallagher and Rachel A. Shelden (Charlottesville: University of Virginia Press, 2012), 85–111.

Chapter 7

1. After a protracted two-month contest in December 1859 and January 1860, Republican leaders finally dropped Sherman and brought forward a compromise candidate, William Pennington of New Jersey, who got the extra few votes needed to prevail.

2. John Sherman to William Tecumseh Sherman, Nov. 26, 1860, Dec. 22, 1860, William T. Sherman Papers, LC.

3. Sherman notwithstanding, some modern scholars consider the Deep South's

hysteria entirely accurate: James Oakes, *The Scorpion's Sting: Antislavery and the Coming of the Civil War* (New York: W. W. Norton, 2014), 22–50.

4. Letters to John Sherman from James T. Smith, Dec. 10, 1860, W. F. Panam, Jan. 1, 1861, H. C. Johnson, Jan. 1, 1861, Z. Phillips, Jan. 10, 1861, Thomas J. Butman, Feb. 13, 1861, John Sherman Papers, LC.

5. Letters to John Sherman from James D. Whitney, Dec. 15, 1860, Henry F. Page, Dec. 17, 1860, C. Hade, Dec. 24, 1860, A. P. Stone, Jan. 7, 1861, R. P. Spaulding, Feb. 7, 1861, John Sherman Papers.

6. James T. Hale to Abraham Lincoln, Jan. 6, 1861, Lincoln Papers. Hale, like John Sherman, was a member of the so-called Border State Committee. The letter reflected Sherman's views.

7. *CG*, 36:2 (Jan. 18, 1861), 450–52.

8. Ibid., 455. Sherman might have been willing to bend a little more toward the South. James T. Hale of Pennsylvania, Sherman's Republican colleague on the so-called Border State Committee, floated a trial balloon that would have barred Congress from legislating against slavery in the New Mexico Territory, but Lincoln firmly quashed this potential concession to Southern sensibilities on the territorial issue. New Mexico statehood was a scheme to bypass the territorial tangle. See Lincoln to Hale, Jan. 11, 1861, *CWAL*, 4:172; and Crofts, *Reluctant Confederates*, 202–3, 232–34.

9. *CG*, 36:2 (Jan. 18, 1861), 454.

10. Nathaniel G. Foster to John Sherman, Jan. 10, 1861, John Sherman Papers.

11. Foster to John Sherman, Jan. 21, 1861, John Sherman Papers. This letter alludes to a response from Sherman.

12. *CG*, 36:2 (Jan. 18, 1861), 454–56.

13. The most detailed modern study of nullification challenges Corwin's generalization and finds instead that it gained substantial support elsewhere in the South, especially Georgia and Virginia. Richard E. Ellis, *The Union at Risk: Jacksonian Democracy, States' Rights and the Nullification Crisis* (New York: Oxford University Press, 1987). But in the end, a compromise was arranged and South Carolina did back down.

14. *CG*, 36:2 (Jan. 21, 1861), A72–76; Josiah Morrow, ed., *Life and Speeches of Thomas Corwin: Orator, Lawyer, and Statesman* (Cincinnati, OH: W. H. Anderson, 1896), 457–77.

15. Carl Schurz, *The Reminiscences of Carl Schurz*, vol. 2, *1852–1863* (New York: McClure, 1907), 214–15; "Sigma," Letter from Washington, Jan. 22, 1861, in *Cincinnati Commercial*, Jan. 28, 1861.

16. "Southern Rights," Dresden (TN), Apr. 1, 1861, in *Memphis Avalanche*, Apr. 6, 1861; Crofts, *Reluctant Confederates*, 31–34; Daniel W. Crofts, "No Better Southern Man," *NY Times*, Disunion (blog), Jan. 22, 2011, http://opinionator.blogs.nytimes.com/2011/01/22/no-better-southern-man/.

17. Robert Hatton to Sophia Hatton, Dec. 16, 1859, Jan. 16, Feb. 8, 1860, in James Vaulx Drake, *Life of General Robert Hatton, Including His Most Important Public Speeches; Together, with Much of his Washington and Army Correspondence* (Nashville, TN: Marshall and Bruce, 1867), 181–82, 217–18, 232; Charles Faulkner

Bryan Jr., "Robert Hatton of Tennessee" (MA thesis, University of Georgia, 1971), 74–75; *NY Times*, Dec. 23, 1859.

18. Daniel W. Crofts, "The Southern Opposition and the Crisis of the Union," in *A Political Nation: New Directions in Mid-Nineteenth-Century American Political History*, ed. Gary W. Gallagher and Rachel A. Shelden (Charlottesville: University of Virginia Press, 2012), 85–111.

19. *CG*, 36:2 (Jan. 23, 1861), A111–16.

20. "Sigma" (Ben Perley Poore), Jan. 23, 24, 25, 1861, in *Cincinnati Commercial*, Jan. 26, 28, 1861.

21. *CG*, 36:2 (Jan. 26, 1861), 580–83; John A. Gilmer to Thurlow Weed, Jan. 12, 1861, Weed Papers.

22. Crofts, *Reluctant Confederates*, 34–36, 222–29, 245–47; Daniel W. Crofts, "John Gilmer's Last Stand," *NY Times*, Disunion (blog), Mar. 11, 2011, http://opinionator.blogs.nytimes.com/2011/03/11/john-gilmers-last-stand/.

23. *CG*, 36:2 (Jan. 26, 1861), 580–83.

24. *Baltimore Clipper*, quoted in *Salisbury* (NC) *Carolina Watchman*, Feb. 5, 1861; Gerald W. Johnson, "John Adams Gilmer, 1805–1868," in *Founders and Builders of Greensboro, 1808–1908*, ed. Bettie D. Caldwell (Greensboro, NC: J. J. Stone, 1925), 94–102; Crofts, *Reluctant Confederates*, 36, 124–25, 206–7.

25. Henry Adams to Charles Francis Adams Jr., Jan. 17, 24, 28, 1861, in *The Letters of Henry Adams*, ed. J. C. Levenson et al., 6 vols. (Cambridge, MA: Belknap Press of Harvard University Press, 1982–88), 1:221–26; CF Adams Diary, Jan. 31, 1861.

26. *CG*, 36:2 (Jan. 31, 1861), A124–27, and in the following paragraphs; Crofts, *Reluctant Confederates*, 13–17, 234–40; Daniel W. Crofts, "The Adams Family," *NY Times*, Disunion (blog), Mar. 23, 2011, http://opinionator.blogs.nytimes.com/2011/03/23/the-adams-family/.

27. Nick Bunker, *An Empire on the Edge: How Britain Came to Fight America* (New York: Alfred A. Knopf, 2014), 249–52, 257–66.

28. Martin B. Duberman, *Charles Francis Adams, 1807–1886* (Boston: Houghton Mifflin, 1961); Paul C. Nagel, *Descent from Glory: Four Generations of the John Adams Family* (New York: Oxford University Press, 1983), 161–238.

29. Charles Sumner to Salmon P. Chase, Jan. 19, 1861, Salmon P. Chase Papers, LC; *CG*, 36:2 (Jan. 31, 1861), A124–27.

30. CF Adams Diary, Jan. 31, 1861.

31. Henry Adams to Charles Francis Adams Jr., Feb. 5, 1861, in Levenson et al., *Letters of Henry Adams*, 1:227–29; CF Adams Diary, Jan. 31, 1861; *CG*, 36:2 (Jan. 25, 1861), A108; *Louisville Daily Journal*, Feb. 9, 1861.

32. Crofts, *Reluctant Confederates*, 136–43, 159–63; James D. Davidson to James B. Dorman, Feb. 13, 1861, James D. Davidson Papers, copy in U. B. Phillips Papers, Yale University; "Bell-Everett," in *Wheeling Daily Intelligencer*, Jan. 22, 1861.

33. Charles Francis Adams Jr. to Charles Francis Adams, Feb. 6, 1861, Adams Family Papers, Massachusetts Historical Society (microfilm edition); Stevens quoted in *Richmond Dispatch*, Feb. 9, 1861; Crofts, *Reluctant Confederates*, 153.

34. Gerald S. Henig, *Henry Winter Davis: Antebellum and Civil War Congressman from Maryland* (New York: Twayne, 1973); *CG*, 36:2 (Feb. 7, 1861), A181–85.

35. "Letter from Washington," Feb. 7, 1861, in *Boston Advertiser*, Feb. 11, 1861; Mark J. Stegmaier, *Henry Adams in the Secession Crisis: Dispatches to the Boston Daily Advertiser, December 1860–March 1861* (Baton Rouge: Louisiana State University Press, 2012), 198–205; "Sigma," Feb. 7, 1861, in *Cincinnati Commercial*, Feb. 9, 1861; "Independent" (James E. Harvey), Feb. 7, 1861, in *Philadelphia North American*, Feb. 8, 1861; *New York World*, Feb. 9, 1861, Washington Correspondent, Feb. 7, 1861.

36. *CG*, 36:2 (Feb. 7, 1861), A181–85.

37. *NY Times*, Jan. 16, 1860; Robert Hatton to Sophia Hatton, Feb. 8, 28, 1860, in Drake, *Life of Hatton*, 232, 241; Crofts, *Reluctant Confederates*, 1–7; Daniel W. Crofts, "No Better Southern Man," *NY Times*, Disunion (blog), Jan. 22, 2011, http://opinionator.blogs.nytimes.com/2011/01/22/no-better-southern-man/.

38. *CG*, 36:2 (Feb. 8, 1861), A171–74.

39. Hatton to William Bowen Campbell, Feb. 16, 1861, Campbell Family Papers, Duke University; Campbell to Hatton, Feb. 12, 1861, Seward Papers; Crofts, *Reluctant Confederates*, 1–7, 144–52; Jonathan M. Atkins, *Parties, Politics, and the Sectional Conflict in Tennessee, 1832–1861* (Knoxville: University of Tennessee Press, 1997), 228–44.

40. *NY Times*, Feb. 11, 12, 1861.

41. Henry Adams to Charles Francis Adams Jr., Feb. 8, 1861, in J. C. Levenson et al., *Letters of Henry Adams*, 1:229–30.

42. *Springfield Republican*, Feb. 8, 1861, "Van" from Washington, Feb. 6, 1861.

43. James Barbour to William H. Seward, Feb. 8, 1861, Seward Papers; Robert Eden Scott, letter to Committee of Thirty-Three, Dec. 20, 1860, in *Alexandria Gazette*, Dec. 21, 1860; J. W. Merriam to Horatio King, Feb. 12, 1861, Horatio King Papers, LC; Crofts, *Reluctant Confederates*, 210, 270; Potter, *Lincoln and His Party*, 148–49; Seward to Lincoln, Dec. 28, 1860, Jan. 15, 27, 1861, all in Lincoln Papers.

44. Campbell to Robert Hatton, Feb. 12, 1861, J. R. Bailey to Seward, Feb. 11, 1861, both in Seward Papers.

Chapter 8

1. Jabez Woodman to Seward, Dec. 5, 1860, Seward Papers; Robert J. Cook, *Civil War Senator: William Pitt Fessenden and the Fight to Save the American Republic* (Baton Rouge: Louisiana State University Press, 2011), 68; http://civilwarthosesurnames.blogspot.com/2012/09/woodmans-throught-history.html.

2. Gaillard Hunt, *Israel, Elihu, and Cadwallader Washburn: A Chapter in American Biography* (New York: Macmillan, 1925); Mark Washburne, *A Biography of Elihu Benjamin Washburne: Congressman, Secretary of State, and Envoy Extraordinary*, 4 vols. (Bloomington, IN: Xlibris, 2001–7); Michael Hill, ed., *Elihu Washburne: The Diary and Letters of America's Minister to France during the Siege and Commune of Paris* (New York: Simon and Schuster, 2012). Maine remained a part of Massachusetts until achieving separate statehood in 1820.

3. http://www.granthome.com/washburne_house.htm.

4. Washburne, *Elihu Benjamin Washburne*, 1:242–49. Washburne's 7,392 votes edged the Democratic incumbent, who collected 7,106 votes. The Free Soil candidate polled 2,200 votes.

5. Washburne, *Elihu Benjamin Washburne*, 1:258–71; Michael F. Holt, *The Rise and Fall of the American Whig Party: Jacksonian Politics and the Onset of the Civil War* (New York: Oxford University Press, 1999), 827, 829–30, 869. In 1858 Stephen A. Douglas hammered Washburne's pledge to oppose admitting any more slave states and attempted to tie Lincoln to this quasi-abolitionist position. Washburne, *Elihu Benjamin Washburne*, 1:359–62. Cadwallader Washburn, the youngest of the three brothers, first was elected to Congress from Wisconsin in 1854, amid that year's enormous political upheaval. The three Washburn brothers held seats in the House together starting in 1855, when Cadwallader's term began.

6. William B. Dodge to Washburne, Aug. 16, 1858, Dec. 17, 1859, Jan. 13, Apr. 14, 20, 1860, Elihu B. Washburne Papers, LC.

7. In an era when unexpected treasures sometimes emerge through a web search, the tale in this paragraph about William Bradford Dodge (1784–1869) stands out. The gift from the African chief is now held in the Newton (Massachusetts) History Museum; it is displayed on a helpful website that includes documentation in Dodge's handwriting: http://apps.newtonma.gov/jackson/seeking-freedom/02.html. The information about his church's reaction to John Brown—almost certainly written by Dodge himself—may be found in Mark Hubbard, *Illinois's War: The Civil War in Documents* (Athens: Ohio University Press, 2013), 46–47. Other pertinent sources include the website for the Historic Millburn Community Association: http://www.hmca-il.org/, a history of the Millburn church, extracted from John J. Halsey, ed., *A History of Lake County, Illinois* (Chicago: Roy S. Bates, 1912), two 1869 obituaries for Dodge (http:/www.hmca-il.org/c1869_04.htm), which include the recollections of Robert Morris (1823–1882), and Jill Rebman Martin, "Conventions and Sentiments of Civil War Correspondence in the Minto Letters," *Journal of Illinois History* 5 (Summer 2002): 137–54, esp. 138. On Morris, see Stephen Kendrick and Paul Kendrick, *Sarah's Long Walk: The Free Blacks of Boston and How Their Struggle for Equality Changed America* (Boston: Beacon, 2004), 3–20; and Stephen Kantrowitz, *More Than Freedom: Fighting for Black Citizenship in a White Republic, 1829–1889* (New York: Penguin Books, 2012), 137–39, 170–71, 214–18, 403–4.

8. Washburne, *Elihu Benjamin Washburne*, 1:416–17, 2:180–82, 206.

9. Jane Addams, *Twenty Years at Hull-House with Autobiographical Notes* (New York: Macmillan, 1910, often reprinted as *Twenty Years at Hull-House*); Allen F. Davis, *American Heroine: The Life and Legend of Jane Addams* (New York: Oxford University Press, 1973).

10. Letters to Washburne from A. J. Betts, Nov. 27, Dec. 30, 1860, C. G. Cotting, Dec. 2, 1860, Volney Armour, Dec. 21, 1860, E. Chamberlain, Dec. 21, 1860, William B. Dodge, Dec. 22, 1860, John H. Addams, Jan. 9, 1861, Washburne Papers.

11. Letters to Washburne from Cotting, Dec. 2, 1860, C. K. Williams, Dec. 31, 1860, M. D. Hoy, Jan. 17, 1861, Ebenezer Tucker, Jan. 28, 1861, Washburne Papers.

12. Letters to Washburne from Chamberlain, Dec. 21, 1860, D. Mackay, Jan. 1, 1861, Washburne Papers.

13. Letters to Washburne from Chamberlain, Dec. 21, 1860, Harley Wayne, Dec. 21, 1860, Stephen A. Hurlbut, Dec. 18, 1860, Sidney Disbrow, Jan. 6, 1861, Dodge, Jan. 19, 1861, Washburne Papers.

14. Letters to Washburne from Armour, Dec. 21, 1860, L. H. Bowen, Dec. 21, 1860, Thomas Graygins, Dec. 24, 1860, R. H. McClellan, Jan. 16, 1861, Washburne Papers.

15. W. Hart Jr. to Washburne, Jan. 7, 1861, Dodge to Washburne, Dec. 22, 1860, Washburne Papers.

16. Armour to Washburne, Dec. 21, 1860, McClellan to Washburne, Jan. 16, 1861, Washburne Papers.

17. Dodge to Washburne, Jan. 13, 1860, Washburne Papers.

18. Letters to Washburne from Dodge, Dec. 22, 1860, John James, Jan. 16, 1861, J. W. North, Jan. 17, 1861, Washburne Papers.

19. Letters to Washburne from Henry R. Bass, Dec. 22, 1860, Horace White, Dec. 30, 1860, W. H. Baldwin, Jan. 4, 31, 1861, N. J. Tompkins, Feb. 5, 1861, Washburne Papers.

20. Letters to Washburne from Betts, Dec. 31, 1860, Charles L. Stephenson, Jan. 15, 1861, B. F. Baird, Jan. 16, 1861, James, Jan. 16, 1861, Washburne Papers.

21. Letters to Washburne from O. M. Cooley, Jan. 2, 1861, Baldwin, Jan. 4, 31, 1861, N. A. Vose, Jan. 27, 1861, Tucker, Jan. 28, 1861, H. C. Burchard, Jan. 28, 1861, Washburne Papers.

22. Dodge to Washburne, Feb. 1, 1861, Washburne Papers, LC.

23. Letters to Washburne from Williams, Dec. 31, 1860, Baldwin, Jan. 4, 1861, James, Jan. 16, 1861, E. G. Howe, Feb. 19, 1861, Tompkins, Feb. 5, 1861, Washburne Papers.

24. *CG*, 36:2 (Feb. 26, 1861), 1237–40.

25. *NY Tribune*, Feb. 26, Apr. 10, 1861; Bernard Weisberger, "Horace Greeley: Reformer as Republican," *Civil War History* 23 (March 1977): 5–25.

26. "Warrington," Feb. 28, 1861, in *Springfield Republican*, Mar. 2, 1861.

27. *NY Tribune*, Mar. 2, 4, 1861.

28. *Boston Evening Transcript*, Feb. 5, 1903.

29. Henry L. Dawes to Ella Dawes, June 10, 1860, box 12, Henry L. Dawes Papers, LC; *Charles Sumner: His Complete Works*, 20 vols. (Boston: Lee and Shepard, 1900; reprint ed., New York: Negro Universities Press, 1969), 6:113–286, esp. 120–21, 239–41.

30. David Donald, *Charles Sumner and the Coming of the Civil War* (New York: Alfred A. Knopf, 1960), 363–65.

31. Henry L. Dawes to Ella Dawes, Dec. 9, 10, 14, 15, 1860, Ella Dawes to Henry L. Dawes, Dec. 11, 1860, box 12, Dawes Papers.

32. Letters to Henry L. Dawes from E. H. Owen, Dec. 11, 1860, F. E. Patrick, Dec. 13, 1860, William M. Walker, Dec. 25, 1860, box 17, P. K. Clark, Jan. 4, 1861, E. H. Gray, Feb. 12, 1861, box 18, Dawes Papers.

33. Henry L. Dawes to "My Dear Colt," Dec. 23, 1860, box 17, Moses Kimball to Henry L. Dawes, Jan. 9, 1861, box 18, Dawes Papers.

34. W. P. Porter to Henry L. Dawes, Jan. 1, 1861, Amasa Walker to Henry L. Dawes, Jan. 21, 1861, box 18, Dawes Papers.

35. Clark to Henry L. Dawes, Jan. 4, 1861, box 18, Dawes Papers.

36. Letters to Henry L. Dawes from D. W. Alford, Feb. 13, 1861, Nelson Clark, Feb. 11, 1861, Patrick, Jan. 23, 1861, box 18, Dawes Papers.

37. Letters to Henry L. Dawes from H. Hubbard, Feb. 19, 1861, Charles Wright, Feb. 22, 1861, A. H. Laflin, Feb. 23, 1861, box 18, Dawes Papers.

38. Henry Chickering to Henry L. Dawes, Feb. 18, 1861, box 18, Dawes Papers.

39. Samuel Bowles to Henry L. Dawes, Feb. 26, 1861, box 18, Dawes Papers.

40. *Springfield Republican*, Mar. 2, 1861; Washington correspondence by W. D., Mar. 2, 6, 1861.

41. "Warrington," Feb. 28, Mar. 7, 1861, in *Springfield Republican*, Mar. 2, 9, 1861; William S. Robinson, *"Warrington" Pen-Portraits: A Collection of Personal and Political Reminiscences from 1848 to 1876* (Boston: Mrs. W. S. Robinson [Harriet Jane Hanson Robinson], 1877).

42. James Dixon to Gideon Welles, Dec. 8, 22, 1860, Gideon Welles Papers, LC.

43. Allan Nevins, *Hamilton Fish: The Inner History of the Grant Administration* (New York: Dodd, Mead, 1936), 50–64; Fish quoted on 61.

44. Hamilton Fish to Thomas G. Turner, Dec. 7, 1860, Fish to Charles S. Davies, Jan. 18, 1861, letterbook, container 187, Hamilton Fish Papers, LC; Nevins, *Hamilton Fish*, 81.

45. Fish to William S. Thayer, Dec. 15, 1860, letterbook, container 187, Fish Papers.

46. Fish to William H. Seward, Dec. 10, 1860, Fish to William P. Fessenden, Dec. 11, 1860, letterbook, container 187, Fish Papers; *CG*, 36:2 (Dec. 10, 1860), 32–33.

47. Seward to Fish, Dec. 11, 1860, container 47, Fish Papers. Dixon, Seward, and Fish drifted away from the Republican orbit. All three stood apart from the party consensus in the immediate postwar years. Dixon lauded Andrew Johnson as "the most popular President since the days of Washington" and displayed a "passion against Republican radicals," noted historian Eric McKitrick. Seward was a more complex case. Gravely wounded by one of John Wilkes Booth's co-conspirators on that terrible night in April 1865, he recovered and continued as secretary of state under Johnson. Eager to pursue an ambitious plan for overseas acquisitions, he sided uncomfortably with Johnson after the obstinate president broke with the Republican Party. Fish avoided partisan involvement during wartime and the early years of Reconstruction; he remained on the sidelines until Grant became president. Eric McKitrick, *Andrew Johnson and Reconstruction* (Chicago: University of Chicago Press, 1960), 81–83, 275; Walter Stahr, *Seward: Lincoln's Indispensable Man* (New York: Simon and Schuster, 2012), 446–529; Nevins, *Hamilton Fish*, 64–67, 88, 99–101.

48. William P. Fessenden to Fish, Dec. 15, 1860, container 47, Fish Papers.

49. Cook, *Civil War Senator*, 86–90, 103–4, 124–31, 152, 168, 241.

50. Woodbury Davis to William Pitt Fessenden, Jan. 14, 1861, J. P. Fessenden to William P. Fessenden, Jan. 10, 1861, William Pitt Fessenden Papers, LC.

51. William Pitt Fessenden to William Fessenden, Feb. 10, 1861, William Pitt

Fessenden to Samuel Fessenden, Feb. 16, 1861, box 9, William Pitt Fessenden Papers, Bowdoin College.

52. R. W. McDade to Seward, Feb. 4, 1861, R. T. C. to Seward, Feb. 4, 1861, J. H. Fait to Seward, Feb. 17, 1861, Seward Papers.

53. Henry Willis to Seward, Feb. 17, 1861, Seward Papers.

Chapter 9

1. *CG*, 36:2 (Jan. 29, 1861), 621–24.

2. Hans L. Trefousse, *Thaddeus Stevens: Nineteenth-Century Egalitarian* (Chapel Hill: University of North Carolina Press, 1997), chap. 9, 100–110, covers the presidential election of 1860 and the secession crisis.

3. Edward Magdol, *Owen Lovejoy: Abolitionist in Congress* (New Brunswick, NJ: Rutgers University Press, 1967), chap.13, 260–75, addresses the secession crisis; Owen Lovejoy, *His Brother's Blood: Speeches and Writings, 1838–64*, ed. William F. Moore and Jane Ann Moore (Urbana: University of Illinois Press, 2004), 250–61; Frederick J. Blue, "The Barbarism of Slavery: Owen Lovejoy and the Congressional Assault on Slavery," in *No Taint of Compromise: Crusaders in Antislavery Politics* (Baton Rouge: Louisiana State University Press, 2005), 90–116; Abraham Lincoln to David B. Davis, July 7, 1856, in *The Collected Works of Abraham Lincoln, First Supplement*, ed. Roy P. Basler, 9 vols. (Westport, CT: Greenwood, 1973), 27.

4. *CG*, 36:2 (Jan. 23, 1861), A84–87.

5. *Congressional Globe*, 36th Cong., 1st Sess. (Jan. 25, 1860), 586; 35th Cong., 2d Sess. (Feb. 21, 1859), A196–99; Beverly Wilson Palmer and Holly Byers Ochoa, eds., *The Selected Papers of Thaddeus Stevens*, 2 vols. (Pittsburgh, PA: University of Pittsburgh Press, 1997–98), 1:163–65; Lovejoy, *His Brother's Blood*, 175–78; Magdol, *Owen Lovejoy*, 223–25.

6. *CG*, 36:2 (Jan. 23, 1861), A85.

7. Daniel W. Crofts, *A Secession Crisis Enigma: William Henry Hurlbert and "The Diary of a Public Man"* (Baton Rouge: Louisiana State University Press, 2010), 209–10. The Lincoln Legend looms large in Harold Holzer, *Lincoln President-Elect: Abraham Lincoln and the Great Secession Winter, 1860–1861* (New York: Simon and Schuster, 2008); James Oakes, *Freedom National: The Destruction of Slavery in the United States, 1861–1865* (New York: W. W. Norton, 2013), 49–54; James Oakes, *The Scorpion's Sting: Antislavery and the Coming of the Civil War* (New York: W. W. Norton, 2014), 22–50.

8. Woodbury Davis to William P. Fessenden, Jan. 14, 1861, William Pitt Fessenden Papers, LC; *Reading Berks and Schuylkill Journal*, Dec. 15, 1860, in *Northern Editorials on Secession*, Howard Cecil Perkins, 2 vols. (New York: D. Appleton-Century for the American Historical Association, 1942), 1:118–21.

9. Potter, *Lincoln and His Party*, 307–9; Crofts, *Reluctant Confederates*, 138–39, 207–13; CF Adams Diary, Feb. 5, 1861; *Baltimore American*, Feb. 4, 1861, Washington correspondent, Feb. 4, 1861. Many reports corroborated that Corwin held back his proposals during February: *New York Evening Post*, Feb. 7, 1861; *Newark Daily Mercury*, Feb. 11, 1861; *NY Herald*, Feb. 16, 1861.

10. Robert Gray Gunderson, *Old Gentlemen's Convention: The Washington Peace Conference of 1861* (Madison: University of Wisconsin Press, 1961); Crofts, *Reluctant Confederates*, 138, 206–13.

11. Gunderson, *Old Gentlemen's Convention*, 10–13, 95–96; Adam Goodheart, *1861: The Civil War Awakening* (New York: Alfred A. Knopf, 2011), 85–88, 397n70; *Springfield Republican*, Feb. 8, 1861, "Van" from Washington, Feb. 6, 1861.

12. L. E. Chittenden, *A Report of the Debates and Proceedings in the Secret Sessions of the Conference Convention for Proposing Amendments to the Constitution of the United States, Held at Washington, D C., in February, A. D., 1861* (New York: D. Appleton, 1864; reprint ed., New York: Da Capo, 1971), 47–52, 292–95, 440–43; Crofts, *Reluctant Confederates*, 208–13.

13. Chittenden, *Report of the Conference Convention*, 443–44.

14. Ibid., 91–98, 125–28, 150–56.

15. Ibid., 165.

16. Ibid., 175–76.

17. Ibid., 428–29.

18. Ibid., 278. For corroboration regarding the campaign in Pennsylvania in 1860, see the *Philadelphia North American*, Nov. 7, 1860, in Perkins, *Northern Editorials on Secession*, 1:80–83; and James L. Huston, *The Panic of 1857 and the Coming of the Civil War* (Baton Rouge: Louisiana State University Press, 1987), 249–56, 264–68.

19. Chittenden, *Report of the Conference Convention*, 399–400.

20. *CG*, 36:2 (Feb. 6, 1861), 763–66; Potter, *Lincoln and His Party*, 277–78.

21. Potter, *Lincoln and His Party*, 278; Crofts, *Reluctant Confederates*, 255; Nichols, *Disruption*, 467; Robert W. Johannsen, *Stephen A. Douglas* (New York: Oxford University Press, 1973), 830–31; Michael Burlingame, *Abraham Lincoln: A Life*, 2 vols. (Baltimore: Johns Hopkins University Press, 2008), 1:758.

22. *Philadelphia North American*, Feb. 5, 18, 1861, "Independent," Feb. 4, 17, 1861.

23. *CG*, 36:2 (Feb. 1, 1861), 695–97.

24. *CG*, 36:2 (Feb. 7, 1861), 801–3. Junkin was a lame duck, having been defeated for reelection.

25. John F. Coleman, *The Disruption of the Pennsylvania Democracy, 1848–1860* (Harrisburg: Pennsylvania Historical and Museum Commission, 1975), 148–49. Other scholars corroborate Coleman. Republicans knew the "vital necessity of obtaining the Keystone State's twenty-seven electoral votes," writes James L. Huston. Accordingly they recognized "the primacy of the tariff issue there." Economic issues rather than "slavery extension" tipped the balance in this all-important state. Huston, *Panic of 1857*, 249, 264–68. Few Republicans in Pittsburgh condemned slavery as a "moral wrong." They "played down their antislavery appeal and spoke instead of white men's rights." The party tapped into "the virulent animosities between Protestants and Catholics" and did nothing to challenge "the anti-Negro prejudices of many of the people in the city." Michael Fitzgibbon Holt, *Forging a Majority: The Formation of the Republican Party in Pittsburgh, 1848–1860* (New Haven, CT: Yale University Press, 1969), 6–7, 311. A study of public opinion in Philadelphia during the antebellum and Civil War eras surmises that the "political

atmosphere" there was comparable to "the large area extending from New York City and much of New Jersey, through southern Pennsylvania, to the southern parts of Ohio, Indiana, and Illinois." Because antiblack sentiment was prevalent in the border North, Republicans made headway only by distancing themselves from abolition and by emphasizing their devotion to the interests of Northern white men. No Philadelphia Republican voted against the prospective thirteenth amendment. William Dusinberre, *Civil War Issues in Philadelphia, 1856–1865* (Philadelphia: University of Pennsylvania Press, 1965), 11, 28–29. For a related account of the clamor in late 1860 and early 1861 to repeal Pennsylvania's Personal Liberty Law, see David G. Smith, *On the Edge of Freedom: The Fugitive Slave Issue in South Central Pennsylvania, 1820–1870* (New York: Fordham University Press, 2013), 159–73.

26. *CG*, 36:2 (Feb. 19, 1861), 1040–43. See Matthew Salafia, *Slavery's Borderland: Freedom and Bondage along the Ohio River* (Philadelphia: University of Pennsylvania Press, 2013).

27. *CG*, 36:2 (Jan. 31, 1861), A127–29. The next two paragraphs draw from the same source.

28. *CG*, 36:2 (Jan. 25, 1861), 568–71. The next two paragraphs draw from the same source.

29. *CG*, 36:2 (Feb. 9, 1861), A199–203. The next two paragraphs draw from the same source.

30. *CG*, 36:2 (Feb. 19, 1861), A228–30, and for the following paragraph. On Edward Wade, see Frederick J. Blue, "The Plight of Slavery Will Cover the Land: Benjamin and Edward Wade, Brothers in Antislavery Politics," in *No Taint of Compromise: Crusaders in Antislavery Politics* (Baton Rouge: Louisiana State University Press, 2005), 213–37, esp. 217–26.

31. Mark J. Stegmaier, *Henry Adams in the Secession Crisis: Dispatches to the Boston Daily Advertiser, December 1860–March 1861* (Baton Rouge: Louisiana State University Press, 2102), 199–200, 204–5; *CG*, 36:2 (Feb. 7, 1861), 795–98; Charles Sedgwick to Deborah G. Sedgwick, Jan. 8, 1861, Charles Baldwin Sedgwick Papers, Syracuse University Library Special Collections, quoted in Earle Field, "Charles B. Sedgwick's Letters from Washington, 1859–1861," *Mid-America* 49 (April 1967): 137–38.

32. *CG*, 36:2 (Jan. 25, 31, 1861), A109, A118–21.

33. *CG*, 36:2 (Jan. 29, 1861), 622.

34. *CG*, 36:2 (Feb. 16, 1861), 967–69. The next paragraph draws from the same source.

35. Benjamin W. Arnett, ed., *Duplicate Copy of the Souvenir from the Afro-American League of Tennessee to Hon. James M. Ashley of Ohio* (Philadelphia: A. M. E. Church, 1894), 113, 628–29; *CG*, 36:1 (May 29, 1860), A374–76. Ashley comes alive in a modern biography, Robert F. Horowitz, *The Great Impeacher: A Political Biography of James M. Ashley* (New York: Brooklyn College Press, 1979), physical description on p. 1.

36. Arnett, *Ashley*, 605, 623–24.

37. *CG*, 36:2 (Jan. 17, 1861), A61–70, quotations on 62, 68–70; Arnett, *Ashley*,

116–64; Leonard L. Richards, *Who Freed the Slaves? The Fight over the Thirteenth Amendment* (Chicago: University of Chicago Press, 2015).

38. For a compelling biography of Bingham, see Gerard N. Magliocca, *American Founding Son: John Bingham and the Invention of the Fourteenth Amendment* (New York: New York University Press, 2013), 3. The quoted segment is from the *New Hampshire Statesman*, Feb. 13, 1863.

39. *CG*, 36:2 (Jan. 22, 1861), A80–84.

40. James Ashley also touched what Adams had said about the war powers, but only in passing. *CG*, 36:2 (Jan. 17, 1861), A66.

41. Reporters were startled by Bingham's "extremely radical anti slavery speech," the most outspoken of the session. "Not that Mr. Bingham was furious in manner, or loose in his language; — the speech was composed with extreme care, and what is more, thoroughly committed to memory." It was evident "that Mr. Bingham represents a constituency of most decided anti slavery sentiments." "Sigma," Letter from Washington, Jan. 22, 1861, in *Cincinnati Commercial*, Jan. 28, 1861.

42. *CG*, 36:2 (Feb. 1, 1861), A129–33.

43. *CG*, 36:2 (Feb. 8, 1861), A185–89.

44. *CG*, 36:2 (Jan. 30, 1861), 649–52; see also John Hutchins, *CG*, 36:2 (Feb. 9, 1861), A199–203. Conkling, however, changed his mind and did vote for the amendment.

45. At the start of the lame-duck session of Congress, on December 3, the House voted to establish a special committee, with one member from each state, to consider the crisis facing the Union. As noted in chapter 6, this measure passed without debate, 145 to 38. Republicans voted 62 to 38 to form what soon would be called the Committee of Thirty Three, but a substantial minority of hard-line Republicans opposed organizing the committee in the first place. *CG*, 36:2 (Dec. 4, 1860), 6; Potter, *Lincoln and His Party*, 88–92. Bingham's vote in favor of the February 11 resolution was consistent with his view that in time of war, the president and the commander of the army *could* move against slavery (even if Congress and the free states had no such power).

46. *CG*, 36:2 (Feb. 11, 1861), 855–58.

47. Nichols, *Disruption*, 475.

Chapter 10

1. Michael Burlingame, *Abraham Lincoln: A Life*, 2 vols. (Baltimore: Johns Hopkins University Press, 2008), 32–39; Harold Holzer, *Lincoln President-Elect: Abraham Lincoln and the Great Secession Winter, 1860-1861* (New York: Simon and Schuster, 2008), 377–96. Was William H. Seward also at the depot? Two modern assessments explore the question and address the larger issue of his behind-the-scenes role: Daniel W. Crofts, *A Secession Crisis Enigma: William Henry Hurlbert and "The Diary of a Public Man"* (Baton Rouge: Louisiana State University Press, 2010), 85–87; and Walter Stahr, *Seward: Lincoln's Indispensable Man* (New York: Simon and Schuster, 2012), 237–38, 601-2n59.

2. CF Adams Diary, Feb. 11, 19, 1861.

3. Burlingame, *Abraham Lincoln*, 2:40–45. The setting for the Peace Conference is described in Adam Goodheart, *1861: The Civil War Awakening* (New York: Alfred A. Knopf, 2011), 85.

4. Nichols, *Disruption*, 475; Crofts, *Reluctant Confederates*, 245, 425n71. The CF Adams Diary, Feb. 24, 1861, places Corwin among the visitors who spoke with Lincoln that day.

5. *Journal of the Committee of Thirty-Three*, 36th Cong., 2d Sess., H.R. Rep. No. 31, Dec. 28, 1860, 19.

6. *CG*, 36:2 (Feb. 26, 1861), 1234–36.

7. Nichols, *Disruption*, 476; "Sigma," Letter from Washington, Feb. 27, 1861, in *Cincinnati Commercial*, Mar. 1, 1861; CF Adams Diary, Feb. 26, 1861; *CG*, 36:2 (Feb. 26, 27, 1861), 1232–43, 1258–65. The hard-line statement proposed by Elihu Washburne of Illinois is on 1240. The key votes are on 1263–65.

8. *CG*, 36:2 (Feb. 27, 1861), 1264–65. Ibid., 1264, shows a vote of 123–71, but the *House Journal*, 36th Cong., 2d Sess. (Feb. 27, 1861), tallies a vote of 120–71.

9. CF Adams Diary, Feb. 27, 1861.

10. *CG*, 36:2 (Feb. 28, 1861), 1283–84; "News of the Day," *NY Times*, Mar. 1, 1861; "Sigma," Letter from Washington, Feb. 28, 1861, in *Cincinnati Commercial*, Mar. 4, 1861. Benjamin Stanton, not to be confused with Edwin Stanton, the U.S. attorney general who would presently become Lincoln's secretary of war, included an impolitic plea to recognize Confederate independence. This did not please Republicans, but it elicited "applause and cries of 'That's right' from the Democratic benches," and Stanton was "subsequently congratulated by Southern members." He continued to display a penchant for placing himself on the wrong side of history by demanding that Ulysses S. Grant be shot after the Battle of Shiloh in 1862. For understandable reasons, he faded into political obscurity.

11. *Washington National Republican*, Mar. 1, 1861; *Springfield Republican*, Mar. 2, 1861, "W. D." from Washington, Mar. 2, 1861, in Mar. 6, 1861. The editorial writer for the *Washington National Republican* assumed that Arkansas was likely to join the Confederacy, so that there would have been seven slave states and nineteen free states remaining in the Union.

12. *CG*, 36:2 (Feb. 28, 1861), 1283–84.

13. "News of the Day," *NY Times*, Mar. 1, 1861; *CG*, 36:2 (Feb. 28, 1861), 1285.

14. "Sigma," Telegraphic correspondence, Mar. 1, 1861, "The New Administration Party—The Necessities of an Affirmative Policy," both in *Cincinnati Commercial*, Mar. 2, 1861; "W. D.," Mar. 2, 1861,"Warrington," Mar. 7, 1861, in *Springfield Republican*, Mar. 6, 9, 1861. As explained in chapter 1, Spooner contended that slavery was contrary to the Constitution.

15. Crofts, *Reluctant Confederates*, 227–29, 243–47. Samuel Bowles, editor of the *Springfield Republican*, privately complained that the jousting within the Republican Party in late February was "more about getting Mr. Seward out of the Cabinet than anything else." Bowles to Henry L. Dawes, Feb. 26, 1861, box 18, Henry L. Dawes Papers, LC. On February 27, Sherman announced that he was paired with an Arkansas congressman, Thomas Hindman, who opposed the amendment. *CG*, 36:2 (Feb. 27, 1861), 1259, 1264.

16. Two classic studies deserve mention here: Whitney R. Cross, *The Burned Over District: The Social and Intellectual History of Enthusiastic Religion in Western New York, 1800-1850* (Ithaca, NY: Cornell University Press, 1950); and Lee Benson, *The Concept of Jacksonian Democracy: New York as a Test Case* (Princeton, NJ: Princeton University Press, 1961).

17. The twelve included Freeman Morse, Ezra French, and John J. Perry from Maine; Martin Butterfield, James A. Graham, and George W. Palmer from New York; Thomas Theaker from Ohio; John L. N. Stratton from New Jersey; John Covode from Pennsylvania; David Kilgore from Indiana; and Cyrus Aldrich from Minnesota. John Sherman from Ohio, who was paired in favor of the amendment on February 27, voted for it the next day. So eleven actually voted differently. The assessments that follow draw in part from the online *Biographical Dictionary of the United States Congress*, supplemented by Wikipedia.

18. *CG*, 36:2 (Jan. 24, 1861), 550–54, quotation on 553. Governor Israel Washburn appointed all six of Maine's House members and two Senate members to serve as delegates to the Peace Conference. It appears unlikely that most found a way to juggle this added assignment to their already substantial duties. Only twice did anyone from Maine participate in Peace Conference discussions. L. E. Chittenden, *A Report of the Debates and Proceedings in the Secret Sessions of the Conference Convention for Proposing Amendments to the Constitution of the United States, Held at Washington, D. C., in February, A. D., 1861* (New York: D. Appleton, 1864; reprint ed., New York: Da Capo, 1971), 144–50, 409. Daniel Somes, the Maine representative introduced in the last chapter, continued to vote against the amendment. His speech marked him as having deeply held antislavery convictions.

19. George W. Palmer to Thurlow Weed, Nov. 19, 1860, Jan. 5, 29, 1861, Weed Papers.

20. Arthur Andrew Olson III, "Pioneer and Civil War Era Indiana Politics: The Political Career of David Kilgore" (self-published, 2012), 74, 79, 86–88, 93. I thank Gregory Peek for calling my attention to this carefully researched study.

21. *CG*, 36:2 (Feb. 28, 1861), 1285; Nichols, *Disruption*, 285; John F. Coleman, *The Disruption of the Pennsylvania Democracy, 1848-1860* (Harrisburg: Pennsylvania Historical and Museum Commission, 1975), 122–23; Erwin Stanley Bradley, *The Triumph of Militant Republicanism: A Study of Pennsylvania and Presidential Politics, 1860-1872* (Philadelphia: University of Pennsylvania Press, 1964), 57–58, 163, 258–59. Besides Millward, only one other Republican failed to vote either on the 27th or the 28th—he was Samuel R. Curtis of Iowa, the future Union general, who announced that he was paired with Thomas L. Anderson of Missouri, an Independent Democrat and former Whig and American who had been "called home by illness in his family." Officially Curtis would have voted against the amendment and Anderson would have favored it. *CG*, 36:2 (Feb. 27, 1861), 1264. But Curtis may have welcomed the chance to avoid casting a "no" vote. He had been a delegate to the Peace Conference and had indicated there that he was open to concessions other than a territorial compromise. He was willing to admit New Mexico as a state: "If this is acceptable to the South, I will go for it." He also indicated that he could accept restoration of the Missouri line, so that there would

be no restriction against slavery in territories south of 36° 30′. Chittenden, *Report of the Conference Convention*, 71–73, 298–99. Because both senators from Iowa voted for the amendment several days later, there is reason to surmise that Iowa Republicans may have coordinated their stance. As will be seen, Maine's Republicans certainly did so: five of Maine's eight representatives and senators—all of them Republicans—either voted for the amendment or did not vote.

22. New Jersey's William Pennington, Speaker of the House, was prevented by custom from voting, but he was known to share Corwin's and Sherman's proamendment position.

23. John and LaWanda Cox, *Politics, Principle, and Prejudice, 1865–1866: Dilemma of Reconstruction America* (New York: Free Press, 1963), 1–30. Three Northern Democrats who missed the vote on February 27 added their support on February 28. John T. Hubbell, "The Northern Democracy and the Crisis of Disunion, 1860–1861" (Ph.D. diss., University of Illinois, 1969), 123. So the effort to poll a full vote for the amendment on February 28 had a bipartisan dimension.

24. Bernard Weisberger, "Horace Greeley: Reformer as Republican," *Civil War History* 23 (1977): 5–25; Crofts, *Secession Crisis Enigma*, 83–85.

25. *NY Tribune*, Feb. 26, 28, Mar. 1, 1861.

26. Ibid., Mar. 4, 5, 1861.

27. Crofts, *Reluctant Confederates*, 292; Harold G. Villard and Oswald Garrison Villard, eds., *Lincoln on the Eve of '61: A Journalist's Story* (New York: Alfred A. Knopf, 1941).

28. *NY Herald*, Mar. 5, 1861; Philip S. Foner, *Business and Slavery: The New York Merchants and the Irrepressible Conflict* (Chapel Hill: University of North Carolina Press, 1941). Hardly any Republican, no matter how moderate or conservative, would touch the Crittenden Compromise, which demanded a constitutionally protected right to hold slaves in present and future territory south of the old Missouri Compromise line, 36° 30′. And William Lloyd Garrison would have been the first to dispute that he was a Republican.

29. *NY Herald*, Mar. 1, 2, 4, 1861.

30. Ibid., Mar. 1, 1861.

31. Ibid. The *Herald* account was picked up in the evening edition of *New York Tribune* that same day. Ibid.

32. Ibid.

33. Ibid.

34. *CG*, 36:2 (Mar. 1, 1861), 1327–31; Potter, *Lincoln and His Party*, 301–2; CF Adams Diary, Feb. 28, Mar. 1, 1861; *NY Tribune*, Mar. 2, 1861; *St. Louis Democrat* quoted in *Springfield Republican*, Feb. 28, 1861; Mark J. Stegmaier, "'An Imaginary Negro in an Impossible Place?' The Issue of New Mexico Statehood in the Secession Crisis, 1860–1861," *New Mexico Historical Review* 84 (2009): 263–90.

35. *CG*, 36:2 (Mar. 1, 1861), 1328–31; William H. Seward to Abraham Lincoln, Dec. 26, 1860, Seward Papers, with a copy in Frederick W. Seward, *Seward at Washington, as Senator and Secretary of State: A Memoir of His Life, with Selections from His Letters*, 2 vols. (New York: Derby and Miller, 1891), 2:484–85.

36. Crofts, *Reluctant Confederates*, 245–47.

37. The protracted Senate consideration of the amendment was all part of the "legislative day" of March 2: *CG*, 36:2 (Mar. 2, 3, 4, 1861), 1338–74, 1374–1402. So the official proceedings in the *Congressional Globe* all indicate the date of March 2. For the remainder of the chapter, I shall not include a date when citing the *Congressional Globe*.

38. "Two Nights in the Senate," *Harper's Weekly*, Mar. 16, 1861, 162.

39. *CG*, 36:2, 1366–67, 1384–86.

40. Ibid., 1384–85.

41. "Two Nights in the Senate," 162.

42. *CG*, 36:2, 1400–1402.

43. "Two Nights in the Senate," 162; *CG*, 36:2, 1403. Fessenden resumed voting after the amendment had passed. The *NY Herald*, Mar. 5, 1861, appears the best source for determining the time of the vote.

44. *CG*, 36:2, 1392–93. Morrill also played an active role at the Peace Conference, where he scathingly indicted Virginia for providing Deep South secessionists with "aid and comfort." Chittenden, *Report of the Conference Convention*, 146.

45. Robert J. Cook, *Civil War Senator: William Pitt Fessenden and the Fight to Save the American Republic* (Baton Rouge: Louisiana State University Press, 2011), 111, 115, 123, 128, quotation on 128. Cook repeatedly depicts the relationship between Fessenden and Morse as friendly. Cook, *Civil War Senator*, 66, 159, 211, 222, 224, 233–34, 241. The possibility of getting the Portland Custom House for Morse is addressed in William Fessenden to William Pitt Fessenden, Mar. 3, 1861, William Pitt Fessenden Papers, Bowdoin College.

Cook, author of the fine modern Fessenden biography, depicts his subject as having "refused to vote for a constitutional amendment to prohibit the federal government from interfering with slavery in the states." *Civil War Senator*, 128. Although technically correct, this statement is misleading: Fessenden could have defeated the amendment but chose not to. Fessenden's early biographer did not touch the subject: Francis Fessenden, *The Life and Public Services of William Pitt Fessenden*, 2 vols. (Boston: Houghton Mifflin, 1907), 1:125–26. So far as I have been able to learn, Fessenden's nonvote never attracted public attention. But one insightful veteran of Maine and national politics, James G. Blaine, did acknowledge it long after the fact, as noted in the Bibliographical Postscript. Blaine recognized that Fessenden and several of "the weightiest Republican leaders" had failed to vote and thereby had "consented to the passage of the amendment." James G. Blaine, *Twenty Years in Congress, From Lincoln to Garfield*, 2 vols. (Norwich, CT: Henry Bill, 1884), 1:265–66.

46. William Pitt Fessenden to William Fessenden, Feb. 17, 1861, Fessenden Papers; two memoranda dated Mar. 15, 1861, *CWAL*, 4:284; draft letter from Fessenden to Lincoln, Mar. 25, 1861, Fessenden Papers, Bowdoin. 47. Fessenden to Elizabeth (Lizzy) Warriner, Jan. 12, 1861, Fessenden to William Fessenden, Feb. 17, 1861, Fessenden Papers, Bowdoin.

48. McClintock, *Lincoln and the Decision for War*, 185; Crofts, *Reluctant Con-*

federates, 243–53, Virginia reaction on 251; Crofts, *Secession Crisis Enigma*, 109–11; Stahr, *Seward*, 244–45. Stahr alertly noticed that Seward cast a vote on March 3, soon after the evening session began. *CG*, 36:2, 1375.

49. McClintock, *Lincoln and the Decision for War*, 209–12; *CG*, 36:2, 1360.

50. *CG*, 36:2, 1395–96.

51. Dispatch from Springfield, IL, Dec. 19, 1860, in *NY Herald*, Dec. 24, 1860, in *Recollected Words of Abraham Lincoln*, ed. Don E. Fehrenbacher and Virginia Fehrenbacher (Stanford, CA: Stanford University Press, 1996), 456; Michael Burlingame, *Abraham Lincoln: A Life*, 2 vols. (Baltimore: Johns Hopkins University Press, 2008), 2:120. The source for the latter is an 1879 recollection by H. Chrisman, a resident of Galesburg, Illinois, who came from Virginia. Contemporary evidence from early 1861 shows that Chrisman visited Springfield, talked with Lincoln, and was attempting to reassure pro-Union Virginians regarding Lincoln's benign intentions. H. Chrisman to William C. Rives, Feb. 4, 7, 1861, William Cabell Rives Papers, LC.

52. As noted at the start of this chapter, Roy Franklin Nichols depicted the constitutional amendment as a tactical expedient by which Republicans deflected pressures to accept a more substantive territorial compromise. Nichols, *Disruption*, 475.

53. Charles S. Morehead to John J. Crittenden, Feb. 23, 1862, John J. Crittenden Papers, LC, in Mrs. Chapman Coleman, *The Life of John J. Crittenden*, 2 vols. (Philadelphia: J. B. Lippincott, 1871), 2:336–43; Charles S. Morehead, speech to the Southern Club at Liverpool, England, Oct. 9, 1862, in David Rankin Barbee and Milledge L. Bonham Jr., "Fort Sumter Again," *Mississippi Valley Historical Review* 28 (1941): 63–73. See McClintock, *Lincoln and the Decision for War*, 196–97, 319n19; and Crofts, *Reluctant Confederates*, 250. Lincoln's five visitors were Virginians George W. Summers and William Cabell Rives; James Guthrie and Charles Morehead from Kentucky; and Alexander W. Doniphan from Missouri. All but Guthrie were former Whigs. Summers was the leading Unionist at the Virginia Convention and a key behind-the-scenes link to Seward and the incoming Lincoln administration. Despite some confusion about the date of this meeting, it occurred on the evening of February 27. There is no reason to believe that any others were present besides these five and Lincoln.

54. *Philadelphia North American*, Mar. 4, 1861, "Independent" on Mar. 3, 1861; Henry Adams, "The Great Secession Winter," in *The Great Secession Winter of 1860–61 and Other Essays*, ed. George Hochfield (New York: Sagamore, 1958), 27. Adams's "Great Secession Winter" was composed before he left for England in May.

55. Charles Eugene Hamlin, *The Life and Times of Hannibal Hamlin* (Cambridge, MA: Riverside, 1899), 380.

56. Cook, *Civil War Senator*, 74–75, 84–85, 100, 116; Hamlin, *Life and Times of Hannibal Hamlin*, 69, 151, 358.

57. *NY Herald*, Mar. 1, 1861. An alternate scenario might be suggested—that Hamlin took a cue from Seward rather than Lincoln. But Hamlin was not regarded as someone who supported Seward's Union-saving schemes. He came from the Democratic wing of the Republican Party, which disliked any idea of concession

or compromise. Even though Hamlin was to play little role in Lincoln's administration, he would have been Lincoln's man during the tense week preceding the inauguration. See H. Draper Hunt, *Hannibal Hamlin of Maine: Lincoln's First Vice-President* (Syracuse, NY: Syracuse University Press, 1969).

Chapter 11

1. Nelson Lankford, *Richmond Burning: The Last Days of the Confederate Capital* (New York: Viking, 2002), 135–45, 157–67.

2. Duff Green, *Facts and Suggestions: Biographical, Historical, Financial and Political* (New York: Lippincott, 1866), 232–34. This source was called to my attention by David E. Woodard, "Abraham Lincoln, Duff Green, and the Mysterious Trumbull Letter," *Civil War History* 42 (1996): 218–19.

3. Michael Burlingame, *Abraham Lincoln: A Life*, 2 vols. (Baltimore: Johns Hopkins University Press, 2008), 1:259–60, 273, 299, 713; William J. Cooper, *We Have the War upon Us: The Onset of the Civil War, November 1860–April 1861* (New York: Alfred A. Knopf, 2012), 107–8; Kenneth J. Winkle, *Lincoln's Citadel: The Civil War in Washington* (New York: W. W. Norton, 2013), 5–8. Green's nephew, Ninian W. Edwards, was married to Mary Todd Lincoln's sister, Elizabeth (Green also was directly connected by marriage to Calhoun—Green's daughter Margaret married Calhoun's son, Andrew). See Cooper, *We Have the War upon Us*, 107–8; and James Hickey, ed., "A Family Divided," *Journal of the Illinois State Historical Society* (February 1977): 22–26. The modern biography, W. Stephen Belko, *The Invincible Duff Green: Whig of the West* (Columbia: University of Missouri Press, 2006), focuses on the Jacksonian era.

4. Green, *Facts and Suggestions*, 232; Woodard, "Abraham Lincoln, Duff Green, and the Mysterious Trumbull Letter," 219. Two other sources, both published decades later, purport to recount the interview between Lincoln and Green. One recalled that a hostile Green refused even to shake Lincoln's hand. See David Dixon Porter, *Incidents and Anecdotes of the Civil War* (New York: D. Appleton, 1885), 306–8; and William Henry Crook, *Through Five Administrations: Reminiscences of Colonel William H. Crook* (New York: Harper and Brothers, 1910), 56–57. But the most detailed modern account of Lincoln's visit to Richmond warns that Porter's work often was "sensationalized and amplified" and that "Crook's memoir reeks of embellishment and romanticism." Michael D. Gorman, "A Conqueror or a Peacemaker? Abraham Lincoln in Richmond," *Virginia Magazine of History and Biography* 123 (2015): 3–88, quotations on 77n19, 77n25. Gorman broadly accepts Crook's account of a frosty Lincoln-Green interview. But he does not use Green's own account, which was more contemporaneous and, to my way of thinking, more plausible. Ibid., 63–64, 87n174–76.

5. Green, *Facts and Suggestions*, 233–34.

6. Abraham Lincoln, First Inaugural Address, Mar. 4, 1861, *CWAL*, 4:270. For a precise and detailed account of the proceedings on March 4, see Harold Holzer, *Lincoln President-Elect: Abraham Lincoln and the Great Secession Winter, 1860–1861* (New York: Simon and Schuster, 2008), 446–58. Why did Lincoln use

the word "irrevocable"? He likely regarded any constitutional amendment as permanent. But his use of the word "irrevocable" obscured the distinction between the original version of the amendment and the revised version that Corwin and his allies had battled so hard to substitute for the original.

7. Nichols, *Disruption*, 486; *NY Times*, Mar. 5, 1861; *NY Herald*, Mar. 5, 1861. Did Douglas also hold Lincoln's hat during the inaugural address? Although the evidence is inconclusive, I am not alone in finding the story plausible. See my review of the evidence: Daniel W. Crofts, *A Secession Crisis Enigma: William Henry Hurlbert and "The Diary of a Public Man"* (Baton Rouge: Louisiana State University Press, 2010), 8, 18–19, 112–13, 254.

8. CF Adams Diary, Mar. 4, 1861. Newspaper accounts sometimes referred to the "Adams Amendment."

9. *CWAL*, 4:262–71, quotations on 264–66, 271; Burlingame, *Abraham Lincoln*, 2:67.

10. Abraham Lincoln, Second Inaugural Address, Mar. 4, 1865, *CWAL*, 8:332. Cameron soon was overwhelmed by wartime responsibilities and was replaced as secretary of war by Edwin Stanton in January 1862.

11. Frederick Douglass, "The Danger of the Republican Movement," *Radical Abolitionist*, July 1856; "The Inaugural Address," *Douglass' Monthly*, April 1861, in Philip S. Foner, ed., *The Life and Writings of Frederick Douglass*, 5 vols. (New York: International Publishers, 1952), 3:73–74, 5:385–90; David W. Blight, *Frederick Douglass' Civil War: Keeping Faith in Jubilee* (Baton Rouge: Louisiana State University Press, 1989), 68, 71, 73, 78; David W. Blight, "Lincoln, Douglass and the 'Double-Tongued Document,'" *NY Times*, Disunion (blog), May 6, 2011, http://opinionator.blogs.nytimes.com/2011/05/06/lincoln-douglass-and-the-double-tongued-document/. See also John Stauffer, *Giants: The Parallel Lives of Frederick Douglass and Abraham Lincoln* (New York: Twelve, 2009), 213–19.

12. David W. Blight, *Race and Reunion: The Civil War in American Memory* (Cambridge, MA: Harvard University Press, 2001), 1–5. See also David W. Blight, *American Oracle: The Civil War in the Civil Rights Era* (Cambridge, MA: Harvard University Press, 2011).

13. *CG*, 37:4, Special Senate Session (Mar. 6, 1861), 1436–37; Robert W. Johannsen, *Stephen A. Douglas* (New York: Oxford University Press, 1973), 845–48; T. A. R. Nelson to William G. Brownlow, Mar. 13, 1861, in *Brownlow's Knoxville Whig* (weekly edition), Mar. 23, 1861, and *National Intelligencer*, Mar. 25, 1861; *Richmond Whig*, Mar. 9, 1861; *Lynchburg Virginian*, Mar. 11, 1861; *Raleigh Semi-Weekly Register*, Mar. 16, 1861; Crofts, *Reluctant Confederates*, 261–62.

14. *Springfield Republican*, Mar. 5, 1861; *CG*, 37:4, Special Senate Session (Mar. 6, 7, 1861), 1438–39, 1442–43, 1445–46.

15. *CG*, 37:4, Special Senate Session (Mar. 7, 1861), 1443–46; Nelson to Brownlow, Mar. 13, 1861, in *Brownlow's Knoxville Whig* (weekly edition), Mar. 23, 1861, and *National Intelligencer*, Mar. 25, 1861; *Baltimore American*, Mar. 6, 1861; John A. Gilmer to Stephen A. Douglas, Mar. 8, 1861, Stephen A. Douglas Papers, University of Chicago; Crofts, *Reluctant Confederates*, 255–56.

16. *CWAL*, 4:266; Crofts, *Reluctant Confederates*, 273–74.

17. *CG*, 37:4, Special Senate Session (Mar. 6, 7, 1861), 1437, 1443–46; Mc-Clintock, *Lincoln and the Decision for War*, 200–212, esp. 212; Nichols, *Disruption of American Democracy*, 486–87.

18. Gilmer to Seward, Mar. 7, 8, 12, 1861, Seward Papers, excerpted in Bancroft, *Seward*, 2:545–48; Gilmer to Seward, Mar. 9, 1861, Lincoln Papers; Crofts, *Reluctant Confederates*, 257–59. See also Gilmer to Douglas, Mar. 8, 10, 1861, Douglas Papers.

19. These matters are covered in close detail in McClintock, *Lincoln and the Decision for War*, 215–19; Crofts, *Reluctant Confederates*, 273–76; and Crofts, *Secession Crisis Enigma*, 90–93, 214–15, 270. For overviews aimed at a wider audience, see Lawrence M. Denton, *William Henry Seward and the Secession Crisis: The Effort to Prevent Civil War* (Jefferson, NC: McFarland, 2009); and Lawrence M. Denton, *Unionists in Virginia: Politics, Secession and Their Plan to Prevent Civil War* (Charleston, SC: History Press, 2014). The personal impact of the political crisis leaps from the pages of Brent Tarter, *Daydreams and Nightmares: A Virginia Family Faces Secession and War* (Charlottesville: University of Virginia Press, 2015).

20. McClintock, *Lincoln and the Decision for War*, 226–34, quotation on 226; Crofts, *Reluctant Confederates*, 283–90, 355–59.

21. This paragraph and the one that precedes it barely scratch the surface of a complex topic that lies beyond the scope of this study. The most reliable guide is McClintock, *Lincoln and the Decision for War*, 226–80.

Chapter 12

1. John Hay to William Leete Stone, Mar. 15, 1861, in *At Lincoln's Side: John Hay's Civil War Correspondence and Selected Writings*, ed. Michael Burlingame (Carbondale: Southern Illinois University Press, 2000), 5.

2. Richard Albert, "The Ghost Amendment That Haunts Lincoln's Legacy," Cognoscenti (blog), Feb. 18, 2013, http://cognoscenti.wbur.org/2013/02/18/the-other-13th-richard-albert; John A. Lupton, "Abraham Lincoln and the Corwin Amendment," *Illinois Periodicals Online (IPO)*, 2006, http://www.lib.niu.edu/2006/ih060934.html; Brooks D. Simpson, "Lincoln and the Corwin Amendment," Crossroads (blog), Jan. 24, 2011, http://cwcrossroads.wordpress.com/2011/01/24/lincoln-and-the-corwin-amendment/; Daniel Patrick Sheehan, "An 'amazing find' in Allentown," *Morning Call* (Allentown, PA), July 19, 2006 (I thank Steven Thompson of The College of New Jersey for this reference); Phillip W. Magness, "Abraham Lincoln and the Corwin Amendment," article reposted from Kosmosonline.org, http://philmagness.com/?page_id=398. Particular thanks to Phillip Magness, who has generously shared with me his research on the subject.

3. Theodore C. Pease and James G. Randall, eds., *The Diary of Orville Hickman Browning*, 2 vols. (Springfield: Illinois State Historical Library, 1925, 1933), 1:475–76; Michael Burlingame, ed., *With Lincoln in the White House: Letters, Memoranda, and Other Writings of John G. Nicolay, 1860–1865* (Carbondale: Southern

Illinois University Press, 2000), 46; Daniel W. Crofts, *A Secession Crisis Enigma: William Henry Hurlbert and "The Diary of a Public Man"* (Baton Rouge: Louisiana State University Press, 2010), 136.

4. *Raleigh Register,* Mar. 13, 1861; *Brownlow's Knoxville Whig* (weekly edition), Mar. 9, 1861; *Louisville Journal,* Mar. 6, 1861 (L. A. W. from Washington, Mar. 1, 1861), Mar. 9, 16, 1861; T. A. R. Nelson to William G. Brownlow, Mar. 13, 1861, in *Brownlow's Knoxville Whig* (weekly edition), Mar. 23, 1861, and *National Intelligencer,* Mar. 25, 1861.

5. *Portland Eastern Argus,* Mar. 8, 1861.

6. *Journal of the Called Session of the Senate of the Commonwealth of Kentucky* (Frankfort: Kentucky Yeoman Office, 1861), 253.

7. *Louisville Journal,* Apr. 2, 1861 (letter from Frankfort, Apr. 1, 1861), Apr. 3, 5, 10, 1861.

8. Ibid., Apr. 1, 1861 (letter from Frankfort, Mar. 30, 1861).

9. *Journal of the Called Session,* 407; *Louisville Journal,* Apr. 6, 1861 (letter from Frankfort, Apr. 4, 1861).

10. *The Journal of the Senate of the State of Ohio for the Second Session of the Fifty-Fourth General Assembly . . . ,* vol. 57 (Columbus, OH: Richard Nevins, State Printer, 1861), 198 (shows party breakdowns when Sherman was elevated to the U.S. Senate), 286, 289 (vote tally), 389, 391. *Daily Ohio Statesman* (Columbus), Apr. 17, 1861; *Daily Ohio State Journal* (Columbus), Apr. 17, 18, 1861. I thank Steven Thompson of The College of New Jersey for assistance in tabulating the Senate vote.

11. Jerome Mushkat, *A Citizen-Soldier's Civil War: The Letters of Brevet Major General Alvin C. Voris* (De Kalb: Northern Illinois University Press, 2002).

12. *Daily Ohio Statesman* (Columbus), May 14, 15, 1861, available online in the NEH's Chronicling America series. This is a Democratic newspaper, prowar and antiabolition. It gives a breakdown of the house vote in the issue of May 14; *Daily Ohio State Journal* (Columbus), May 15, 1861; *Acts of . . . the Fifty-Fourth General Assembly of the State of Ohio* (Columbus, OH: Richard Nevins, State Printer, 1861), 190; for a roster of senate and house members and their districts, see pp. 354ff.

13. David E. Kyvig, "Ohio and the Shaping of the U.S. Constitution," in *The History of Ohio Law,* ed. Michael Les Benedict and John F. Winkler (Athens: Ohio University Press, 2004), 345–46; Benjamin W. Arnett, ed., *Duplicate Copy of the Souvenir from the Afro-American League of Tennessee to Hon. James M. Ashley of Ohio* (Philadelphia: A. M. E. Church, 1894), 699.

14. *NY Times,* "Rhode Island Politics," Mar. 29, 1861 ("From Our Special Correspondent," "Howard," Providence, Mar. 27, 1861).

15. *Rhode Island Senate Journal, May Session, a.d. 1861* (handwritten), May 31, 1861; *Rhode Island House Journal, May Session, a.d. 1861* (handwritten), May 31, 1861, 236, 239–41; Kenneth Carlson to Phillip W. Magness, e-mail, Aug. 23, 2012; *Providence Evening Press,* June 17, 1861. Both Providence newspapers were under the misimpression that Congress had approved the version of the amendment originally proposed by Charles Francis Adams, rather than the Seward version substituted for the original by Thomas Corwin in late February.

16. *CG*, 38:1 (Feb. 8, 1864), 522–23.

17. *The Brevier Legislative Reports*, vol. 5 (Apr. 30, 1861, May 27, 30, 1861), 34–36, 184, 224–27.

18. Abraham Lincoln, "Drafts of a Bill for Compensated Emancipation in Delaware," Nov. 26, 1861(?), *CWAL*, 5:29–31; James Oakes, *Freedom National: The Destruction of Slavery in the United States, 1861–1865* (New York: W. W. Norton, 2013), 283–85; Patience Essah, *A House Divided: Slavery and Emancipation in Delaware, 1638–1865* (Charlottesville: University Press of Virginia, 1996), 162–71.

19. *Baltimore American*, Jan. 10, Feb. 19, 1862; Oakes, *Freedom National*, 269–77.

20. *Journal of the Proceedings of the House of Delegates of the State of Maryland, January Session, Eighteen Hundred and Sixty-Two, in Extra Session* (Annapolis, MD: Thomas J. Wilson, 1862), 173; *Journal of the Proceedings of the Senate of Maryland of the State of Maryland, January Session, Eighteen Hundred and Sixty-Two* (Annapolis, MD: Schley and Cole, 1862), 97; *Baltimore American*, Jan. 11, 15, 25, Feb. 7, 1862 (Annapolis Letter, Feb. 6, 1862), Feb. 17, 1862. For a brief sketch of emancipation's complex origins in Maryland, see Daniel W. Crofts, "Holding the Line in Maryland," *NY Times*, Disunion (blog), Oct. 22, 2013, http://opinionator.blogs.nytimes.com/2013/10/22/holding-the-line-in-maryland/.

21. *Baltimore American*, Feb. 15, 17, 1862.

22. *Acts of the [Virginia] General Assembly Passed at the Regular Session, Held December 2, 1861, at the City of Wheeling, Joint Resolutions 1861-2* (Wheeling, VA, 1862), 65; *Wheeling Intelligencer*, Jan. 6, 25, Feb. 14, 1862. Snider and Porter both played visible roles in the movement that ultimately led to creating the state of West Virginia. Porter had been a delegate to the Virginia Convention in Richmond in early 1861, both were delegates to the First and Second Wheeling Conventions in May and June 1861, and both are listed on the roster of the latter as members of the House of Delegates of the reorganized state government. See http://www.wvculture.org/history/statehood/delegateswc2.html. A Douglas Democrat in 1860, Snider became a Republican and an officer in the Union army. He spoke out against slavery as a legislator. George Wesley Atkinson and Alvaro Frankin Gibbens, *Prominent Men of West Virginia* (Wheeling, WV: W. L. Callin, 1890), 473; and see http://www.wvculture.org/history/snider/sniderbi.html. Porter died of tuberculosis in 1864 at the age of twenty-nine after having fought the disease for most of his brief adult life. Stanton C. Crawford and Nancy C. Hodges, "George McCandless Porter," *Western Pennsylvania Historical Magazine* 43 (1963): 259–83.

23. *Wheeling Intelligencer*, Feb. 8, 13–15, 21, 25, 1862; "A Virginian," Feb. 14, 1862, "M," Feb. 8, 1862, both in ibid., Feb. 15, 1862.

24. Ibid., Feb. 21, 1862; Oakes, *Freedom National*, 294–300.

25. Oliver Morton Dickerson, *The Illinois Constitutional Convention of 1862* (Urbana: University Press, 1905), 4–8, 13–14, 22–26, 36–37, 54–55; Philip E. Martin, "Illinois' Ratification of the Corwin Amendment," *Journal of Public Law* 15 (1966): 18–91; Drew E. VandeCreek, "The State Constitutional Convention of 1862," Illinois during the Civil War, http://dig.lib.niu.edu/civilwar/narrative3.html; *Chicago Tribune*, Nov. 13, 1861, Feb. 17, June 21, 23, 25, 27, 1862.

26. Michael Vorenberg, *Final Freedom: The Civil War, the Abolition of Slavery, and the Thirteenth Amendment* (Cambridge: Cambridge University Press, 2001), 211–33. New Jersey dragged its feet but did ratify one year later in 1866. Ibid., 232n61.

27. David E. Kyvig, *Explicit and Authentic Acts: Amending the U.S. Constitution, 1776–1995* (Lawrence: University Press of Kansas, 1996), 151, 469, 480; Albert, "Ghost Amendment."

Epilogue One

1. Robert F. Horowitz, *The Great Impeacher: A Political Biography of James M. Ashley* (New York: Brooklyn College Press, 1979), 80–83; *Fremont Journal*, Oct. 17, 24, 1862; *Toledo Commercial* in *Fremont Journal*, Oct. 17, 1862.

2. "Annual Message to Congress," Dec. 6, 1864, *CWAL*, 8:149. The failed House vote is at *CG*, 38:1 (June 15, 1864), 2995.

3. Doris Kearns Goodwin, *Team of Rivals: The Political Genius of Abraham Lincoln* (New York: Simon and Schuster, 2005), 686–90. The House vote is at *CG*, 38:2 (Jan. 31, 1865), 531.

4. Michael Burlingame, *Abraham Lincoln: A Life*, 2 vols. (Baltimore: Johns Hopkins University Press, 2008), 2:745–51; Walter Stahr, *Seward: Lincoln's Indispensable Man* (New York: Simon and Schuster, 2012), 417–21; James M. McPherson, *Battle Cry of Freedom: The Civil War Era* (New York: Oxford University Press, 1988), 838–40. The interested reader should consult Burlingame's full manuscript: http://www.knox.edu/about-knox/lincoln-studies-center/burlingame-abraham-lincoln-a-life, which contains annotation omitted from the published version.

5. J. G. Randall and Richard N. Current, *Lincoln the President: Last Full Measure*, vol. 4 of *Lincoln the President* (New York: Dodd, Mead, 1955), 298–321, quotation on 301.

6. LaWanda Cox and John H. Cox, *Politics, Principle, and Prejudice, 1865–1866: Dilemma of Reconstruction America* (New York: Free Press, 1963), 1–30, quotations on 6, 25.

7. Michael Vorenberg, *Final Freedom: The Civil War, the Abolition of Slavery, and the Thirteenth Amendment* (Cambridge: Cambridge University Press, 2001), 143–46, 150–51, 176–210, quotations on 177–78.

8. Ibid., 183–85. The ambition of the Blairs to organize a new Conservative Party also is a central idea in Cox and Cox, *Politics, Principle, and Prejudice*.

9. Vorenberg, *Final Freedom*, 185–97, quotations on 191–92, 194, 197; E. L. Godkin, "The Constitution and Its Defects," *North American Review* 99 (1864): 117–45, quotations on 120, 123.

10. Vorenberg, *Final Freedom*, 197–210, 242–44, quotations on 198, 208, 243.

11. Leonard L. Richards, *Who Freed the Slaves? The Fight over the Thirteenth Amendment* (Chicago: University of Chicago Press, 2015), 5–6, 56–57; Vorenberg, *Final Freedom*, 49–51; Herman Belz, *Reconstructing the Union: Theory and Policy during the Civil War* (Ithaca, NY: Cornell University Press for the American Historical Association, 1969), 66–82; Horowitz, *Great Impeacher*, 71–73; Benjamin W.

Arnett, ed., *Duplicate Copy of the Souvenir from the Afro-American League of Tennessee to Hon. James M. Ashley of Ohio* (Philadelphia: A. M. E. Church, 1894), 360–69.

12. Richards, *Who Freed the Slaves?*, 7; Horowitz, *Great Impeacher*, 91–94; Belz, *Reconstructing the Union*, 176–87.

13. Vorenberg, *Final Freedom*, 178–79; James Oakes, *Freedom National: The Destruction of Slavery in the United States, 1861-1865* (New York: W. W. Norton, 2013), 476–80.

14. *CG*, 38:2 (Jan. 6, 1865), 138–39.

15. *CG*, 38:2 (Jan. 6, 1865), 141; Arnett, *Ashley*, 257–59.

16. Richards, *Who Freed the Slaves?*, 186–217; Horowitz, *Great Impeacher*, 169. Ashley's own recollections of the great moment are full of human interest: Arnett, *Ashley*, 693–713. He gave special praise to the twenty-four "unselfish and patriotic" Democrats and border state Unionists who voted differently in January than the previous June. Many of them, he noted, "marched to their political death." Ibid., 713.

17. Horowitz, *Great Impeacher*, 149–50, 155–57; Arnett, *Ashley*, 5–6; Richards, *Who Freed the Slaves?*, 4–5.

18. Arnett, *Ashley*, 257; Richards, *Who Freed the Slaves?*, 253–61.

19. Henry Wilson, *History of the Rise and Fall of the Slave Power in America*, 3 vols. (Boston: J. R. Osgood, 1872–77), 3:96–100; Richard H. Abbott, *Cobbler in Congress: The Life of Henry Wilson, 1812-1875* (Lexington: University Press of Kentucky, 1972), 233–38, 258–59.

20. Abbott, *Cobbler in Congress*, 1–63.

21. *CG*, 33:2 (Feb. 23, 1855), A238.

22. *CG*, 34:3 (Dec. 2, 4, 19, 1856), 13–14, 28–29, A64–66; 36:2 (Feb. 21, 1861), 1088–94; Henry Wilson, *Letter of Senator Wilson to Honorable Caleb Cushing* (Washington, DC: National Republican Office, pamphlet dated Dec. 15, 1860); Abbott, *Cobbler in Congress*, 64–90, 100–101, 111–13.

23. Lydia Maria Child to William Lloyd Garrison, *Liberator*, Feb. 19, 1864, quoted in Benjamin Quarles, *The Negro in the Civil War* (Boston: Little, Brown, 1953), 260, and in Larry Gara, *The Liberty Line: The Legend of the Underground Railroad* (Lexington: University of Kentucky Press, 1861), 166.

24. *CWAL*, 3:16, 181, 277, 311, 4:263. The view that emancipation would take place only in the distant future was widely shared among Republicans before the war. Note in the Bibliographical Postscript my critique of Oakes, *Freedom National*, which contends that Republicans were eager to fight a war to end slavery.

25. Don E. Fehrenbacher and Virginia Fehrenbacher, eds., *Recollected Words of Abraham Lincoln* (Stanford, CA: Stanford University Press, 1996), 116, 448–49. The Fehrenbachers give the Truth recollection their highest rating—it captured "direct discourse" and was written down "within a few days after the words were spoken." Ibid., lii.

Epilogue Two

1. Gerard N. Magliocca, *American Founding Son: John Bingham and the Invention of the Fourteenth Amendment* (New York: NYU Press, 2013), 108–27, 187.

2. Jacobus tenBroek, *Equal under Law* (New York: Collier Books, 1965), originally published as *The Antislavery Origins of the Fourteenth Amendment* (Berkeley: University of California Press, 1951), 145–48.

3. Magliocca, *American Founding Son*, 114–15, 186; see also Magliocca, "The Father of the 14th Amendment," *NY Times*, Disunion (blog), Sept. 17, 2013, http://opinionator.blogs.nytimes.com/2013/09/17/the-father-of-the-14th-amendment/.

4. Magliocca, *American Founding Son*, 8–9, 16.

5. Ibid., 56, 64, 125–26.

6. Garrett Epps, *Democracy Reborn: The Fourteenth Amendment and the Fight for Equal Rights in Post–Civil War America* (New York: Henry Holt, 2006), 11, 165, 227, 268–70.

7. Ibid., 164–83, 222–29; Magliocca, *American Founding Son*, 108–27; cf. Eric McKitrick, *Andrew Johnson and Reconstruction* (Chicago: University of Chicago Press, 1960), 76–77, 257, 340, 453–54, 477–80; Michael Les Benedict, *A Compromise of Principle: Congressional Republicans and Reconstruction, 1863–1869* (New York: W. W. Norton, 1974), 189–91, 211, 218, 225.

8. Magliocca, *American Founding Son*, 1.

9. Juan Williams, *Thurgood Marshall: American Revolutionary* (New York: Times Books, 1998), 219–22.

10. Taylor Branch, *Parting the Waters: America in the King Years, 1954–63* (New York: Simon and Schuster, 1988), 823–24, 881–82, 887.

11. Ira Berlin et al., eds., *Freedom: A Documentary History of Emancipation, 1861–1867*, series 1, volume 1, *The Destruction of Slavery* (Cambridge: Cambridge University Press, 1985), 1–56.

12. Abraham Lincoln to James C. Conkling, Aug. 26, 1863, *CWAL*, 6:406–10.

13. Branch, *Parting the Waters*, 272–632.

14. Taylor Branch and Haley Sweetland Edwards, "A Second Emancipation," *Washington Monthly*, January–February 2013; Branch, *Parting the Waters*, 673–845, quotation on 777, "Letter from Birmingham Jail" on 737–45, 804.

Bibliographic Postscript

1. James G. Blaine, *Twenty Years of Congress, from Lincoln to Garfield*, 2 vols. (Norwich, CT: Henry Bill, 1884–86), 1:258–59.

2. Ibid., 269–72.

3. Ibid., 259–61.

4. Ibid., 261–65.

5. Ibid., 265–66.

6. Ibid., 282, 287, 290.

7. Ibid., 267.

8. Jonathan Zeitz, *Lincoln's Boys: John Hay, John Nicolay, and the War for Lincoln's Image* (New York: Viking, 2013), 253–57.

9. John G. Nicolay and John Hay, *Abraham Lincoln: A History*, 10 vols. (New York: Century, 1890), 3:234–36.

10. James Ford Rhodes, *History of the United States from the Compromise of 1850 to the Final Restoration of Home Rule at the South in 1877*, 7 vols. (New York: Macmillan, 1892–1906), 3:313–15.

11. Potter, *Lincoln and His Party*, 173, 292–93, 301–3, 313–14; Henry Adams, "The Great Secession Winter of 1860–61," *Proceedings of the Massachusetts Historical Society* 43 (1910): 679.

12. Kenneth M. Stampp, *And the War Came: The North and the Secession Crisis, 1860–61* (Baton Rouge: Louisiana State University Press, 1950), 131, 139, 166, 172, 175–76.

13. Allan Nevins, *The Emergence of Lincoln: Prologue to Civil War, 1859–1861*, vol. 4, *Ordeal of the Union* (New York: Charles Scribner's Sons, 1950), 390–410, quotations on 408–10.

14. Roy Franklin Nichols, *The Disruption of American Democracy* (New York: Macmillan, 1948), 445–46, 475–82. Chapter 25, "A Stalemate in Washington," 466–82, has no endnotes starting on page 475, just where he began an eight-page segment on the constitutional amendment that ran for the rest of the chapter. The book's handwritten and typed drafts, held in the Roy Franklin Nichols Papers, Rare Book and Manuscript Library, University of Pennsylvania, include multiple references to the *Congressional Globe* for the concluding part of chapter 25. But the Macmillan Company apparently decided to streamline the published version by deleting annotation to such an obvious source. The entire chapter is carefully researched just like the rest of the book. Nichols had an exceptional command of published and unpublished sources.

15. Patrick M. Sowle, "The Conciliatory Republicans during the Winter of Secession" (Ph.D. diss., Duke University, 1963), 185–86, 202, 432–47, 511–15.

16. R. Alton Lee, "The Corwin Amendment in the Secession Crisis," *Ohio Historical Quarterly* 70 (1961): 1–26, quotation on 3–4. Lee's idea that the amendment originated with Lincoln corroborated a "supposition" first sketched by George Fort Milton, *The Eve of Conflict: Stephen A. Douglas and the Needless War* (Boston: Houghton Mifflin, 1934), 527. As noted in chapter 5, Lee anticipated a view more recently advanced by William J. Cooper, Michael F. Holt, and Phillip Magness. See William J. Cooper, *We Have the War upon Us: The Onset of the Civil War, November 1860–April 1861* (New York: Alfred A. Knopf, 2012), 68, 107–8, 285n74, 291n55; Phillip Magness, "Abraham Lincoln and the Corwin Amendment," *History News Network*, June 20, 2014. Lee correctly noted that the final version of the amendment was identical to the one first proposed by Seward in December. Lee erred, however, in writing that the final version contained the word "ever"—"No amendment shall ever be made to the Constitution which will authorize or give to Congress the power to abolish or interfere, within any State, with the domestic institutions thereof, including that of persons held to labor or service by the laws

of said State." The word "ever" was imagined by Lee and not part of Corwin's or Seward's language. *CG*, 36th Cong., 2d Sess. (Feb. 26, 27, 1861), 1236, 1263. Lee's bit of imagination persists in Leonard L. Richards, *Who Freed the Slaves? The Fight over the Thirteenth Amendment* (Chicago: University of Chicago Press, 2015), 22.

17. Norman A. Graebner, "Thomas Corwin and the Sectional Crisis," *Ohio History* 86 (1977): 229–47, quotations on 247. See also Daryl Pendergraft, "Thomas Corwin and the Conservative Republican Reaction, 1858–1861," *Ohio State Archaeological and Historical Quarterly* 57 (1948): 1–23, which focused principally on the election of 1858 and debates in Congress in 1859–60.

18. David M. Potter, *The Impending Crisis, 1846–1861*, ed. Don E. Fehrenbacher (New York: Harper and Row, 1976), 552–53.

19. Ibid., viii, 552–53, 582; Don E. Fehrenbacher, *The Slaveholding Republic: An Account of the United States Government's Relations to Slavery*, ed. Ward M. McAfee (New York: Oxford University Press, 2001).

20. Maury Klein, *Days of Defiance: Sumter, Secession, and the Coming of the Civil War* (New York: Random House, 1997), 287–88, 305–9, quotations on 287, 308.

21. Harold Holzer, *Lincoln President-Elect: Abraham Lincoln and the Great Secession Winter, 1860–1861* (New York: Simon and Schuster, 2008), 428–29. Holzer's book includes an annotated copy of Lincoln's inaugural address, which perforce includes his stated readiness to accept the constitutional amendment, but Holzer does not attempt to grasp the troublesome nettle in the text of his chapter on the inaugural. Ibid., 437–58, 473.

22. Brian Dirck, *Lincoln and the Constitution* (Carbondale: Southern Illinois University Press, 2012).

23. Doris Kearns Goodwin, *Team of Rivals: The Political Genius of Abraham Lincoln* (New York: Simon and Schuster, 2005), 325–26. Goodwin's account is blurred. She thinks Lincoln enlisted Seward in December to support the amendment, which is plausible even if unprovable. See my chapter 5. But she is not aware that both Lincoln and Seward worked to get the measure approved by Congress in late February and early March.

24. Adam Goodheart, *1861: The Civil War Awakening* (New York: Alfred A. Knopf, 2011), 19, 128–31. The first inaugural's peroration—the appeal to "the better angels of our nature" that Lincoln rewrote from Seward's original draft—is in fact widely quoted today.

25. James Oakes, *Freedom National: The Destruction of Slavery in the United States, 1861–1865* (New York: W. W. Norton, 2013), 49–54. See also James Oakes, *The Scorpion's Sting: Antislavery and the Coming of the Civil War* (New York: W. W. Norton, 2014), 22–50.

26. Second Debate with Stephen A. Douglas at Freeport, IL, Aug. 27, 1858, Third Debate with Stephen A. Douglas at Jonesboro, IL, Sept. 15, 1858, Lincoln to Elihu Washburne, Sept. 16, 1858, *CWAL*, 3:40, 58–61, 104–5, 116–17, 138–41, 144–45.

27. Abraham Lincoln to Salmon P. Chase, June 9, 20, 1859, Lincoln to Schuyler

Colfax, July 6, 1859, Lincoln to John Hill, September 1860, *CWAL*, 3:384, 386, 391, 4:104–8.

28. Oakes, *Freedom National*, 52–54; *Chicago Daily Democrat*, Oct. 31, Nov. 8, 1860; *Louisville Courier*, Nov. 12, 1860; *Richmond Enquirer*, Nov. 16m 1860; *Illinois State Journal* (Springfield), Dec. 13, 1860; William Kaufmann Scarborough, ed., *The Diary of Edmund Ruffin*, 3 vols. (Baton Rouge: Louisiana State University Press, 1972–89), 1:498 (Nov. 17, 1860); Michael Burlingame, *Abraham Lincoln: A Life*, 2 vols. (Baltimore: Johns Hopkins University Press, 2008), 1:673. Burlingame sees Wentworth as "a spiteful marplot." Ibid., 1:578. The *Chicago Daily Democrat*, Oct. 31, 1860, may be found in Howard Cecil Perkins, ed., *Northern Editorials on Secession*, 2 vols. (New York: D. Appleton-Century for the American Historical Association, 1942), 1:508–9.

29. Oakes, *Freedom National*, 52–54; *Chicago Daily Democrat*, Oct. 31, 1860; "Fourth Debate with Stephen A. Douglas at Charleston, Illinois," Sept. 18, 1858, *CWAL*, 3:181.

30. Oakes, *Freedom National*, 5, 74.

31. For example, David Brion Davis, "How They Stopped Slavery: A New Perspective," *New York Review of Books*, June 6, 2013, 59–61; Howell Raines, review in *Washington Post*, Jan. 18, 2013. Davis is an eminent authority on slavery and antislavery but not on late antebellum politics; Raines is an award-winning journalist who is working on a Civil War–era novel. Some professional specialists on the Civil War era have also commended the book—e.g., Steven E. Woodworth, *American Historical Review* 119 (2014): 464–66. To the best of my knowledge, Glenn David Brasher, *The Civil War Monitor*, May 1, 2013, and George C. Rable, *Journal of the Abraham Lincoln Association* 35 (Summer 2014): 80–84, are the only reviewers who directly address the shortcomings in *Freedom National*.

32. Robert J. Cook, *Civil War Senator: William Pitt Fessenden and the Fight to Save the American Republic* (Baton Rouge: Louisiana State University Press, 2011), esp. 244–49; William P. Fessenden to Hamilton Fish, Dec. 15, 1860, container 47, Hamilton Fish Papers, LC.

33. Russell McClintock, *Lincoln and the Decision for War*, 94–95, 99–104, 117–19, 145–47, 158–63, 171–75, 185, 199, quotations on 94, 103, 185.

34. Burlingame, *Abraham Lincoln*, 2:47–48, 67.

35. Eric Foner, interview with National Public Radio's Terry Gross, *Fresh Air*, Oct. 11, 2010.

36. Eric Foner, *The Fiery Trial: Abraham Lincoln and American Slavery* (New York: W. W. Norton, 2011), 157–61, quotations on 157–58.

37. Lincoln "expected the Union to be saved, and he expected it to be saved without war." Potter, *Lincoln and His Party*, 318. Immediately after the inauguration, Lincoln "could breathe a sigh of relief and look forward to a peaceable solution to the secession crisis." Burlingame, *Abraham Lincoln*, 2:67.

38. Michael Dobbs, *One Minute to Midnight: Kennedy, Khrushchev, and Castro on the Brink of Nuclear War* (New York: Random House, 2008), xv.

39. Mark J. Stegmaier, *Henry Adams in the Secession Crisis: Dispatches to the*

Boston Daily Advertiser, *December 1860–March 1861* (Baton Rouge: Louisiana State University Press, 2012), 198; "The Great Secession Winter, 1860–1861," in *The Letters of Henry Adams*, ed. J. C. Levenson et al., 6 vols. (Cambridge, MA: Belknap Press of Harvard University Press, 1982–88), 1:203–34.

40. Don H. Doyle, *The Cause of All Nations: An International History of the American Civil War* (New York: Basic Books, 2014), 55; Potter, *Impending Crisis*, 14–16.

41. William J. Cooper. *We Have the War upon Us: The Onset of the Civil War, November 1860–April 1861* (New York: Alfred A. Knopf, 2012), 68, 98, 101–12, 158–60, 206–7, quotation on 79.

42. Thomas J. DiLorenzo, *Lincoln Unmasked: What You're Not Supposed to Know about Dishonest Abe* (New York: Crown Forum, 2006), 12, 24–25, 54, 100, 126, 175–76.

43. Michael Vorenberg, *Final Freedom: The Civil War, the Abolition of Slavery, and the Thirteenth Amendment* (Cambridge: Cambridge University Press, 2001), 9, 20–22. Vorenberg is aware that only a few radicals embraced the idea of an anti-slavery Constitution, and so said that Congress could abolish slavery by statute. Ibid., 12–13, 110, 159, 192–93. Vorenberg misses Corwin's last-minute decision to drop the version of the amendment that he and Adams concocted—which specified that it could not be changed except with support from all the states—and instead to return to the version Seward first proposed in December. So Vorenberg, along with many other historians, depicts the amendment as "unamendable." Kenneth Stampp likewise wrote that the amendment was to be "binding for all time." Stampp, *And the War Came*, 131.

44. Richards, *Who Freed the Slaves?*, 20–23; Benjamin W. Arnett, ed., *Duplicate Copy of the Souvenir from the Afro-American League of Tennessee to Hon. James M. Ashley of Ohio* (Philadelphia: A. M. E. Church, 1894), 699–700. Richards follows R. Alton Lee in adding an additional word to Seward's amendment; see note 16 above. Richards also places Senate ratification on March 2, 1861, as indicated in the *Congressional Globe*. But the "legislative day" of March 2 stretched over three different dates—see prologue, note 1, and chapter 10, note 37.

Index

David M. Potter as an "appallingly greater concession to the South" than a territorial compromise, 10, 275–76; drafted by William H. Seward for Committee of Thirteen, 14, 117–20; alternate version developed in Thomas Corwin's Committee of Thirty Three, 14, 125–41; favored by conciliatory Republicans and Southern Opposition, 14, 145–63; opposed by hard-line Republicans, 14, 165, 208; ratified by six states, 15, 243–54; Lincoln's probable collaboration with Seward, 117–18, 212; irrevocability, 134–35, 235–36, 289n15, 327–28n6, 338n43; hard-line Republicans charged that it might tie the hands of future generations, 139, 178, 201–2, 207, 252; passed by House (Feb. 28, 1861), 213–15; House Republican votes for and against, 217; support from Lincoln, 231–33; never became part of Constitution, 242, 254; bibliographical context, 271–82. *See also* Prospective thirteenth amendment; Would-be thirteenth amendment
Oxford, Maine, 219
Oxford Democrat (Maine), 219

Palmer, George W., 207, 217, 219–20
Palmyra, N.Y., 219
Panic of 1857, 69, 185
Parker, Theodore, 52, 263
Parsons, Richard C., 248
"Pathfinder, The" (John C. Frémont), 53, 204
Patrick, F. E., 178
Peace Conference (Washington, DC, Feb. 1861), 158, 189–95, 208, 214–15, 223, 225, 232, 248, 274, 275; instigated by Seward and his Virginia allies, 189–90, 211–12
Peace Conference Plan, 190–91, 214, 230, 239
Pearce, James A., 129
Pennington, William, 130, 158, 214, 217

Pennsylvania, 9, 19, 20–21, 39, 44, 62, 66, 68, 69, 75, 76, 88, 100, 105, 127, 128, 158, 185, 193, 195–96, 211, 216, 217, 218, 220, 223, 237, 319–20n25; key Lower North target for Republicans (1856–60), 62, 68–69, 75–76; open to conciliation, 193, 195–96; not strongly antislavery, 193, 196. *See also* Stevens, Thaddeus
Pennsylvania Avenue (Washington, DC), 223–24
"People's Party," 218
Perry, John J., 217, 219, 232
Petersburg, Va., 256
Phelps, Edward L., 255
Philadelphia, Pa., 19, 20–21, 66, 100, 211, 220, 223, 319–20n25
Philadelphia North American, 122
Philanthropist, 41
Phillips, Wendell, 29, 46, 85, 100, 123, 173, 181, 204
Pickens, Fort (offshore from Pensacola, Fla.), 98
Pierce, Franklin, 48–49, 53; annual message (Dec. 1856) and responses thereto, 56–66
Pike, James Shepherd, 222
Pike's Peak region (Colo.), 194
Pinckney, Henry L., 36
Pinkerton, Allan, 211
Pitt, William (Lord Chatham), 156
Pittsfield, Mass., 175, 179
Plants, Tobias A., 247
Plattsburgh, N.Y., 219
Polk, James K., 37–39
Pollock, James, 193
Pomeroy, Ohio, 247
Portage County, Ohio, 247
Porter, Albert G., 196–97
Porter, George McC., 252, 331n22
Porter, W. P., 177
Portland, Maine, 165, 229, 245
Portland Eastern Argus, 245
Potomac River, 33
Potter, David M., 10, 34–35, 98, 103–5, 111, 113, 115, 194, 273–76, 280, 307–8n32

Index